Essays on Handel and Italian opera

Essays on
Handel and Italian opera

REINHARD STROHM

Professor of Music History, Yale University

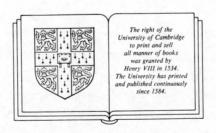

The right of the
University of Cambridge
to print and sell
all manner of books
was granted by
Henry VIII in 1534.
The University has printed
and published continuously
since 1584.

CAMBRIDGE UNIVERSITY PRESS

Cambridge

London   New York   New Rochelle
Melbourne   Sydney

Published by the Press Syndicate of the University of Cambridge
The Pitt Building, Trumpington Street, Cambridge CB2 1RP
32 East 57th Street, New York, NY 10022, USA
10 Stamford Road, Oakleigh, Melbourne 3166, Australia

First published 1985

Printed in Great Britain by
the University Press, Cambridge

Library of Congress catalogue card number: 84–21349

British Library Cataloguing in Publication Data
Strohm, Reinhard
Essays on Handel and Italian opera.
1. Handel, George Frideric
I. Title
782.1′092′4   ML410.H13
ISBN 0 521 26428 6

UP

Contents

Preface

THE ESSAYS assembled in this book were written between 1972 and 1984 – really a very short span when compared with the time-distance between the essays and their subject. There is a similar disparity between my knowledge or understanding of Italian opera of Handel's time and the immense knowledge that Handel himself must have had of it. The reader should not expect too much from information collected over so short a period, from conclusions drawn in such haste. Of my contemporaries who kindly advised me in these pursuits, only a few can be mentioned: Bernd Baselt, Hans Dieter Clausen, Winton Dean, J. Merrill Knapp, Lowell Lindgren, Brian Trowell. The list of authors of the past, who were equally helpful, would be longer. Thanks to the support of Rosemary Dooley and Penny Souster at Cambridge University Press, I can now present the essays to the discriminating Anglo-American readership. Martin Cooper translated all except the two on Vivaldi and Handel's *Orlando*, which were originally written in English. In many places, I have dared change Mr Cooper's translation beyond recognition, a practice not unknown to opera-lovers. I also enjoyed changing my own original text wherever it seemed necessary.

When I was studying the operas of some of Handel's contemporaries, trying to concentrate on the scores of Vinci, Leo, Vivaldi, Porpora or Hasse, Handel's music (particularly his basses) often came to mind. I then believed, in 1972, that I had a chance of understanding Handel better when holding his operas against 'the Italian operatic tradition'. This, with hindsight, is the common goal of all twelve essays. I no longer believe that there is such a thing as 'the Italian operatic tradition' (the change of mind being the result of writing the essays). In 1972, however, there were also many other people who thought that there was one, nobody really knowing it. Moreover, there were more people than there are today who thought that Handel's operas are different from those of his contemporaries simply in that they are better, and fewer people even than today who had any live experience of Baroque opera whether of Handel's or Scarlatti's or Vivaldi's, whether as performers or listeners. The fact is that Handel's operas are far more different from those of his contemporaries than distinctions of aesthetic value or compositional skill can account for.

Winton Dean, in his book *Handel and the Opera Seria* of 1969, also demonstrated that Handel's operas are different from his other music because they are music written for the stage. This recognition, albeit foreshadowed by Edward J. Dent (who knew the Italian operatic tradition if there ever was one), is the real breakthrough, everything else following from it – the need to perform the works on stage in order to appreciate them, the desire to know more about the dramatic subjects, about Baroque stage-craft, singers, libretti, Italian poetry, procedures of borrowing and revising other people's music, of writing and revising performance scores, about impresarios, economic conditions, audiences, about London and Italy as European theatre-landscapes. Only some of these fascinating themes are discussed in detail in this book. With regard to others, I have hardly scratched the surface. Research is now on the way in several countries concerning most of these problems. Also the number of actual performances, and the artistic standards shown in them, have made a happy progress during the last decade, a progress quite uninfluenced by what scholars like myself may have had to say. I feel a sense of gratitude and responsibility for having been a witness.

There may be a case, nevertheless, for some more critical and historical underpinning of the Handel opera experience. The historical perspective can provide an awesome view. If we realise, only to the smallest extent, how much musical theatre must have been present in Handel's mind that is now forever forgotten, it can be electrifying when a good performance makes us Handel's contemporaries. That is possible with his music, which brought the historical characters of his dramas back from the dead. Paradoxically, we may be able to understand Handel even from our modern standpoint because he himself understood his own past so well. His superb hindsight made him a real progressive.

No Handelian can afford, of course, to ignore the works of such men as Alessandro Scarlatti, Pietro Metastasio, Leonardo Vinci and Johann Adolf Hasse. They show us what sweet old Italian opera was really like. Handel knew them well, but he chose to be different.

Vivi felice.

R.S.

Acknowledgements

THE original sources of publication of the essays in this book are given below. The Press is most grateful to the publisher in each case for permission to publish an English translation here. The essay on Vivaldi was originally published in English.

Handel's Italian journey as a European experience
'Il viaggio di Handel come esperienza europea' in *Handel in Italia*, ed. G. Morelli, Istituto Italiano Antonio Vivaldi della Fondazione Giorgio Cini, Venice, 1981.

Alessandro Scarlatti and the eighteenth century
'Alessandro Scarlatti und das Settecento' in *Colloquium Alessandro Scarlatti*, ed. W. Osthoff, Musikverlag Hans Schneider, Tutzing, 1979.

Handel and his Italian opera texts
'Händel und seine italienischen Operntexte' in *Händel-Jahrbuch*, 1975–6.

Francesco Gasparini's later operas and Handel
'Francesco Gasparini, le sue opere tarde e Georg Friedrich Händel' in *Francesco Gasparini (1661–1727): Atti del primo Convegno Internazionale*, Leo S. Olschki, Florence, 1982.

Towards an understanding of the *opera seria*
'Zum Verständnis der Opera Seria' in *Werk und Wiedergabe: Musiktheater exemplarisch interpretiert*, ed. Sigrid Wiesmann, Fehr Verlag 1981, by permission of the Forschungsinstitut für Musiktheater der Universität Bayreuth.

An opera autograph of Francesco Gasparini?
'Ein Opernautograph von Francesco Gasparini?' in *Hamburger Jahrbuch für Musikwissenschaft*, 3, ed. H. J. Marx, K. D. Wagner Verlag, Hamburg, 1978.

Vivaldi's career as an opera producer
   Under the same title in *Antonio Vivaldi: Teatro Musicale Cultura Società*,
   Leo S. Olschki, Florence, 1982.

Handel's pasticci
   Under the same title in *Analecta Musicologica*, 14 (Studien zur italienisch-
   deutschen Musikgeschichte IX, ed. Friedrich Lippmann), 1974, by
   permission of the Deutsches Historisches Institut, Musikgeschichtliche
   Abteilung, Rome.

Leonardo Vinci's *Didone abbandonata* (Rome 1726)
Handel's *Ezio*
   Two chapters in Reinhard Strohm, *Die italienische Oper im 18. Jahrhundert*
   (Taschenbücher zur Musikwissenschaft 25), Heinrichshofen's Verlag,
   Wilhelmshaven, 1979.

Metastasio's *Alessandro nell' Indie* and its earliest settings
   'Metastasios "Alessandro nell'Indie" und seine frühesten Vertonungen',
   in *Probleme der Händelschen Oper*, ed. W. Siegmund-Schultze (Wissenschaftliche Beiträge, Martin-Luther-Universität, Halle-Wittenberg
   1982/21).

The essay 'Comic traditions in Handel's *Orlando*', written in 1984, is
published here for the first time.

Handel's Italian journey as a European experience

GEORGE FRIDERIC HANDEL (1685–1759) is only one of the many Germans who, across the years, have visited Italy as tourists, soldiers, students, artists, scholars, princes, politicians and businessmen. A great many reasons have led these Germans to cross the Alps, and this variety itself gives the 'historical' relations between the two countries their real significance. Such diversity of contact has been a vital element in the various stages of their development in the course of European history, frequently determining the character of its debates and tensions. Yet those Germans whose visits to Italy have turned out, in the long run, to be positive rather than negative in the context of the two nations' bilateral relationship are perhaps in a minority. It is certainly to this minority that Handel belongs.

As a young artist travelling with the twin aims of working and learning from his travels, his journey turned out to be as placid and amiable as might have been expected. His extraordinary personality, overflowing with energy and optimism, contributed to the cultural enrichment of both his homeland and the country he was visiting, not only through the production of a number of musical compositions, but also through the delivery of a clear and meaningful message to Europe as a whole.

More specifically, Handel was one of many German musicians who spent the most important years of their professional training in Italy. Others included Heinrich Schütz (1585–1672), Johann Rosenmüller (1613–84), Johann David Heinichen (1683–1729), Johann Adolf Hasse (1699–1783), as well as Gluck, Johann Christian Bach and Mozart. However, for nearly all these seventeenth- and eighteenth-century musicians the motivation and circumstances of their Italian travels were different, as were the consequences for each individual. Schütz and Heinichen, for example, had set out on the orders of their princely patrons, whose employees they already were, with the aim of completing their own vocational training during a limited stay, and were obliged to return afterwards to Germany, where their jobs – and salaries – awaited them. Study-trips of this kind usually involved the choice of Venice as sole destination and place of residence.

1

Rosenmüller, although from a similar background in Saxony, ended up by being absorbed into Italian life – much more fully, perhaps, than might have been expected. He even went so far as to be converted to Catholicism, like Johann Christian Bach a century later. Bach himself and Gluck, at about the middle of the eighteenth century, made their way to Milan, unlike their older colleagues, who still tended to opt for Venice. They did so in search of suitable openings for careers which, in their early stages, had brought them only economic hardship. Their great successes were still several years off. Mozart's journey, on the other hand, was meticulously planned by his father, with an eye to both his education and his career. He avoided spending too long in any one place, so as to allow the young musician the benefit of as many useful and productive meetings, contacts and changes of surroundings as possible. Much less is known about the first years (1722–5) spent by Hasse in Italy. Although his career, alone among those considered here, was to reach a peak in permanent employment (at the Cappella Reale in Naples), it is not possible to arrive at a coherent explanation of his movements. Hasse seems to have wandered almost at random, working at first (1722–4) in Venice, Rome and Bologna, without producing anything which has survived. It is not so much his studies with Porpora and Alessandro Scarlatti (1724–5) as his work in Naples and Venice and his marriage to the *primadonna* Faustina Bordoni in 1730 which make Hasse the most 'Italianised' of all the German composers, providing a firm basis for his long connection with the host country. Hasse was born near Hamburg and had begun his career in opera-houses as a singer; the Italians called him 'caro Sassone' ('the sweet Saxon'), as they had Handel before him – a fact of which he may well have been aware.

All these fundamental aspects of the journeys made by other German artists are combined in Handel: the cultural background in central northern Germany, the quest for learning, the aspiration to a career, the dependence on patronage, the spirit of adventure. If, like Rosenmüller and Schütz before him, he came south as a musician seeking to perfect his skills in the field of sacred music, he soon showed himself ready to begin a career as, above all, a composer of opera. He arrived in Italy richly endowed with extensive experience of the German tradition at its most profound; he left as an 'international' artist, at the beginning of an age which was to believe firmly in the values of progress and enlightenment.

The most significant aspect of Handel's character during his Italian period is his marked capacity to adapt himself to the whole body of circumstance and influence which surrounded him. This not only involved the output of a considerable body of work, compared with that of his colleagues, within a short space of time (1706–10), but is also visible in the quality and imaginative force of that work, greater than those typical of the products of other German composers active in Italy. Compositions like the psalm

Dixit Dominus (4 April 1707), *La Resurrezione* (8 April 1708), the opera *Agrippina* (1709) and many cantatas, sacred and secular, bear the stamp of the mature Handel; and when the composer incorporated some of this youthful material into later works, the spirit of the Italian period remained fresh and unsullied. Stylistically, most of Handel's Italian compositions are 'revolutionary' in one way or another, while at the same time reaching a level of Italo-German craftsmanship comparable only with that achieved by the young Mozart.

How is such success to be explained? By the timing of Handel's journey? The cultural atmosphere of the places he visited? The Italian audience? Although very little is known about the day-to-day, 'practical' details of Handel's life in Italy, or the relationships he enjoyed with patrons and public, we can certainly say that the Saxon maestro was received with open arms, proving the respect and support offered by public, colleagues and patrons alike. His music enjoyed immediate approbation.

This fact may be very significant in the light of the cultural atmosphere of contemporary Italy, especially as Handel's success was in no way dependent upon servile imitation of the universally popular Italian style. In fact, the limits within which Handel could be appreciated, and which he would constantly have had in mind as a touchstone of conformity, were not stylistic in nature.

He had to show that he possessed flexibility of approach, a willingness to accept any type of commission, the readiness to work at great speed, and an aptitude for cultivating all the genres already practised by his Italian fellow-composers: opera, oratorio, cantata da camera, serenata and Latin church music for the Catholic liturgy. It so happened that he wrote neither instrumental music nor anything for the organ, despite being an excellent organist himself. Similarly, he wrote only two operas (in 1707 for Florence and in 1709 for Venice), whereas in Hamburg a few years before (1705–6) he had written four. He found himself no longer writing sacred music for Protestant rites, even though he had not given up his Lutheran faith. Another limitation in his Italian career was that he did not influence, at least in any recognisable or demonstrable way, any other composer of the period; and he had no Italian pupils. Indeed, there is no evidence that the music he composed in Italy was even performed after 1713. This was because Handel's Italian music had blossomed with the suddenness of a flower in an environment which was changing rapidly. The change was taking place under the influence of particular vested interests: those of a society itself in a state of transition combined with those of a class of clerical patrons who lacked heirs, of princes (like Ferdinando Medici) who died young, of aristocratic circles who were keen to develop highly exclusive forms of entertainment, and of cities which lacked lay educational institutions.

When this picture is compared with that offered by the solidly based institutions, churches and schools of Halle or Hamburg, or with the lively bourgeois culture of a rich metropolis like London, it becomes apparent why it was so important for Handel to return to the north, where he could create, in his work, an imposing monument to his memories of Italy and to Italy herself.

The political and cultural landscape of the country into which Handel had ventured in 1706 was confused and fragmentary. The War of the Spanish Succession (1700–14) had been unleashed in Italy by the dynastic rivalry between the Bourbons and the Habsburgs, and had brought, once again, foreign armies into the countryside and social and cultural crisis into the cities and courts. In 1707 Lombardy and Naples passed from Spanish control into the hands of the Austrians, and the Gonzaga domination of Mantua ended with the installation in the city of a German governor, Philip of Hesse-Darmstadt, which was carried out by the Austrian army after they had expelled the French troops from the district.

The Habsburg claimant to the throne of Spain, the Archduke Charles, had proclaimed himself King Charles III of Spain, and had used northern Italy as a territorial corridor en route to his royal seat, Barcelona, in 1709. He had thus paid a fleeting visit to Milan and Lombardy. Venice, the Medici and the pope had tried to remain in a state of quasi-neutrality, but when the conflict spread and deepened, as a result of the military successes won by the Austrians, they too had to choose sides. Unfortunately, they lined up against each other: Florence and the Papal States with France, Venice with the Austrians. The decaying houses of Este, in Modena and Reggio, and Farnese, in Parma, both fast approaching extinction, were caught up like helpless puppets in the tangled threads of this vast international performance.

The situation had three main consequences for culture, and for music in particular. Chief of these was the collapse of cultural institutions brought about by the instability of political power. Court chapels, academies, theatres, all saw their staff dismissed by the new masters; and the consequences were most visible where the local aristocracy – the most important source of support for musicians, after the Church and the princes – either lost or regained, according to the unpredictable course of events, its influence in the state. This was particularly clear at Naples, where the pro-Hispanic aristocracy disappeared from the scene in 1707, leaving many artists on the breadline. There was also the excessive exploitation of public and court musical life in the pursuit of particular political ends. The texts of operas and celebratory serenades, even oratorios, regularly alluded to political events, military successes, dynastic marriages and legitimate royal successions. This practice, which was initiated in seventeenth-century Venice and later spread to all the courts of Italy, developed to the point where these themes became obsessively frequent in Italian opera, as can still be seen today in the libretti of Silvani and Zeno and operas composed by Pollarolo, Gasparini, Caldara and even Handel himself. Handel's *Rodrigo* (or *Vincer se stesso è la maggior vittoria*), written for Florence in 1707, alludes to the strictly contemporary events of the War of the Spanish Succession – obviously from a Francophile viewpoint. Similarly, his *Agrippina* was written as an anti-Bourbon and anti-papal satire, recounting a tale of court intrigue during a palace coup. Eventually, the climate of political conflict influenced life in the palaces and salons of diplomatic residences and the urban nobility – the places in which the greatest efforts were made to recreate, at a distance, the grandiose atmosphere of the absolutist courts. This was especially the case at Rome and at Venice, where all royal or Imperial birthdays and all visits made by foreign princes were celebrated by every diplomat, Italian or otherwise.

All this meant that, culturally, the times were very much out of joint. The Venetian cardinal, Pietro Ottoboni, an important patron, was banished from his native city for supporting the French cause on behalf of Pope Clement XI, while at the same time another Venetian cardinal, Vincenzo Grimani, Imperial ambassador to the Vatican, lost all his power and influence in Rome. Both envoys were patrons of Handel, as indeed had been the Medici family, who had supported the French; the Duca d'Alvito, a Neapolitan supporter of the Emperor; and the Roman Marchese Ruspoli, who had acted ingloriously enough as a mercenary against the Habsburgs. If to all these are added the two Roman cardinals, Pamphilij and Colonna, both supporters of the French cause, and the various German and English diplomats whom Handel met at Venice and Rome – who were all, for the moment, more or less hostile to France – we have, if not a complete list of Handel's patrons, at least an excellent idea of the political chaos which prevailed in the Italian peninsula at that time.

Was the necessity to serve so wide a range of patrons a constant feature of the practice of the musical profession in this period? Two facts need to be borne in mind here. Firstly, while some musicians of Handel's generation resisted such pressures and stayed in Italy, when the flow of local patronage began to dry up, many others sought protection in foreign courts or embassies. Some created, while others maintained, contacts and commitments abroad; these included the Bononcinis and, later, Caldara in Vienna, Luigi Mancia and Nicola Haym in Germany and London, and Agostino Steffani and Carlo Pietragrua in Düsseldorf. A large part of that splendid tradition of Italian opera outside Italy so characteristic of the eighteenth century owes its origins to the artistic diaspora which took place at this time.

Secondly, various foreign influences, including musical ones, were making themselves felt in Italy, taking advantage of the opportunities offered by new political affiliations and relationships. French influence is obvious in the music, theatre and literature of the Medici court (though this was partly the fruit of a long-standing tradition) and of Rome, where it even managed to find its way into the Accademia dell'Arcadia, while signs of Spanish influence are visible at Naples until 1707. It is also possible to speak, at least to a certain extent, of German and Austrian influence on music. Although France held a dominant position, insofar as French taste was prevalent in many courts, Germany and Austria exported a number of musicians, including, of course, Handel. These were able to turn current political rivalries to their own material advantage, as long as they showed themselves ready and willing to turn out compositions to order with due speed and efficiency. The situation of Italian musicians was different in that, in many cases, they were able to obtain a safe position in the service of some noble family. No such possibility seems ever to have existed for the Germans. Alessandro Scarlatti, for example, changed masters several times, along with his large family, between 1707 and 1709. After having first been under the protection of Ferdinando de' Medici, and later that of Ottoboni, in 1709 he re-installed himself at Naples as a protégé of Ottoboni's political rival Vincenzo Grimani, who was happy to compete with Ottoboni in matters of cultural prestige as well. In such a case – one of the best-known instances – questions of stylistic development in musical practice were bound up with the problems involved in social transformation on a large scale. Scarlatti continued to respect the esoteric and idealist aesthetic standards of an apparently coherent aristocratic class – made up in this case of Roman cardinals – and his refined contrapuntal music acts as a mirror of the past. At the same time, two ambitious composers of the new generation, Porpora and Vivaldi, had begun their careers just before 1710 (in Porpora's case, with his *Agrippina*, written for Naples in 1708), and were to become the founders of the modern 'impetuoso' style in vocal and instrumental music.

It is not without significance that these new composers should have addressed themselves to the Church, to civic institutions (such as conservatories), to bourgeois impresarios and to the German and Austrian nobility in Naples, Mantua or Vienna. Their careers and even their style can be seen as, in some ways, symbolic of Italian music's expansionist tendencies during the eighteenth century.

Corelli, like Alessandro Scarlatti a member of the Accademia dell'Arcadia, and, as far as character goes, perhaps the most withdrawn of the 'integralist' Italian composers, did not allow his orchestral music to be circulated outside Italy during his lifetime; and so works written for the exclusive entertainment of Roman prelates found a large new audience among the bourgeoisie of northern Europe only thanks to the northern music publishers. Only Handel's exact contemporary, Domenico Scarlatti, survived to see his music circulate all over Europe. After his father's death, after giving up vocal music to compose for the keyboard, after emigrating, he at last found his proper creative niche in eighteenth-century Europe.

In Handel all these various types of musician are united. As described above, while working in Italy and executing commissions there, he had been at the service both of the old groups of 'integralist' Italian nobility, at Florence and Rome, and of the patrons of the new order. But when did Handel become involved in these different trends? What were the influences, of patrons or fellow-musicians, which affected his style and ideas? How much of it all did he carry with him when he returned from Italy to northern Europe? Handel's own works are the best guide to a full understanding not only of his character and artistic intentions, but also of his life and the social, aesthetic and political ideas which underlay it. Chrysander is quite right to say that the hundred and more cantatas da camera which Handel wrote in Italy are a kind of musical diary.

Although very many of these are works of extraordinary beauty, they are among the least-known of Handel's compositions. He had probably tried his hand at the genre before; at least, several Italian arias were composed by Handel for his Hamburg operas, and it is also possible to detect exercises in the Italian style in some of his German-texted arias and recitatives. Musicians who were acquainted with Italian vocal music of this kind at Hamburg included Cousser, Keiser and Mattheson, who certainly had access to Italian manuscripts of opera-arias and cantatas. What Handel learned at Rome and Florence while turning out regular contributions to the aristocracy's literary gatherings and pieces for the musical academies (under the patronage of the Ruspoli family, the Roman cardinals, or Ferdinando's court) was the essential immediacy of the interplay between the composition and its performance, encouraged both by improvisations in the cantatas and by the unashamedly exclusive and esoteric approach of his patrons, who dressed up in the garb of Arcadian shepherds and communicated with one another in a refined literary language typical of late Mannerism.

It is known that many composers took part in performances of this kind (including Alessandro Scarlatti, Pasquini and Handel himself, playing the harpsichord) and that the singers (often including female sopranos, who were not allowed to sing in public at Rome) and the cellist providing the accompaniment were often servants or even members of noble households. The texts usually dealt with themes of pastoral love in a lyrical, epic or semi-dramatic style, and were provided by the patrons themselves (Cardinal Pamphilij being one example). Handel was a skilful composer in this genre, and his music is well suited to such pleasant entertainments in an intellectual atmosphere. The cantatas are full of contrapuntal subtleties, startling harmonic effects, virtuoso developments of the vocal line or the cello part, and richly rhetorical embroidery of the text which could only have been understood by a small and sophisticated audience. (The great importance given to the cello part is, in fact, a striking characteristic of the cantata in its Roman form, since it had been developed there thanks to the considerable performing skills of players like Giovanni Bononcini, Giovanni Lulier and Nicola Haym.)

Handel's contribution to the genre is notable not so much for the particular stylistic traits which set it apart from the attempts made in the same field by Scarlatti or Bononcini, as for the singular effect made by each individual piece, through the presence of a highly personal stamp, sometimes surprising, sometimes dramatic, which gives each composition its own particular character. Handel is more concerned with the instrumental parts than Scarlatti, for instance, as is clear from the harmonic continuos and the expressive figurations of the cello line. Yet he does not stand out by virtue of the use of technical devices which differ greatly from those used by other composers. Even the chromaticism which is the basic feature of so many of these works is a fashionable stylistic quirk in Mannerist music.

The most 'Handelian' of the cantatas (such as 'Udite il mio consiglio', one of the earliest, or the larger-scale, three-part *Clori, Tirsi e Fileno*, or the epic cantatas *Agrippina condotta a morire* and *Lucrezia*) are typical more for the power of their melodies to move and the spirited approach that they require than for their academic subtlety. In his Italian works, Handel is a dramatic composer gifted with enormous melodic sweep and an extrovert personality, who can only give full rein to these aspects of his nature, it seems, in the single form of the cantata.

On those occasions when he is able to add violins to the continuo, Handel's treatment is in the grand manner, with many decorative and theatrical effects; to the extent that many of the arias from cantatas with violin accompaniment written at this time were later to be revised and adapted for use in operas and oratorios, including both those written for Italy and those composed in London. In these revisions, however, Handel banishes from the arias all the intrinsic characteristics of chamber music style. Indeed, very few arias in opera are as chromatic and contrapuntal as the cantatas; and when he looks outside his own earlier compositions, Handel chooses colourful dance-tunes, broad, tuneful movements and clear and expressive motifs. His chief concern seems to have been not to contribute to the qualitative development of the typical Roman cantata, but to use the progress made there to characterise his own output as a composer. I suspect that Handel in no way shared the Arcadian aesthetic.

He seems, however, to have admired his frivolous patron, Ruspoli, whom he celebrated in the guise of a shepherd-warrior in the cantata 'Mentre il tutto è in furore' (August 1708), before the marquis launched his feeble military campaign in the Comacchio marshes. This campaign displayed the hollowness of the pastoral fiction by revealing the noble patron's ludicrous inability to understand the nature of military realities. The cantata 'Oh! come chiare e belle' also celebrates Ruspoli, now in the guise of the shepherd Olinto, as well as the River Tiber and Pope Clement XI (the 'star of clemency'). Despite the wealth of agreeable melody which Handel very sensibly decided to employ in it, this is a serious work, as rich in ideas as it is inconsistent. With the aid of many 'borrowings' from various cantatas and even from *Vincer sè stesso*..., Handel put together an impressive cantata to mark the ascent of the Archduke Charles to the Spanish throne. This is the incomplete cantata (though it probably only lacks a brief introductory recitative) 'Io languisco fra le gioie'. Although originally composed in 1709 (the allegorical and political allusions to Charles and his army, as well as to the various European princes involved in the war of succession, can refer to no other period and can only have been conceived at Rome) the cantata proves to have been written on paper used by Handel in London in 1710.

The large-scale secular works, such as the serenata *Aci, Galatea e Polifemo*, are, in fact, unusually long cantatas. At the time there was no common distinction between 'serenata' and 'cantata', both of which referred to dramatic but non-staged works performed in private houses. In these Handel perfected his dramatic style no less evidently than in the shorter cantatas. This particular serenata was written for the Neapolitan Duca d'Alvito, a noble whose family name has not come down to us, who possessed estates in the countryside to the north of the city. He was a supporter of the Austrians, and used Handel's serenata on the occasion of his own wedding (July 1708); in September of the same year, d'Alvito celebrated the Austrian conquest of Sardinia with another, three-part, serenata set to music by Domenico Sarri.

These private celebrations – of weddings, birthdays, victories, public events – were typical of the lives of noble Neapolitan households in this period. Handel probably made d'Alvito's acquaintance through Vincenzo Grimani, whose efforts had previously been devoted to his aim of expelling the Spanish from Naples, and who had become viceroy (30 June 1708) under the new Imperial rule. We know that Handel met other members of the d'Alvito family at Rome; these included Nicolò d'Alvito, a pupil of Filippo Merelli at the Collegio Clementino, who acted in one of the French tragedies which Merelli translated from Racine and other authors. This tragedy was *Tamerlano*, based on Pradon's play, in 1709; the play itself was to be the basis of an opera of Handel's with the same title.

The two oratorios which Handel wrote for the Rome of the prelates, *Il Trionfo del Tempo e della Verità* of 1707 and the *Oratorio per la Risurettione di Nostro Signore* of 1708, are in every way, both in dimensions and function, similar to the serenata *Aci, Galatea e Polifemo*. All these works were written for lavish performance in front of an exclusive audience of invited guests, in ornate and splendidly decorated rooms, without staging as such but with clear individuation of the dramatis personae through the use of musical characterisation, and were based on mythological and allegorical subjects enriched with the colourful music which Handel provided. They also used first-rate singers (the bass, G. M. Boschi, always sang important parts in Handel's works) who were probably not too displeased to have the chance to sing without having to act. In *La Resurrezione* all the instrumentalists are given passages demanding great skill which reach a peak of virtuosity and originality.

It seems clear that in this oratorio Handel was attempting to outdo Scarlatti, one of the best-known specialists in the genre, who had displayed his powers in *La Passione*, with its brilliant musical treatment of the text and its, perhaps, somewhat restrained interpretation. In his setting of the more cheerful subject, the Resurrection, Handel was able to include dance-tunes and even popular songs (such as 'Ho un non sò che nel cor'), thereby emulating Bononcini and Caldara rather more than Scarlatti. He gathers together his various musical numbers as if they were pieces of a mosaic, and some of them turned out to be genuine 'hits', which were used again in later works. This practice, though it impairs the inner unity of the work, makes it possible for each individual piece to impress the audience with its freshness and originality.

Carlo Sigismondo Capeci, one of Arcadia's best poets, wrote the libretto for *La Resurrezione*; several years later Handel was to honour him again by setting two more of his libretti to music (*Tolomeo* and *Orlando*). These had been written for one of Rome's princely theatres in 1711, for use with music by Domenico Scarlatti, and indeed both works were much appreciated by more or less the same audience which had enjoyed *La Resurrezione*, including Cardinal Ottoboni. Handel never returned to *La Resurrezione*, but he did revise both *Aci...* and *Il Trionfo...*, preparing two revisions of each for use in London. These included a good deal of new music, but retained the pastoral and allegorical atmosphere of the pieces. They are both dramatic but non-staged works, in the tradition of the masque and the oratorio, in which Handel seems to recall Italy more intensely than elsewhere. Each re-working must have been like another journey into Italy for the composer, and the very idea of replacing onstage action with purely musical expressive and dramatic details, whether instrumental or harmonic, must have acted as a stimulus in the same way as it did in aristocratic circles in Italy. To this may be added the late borrowings from Italian composers (Stradella, Urio, Erba, all of them linked with Rome or Ferdinando Medici) which he used in the writing of oratorios and other sacred music. Above all, in noting that most of these borrowings are in the field of choral music, we must perhaps recognise that it was not so much theatre-music itself as the theatricality of the Italian approach to choral music and oratorio which constituted Italy's strongest attraction for Handel.

Opera itself had been forbidden at Rome from 1698 to 1709, the pope having ostensibly been worried at the immorality of some of the performances. We may perhaps suggest that during this period those in charge of musical patronage, the cardinals, felt themselves better served by private performances of outstanding quality, which catered very well to their own personal tastes, rather than by performances in the public atmosphere of theatres. Although the theatres of Rome were run by private individuals (from various classes, and including such as Cardinal Ottoboni), both before and after they were placed under interdict, the cardinals probably preferred to exercise monopoly control over serious musical life, which chiefly meant a monopoly of the best singers. Women were allowed to sing in private academies, but not in the Roman theatres. Since Handel spent at least half his stay in Italy at Rome, did he not resent being barred from composing operas during much of this time? The most up-to-date research confirms, however, that he left Rome each winter, at precisely the time when good new operas were being performed in various other cities. He then settled in the towns with the best reputations in the operatic field: Florence and Venice. Although he only wrote one opera for each of these important centres, these two works can be counted among the masterpieces of the period. The obligatory stay at Florence, which attracted him every autumn from 1706 to 1709, owed its fascination to the exclusive operas commissioned by Ferdinando in his country house, the Villa di Pratolino.

The prince was a truly fanatical opera-lover who had, incomprehensibly, invited Handel to come from Hamburg without having any precise knowledge of his skills as a dramatic composer. This may explain why Handel's first commission was extended by the Teatro Civico Accademico (in the Via del Cocomero, i.e. of 'the Watermelon'), while the contracts for Pratolino were intended for Italian composers who had served Ferdinando for many years: first Alessandro Scarlatti, later G. A. Perti. All the scores composed for Pratolino have long since vanished, and today the operas are only known through the libretti written for them by the Court physician, Antonio Salvi. Each of Salvi's libretti from the years 1707–10 was set to music by Handel in London some years later: they were *Sosarme*, *Berenice*, *Ariodante*, and *Rodelinda*. Undeniably the experiences of the Pratolino theatre left their mark on Handel's artistic personality.

The opera which Handel wrote for Florence, *Vincer se stesso è la maggior vittoria* (*Rodrigo*), stands out as a curious exception in this repertoire; it is a brutal tragedy in the Venetian style, written by Francesco Silvani and set by Handel to a score which includes many reminiscences of Hamburg and not a few borrowings from *Almira* and from Keiser.

Its elements of heroic determination and sentimentality make it perhaps the most 'modern' opera Handel wrote before *Radamisto* in 1720; it is a genuine 'opera seria' in the eighteenth-century sense. On the strictly musical level, however, *Rodrigo* is still much less developed than even Handel's first work for London, *Rinaldo* (1711), although that opera is crammed with borrowings from *Rodrigo* itself and many other Italian compositions. Comparison of these two operas shows just how noteworthy was the progress which Handel had made in his dramatic art between his arrival in Italy and his arrival in London. Halfway along this line of development stands *Agrippina*, performed at Venice just before Handel's departure for Germany in 1710. Can this work be seen as the summation of his Italian experiences? It is, once more, a kind of pastiche made up of the most popular arias he had written during his time in Italy, but the composer's sense of dramatic balance gives this anthology a unity of its own.

Grimani's text is perhaps the most entertaining theatrical libretto which Handel ever set to music, skilfully organised, ironic, moving and full of surprises. Handel seems to have met Grimani in Rome as early as 1708, at the time when the cardinal was writing his libretto, and some of the composer's wishes (such as, perhaps, the inclusion of arias taken from a variety of earlier works) may have been discussed between them then. As stated above, Grimani's satire is political, poking fun at Pope Clement XI and his involvement in the intrigues surrounding the succession to the Spanish throne (though the setting, in accordance with well-established theatrical convention, is ancient Rome). Grimani's protector, the Archduke Charles, was sent a copy of the score – perhaps more than one – and must have enjoyed it.

Although written by a Venetian, and one who had a half-share in a theatre at that (the S. Giovanni Grisostomo), the opera appears as something of an anomaly in the Venetian theatre of the time, particularly as far as the libretto is concerned. In Venice, as opposed to Florence, dramas of the type of *Vincer se stesso...* had become more popular. It is no longer possible to attempt an accurate historical evaluation of the music's quality in terms of the characteristics of the Venetian tradition, as most of the scores written between 1700 and 1710 have failed to survive. Further, it is not easy to declare – though the claim has been made – that *Agrippina* has a generic similarity of style shared with the operas of older Venetian composers such as Cavalli and Legrenzi. We have already pointed out that Handel tends to avoid imitating the models offered by his predecessors. The structure of *Agrippina* could, however, be similar to that of his contemporaries Caldara, Gasparini, Albinoni, Pollarolo, Ruggieri, Lotti, Bononcini and Mancia, all of whom composed for Venice at the time, and whose style may already have been a response to prevailing taste and a particular audience. It may easily be imagined that comparison would favour *Agrippina* over the other works involved, but the aim of such comparison ought not to be simply to establish their respective value and qualities; it should seek to identify the compositional and dramatic techniques which Handel learned at Venice and the ways in which he adapted them. He must, indeed, have seen a great many operas, and he must have understood the Venetians pretty well, since *Agrippina* was to have such splendid success, crowned with a total of no fewer than twenty-seven performances. We may recall that Scarlatti's *Mitridate* of 1707, though also commissioned by Grimani, had been a fiasco. By studying the score we can come to appreciate the Venetians' attitude, but if we do not understand Scarlatti's failure we cannot hope to understand the reasons for Handel's success.

In the strictly technical sense *Rinaldo* has much in common with *Agrippina*, but since, by that time, Handel was no longer writing for the Italian theatre, a certain spirit of reciprocal understanding between Handel and his audience – which had been a crucial factor in the Venetian performances – had disappeared for ever.

Handel's achievements in Italian church music are perhaps more difficult to understand. Two of his earliest compositions for Rome, *Dixit Dominus* and *Salve Regina*, are certainly very ambitious works. They may be considered more Handelian than Italian, and both recall Halle or Hamburg. In the choral sections of *Dixit Dominus*, in particular, a kind of interior drama is clearly discernible in the treatment of the combined vocal forces as if they were one individual, which is to be the distinguishing mark of the choral works of the composer's maturity.

This can be identified by comparing Handel's work with the almost contemporary setting by Scarlatti. Scarlatti shows himself to be a more moderate and restrained composer, just where the young German is creating structures of Baroque architecture reminiscent of Bernini. This is that 'theatrical' splendour which was mentioned above in discussing the oratorios, and the *Resurrezione* oratorio in particular. One ought to add that Handel, a Saxon who had begun his professional life high up in the organ-loft of a Gothic church in Halle, must have had no small difficulty in responding to the Catholic sentiments of the Marian antiphon, as well as in producing a sound so strikingly un-German as that of the 'cantus firmus' sections of the psalm. The latter work was commissioned by Cardinal Colonna, and was probably performed as part of the annual celebrations at the church of the Madonna del Carmine at Rome, in an environment at once monastic and aristocratic. Handel pays his tribute to popular Catholic devotion with perfect composure, especially in the Marian works with Italian texts: the great motet-cantata *Donna che in ciel* and the serenely beautiful fragment which begins with the words 'Ah che troppo ineguali'.

Donna che in ciel was certainly commissioned for one of the yearly festivals commemorating the deliverance of Rome from the afflictions of the 1702 earthquakes, and performed on the feast of the Purification (2 February). It is not known in which year it was first performed – the style suggests 1707, but it may possibly have been 1709, whilst on 2 February 1708 Handel was almost certainly in Venice. 'Ah che troppo ineguali' is a prayer to the Madonna for the restoration of peace, and was probably written for Rome in the winter of 1707–8. Both these Marian works are written in a highly personal style, and often expand expressively on the Italian religious text, with the result that they appear to be the work at least of a believer, if not of a downright fanatic. The puzzle posed by these pieces of church music may be solved by taking into consideration not the immediate Italian influence on Handel, but the tradition of orthodox Lutheran music in Germany itself, which had for generations been influenced by Italian precedent. At the beginning of this essay mention was made of Schütz, who came to Venice to study with Gabrieli and Monteverdi, as well as of the Italianised Rosenmüller. Handel's teacher, Zachow, left at least one *Magnificat*, not only written in the modern style but shot through with 'galant' and operatic elements. The founders and administrators of the Hamburg Opera, the city's Lutheran clergy, and Handel's tutors, Mattheson and Keiser, were internationalists, even in church music. Handel takes only one step forward in this direction: he combined the brilliant musical artifice of the instrumental concertato style and the expressivity of large choral units with the details of pronunciation, a pronunciation which seems to be born with absolute spontaneity from the Latin or Italian words. His handling of metre is always correct (though not as refined as Scarlatti's), but that is not the point here.

The melodic gesture accorded to pronunciation in the aria 'O del Ciel Maria Regina' (which follows the recitative 'Ah che troppo ineguali') goes beyond accentuation: it actually 'incorporates' the words, and makes the narrator, the singer, a 'real' person. This is Handel's achievement, the 'personification' of language, stemming from a double source, the tradition of his German ancestors and the practice of his Italian contemporaries.

According to a tradition reported by Mainwaring (Deutsch, p. 18), Handel rejected entreaties made to him to become a Catholic; one wonders whether this story is supposed to explain his return to the North. This seems to be somewhat at odds with the image of the internationalist Handel, the intellectual at home with both denominations, described for us by, among others, Paul Henry Lang. His Italian church music may, however, suggest a new approach to the question: given his extreme (poetic) assimilation to papalism and devotion to Mary, may the composer not have felt himself threatened by the danger of the loss of his spiritual identity? May his departure from Italy not have been a retreat, a flight? It was, at all events, a departure which left behind it a set of profoundly memorable experiences and a personal awareness of European culture, which were to be drawn on often in the future, with all the pride of the émigré.

Alessandro Scarlatti and the eighteenth century

THERE IS perhaps a lesson to be learned from the case of Alessandro Scarlatti, and from the fact that attempts to relate him intelligibly to his age and his background have failed already more than once. Scarlatti was neither the leader of a Neapolitan school nor the last notable representative of a Venetian school; nor was he a forerunner of Mozart, as supposed by a succession of earlier scholars. We should re-phrase the question of the nature of his specific achievements, bearing in mind the danger of repeating the mistakes of past scholarship. The present article is an attempt to do this from the perspective of the eighteenth century.

'Placing' and 'understanding' composers of the past presupposes above all a practical acquaintance with their music, and in saying this we may already have put our fingers on one shortcoming of earlier generations. Insufficient knowledge of Scarlatti's works is, however, not the only reason why his style and historic contribution have been misrepresented. There was, and still is, a mistaken concept of history in general which has replaced the import of concrete human beings with that of abstract ideas. History of music has been made to consist of 'style periods', 'schools', 'influences', 'reform', of 'tradition' and 'progress', and in turn too little attention has been paid to the active parts played by the individuals and groups who in fact make history – and who, in their turn, make use of general ideas only in order to explain and promote their own activity. Slogans such as 'tradition' and 'progress' are raised as banners in the historical struggle – though in fact all depends on those who bear these banners. We shall be helped in our understanding of Scarlatti quite as much by his personal decisions, both as man and artist, as by the tendencies that he did or did not represent or the circumstances of his age to which he could not choose but adapt himself.

I want to attack the problem – if only in outline – from several angles. First, I want to draw attention to some contemporary remarks concerning questions of musical style and taste relevant to Scarlatti. I shall then examine the part played by Scarlatti's operas in the repertory of the early eighteenth

15

century, and, finally, go on to say what has struck me most in comparing Scarlatti's works with those of some of his contemporaries.

1. The comments of Scarlatti's contemporaries

There is a relatively large number of contemporary references to regional musical traditions, or at least to tensions between groups and individuals subject to local influences: Bologna–Venice; Corelli–Naples; Bologna–Scarlatti; Italy–France etc. (see particularly Appx, nos. 1–4). Many of these comments are of a polemical nature and also reflect professional jealousies, but do not at first touch on the question of tradition and progress. Scarlatti's own correspondence with Ferdinando de' Medici (Appx, no. 5) throws a clear light on the question of taste in the composer's struggle for existence, but reveals only a posteriori the fact that in 1706–7 Scarlatti was no longer willing or able to follow the developments of the prince's taste. On the other hand we find attitudes to contemporary music, commonly expressed in print, which defend on principle the achievement of the older generation, including Scarlatti, against innovations of the day (Appx, nos. 6 and 8). Despite their notorious local Bolognese patriotism we find Martello and Tosi praising Scarlatti, and this is all the more remarkable if we compare them with Pistocchi (Appx, no. 4). Tosi stops short of actually naming Scarlatti but goes so far as to appeal against the younger composers to styles such as 'il patetico', from which even Scarlatti himself, in his letters to Ferdinando de' Medici, protests that he is trying to escape. Tosi's aggressive conservatism, like Marcello's in his *Teatro alla moda* of 1720, is allied to social elitism. In unambiguous opposition to this stands the Bolognese Zambeccari (Appx, no. 7) who, as impresario in Naples, attacks Scarlatti for his exclusive, chamber-music style, quoting as a model – the operatic taste of Venice. If we also take into consideration the later documents (Appx, nos. 9–12), we can see that there really was a 'trend' that was not represented by Scarlatti and which he only occasionally followed, and then under protest (see the contrasting of 'facile' and 'malinconico' in his last letter to Ferdinando). The documents of course reveal very clearly the personal interest of their authors but seem to agree on one point – that Scarlatti had difficulty in asserting his own personal style and had to face criticism from individuals (such as must have been contained in the lost letters of Ferdinando). It was only rather later that a historical element also appeared and that Scarlatti was adopted by the conservative party. There is no evidence of his being positively allied to any local taste. This does not mean that no local traditions existed, but their borders followed different lines from those generally supposed. What it does mean is that Scarlatti stood rather for his own, individual views.

2. Operatic life and repertory in the opera centres of Italy

a. Rome after about 1690

We might characterise operatic life in Rome by an increasing tension between ecclesiastic claims to a monopoly in art patronage and the interests of more commercially oriented lay patrons such as the aristocrats Alibert and Capranica, a tension which must have contributed to the breakdown of opera performances after 1697 following papal prohibition of 'public' opera. Before that time, there had been an enormous increase in the sheer quantity of operas performed year by year, owing to the rivalry between the musical institutions. Many of those institutions were in clerical hands and were, therefore, aimed less at continuity over generations than at an immediate display of power and wealth. In these chapels and theatres, foreign or visiting artists were employed as well as Romans. Although Pollarolo (Venice), Perti (Bologna) and Scarlatti (Naples) received regular commissions, many local composers worked for the opera (G. Bononcini, F. Gasparini, C. F. Cesarini, G. Lulier, L. Mancia, S. de Luca, F. Lanciani, N. F. Haym, P. P. Bencini and others). In this situation Scarlatti began unmistakably to lose ground about 1695. But the disappearance of 'public' opera after 1697, which represented a temporary victory for the kind of patrons whose interest was not confined to the 'public' stage, i.e. the Roman cardinals, must have benefited Scarlatti. If it were not so, he of all people would hardly have settled in Rome (1703), where there was no opera, as a composer of oratorios, cantatas and church music, while Gasparini, Bononcini and Haym emigrated. Beside him, only composers who enjoyed no more than a local reputation – men like Lulier and Cesarini – stayed in Rome and adapted themselves to the new conditions (Cesarini became *maestro di cappella* to Cardinal Pamphilij in 1707). Rome in any case possessed no educational institutions for musicians (a result of the individualism of clerical supporters), and when operatic life started again in 1708, there were no outstanding local composers of opera. Either composers had to be engaged from elsewhere, none of whom stayed long, or opera commissions went to outsiders; this gave Scarlatti his chance, since his artistic individualism was well suited to that of the princely patrons, some of whom (e.g. Ruspoli) were laymen. After 1709 we can no longer speak of a specifically Roman tradition in opera, although – or rather precisely because – all the outstanding composers of the day fulfilled commissions for Rome at one time or another.

b. Naples after about 1690

Opera in Naples always received at least a subvention from the Spanish viceroys; and it is essential for us to know how far this meant a standing commission for the head of the Real Cappella – a post held by Scarlatti from 1684 onwards – and more generally what effect this institutional link between the Real Cappella and S. Bartolommeo had on both those bodies. (There are no comparable problems elsewhere in Italy, only in London in Handel's time.) Two remarkable facts have to be taken into account – first that in the seventeenth century it was the viceroys, who were appointed to Naples from Rome (Ognatte, Carpio, Medinaceli and, later, Grimani), who stimulated the production of native Neapolitan opera-composers[1], and secondly that, in spite of this, Scarlatti alone was responsible for new productions during the period roughly between 1680 and 1700. There is no Neapolitan tradition as such, only Venetian importations on the one hand and Scarlatti's series of operas on the other. Recent studies of source materials conclude from this tendency that in the years between 1690 and 1700 Scarlatti concerned himself far less with adaptations than has been hitherto supposed: he generally wrote entirely new music, even for Venetian libretti, or else the adaptations ascribed to him were in fact by other hands[2]. In fact contemporary Venetian works concerned him far less than has been suggested. Medinaceli always gave more commissions, whether for adaptations or for new works, to musicians outside Naples (Bononcini, Gasparini, S. de Luca and Luigi Mancia all came from Rome, which was Medinaceli's previous post) and this, combined with financial difficulties, may account for Scarlatti's leaving Naples. However that may be, it was only in the years after Scarlatti's departure (1702–8) that Naples found her bearings again: Venetian importations suddenly increased but we also suddenly find a whole list of native composers active – Mancini, de Mauro, Sarri, Vignola, Porsile, de Bottis, Orefice – none of whom is mentioned anywhere during the years of Scarlatti's 'rule'. So far as we can gather from their surviving music, they were all followers of the famous Venetians such as Pollarolo, Albinoni and Gasparini rather than of Scarlatti. Whereas Scarlatti's operas were still favourites in Florence for example, and often performed there, Naples in the years 1708–9 (i.e. not until after the city passed into Austrian hands) saw only three revivals of his operas, L'humanità nelle fere, Rosmene, Teodora. These were put on by, among others, Nicola Serino, who had been the impresario for the first performance. He probably had all the arias newly set by Giuseppe Vignola, however, using the poetry as a flimsy excuse for not having retained the original music in many cases; apparently, he was hoping that Scarlatti's name would be enough to attract the public without his music.[3]

Scarlatti's reinstatement in Naples (1708–9) by Cardinal Vincenzo

Grimani was primarily a political move – the Emperor's instructions were to restore old rights that the Spanish had infringed – and financially it was, we may suppose, his salvation. Opera in Naples continued, however, on the lines established before 1708 – importation and arrangements of Venetian works – to which was now added the distressingly successful local *commedia per musica*. This must have put Scarlatti in a more difficult position than he had experienced before 1700. He made attempts to gain a footing with the native audiences of the *commedia*, especially with his *Il trionfo dell'onore* of 1718 – an unsuccessful venture as far as it was intended to 'nobilitate' the tastes in the new genre. For his *drammi per musica*, he was very soon procuring new commissions from Rome (in addition to the works written for Naples) and in general succeeded in establishing relations with Roman patrons such as Cardinal Ottoboni and above all Francesco Maria Ruspoli, who was the patron of the Teatro Capranica.

c. Florence and Tuscany

It may perhaps be said that a relatively independent operatic life had been established in Tuscany during the seventeenth century. Apart from the court itself, supporters were to be found among the comparatively broad class of intellectuals who had organised themselves into the numerous academies of Florence, Siena and Livorno. Both of the regular theatres in Florence, the Pergola and the Cocomero, belonged to academies, and smaller academies primarily devoted to oratorio (and comparable to the oratorio-brotherhoods in Rome and Naples) may well have been founded primarily for musical purposes. Between about 1690 and 1706 Scarlatti seems to have been the most frequently performed composer in these 'academic' theatres and oratorio-halls. It was here that his whole life's work in both genres had its greatest effect, greater than anywhere else in the whole of Italy. What we still do not know is why, in spite of this, Scarlatti was actually commissioned only by the court i.e. Ferdinando, whose patronage was modelled on that of the Roman cardinals, and more particularly on his own family tradition. From 1702 to 1706 Scarlatti was continuously active for Ferdinando, and it may be that almost one half (i.e. more than hitherto indicated) of the operas given at the Teatro Cocomero were his. There may be a number of works adapted by him concealed among them.[4] It is easy to see that he was looking for a regular post in Florence in 1702: what still needs explaining is why he then went to Rome and ostensibly contented himself with a subordinate post as a church composer such as he could certainly have obtained in Florence. (It is probable that Ottoboni paid him a regular salary in Rome, or he would hardly have composed such works as the series of solo cantatas.) Ferdinando's polite dismissal of him in 1707 cannot have been simply a private matter between two individuals: it would be interesting to know, for instance, in what way Perti was superior to Scarlatti. It is significant that in precisely the same year performance of Scarlatti's music by the academies suddenly stops and its place in the repertory is taken mostly by works imported from Venice, as was the case in Naples in the years after 1702. Apparently there was a growing opposition to Scarlatti, and possibly to his operatic style. Could this be associated with the fact that here too the whole system of *accademie* was collapsing and giving way to that of the impresario?

d. Venice

Here I can be brief, since Scarlatti had virtually no relations with Venice. No opera of his (and as far as we know at present no oratorio) was given a second performance there, and this can only mean that the Venetian impresarios knew Scarlatti's style and were anxious to avoid the fiasco of 1707 with the works commissioned by Ottoboni. Dotti's satire on Scarlatti's appearance in that year does contain some hints (Pagano et al., pp. 185ff). There is no direct attack on Scarlatti's reputation, only ironical comment. Dotti could have written, as Zambeccari wrote for Naples – 'Per essere così buono, riesce cattivo' (Appx, no. 7). Two things have struck me about the score of *Mitridate*: (1) the unusual number of 'allegrissimo' tempi – note the composer's own fear (Appx, no. 5) that his tempi would be taken too slowly (possibly on account of the complexity of the music?) and that the music would therefore make too melancholy an effect. (2) the series of mistakes made by the professional theatre copyist in Venice, including mistakes in the underlay of the text. Was he perhaps too little acquainted with Scarlatti's setting of words?

e. Dissemination of Scarlatti's operas in general

Scarlatti's output was enormous – 114 operas according to his own reckoning, for sixty-six of which Rostirolla[5] can find titles (Termini finds eighty-two in the case of Pollarolo).[6] A very large number of these, however, were works composed during the years when he held a regular post in Naples (and were possibly a condition of that post). Two facts stand out as worthy of note: (1) Scarlatti hardly ever received *scritture* from foreign impresarios, whereas other composers, e.g. Pollarolo and Gasparini, received many commissions. What fees did Scarlatti demand, or receive? (2) Repeat performances of his operas in other towns, which would furnish clear evidence of their popularity and would have involved no question of fees, are frequent up to about 1700, though only south of the Appenines. After that they quickly become rarer, except in Florence where they were frequent up to 1706. One thing is quite clear – Alessandro Scarlatti was *not* an influential opera composer in the eighteenth century.

3. Comparison with contemporaries

In 1694 Scarlatti's reputation was at its height and he was thoroughly mature when he collaborated in the composition of *La Santa Genuinda,* an opera which Cardinal Pamphilij had performed as a *dramma sacro* in his Roman palazzo. We cannot here go into all the problems raised by collaborative productions of this kind (did the composers concerned come to an agreement in advance, or know each other's contributions?). All we can say is that Scarlatti must have known that his Act II was competing with Giovanni del Violone's Act I and Pollarolo's Act III. The metre, syntax and content of the text of Scarlatti's aria 'Cara destra che sparsa di neve' resembles that of Pollarolo's 'Vaghi lumi ch'il seno ferite'; the rhythmic character of the two arias is correspondingly similar (see Examples 1 and 2).[7] Although the tempo of the two pieces may well have corresponded also (Pollarolo's aria is at least 'allegro'), the rhythmic and melodic movement of Scarlatti's music is noticeably more short-breathed, more varied and indeed more playful than

Example 1
Scarlatti, *La Santa Genuinda* II, 17

Example 1 (*cont.*)

fiam-me, por - ti fiam - me al - l'ac - ce - so mio cor. Quan - to vez - zo - sa,

tan - to pie - to - sa, do - na-mi in bre - ve pa - ce, pa - ce ed a - mor.

[Da Capo]

[written out in the original]

Example 2
Carlo Francesco Pollarolo, *La Santa Genuinda* III, 14

ROSALBA

Va - ghi lu - mi, __   va - ghi lu - mi ch'il se - no __ fe - ri - te, __

Example 2 (*cont.*)

e de - sta - te_ nel - l'al - ma gli ar - do - ri,   e_ de -

the wide spans of Pollarolo's melody. Whereas Pollarolo's line, moving mostly stepwise, builds up to regular two- and four-bar units, sometimes making use of sequences, Scarlatti introduces new impulses of movement at least in every bar and often from one crotchet to the next. He also breaks up the text, repeating portions of it successively with different music and interrupting the line with inserted repetitions and with alternations between small and large intervals. What astonishes about Pollarolo's aria is its dance-like buoyancy, supported by the waltz-like accompaniment pattern of the violins. Scarlatti's bass is a severe ostinato with energetic intervallic gestures; Pollarolo's bass keeps to the tonic degrees, meekly accompanying the vocal line. Despite the spontaneity of the voice-part, Scarlatti's setting is full of calculated tension, whereas Pollarolo rather aims at an *al fresco* general impression. The natural tendency of performers would be to play Scarlatti too slow and Pollarolo too fast.

The text of the solo cantata 'Qualor l'egre pupille' was set by Scarlatti in Rome between 1702 and 1710 and by Handel before 22 September 1707 (see Example 3).[8] It suggests a brooding intellectual atmosphere perfectly captured by Scarlatti. In the first aria, 'Il pensiero' is compared to a ship on a stormy sea, and Scarlatti depicts the rolling of the waves by rolling passages in both the continuo and the voice-part. The voice is also given its own counter-motif for 'duro scoglio' and thus concentrates the listeners' attention on itself. Scarlatti relies more on the illustrative powers of the voice, Handel more on those of the instruments. Moreover, Handel's instrumental figuration itself demands a virtuoso cellist, whereas the voice is given less noticeable and less rewarding figures (*saltus duriusculus* for 'duro scoglio'?). Scarlatti elaborates the apparently profound maxim contained in the final lines into a long and demanding arioso (in which the harmony,

Example 3
Scarlatti, Cantata 'Qualor l'egre pupille', aria and closing recitative

Example 3 (*cont.*)

except on the word 'inganno', is simpler than it seems to the eye!) Handel makes these last lines, conceived by the poet as the climax of the work, a recitative of the simplest kind; and this seems to me the bolder and more theatrical solution, though audiences may well have expected something more. Scarlatti on the other hand faithfully fulfils the intellectual demands of the text.

Scarlatti's and Handel's settings of the *Salve regina* for solo voice and instruments are two very remarkable works to which too little attention has been paid (see Example 4).[9] Scarlatti's setting, which should be regarded as a late work, contains much that we, with our hindsight, could describe as 'Neapolitan', although it may well have nothing to do with Naples. Both composers aim at the greatest intensity of affect almost to the point of neglecting structural considerations, and both sacrifice 'stylistic unity' to effect. Handel achieves this effect in four ways: (a) by technical means, including virtuosity (b) by glaring differences between the individual

Example 4
Scarlatti, *Salve Regina*

Example 4 (*cont.*)

movements (c) by gestures of extreme pathos, particularly in the voice-part, and (d) by theatrical licences ('audacities'). Scarlatti is more reticent, and indeed more archaic and more ecclesiastical in the first movement, with its ostinato-like bass. Yet it seems to me that this moving bass-line, on which everything is at first concentrated, is also used to produce an effect of melancholy, whereas Handel's elaborate violin part is designed to astonish rather than to move the listener. It is only in the later movements that Scarlatti seems – for all his rhetoric and use of traditional techniques, such as an aria with ostinato bass – nearer to the eighteenth-century aesthetic of 'pleasing and touching' than the technically more ambitious Handel. What characterises Scarlatti's third movement, 'Ad te suspiramus', for instance, is not the illustrative chromaticism of 'flentes' and 'lacrimarum' but the highly emotional mood of the whole piece, its unremitting and insistent rhythm and its melodic manner. The penultimate section, 'Et Jesum', is purely a matter of harmonic colour, not extravagant but painted, as it were, with broad brush-strokes. The almost exaggeratedly 'Neapolitan' character of the siciliano with which Scarlatti ends the work suggests to me a conscious statement. Are we perhaps being given to understand by this topical inclusion of a popular 'folk' element that devotion to the Virgin is something open and familiar to the very simplest – something with a universal appeal to the human heart? On the other hand the artistic demands of Handel's corresponding movement give it an esoteric character: he is aiming here to give expression not to the familiar but to the extraordinary. This represents an apparent reversal of fronts, Scarlatti being most commonly accused of exclusiveness while Handel later aimed consciously at, and gained, a wider public. This contradiction remains no more than relative if we bear in mind the probable difference between the audiences of the two works – but it does show that Scarlatti could appeal to other audiences besides that of connoisseurs.

In other compositions Scarlatti and Handel are closer, and Handel's operas in particular must be considered when weighing up Scarlatti's importance for the eighteenth century. But Handel is not the sole measure of what later generations may have owed to Scarlatti. The only composer of importance who is known certainly to have been Scarlatti's pupil is in fact the composer who must concern anyone who seeks to interpret the stylistic changes of the early eighteenth century in opera and church music: Johann Adolf Hasse. But whoever compares the operas and solo cantatas written by the 'caro Sassone' in Naples (1724–30) with the late works of Scarlatti, will wonder whether Hasse's studies with Scarlatti went at all beyond elementary counterpoint – things, in fact, which Hasse no longer needed to learn since he, like Handel, was already a trained composer when he came to Italy. The characteristic features of Hasse's early works were melodies built on the triad, frequent use of sequences, schematic articulation of phrases, rather flat and rhythmically simple instrumental accompaniments and a tendency to periodic and easily graspable structure. All of these are in direct contradiction to Scarlatti's achievements as seen in the more significant works of any period in his life, with their care for characteristic and spontaneous-sounding detail, their polyphonic and concertante style and their ability to transform the lines even of an operatic libretto into, as it were, expressive prose. Fortunately we possess a direct object of comparison in Hasse's arrangements of the original arias from Scarlatti's last opera, *Griselda* (1721). These arrangements generally confirm what has been said above, even though details in them reveal that Hasse had an excellent understanding of what was characteristic in Scarlatti's setting of words and indeed tried – though not very successfully – to imitate it (see Strohm 1975, pp. 225–31). Hasse, however, either invented his new technique of composition himself or, more probably, developed it *from other sources*. And the same thing appears to be true of other, only slightly older, Neapolitan composers such as Sarri, Vinci and Leo, at any rate in their *operatic* writing. Did they learn from some place where Alessandro Scarlatti had not been appreciated for years and from whence Neapolitan impresarios had regularly imported operas up to 1720 – namely Venice? And is it not a remarkable fact that the operas of these Neapolitan composers, which immediately achieved an enormous popularity, were almost without exception commissioned by impresarios and not by courts or private patrons? This is a question I must leave unanswered, but confess that Pollarolo's aria of 1695 reminds me more of Vinci or Hasse than much of Scarlatti. But of what is Scarlatti's own music reminiscent? Or, more pertinently phrased, where and by whom did Scarlatti *wish* to be understood?

Scarlatti wrote his *Griselda* for Prince Ruspoli and there were no subsequent performances in any theatre. He composed almost fifty arias for this opera, by no means all of which were performed; despite some revisions, the autograph of the work[10] shows an almost devout precision only matched in calligraphy by works such as the Mass written for Ottoboni. In striking contrast to more successful eighteenth-century opera composers, Scarlatti very rarely borrowed from his own works. He must have been aware of this extravagance, and he consciously renounced any claim to popularity. The gratitude of his princely and ecclesiastic patrons can be seen in Ottoboni's epitaph, which describes him as 'optimatibus regibusque apprime carus'. This, however, was not the whole Scarlatti.

Although the majority of his works were written for the world of 'courts and princely patrons', this majority is concentrated in definite musical genres – the exclusive solo cantatas, serenatas with instrumental accompaniment, most of the oratorios and those operas that were individual court commissions. Other oratorios, and probably the most important of his instrumental works – the *Sinfonie di concerto grosso* – were addressed to an audience that was both aristocratic and academic. Only a fraction of his complete output – and that in a limited number of genres – was addressed to a wider public, or indeed to the 'public' in the modern sense: the series of operas written exclusively for Naples and in response to a long-standing obligation, and containing comic scenes; the relatively isolated single essay in the genre of the *commedia per musica*: and finally those of his church works meant for simple congregations. This latter group would include the *Salve regina* discussed above. The different styles to be found in Scarlatti's music should in fact be studied in relation to the different audiences addressed, and distinguished accordingly. If we went further and, for instance, made a comparative study of Scarlatti's concerted church music and that of other Neapolitan composers such as Leo, Feo and Durante, we might arrive at important conclusions about Scarlatti's significance for the eighteenth century. It seems very possible that his influence on that century was strongest in works written for the socially least exclusive public, whereas his most concentrated achievements stand isolated, as it were, having lost their appeal with the disappearance of the society for whose aesthetic needs they catered.`

Appendix

1. Giovanni Bononcini, Letter to G. A. Colonna, 8 February 1698, from Venice

'Regarding the compositions of your good father and my dear master [G. P. Colonna] it would seem a crimen laesae majestatis to use good stuff for these ruffians here, since (so far as I can make out) they do nothing but sarabands and jigs, and God knows I am telling the truth as regards not having answered earlier, I have thought it more diligent to be able to signify to you that there is no market here for such precious things.'
(A. Ademollo, 'Haendel in Italia', *Gazzetta Musicale di Milano* 44 (1889), pp. 258ff)

2. Charles Burney, *A General History of Music*, on Corelli

'At the time that Corelli enjoyed the highest reputation, his fame having reached the court of Naples, and excited a desire in the King to hear him perform; he was invited, by order of his Majesty, to that capital. Corelli, with some reluctance, was at length prevailed on to accept the invitation: but, lest he should not be well accompanied, he took with him his own second violin and violoncello. At Naples he found Alessandro Scarlatti, and several other masters, who entreated him to play some of his concertos before the King; this he for some time declined, on account of his whole band not being with him, and there was no time, he said, for a rehearsal. At length, however, he consented; and in great fear performed the first of his concertos. His astonishment was very great to find that the Neapolitan band executed his concertos almost as accurately at sight, as his own band, after repeated rehearsals, when they had almost got them by heart, "Si suona" (says he to Matteo, his second violin) "a Napoli!"

After this, being again admitted in to his Majesty's presence, and desired to perform one of his sonatas, the King found one of the adagios so long and dry, that being tired, he quitted the room, to the great mortification of Corelli. Afterwards, he was desired to lead in the performance of a masque composed by Scarlatti, which was to be executed before the King; this he undertook, but from Scarlatti's little knowledge of the violin, the part was somewhat awkward and difficult: in one place it went up to F; and when they came to that passage, Corelli failed, and was unable to execute it; but he was astonished beyond measure to hear Petrillo, the Neapolitan leader, and the other violins, perform that which had baffled his skill. A song succeeded this, in C minor, which Corelli led off in C major; "ricomminciamo", said Scarlatti good-naturedly. Still Corelli persisted in the major key, till Scarlatti was obliged to call out to him and set him right. So mortified was poor Corelli with this disgrace, and the general bad figure that he had made at Naples, that he stole back to Rome in silence.'

(Burney, vol. 2, pp. 439ff)

3. John Mainwaring, *Memoirs of the life of the late G. F. Handel*

Mainwaring recounts a similar 'failure' of Corelli's in an instrumental composition of Handel's (1707?), when Corelli is said to have excused himself: 'Ma, caro Sassone, questa musica è nello style francese, di ch'io non m'intendo.'

(Mainwaring, p. 55)

4. F. A. Pistocchi, Letter to G. A. Perti, from Florence

'Now the aforesaid Scarlatti is composing another motet, a large one I believe with solos, for the birthday of the Grand Duke which is this very next Wednesday; and they are saying in the town that he is using three subjects in the finale. I do not know how fortune in the world is clothed or depicted, as I, who am a nothing in this profession, have composed works with 2 and 3 subjects, and no one has remarked upon it, and now I hear all this fuss...Florence the 12th of August 1702.'

(Fabbri 1961, p. 45)

5. From the correspondence of Alessandro Scarlatti and Ferdinando de' Medici

'Throughout the opera I have observed a style more pleasing and melodious than learned, having been given to understand by the enlightenment of Sig. Stampiglia, that

H.R.H. enjoys music that is charming and compendious. Hence, in obedience to the royal instructions, I have attempted to execute this to the best of my ability.

The pace of the arias, beside being noted at the proper places, I have given in detail to Sig. Matteuccio, as being a virtuoso familiar with my style...'

Scarlatti on 9 August 1704 (Fabbri 1961, p. 55)

'I have tried diligently, in the fashioning of the same, to follow the respected instructions of H.R.H., and to conform with the wishes of Sig. Silvio Stampiglia, author of the opera (as I shall continue subsequently to do in the other two acts), and to whom I have described at length the manner and the tempo to be adopted in the arias in composing which I have consulted the mixed character of the audience rather than the promptings of my own poor pen: exactly as the author of the opera appears to wish, and as perhaps may be more agreeable to those wishing to take home with them arias that are easily retained in the memory and may be sung by all.'

Scarlatti on 27 June 1705 (Fabbri, p. 62)

'I shall be pleased if you would provide music that is preferably easy and noble in character and that, where this is possible, you should preferably keep it cheerful.'

Ferdinando on 8 April 1706 (Fabbri 1961, p. 69)

'H.R.H. will find spirit in the music, and at the same time all possible facility of understanding; nothing melancholy. And in those places where such a mood seems indispensable, it is not present and yet appears to be; hence it is enough that the pace of the music be chosen with good taste, without prejudice to its lyrical character (*Senza indebolir l'arioso*). I have marked the correct tempo at the beginning of each aria; and, at opportune moments, the loudness and softness of the instruments, which is simply the chiaroscuro that gives charm to any singing and playing.'

Scarlatti on 29 May 1706 (Fabbri 1961, p. 73)

6. Pier Jacopo Martello, *Della tragedia antica e moderna* (Rome 1713)

'And this music is therefore one of the most marvellous and perfect arts in the world, which does not perish in later years as do its authors or the voices or the instruments [which perform it]. Its characteristics give it perpetuity in men's eyes and minds, and these artists, who are as worthy of veneration as they are of love, deserve fame no less than do great poets and philosophers. Pasquini, Colonna, the two Scarlattis, Perti, Bononcini, Albergati, Ariosti, Zanettini, Benati, Pollaroli, Pistocco and many others whom it would take too long to enumerate will live as long as time lasts (*a par dei secoli*). In the anatomy of notes these have reached a point to which refinement of taste has never before penetrated and are the equals of our ancient Greek sculptors...'

(P. J. Martello, *Scritti*...ed. Hannibal S. Noce, in *Scrittori d'Italia* (Bari, 1963), vol. 225, p. 295)

7. The impresario F. M. Zambeccari in a letter from Naples on 16 April 1709

'As for those Gratians who are now meddling in the opera, I can only say you must know that Contarini is master at the theatre, but makes no appearances, forcing this role on Scarlatti [instead], who made the last opera, which pleased no one; so there will be the perpetual annoyance to have to hear him.

He is a great man, so great indeed that he fails because his compositions are extremely difficult and [resemble] chamber works, which do not succeed in the theatre. *In primis* any one who understands counterpoint will admire him, but in a theatre audience of a thousand, there are not twenty who do understand it and the rest are bored when they do not hear cheerful and theatrical stuff. Then the stuff being so difficult, performers have to pay the closest attention not to make a slip and have no liberty to make the gestures that come naturally to them, being simply too tired; hence speaking generally his style is not acceptable in the theatre, where what is needed is cheerful stuff and saltarelli, such as they give in Venice.'

(Lodovico Frati, 'Un impresario teatrale del settecento e la sua biblioteca', *RMI* 18 (1911), p. 69)

8. Pier Francesco Tosi, *Opinioni de' Cantori antichi e moderni*, Bologna 1723

'To composers – Gentlemen (To those of distinction I speak with due reverence), music has changed its style three times in my lifetime; the first style, popular in the theatre and in private gatherings, was that of Piersimone and Stradella : the second is that of the best living composers – and I leave it to others to judge whether they be modern or young men. Of your own style, which is by no means yet established in Italy and has no credit whatever north of the Alps, posterity will soon be speaking, since fashions do not last. But if the profession is to continue, and end with the world, either you will disenchant yourselves or your successors will carry out a reform. Do you know how? By removing abuses, and by recalling the first, the second and the third mode to relieve the fifth, the sixth and the eighth, overcome by their labours. They will resurrect the fourth and the seventh, which are dead for you and buried in church with the finals of the modes. To suit the taste of both singers and connoisseurs we shall have allegros interspersed here and there with moments of pathos. Arias will not be completely drowned by the indiscretion of instruments which overwhelm the studied colours of *piano* and voices that are either delicate or unwilling to shout. The importunate vexatiousness of unisons – invented by ignorance to conceal from the crowd the weaknesses of so many artists of both sexes – will no longer be tolerated. The lost harmony of instruments will be restored. Composers will write more for singers than for players : the voice part will no longer have the mortification of yielding its place to the violins. Soprani and contralti will not perform arias written for basses, disregarding a thousand octaves. And we shall have arias that are more tasteful and less similar : more natural and suited to the voice; more carefully studied and less painful to the ear : and the more noble the further they are removed from the common people.'   (pp. 72ff)

9. Contemporary handwritten comment in a libretto of L. Leo's *Il Cid* (Rome 1727)

'Not a success, the drama being too gloomy and the music not very good.'   (I-Vgc)

10. Contemporary opinion of F. Feo's *Ipermestra* (Rome 1728)

'...proved rather melancholy'.

(A. Cametti, 'Leonardo Vinci e i suoi drammi in musica al Teatro delle Dame', *Musica d'oggi* 6 (1924))

11. *Avvisi di Napoli* of 26 January 1723 on Mancini's *Trajano*, which had to be removed from the season's programme to make way for Sarri's *Partenope*

'...although good, it nevertheless proved tedious, being rather tragical and long'.

12. **Charles de Brosses' judgement of D. Sarri (1739) on the occasion of a performance of his *Partenope* in Naples**

'a learned composer, but arid and gloomy'.

(*Lettres familières sur l'Italie*, ed. Y. Bezard (Paris, 1931), vol. 1, p. 429)

Handel and his Italian opera texts

THE FOLLOWING deals with the texts of Handel's operas from *Rodrigo* to *Deidamia*, including the fragments and pasticci of his own composition, with some preliminary remarks about *Almira*. The object of the enquiry is to contribute to the knowledge and interpretation of Handel and of the conditions of his opera-writing, not to describe the content or to give a literary estimation of each individual opera text. The latter has in many individual cases already been done without always providing any concrete information about the composer.

Is it in fact possible to draw conclusions about the man from the study of these libretti? The immediate assumption is that the texts had something to do with him by the simple fact that they were once composed by him. That is of course a reasonable assumption; but in order to prove rather than simply suppose this, and to validate the thesis that Handel's music was not merely a supplementary addition to these texts, we must examine the origin of the operas as a whole and study the presuppositions of both music and text. In the case of Handel's operas particularly, the creative process begins before the writing of the first notes, which is only a part of the creative work. The first impulses and ideas for any opera can often be traced to some libretto upon which the composer chanced and often, too, to other vaguer stimuli more difficult to identify. These are the suppositions that I propose to examine, and my aim is to establish the elusive point of transition at which these ideas and impulses became factors in Handel's own creative process.

In order to do this we must make three clear distinctions which scholars have hitherto more or less shirked. In the first place, chronologically and with regard to the literary texts, we must distinguish between predecessors and sources, i.e. between texts which Handel did not use and may never have known and those which he actually used.[1] (Further distinctions must then of course be made with regard to *what* he knew about any projected text, whether it was only the fact of its having been set and performed or whether he was also aware of the occasion and the circumstances – whether he was acquainted only with the libretto or also with the music etc.) In the second place a distinction must be made between what was already in existence and what Handel composed. Neither Handel nor Haym was responsible for the recitative 'Alma del gran Pompeo' in *Giulio Cesare*: it was in the original text (see Knapp 1968). The dramatically superfluous part of Oberto in *Alcina* was not an invention of the original author but was added by Handel and his assistants. Thirdly, we must distinguish between what Handel himself wrote, or meant to write, and the part played by other hands in the production of these operas, whether with his assistance, his approval or even without his consent.[2] The point is not to separate these alien contributions from the rest of the work, but simply to understand how they fit in.

We must remember that Handel was writing operas in London, where the opera was of major political importance and inseparable from very concrete social conditions, and that he himself played a part in the development of those conditions. It is no secret, for example, that contemporary political events played a part in determining the choice of an opera's subject. The question is how the artist translated such subjects, whether he played them down or accentuated them, removed or actually restored their topicality (in the case, for instance, of some older libretti whose social or political relevance is thus to be discovered). Questions of this kind are relevant not only to the contents of opera plots: Lucchini's *Giove in Argo*, given as a 'festa teatrale' at Dresden in 1717, served a quite definite social purpose which was entirely absent when it was set and performed by Handel; and this put the whole *genre* in a new light.

Equally important in determining the character of Handel's works is the whole Italian operatic tradition. Present-day criticism of the dramatic or literary qualities of many Handel libretti cannot really escape responsibility by making the *opera seria* responsible for everything that we now find hard to accept. The *dramma per musica* of Handel's day was not, even from the literary point of view, a monolith of conventions from which there was no escape. Handel had the choice of various tendencies in both style and form, and his selection (insofar as it was his) shows very clear preferences for certain distinct elements in the tradition – we should remember on the other hand his problematical relationship with Metastasio and his attitude of indifference to Zeno.[3] One of these elements was certainly Italian operatic practice in the Germanic states which, through the Hanoverian dynasty, affected England. Handel was not free to suit himself in his choice of libretti. A certain section of the public was aware of their earlier history, and members of the aristocracy and the Court could recognise in the subject of an opera Handel's own attitude to tradition. The distribution of roles, for instance, and especially the ensemble demanded by Handel, entailed decisions which were by no means unimportant to London patrons and dilettanti. The same applied to Handel's behaviour with regard to *opera buffa*, then in its infancy. The majority of the public were of course less interested in the content of a libretto than in the singing and the production of a work, demanding of opera almost the exact opposite of what the English theatre generously provided. The Royal Academy represented the apparently absurd attempt to transplant, to a city which had the most varied and most aware theatrical tradition in Europe, a theatrical genre that, because it enjoyed a virtual monopoly in its land of origin, served much more general needs and was therefore unable to provide any intense individual satisfaction. The fact that Handel succeeded – whereas a Bononcini or a Porpora failed – in transforming what had been an experiment into continuous theatrical practice is only partially explained by his artistic superiority; this superiority was the product of a quite special coming to terms with tradition, and one which, in Handel's place of origin had itself become a tradition. It may well have been of more importance subsequently than is generally admitted that most of his time in Italy was spent in Rome, where there was then no opera: this at least prevented him from taking every operatic convention for granted.

Handel did not see the *opera seria* tradition as unified, and his solutions of its problems were just as varied. The obstinacy with which for decades Handel pursued his operatic plans and the resulting 'monumental' body of work are misleading. In the first place categories of style are diffuse and almost as difficult to reduce to a common denominator as in the oratorios; and in the second, there was a process of evolution which has certainly been underestimated by interpreters of Handel's music. The fact is that this evolution moved in waves; Handel was increasingly bold in linking advances into new territory with returns to a very early tradition – think only of such 'paired' works as *Lotario* and *Partenope* or a single work such as *Serse* – and there is therefore no parallel between him and the development of opera in general. Handel's dramatic ideas did not only change: under the pressure of circumstances, and simultaneous counter-pressure on his own part, they changed *very often*, and it often seems as though he were experimenting. Almost of necessity he kept returning to positions that he had already abandoned, and in this way his work gives the modern observer an impression of continuity, smoothness indeed, whereas in fact he was advancing step by step into a future that was for the most part uncertain. The interplay of tradition and progress in Handel's music, and the tension between individual and general artistic development, may be interpreted as a single dialectic: *his relationship to his own past*. Perhaps the most striking constant in Handel's operatic writing is the fact that he never set new texts, only those already in existence and quite regardless of whether his librettists were able or not to produce a new work. His starting point for a libretto, as in other things, was preferably something given, something that must first catch his imagination. As I hope to show in the following pages, these 'data' were in the case of operas often associated with his own past. Libretti and scores which he had encountered earlier, performances that he had seen, authors whom he had met personally – these provided the stimuli for operas which may only have been written many years later. Handel's decision to set a particular subject or libretto was thus often the result of something like a reminiscence, or even something autobiographical. Apart from Italian operatic practice in his native land, already referred to, Handel's richest experiences were those of Italian – and particularly Roman – musical life. The influence of this can be felt even in the oratorios.[4] But if personal experience was to be the basis of his ideas, this means refusing to accept ready made the achievements of other composers. He did not, in fact, set ready-made libretti but preferred, if possible, those still in the process of being written, commissioning librettists only at a point where his own imagination was already involved. The original author's ideas were, so to speak, re-developed and changed in the process.[5] In fact Handel's treatment of his opera texts is analogous to his musical 'borrowings', and his shaping of these texts shows all the same nuances that we find in those 'borrowings'.

The origins of *Almira* (8 January 1705)

The following is what we know about the earlier history of the text of *Almira*:

(a) Friedrich Christian Feustking took as his model the Italian opera *Almira*, performed in Brunswick in 1703 with music by Ruggiero Fedeli, the text of which goes back to a Venetian libretto by Giulio Pancieri (1691). This is clear from a comparison of the two libretti and scores.[6]

(b) In the preface to the libretto of his opera *La fedeltà coronata* of 1706 Reinhard Keiser says 'I have inserted some arias from my Almira because these had already been composed two years ago, before Almira was performed here...' (quoted from Chrysander, vol. 1, pp. 131ff).

(c) Mainwaring tells us that 'KEYSAR, from his unhappy position, could no longer supply the Manager, who therefore applied to HANDEL, and furnished him with a drama to be set. The name of it was ALMERIA' (Mainwaring, p. 37). Here we have Mainwaring interpreting the situation in a way that is demonstrably mistaken, saying that Keiser gave Handel the text because he himself could no longer remain with the management of the Opera. And in fact we may dismiss as 'interpretation' everything else that has been said about Keiser's part in the early history of Handel's *Almira* after Chrysander, including the statement that Keiser had not completed his *Almira* before Handel.

Feustking's text was in fact based not on one earlier version but on two, the Fedeli libretto mentioned above which therefore has nothing to do with Keiser and '"ALMIRA" Queen of Castile/ presented/ on the/ stage/ of the New Augustus-Burg in Weissenfels/ .../in an /OPERA/ d.(30) July,

ANNO 1704./' No composer is mentioned in the libretto. Renate Brockpähler gives 'Reinhard Keiser' as the composer and given the information quoted under (b) above and the fact of Keiser's relations with the court at Weissenfels, this is quite plausible.⁷

The libretto is a fairly independent German translation and a development of the Brunswick text from which the seventeen inserted Italian arias have of course been taken over. Feustking for his part follows far more closely the Weissenfels text, from which he often quotes verbatim (in many German arias, among other places) and only follows the Brunswick text in some details of the action e.g. the inclusion of the character of Raymondo, who does not appear in the Weissenfels libretto. On the other hand, Bellante, who appears in the Weissenfels libretto, is not in the Brunswick version. All of Feustking's Italian arias but one ('Mi da speranza al core') are to be found in the Weissenfels version. In some cases Feustking rewrites the Italian text of the Brunswick version and in others he takes his cue from the prose translation there (e.g. 'Almire, regiere und beherrsche selbst das Glücke').

The above facts may serve as the basis for a new enquiry into the origin of *Almira* and may point to some influence of Keiser's *Almira* of 1704 on Handel's opera.⁸

The operas in Italy: *Rodrigo* and *Agrippina*

The two operas that Handel wrote in Italy are the subject of my article in the *Rivista Italiana di Musicologia* (Strohm 1974). The following is a brief summary of its contents.

Copies of the libretto of *Rodrigo* are to be found in I-Bc (7355) and I-Bu (Aula V.Tab.1.A.III,Caps.99.11). The title-page runs thus:

VINCER SE STESSO/ È/ LA MAGGIOR VITTORIA/ DRAMA PER MUSICA/ Rappresentato /IN FIRENZE/ NELL' AUTUNNO/ Dell' Anno 1707./SOTTO LA PROTEZIONE/ DEL SERENISSIMO/ PRINCIPE/ DI TOSCANA./ Per Vincenzio Vangelisti. Con licenza de' Sup./

The names of poet and composer are not given, and there is no dedication. The list of characters and performers is on page 7:

RODRIGO Re delle Spagne – Il Sig. Stefano Frilli.
ESILENA sua Moglie – La Sig. Anna Maria Cecchi detta la Beccarina.
FLORINDA Sorella di Giuliano Conte di Ceuta – La Sig. Aurelia Marcello.
GIULIANO Conte di Ceuta, e fratello di Florinda – Il Sig. Francesco Guicciardi.
EVANCO figlio di Vitizza già Re d'Aragona – La Sig. Caterina Azzolina detta la Valentina.
FERNANDO Generale di Rodrigo – Il Sig. Giuseppe Perini.
Un Bambino che non parla, figlio di Rodrigo, e di Florinda.

The following are the major differences between the libretti and the *Gesamtausgabe* (HG):

Act I, Scene 1 (missing in HG):
           Recitative Florinda, Rodrigo: 'Ah mostro, ah furia...'
           Aria Rodrigo. 'Occhi neri–voi non siete a pianger soli'
I,2:   Recitative Florinda solo
           Aria Florinda (not Rodrigo) 'Pugneran con noi le stelle'
I,3:   (Aria Esilena 'Nasce il sol' missing)
I,5:   (Aria Giuliano 'Dell' Iberia al soglio invitto' missing)
I,6:   Aria Evanco (not Evaneo). 'Vibri pur iniqua sorte' instead of 'Heroica fortezza'
I,7:   (missing in HG) Recitative Giuliano
           Aria Giuliano. 'Con voci care in petto' (Arioso?)
(I,8 = I,7   in HG etc.)
II,1:   Opening aria Giuliano. 'Quanto belle, quanto care'
II,4:   Aria Florinda. 'Vanne pur tenero affetto' instead of 'Fredde ceneri'
II,6:   Aria Esilena. 'Ti conforta oh caro, spera' instead of 'Empio fato'
III,1:   (missing in HG) Recitative Rodrigo solo
           Aria Rodrigo. 'Qua rivolga gli orribili acciari'
III,2:   Recitative Esilena, Rodrigo
           Aria Rodrigo. 'Sposa diletta io parto' instead of the duet
III,7:   Aria Florinda (not Evanco). 'Così m'alletti'
III,9:   Aria Evanco. 'Io son vostro oh luci belle' instead of 'Lucide stelle'

Final scene (= III,10; missing in HG): Tutti. Recitative Rodrigo Coro. 'L'amorosa Dea di Gnido'

The title of the opera normally in use – *Rodrigo* – is only that handed down by Mainwaring. The title of the libretto was, as in the case of some contemporary operas, a hendecasyllable resembling a proverb: it may well have had little interest for Handel and therefore been forgotten. As the libretto shows, Handel's opera was not performed at the Villa di Pratolino but in Florence. R. and N. Weaver have established that it must have been given in the theatre in the Via del Cocomero, as the cast is nearly identical to that of the opera *Stratonica* by Francesco Gasparini, performed in that theatre in October 1707 (Weaver and Weaver, pp. 209f). It seems significant that the well-known singer 'Vittoria' (Tarquini, detta la Bombace), who plays a part in Mainwaring's account of Handel's stay in Florence, did not appear in his opera; she sang at Pratolino only.[9] R. and N. Weaver suggest that *Rodrigo* was performed in November/December 1707; even so, it is likely that Handel, who was in Rome until the end of September,[10] completed part of the composition before his arrival in Florence. This would mean that he would have received the *scrittura* for the opera from Ferdinando de' Medici (or from the impresario) either by letter or already during his visit to Florence in 1706. The differences between the autograph score and the printed libretto also suggest that the work was mainly composed in Rome. The texts, or versions, used by Handel in Acts I,3, II,4 and III,9 are closer to the model libretto of 1700 than are those of the final, printed text. An earlier version of the text may have been despatched to

Handel in Rome; after his arrival in Florence with the almost finished score, it was found necessary to make changes which were not entered in his manuscript, and these have therefore – with the exception of three arias – disappeared.[11] The libretto-model is F. Silvani's *Il duello d'amore, e di vendetta*, which was performed with music by M. A. Ziani during Carnival, 1700 at the Teatro S. Salvatore in Venice. There is a second, variant edition of this dating from the same season.[12] Handel's text is closer to the first edition. The revision of the text was probably made by Ferdinando's Court poet, Antonio Salvi, with whom Handel must have become acquainted at the time.

The story of the composition of *Agrippina* has to be reconstructed if only because it is still quite uncertain to what extent Handel, in the years before 1709/10 could have imitated Venetian models i.e. whether he had even encountered Venetian opera.[13] Apart from indirect experience at the Hamburg Opera there is a probability that Handel was in Venice during the Carnival of 1708 (Strohm 1974 pp. 164ff). He may then have also met a number of the singers (Boschi, Durastanti) who were later to sing in *Agrippina*: he certainly had dealings with them later that year in Rome and Naples. The librettist of *Agrippina* was Cardinal Vincenzo Grimani, who was Imperial Ambassador to the Vatican before his appointment as Viceroy of Naples on 1 July 1707. He was a sworn political opponent of the Pope, Clement XI, and the libretto is an open attack, half satirical and half realistic, on the Papal Court. He may well have had the Pope himself in mind as the Emperor Claudius. The handsome manuscript copy of the score in Vienna[14] is probably the dedication-copy presented by Grimani to his Habsburg master, the then King Charles III of Spain. Grimani's text is possibly only a reworking of an older libretto, either his own or another poet's. The political references that Grimani himself may have added were possibly a particular reason for his wishing the work to be performed. Handel may well have made Grimani's acquaintance as early as 1707, or at the latest spring 1708, in Rome. Grimani's Neapolitan connections will have enabled him to recommend Handel to a patron in Naples, the Duca d'Alvito, who was a supporter of the Habsburgs.[15] Handel left Naples in mid-July 1708[16] and there is no evidence of his having any further contact with Grimani, who will hardly have had time for operatic plans, let alone writing libretti, in the period immediately after taking up his post in Naples. Most probably therefore the writing of the libretto and the commissioning of Handel took place *before* the summer of 1708, possibly even in 1707, and in Rome.

Rinaldo (24 April 1711)

The history of *Rinaldo* is attested by the prefaces supplied by the librettists Aaron Hill and Giacomo Rossi (Deutsch, pp. 32ff; Fassini, pp. 26ff), though it is not quite clear how much Hill actually contributed. He was obviously concerned to make Rossi's contribution appear as large as possible, he himself being well enough known in London while Rossi needed all the recommendation he could get. We may suppose that Rossi translated Hill's prose dialogue into Italian verse and may, on internal evidence, have supplied new texts for a number of arias ('to fill up the model I had drawn' according to Hill). In some cases he had to take into account an already existing prosody in order to facilitate the use of music already composed by Handel. This was a poetical technique by which he later made himself useful to the composer, providing him after 1729 with some skilful 'parody' texts for his pasticci.

Hill must have been acquainted with Tasso's poem and its historical material and perhaps felt no need to take as models earlier *Rinaldo* libretti, though he does mention them in passing. The most recent of these was F. Silvani's *Armida al campo* (Venice 1707), on which Hill does not depend. Hill departs from Tasso in the matter of the action but emphasises the fundamental poetic character of Tasso's poem, in which military, knightly elements alternate with the religious or moral. In addition to these there is an important further interest, namely magic, which also plays a part in Tasso.

Aaron Hill wanted to give Italian opera in London a new direction, something more in accordance with 'tastes and voices' in England and that would provide the eye with more sumptuous spectacle. The stage-sets and machines in *Rinaldo*, for which Heidegger was partly responsible, were to prove a lasting success (and from this time on the operas that succeeded best in London have always been the most handsome productions!). But it is hard at first sight to see how *Rinaldo* was any more in accordance with English taste than, say, *Almahide* or *Idaspe*. Hill now even wanted to develop an English opera to challenge the Italian. But he was not even able to get rid of the castrati – whom he probably had in mind when he spoke of English 'tastes and voices'. But it is perhaps of importance that he did not confine his appeal to aristocratic audiences, addressing the libretto to 'the Gentlemen of my Country', thus including the cultivated middle class. Both Hill and Handel himself were moving in middle-class circles in London at this time, where there was considerable opposition to Italian opera (see in particular Lang 1966, pp. 120ff). This appeal to the middle class and the emphasis on commonsense ethics and Christian morality constitute, with the knightly and magic in *Rinaldo*, characteristics which clearly look forward to *Orlando* and *Alcina*. Is it a matter of chance that Hill again mentions his dream of an English opera, in an exactly corresponding sense, a few weeks before the performance of *Orlando* (letter to Handel dated 5 December 1732 see p. 66)? If it is another twenty years before we find Handel returning to the aesthetic of *Rinaldo* and to the same cultural attitudes, the explanation doubtless lies in his closer connections with the London aristocracy during those years.

Il Pastor fido (22 November 1712)

Who was responsible for the production of this opera, which many scholars have considered a blunder? A possible theory is that Giacomo Rossi, having had success with his *Rinaldo* based on Tasso, wanted to follow this with a work based on Guarini but came to grief because he no longer had Hill as his collaborator. (We do not know whether on this occasion Rossi worked directly from any existing libretto.) There is however too much against this theory. In the first place the poor success of the work with the public is more plausibly explained by Owen Swiny's management, which was responsible for the unattractive sets and mediocre ensemble. Secondly, Rossi did not here exhibit any faults, from the purely literary point of view, that were not to be found in *Rinaldo*. More important than either of these considerations is the fact that the shift in fashion from the chevaleresque and the spectacular to classicistic pastoral was not confined to Rossi and Handel – Nicola Haym's pasticcio *Dorinda*, produced on 10 December 1712, was also a pastoral piece and also failed. It seems rather that the London aristocracy with its taste for the classical had begun to play a larger role in operatic affairs; and chief among them was Richard Boyle, Earl of Burlington, who had been one of Handel's protectors at least since 1713 and may well have liked both the text and the music of *Il Pastor fido*. Guarini's poem was in any case well known in London, and there was even an English translation.[17]

It is however still possible that Handel himself was responsible for the choice of this precise subject. There is an Italian setting of *Il Pastor fido* in the library at Hanover, where Handel was active in 1711/12, a work that had been commissioned by Duke Johann Friedrich who died in 1679.[18] An operatic version of Guarini's poem seems also to have been known at the Düsseldorf court,[19] which Handel visited in 1711. Handel's *Pastor fido* shares a number of features with a later commission, *Atalanta*, and these might be related not simply to the genre, but to the circumstances in which the two works were written.

Teseo (10 January 1713)

An entry in the *Opera Register* (p. 201) for the beginning of 1713 runs thus: 'Mr. O. Swiny ye Manager of ye Theatre was now setting out a new Opera, Heroick, all ye Habits new and richer than ye former with 4 New Scenes, and other Decorations and Machines. Ye Tragick Opera was called Theseus...'

The failures of *Pastor fido* and *Dorinda* had shown that no profit could be made in London with operas that were poorly produced. Swiny, Handel and Haym now set out together to remedy this situation. *Teseo* represents a change from pastoral opera not only in theatrical presentation, which rivalled the still popular *Rinaldo* in magnificence, but also stylistically. The compiler of the *Opera Register*, generally very sparing with nice distinctions of style, calls the opera 'Heroick' as well as 'Tragick'. No Italian opera at the Haymarket before or since was so markedly a classical tragedy as Handel's five-act *Teseo*. Meanwhile the work still remained strictly within the limits of that classicistic taste as now unmistakably drawn by Burlington House. Haym dedicated the libretto to Lord Burlington, who may also have been responsible for the suggestion of introducing Quinault's *Thésée* (Paris 1675 with music by Lully) as an Italian opera.[20] Such direct links with the Court opera of Louis XIV have no parallel, except occasionally in Germany.

There was a political background to this artistic decision: England's new pro-French policy in this last phase of the War of the Spanish Succession. The career of the Duke of Marlborough, Louis XIV's greatest enemy, had already been truncated by this volte-face in Anglo-French relations, which was primarily the work of the aristocracy, including Lord Burlington.

Dean (1969, p. 83) describes *Teseo* as 'a hybrid between the classical-heroic and magic types'. It is an important fact that the Christian-moral element that we observed in *Rinaldo* is absent here. If there is a direct line from *Rinaldo* to *Orlando* and *Alcina*, the line from *Teseo* leads to the next works designed to please Lord Burlington, *Silla* and *Amadigi*.

Lucio Cornelio Silla (June 1713)

J. Merrill Knapp, who discovered the libretto of this work, has described the particular circumstances in which the performance took place.[21] It may be significant that an opera with a classical Roman plot should have been given at Burlington House in honour of the French Ambassador, Louis d'Aumont.[22] The fact that Giacomo Rossi, who signed the dedication to the ambassador, was responsible for the text, suggests the existence of an earlier Italian libretto, though none has so far been identified. The text may have had something to do with d'Aumont's personal taste: he is described in the *Opera Register* of 1713 (p. 203) as being an enthusiastic frequenter of Italian opera. Earlier i.e. pre-1713 Italian operas on Silla include *Silla* with music by D. Freschi (Venice 1683), and with music by F. Mancini (Naples 1703); *Il tiranno eroe* by Vincenzo Cassani, music by T. Albinoni (Venice 1711). None of these three texts[23] can have served Rossi as a direct model, though it is possible that he worked from a version of the 1683 text.

Amadigi di Gaula (23 May 1715)

The production of *Amadigi* shows Handel still under the spell of Burlington House and the classicistic, French-orientated taste of the aristocracy. Haym

(*Teseo*) and Rossi (*Silla*) are now joined by J. J. Heidegger, a new member of the circle, and it was he that signed the dedication of the work to Burlington, not as author of the libretto but as impresario. The fact that *Amadigi* is another translation from the French points to Haym as the librettist.[24]

Handel as opera-composer was at that time tied only to Burlington, whereas Haym and Heidegger had spread their activities far wider and were pursuing different artistic aims in their other operas, more particularly pasticci of recent Venetian works, the libretti of Zeno and Silvani and the scores of Gasparini.[25] Handel's lack of interest in operatic imports of this kind is particularly remarkable when we consider his later activities.

Radamisto (27 April 1720)

The object of the Royal Academy of Music was to establish Italian opera in London on a firm footing. In 1720 the opera seemed to be materially ensured for years ahead; with Handel at the artistic centre of the undertaking, a new period in the operatic history of London could begin. He was now, as never before, responsible not only for engaging soloists, but also for adapting operas from abroad and for providing possible libretti for his own use, generally obtained from Italy. He personally dedicated the libretto of *Radamisto* to the king, and the dedication contains no mention of Haym, who had adapted the text for London.

Handel obtained the libretto model from Florence. Domenico Lalli's *L'amor tirannico* had had its first performance at Venice in the autumn of 1710, and Gasparini's setting – with the music probably revised by the composer himself – was staged at the Teatro del Cocomero in Florence during the Carnival season of 1712. The text of this second version provided the basis for Handel's.[26] The *argomento* of the 1712 libretto is quoted by Handel verbatim. On the title-page (1712) we read that the performance took place 'sotto la protezione del Serenissimo Principe di Toscana'. Handel must in fact have remained in contact with the court of Ferdinando de' Medici (who died 30 October 1713) after he reached London, as is also suggested by his use of the text of *Rodelinda* of 1710. It is interesting that he preferred Lalli's version to earlier treatments of the same material, including a *Radamisto* which he may himself have seen in Florence during the autumn of 1709.

Haym's alterations to the original libretto, which cannot be detailed here, were made under Handel's supervision; and it is noticeable that the text of Zenobia's final aria ('O scemami il diletto') came from another libretto in Handel's possession, *Ginevra principessa di Scozia* (1708) on which *Ariodante* was to be based.

The new versions of *Radamisto* given in the seasons of 1720/1, 1721/2 and 1727/8 (see Clausen, p. 204) diverge further from the original.

Muzio Scevola (15 April 1721)

The text of this opera by Paolo Rolli is printed in the first volume of his *Componimenti poetici* (see Fassini, p. 44), but there were earlier models. Nicolò Minato wrote a *Muzio Scevola* for Venice as early as 1665, and one of the many reworkings of this was given at Wolfenbüttel in 1692. This was followed by a number of German versions mostly based on a translation by J. C. Bressand made for Hamburg in 1695 and entitled *Clelia*.[27] Later works belonging to the same tradition are in the first place a reworking of the subject by Piovene for Venice in 1712 (*Porsenna* with music by Lotti) and further performances, and then a *Muzio Scevola* by S. Stampiglia, set by G. Bononcini in Vienna (1710).[28] Rolli's libretto seems to be partly indebted to Stampiglia, although none of Bononcini's 1710 music appeared in his London setting of the second act.

The choice of the libretto, and its rewriting, seems to have been determined less by Handel than by the aristocratic party behind Bononcini and Rolli. Their interests, in fact, determined both the apportioning of the composition (Amadei seems to have been a favourite with them) and also, at a higher political level, the kind of peace-offering to the king that is to be found in Rolli's dedication to George I[29] and can be read into the dramatic action of the piece. In this the conservative aristocracy are identifiable with the defenders of Roman republican liberty, while George I is identified with the Etruscan king Porsenna who represents a threat to that liberty but who in the end nobly abandons his plans of conquest and betroths his daughter to the Roman hero Orazio – a detail introduced into the original by Rolli. Rome's own native oppressor, Tarquinius, is not included in this political compromise. The most formidable enemy of the London aristocracy at this time was the Whig leader, Sir Robert Walpole, who was prime minister after 1722. In fact the Tories' disguised offer to drop the traitor 'Tarquinius' did not therefore succeed with the king. Musically speaking, too, the effect of *Muzio Scevola* was not quite what was expected; contemporary reactions interpreted this communal production not as an offer of reconciliation but as a challenge in which Handel is named as 'victorious' (see Deutsch, pp. 126ff; Fassini, p. 60).

Floridante (9 December 1721)

Konrad Sasse has traced references to contemporary politics in Rolli's *Floridante*.[30] His interpretation can be expanded if we look at the libretto on which Rolli based his. Fassini (p. 60) gives its title as *La costanza in trionfo*, written by F. Silvani and first performed in Venice in 1696.[31] Although Rolli changed all the names of the roles and the site of the action, the story remains identical.

Silvani 1696	Rolli 1721
Gustavo tiranno di Norvegia	Oronte re di Persia
Leonilde che si crede sua figlia	Elmira figlia supposta d'Oronte
Sveno principe di Sarmatia generale dell'armi Norvegie	Floridante principe di Tracia
Marianne figlia di Gustavo	Rossane vera figlia d'Oronte
Lotario principe francese sconosciuto, fatto prigioniero di guerra da Sveno, sotto nome di Daliso	Timante principe di Tiro prigioniero al nome di Glicone
Flavio capitano	Coralbo satrapo Persiano
Riccardo servo	(—)

Sasse cleverly identifies Rolli's title-role with John Churchill, Duke of Marlborough, conqueror of the French in the War of the Spanish Succession, an ally of the conservative aristocracy and a patron of Bononcini. The dramatic action of the piece involves the reconciliation of the 'Generale' (Sveno/Floridante) with his former French enemy (Lotario/Timante) to unite against the 'Tiranno' (Gustavo/Oronte) of Norway, easily identified with Great Britain. The tyrant and usurper is eventually dethroned. In the circumstances in which Britain found herself in 1721 the piece could be seen as a challenge to George I, the Hanoverian intruder, who himself pursued a pro-French policy, but only when he had reasons to fear too close a link between his own nobles and France. If Walpole was the object of attack in *Muzio Scevola*, in *Floridante* it is the king himself. On this occasion Rolli dedicated the libretto not to the king but to the Prince of Wales. We may wonder why Handel set such an anti-Hanoverian work; but he was dependent on the directors of the Academy, and it was Rolli's and Bononcini's friends among them who were at that time in the majority. Handel may have insisted on the change of setting and names (already undertaken by the librettist) as a condition of his collaboration, unless this precaution was already part of the commission; in any case it considerably weakens the polemical character of the piece. There was a contemporary instance of a 'transposition' of this kind in the opera *Arsace* (1 February 1721). It was an open secret in London that in Salvi's libretto (which was originally entitled *Amore e maestà*) events of English history were presented under an oriental disguise.[32] Later Handel was to change a name in *Lotario* and transpose roles and scene of action in *Sosarme* – only while he was actually engaged in composing and for a different reason, though here again in order to avoid a historical reference.

There is no exact evidence to show which version of *Costanza in trionfo* Rolli used. The libretti used at Venice in 1696 and 1697, at Ferrara in 1697 and Livorno in 1706 have no aria texts in common with *Floridante*, though this does not exclude any of them as original models. It is worth mentioning a German version performed several times after 1704 with the title *Leonilde oder die siegende Beständigkeit*.[33]

Ottone (12 January 1723)

Ottone is the first – but not the last – of the operas with whose original text Handel became acquainted through a performance. He must have been present at one of the performances of Lotti's *Teofane* given at Dresden in September 1719. Apart from the singers, whom he had come to engage,[34] and Pallavicino's libretto, he must also have been interested by Lotti's music. As late as 1725 he included in the pasticcio *Elpidia* two bass arias for Giuseppe Boschi who had sung them in *Teofane* (see pp. 167–9 below). Handel knew almost all the singers performing at Dresden in 1719 from his Italian days – not only Senesino, whom he was to engage as his chief artist for London, but also Margherita Durastanti, Boschi (*Agrippina*), Guicciardi (*Vincer se stesso*), Matteo Berscelli and the *primadonna* Santa Stella Lotti. Had Handel been able to engage all these singers for London then and there, it may well be that his first opera for the Academy would not have been *Radamisto* but *Ottone*. The importance he attached to the chief female role in *Ottone* can be seen from the fact that he did not produce this work in 1720/1, when Senesino, Durastanti, Boschi and Berscelli were all in London, but waited until the following season (1722/3) when Francesca Cuzzoni was available. He gave greater importance to her part, which Santa Stella Lotti had sung in Dresden, by adding a number of arias. On the other hand the tenor role of Isauro was entirely omitted, because Handel could not get Guicciardi or any other tenor. Handel's autograph (Squire, pp. 56ff) reveals a large number of cuts or substitutions, and a majority of these alterations relate to Cuzzoni's role and only became necessary after her arrival in London. Haym was responsible for the new version of the text, which he dedicated to his patron, the Earl of Halifax (Fassini, p. 68), and he turned for some of the later additional arias to Pallavicino's original texts ('D'innalzar i flutti').

The occasion for which *Teofane* was written was a marriage, and this is reflected in the subject of the work – the marriage of the Saxon Emperor Otto II to the Byzantine princess Theophanu. At the time (A.D. 972) this was a clever political move, which the Elector of Saxony was now trying to imitate by allying his house to the Habsburgs. It was common practice of German courts in Handel's day to choose as subjects for operas historical events which glorified the reigning monarch in the person of some character famous in national or local history. Examples of this are to be found in Steffani's *Enrico Leone* (Hanover 1689), *Arminio* (Düsseldorf 1707) and *Tassilone* (Düsseldorf 1709); Schürmann's *Heinrich der Vogler* (Brunswick 1718), *Rudolphus Habspurgicus* (Brunswick 1723) and *Ludovicus Pius* (Brunswick 1726). In the same category as these are the operas given in Hamburg, which had a more restricted historical reference, such as Keiser's *Störtebecker* (1701) and Telemann's *Emma und Eginhard* (1728). 'Germanic' subjects of this kind were preferred even in the case of imported Italian operas: an *Ottone* by Frigimelica-Roberti and Pollarolo (Venice, 1694) was dedicated to Ernst August of Hanover and reached the Brunswick stage in 1697.[35] The subject in this case was Otto III, while the libretto of Antonio Salvi's *Adelaide* – written for the marriage of the Bavarian Electoral Prince Karl Albert, also with a Habsburg archduchess – concerns Otto I, Handel's later *Lotario* (see pp. 59f.).

Handel's predilection for 'historical truth', which is perceived by Sasse,[36] was not a matter of chance; it had been a concern of German theatres for two generations, and not least in Hanover, where Duke Ernst August had employed Steffani. Just as there is an artistic link between Handel and Steffani, so opera in London during the reign of George I is in a sense a continuation of opera in Hanover under his father Ernst August. The choice of subject in *Ottone* is to be explained even more obviously by politics and history because the Guelf dynasty had almost greater justification in considering themselves heirs of the Saxon emperors than the Wettin Elector in Dresden. In opera libretti of the Baroque period, and not only in Handel's, all representations of history have some bearing on the present. In London *Ottone* was a topical work, whether or not the figure of Adalberto was an allusion to the Pretender, James Stuart (see Sasse and others). On the other hand the references in the libretto to a royal marriage would be lost on a London audience, and the final scene of a *Germania ex machina* was of course cut. Handel's opera was performed in Germany soon afterwards, when it was given at Brunswick with the title *Ottone re di Germania* (summer 1723).[37]

Flavio (14 May 1723)

The libretto of Handel's *Flavio* was based by Haym on a work given in 1696 at the Teatro Capranica in Rome with the title *Il Flavio Cuniberto*.[38] Haym was a cellist in Rome at that time and must have been responsible for bringing the libretto to Handel's notice. An earlier version with the same title, by Matteo Noris (Venice 1682), was not used by Handel, who probably did not know it. Most of the aria texts had already been substituted in 1696, when the version used may have been Silvio Stampiglia's. In the 1696 preface there are references to further performances of the libretto in Naples, Milan, Genoa, Modena and Livorno. The last two are nearest to the Roman version, which was composed by Luigi Mancia (communication from Prof. L. Lindgren). A. Scarlatti set the text for Pratolino in 1702. Apart from this there were performances in Venice (1687), Florence (1697) and Genoa (1702).[39] Handel's original title for the opera was *Emilia* and this was clearly changed in order to avoid possible confusion with Bononcini's similar-sounding *Erminia* (30 March 1723).

The many alterations to which this work was subjected even before performance still need investigating and are probably to be explained by a mixture of dramaturgical problems raised by the rewriting of the text and casting difficulties. Some of the arias that were either shifted or 'parodied' had possibly been composed before Haym had really finished work on the libretto.

Giulio Cesare in Egitto (20 February 1724)

H. Chr. Wolff has already established that this libretto is by G. F. Bussani and was set in 1677 by Sartorio for the Teatro S. Salvatore in Venice.[40] After comparing the two versions of 1677 and 1724, J. Merrill Knapp is of the opinion that Haym must have worked from a third version, since many of the arias are different (Knapp 1968). Even so Handel also set five aria-texts from the 1677 version ('V'adoro pupille', 'Belle dee di questo core', 'Nel tuo seno amico sasso' and two others which were cut before the first performance – 'Speranza nudrice' and 'Questo core incatenato'). All five of these texts also appear in the libretto of a performance given in Naples in 1680.[41] Wolff assumes that Handel was acquainted with the subject before he left Germany, and this is in any case possible in the case of F. C. Bressand's Cleopatra (Brunswick 1691), which may be based on an Italian source (score or libretto) which reached Germany through the Hanover court. The Duchess Sophie certainly attended the 1677 performance in Venice, and the score of a twin work – Antonino e Pompeiano by Bussani and Sartorio (S. Salvatore 1677) – reached Hanover through either its dedicatee, the Duchess Benedikta Henriette, or Sartorio himself.[42]

In London there were casting difficulties which involved among other changes the elimination of one part even before the performance (the character of Berenice, corresponding to Bussani's Rodispe). During the 1724/5 season the part of Nireno was also cut, or rather replaced by a Nerina, who could have been sung by the contralto Benedetta Sorosina, who was a member of Handel's company in 1725.

Deutsch (p. 280) mentions a performance of Handel's Giulio Cesare in Vienna (1731). The name of the composer is not given in the libretto (A-Wn), but it was probably Luca Antonio Predieri, who set the text for the first time in 1728 and had connections with the Vienna Court in 1732, if not earlier.

Tamerlano (31 October 1724)

The history of Tamerlano is very complicated and is the subject of a detailed study by J. Merrill Knapp (1970). According to Knapp Handel composed the work on a text adapted by Haym, Agostino Piovene's Il Tamerlano, given at the Teatro S. Cassiano, Venice in 1711 (the '1710' on the libretto is an old-style dating), with music by F. Gasparini. Handel's autograph bears the dates 3–23 July 1724; but in the final version of the opera he made use of a still later version of the text, namely *Il Bajazet* (Reggio Emilia 1719), again with music by Gasparini, who was obliged to re-set almost all the arias owing to changes in the text.[43] It was primarily in the opening and closing scenes that Handel borrowed from this more recent version. His autograph contains, besides the final version, rejected passages from the first version and intervening stages of the composition. So much for Knapp's information: he leaves open the question of when and why Handel made these changes. The final date on the autograph (23 July) represents the *terminus a quo*, since it can only refer to the original version. Some alterations (though not those in the scenes mentioned above) were made so late that they are not even taken into account in the original version of the conducting score, which was certainly not begun until a few weeks before the performance. (see Clausen, pp. 237ff). But the interjacent alterations – mostly in the part of Bajazet – are the most important. Handel never made such extensive alterations to his original conception of an opera simply because he had in the meantime come upon another version of the libretto.

On the other hand he often allowed himnself to be influenced by the wishes of newly engaged singers (in *Ottone*, for instance) and in this case it was the tenor Francesco Borosini, who had been engaged from Vienna for the part of Bajazet, and may well not have arrived in London until after Handel had completed his autograph. Borosini would naturally bring a copy of the 1719 libretto of *Bajazet* with him, as he had sung the title-role in this opera, which had been reshaped in accordance with his wishes. He probably even had a copy of Gasparini's score, which he would have shown to Handel, who borrowed a number of Gasparini's ideas (see the music examples in Knapp 1970): Bajazet's first aria ('Lacci, ferri'), which was planned at an intermediary stage, and the aria 'Lieto, e forte' in the final version resemble Gasparini's 'Lieto, e forte' of 1719. A score of the 1719 opera, now in the Staatliche Museen at Meiningen, was presented in 1727 by Borosini to Duke Anton Ulrich of Sachsen-Meiningen.[44] It is an Italian copy and I suspect it to be the one used by Handel in 1724. The title-page, which was added at a later date in Germany, runs: BAJAZET/ Drama per Musica/ Che fu rappresentata a Reggio di Modena/L'Anno 1721, [an error!] La Poesia è del Nobile Venetiano Pioveni/ Toltone l'ultima Scena che fù composta dal Zanella secondo/ L'Idea del Sig.^{re} Borosini Questo Zanella è un Poeta illustre Modonese./ La Musica è del Sig.^{re} Gasparini/.' The 'last scene', which is thus a joint production of Ippolito Zanella and Francesco Borosini, means of course Bajazet's last scene. Handel was not the first to encounter a dramaturgical problem at the end of the piece, after Bajazet's departure, i.e. the transition to the final chorus and the *lieto fine*:

this had presented difficulties at Reggio in 1719. Asteria's transitional scene with the aria 'Padre amato a te verrò' does not appear in the scores, though it is printed in the libretto. Exactly how Handel managed the final scenes is not explained even by Knapp. It looks as though the earliest version already contained the new final chorus 'D'atra notte' which is followed in the autograph by the date (f.27v; see Squire, p. 87): also f.126 (sc.11, 'Dopo l'aria d'Asteria') might also belong to the earliest version. What was originally sc.10, with Asteria's aria 'Svena uccidi' from the 1711 libretto, was cut when the new scenes with the 1719 text were inserted, among them Asteria's aria 'Padre amato in me riposa' (ff. 113–25: HG, pp. 132–41, Version A). The shortening of the final scenes described by Knapp came later and Handel may have got the idea of this from the comparable solution in the Meiningen score (as used for the 1719 production). Although Handel had jotted down a number of alternative lines for his own and Haym's final chorus ('D'atra notte') this was not touched at any stage in the preparations.[45]

Il Gran Tamerlano (Antonio Salvi, music by A. Scarlatti) may have been the very first opera that Handel saw in Italy. Written for Ferdinando de' Medici, it was given at Pratolino in the autumn of 1706, when Handel had probably just arrived in Florence.[46] It is a remarkable fact that he preferred Piovene's version to the rather similar drama by Salvi.

Rodelinda (13 February 1725)

Rodelinda is Handel's first setting of a drama written by Antonio Salvi for Ferdinando de' Medici's theatre at Pratolino, and begins the series that continues with *Sosarme*, *Ariodante*, *Arminio* and *Berenice*. There is nothing surprising in Handel's interest in Salvi, which must date from his stay in Florence. Indeed he had long been in possession of a number of Salvi's libretti, so that we need some explanation of why he did not embark on this series before 1725 and also why his first choice was a work that he had not actually seen.

Emilie Dahnk-Baroffio has established that a play of Pierre Corneille's was the model of Salvi's *Rodelinda*.[47] In fact this opera also belongs to another category – Italian remodellings of seventeenth-century French classical tragedies, on which many early eighteenth-century libretti are based. This is particularly true of Salvi, who began his career in 1701 with a reworking of Racine's *Andromaque*, and used French subjects for the majority of his texts (including intermezzi). Haym, who reworked texts for Handel, had started his career as a librettist before 1720 by drawing on quite different sources, but after *Rodelinda* had the opportunity to adapt Salvi's *Astianatte* of 1701 for the Royal Academy.[48] This was set by Bononcini in 1727: both subject and composer had already been decided by the autumn of 1725, though Haym had not yet been engaged to rework the text.[49] What remains unexplained is the reason why Handel went on working with Rolli from 1725/6 while the Bononcini party's plans for *Astianatte* represented an attempt to continue a line which might be considered to be Handel's own and which had achieved a first major success with *Rodelinda*.

Scipione (12 March 1726)

Handel employed Paolo Rolli to prepare the text of this opera, a collaboration which continued in the operas that were to follow, while Haym, as official poet of the Royal Academy, was working for Bononcini and Ariosti during the same period. The reasons for this change have not yet been studied. As early as January 1726 Haym appeared as the arranger of a pasticcio *Elisa* assembled, probably by Ariosti, from arias by Porpora (see p. 169 below). The subject of this was also a Scipio, in this case Scipio Africanus Major whereas the background of Rolli's libretto was the Spanish conquests of the younger Scipio.

Handel seems to have composed his score in some haste; he certainly made use of the sinfonia that he had already written for his next opera *Alessandro* (see Clausen, p. 221), and the interval between his completing the autograph (see Squire, p. 77) on 2 March and the performance on 12 March was a relatively short one. The reason in each case may have been that Handel had planned *Alessandro* as the first opera of the season, with the new prima donna Faustina Bordoni who had been expected in London since the autumn of 1725 (Deutsch, pp. 185 and 187). Since she had still not arrived in March, Handel was obliged at short notice to change his plans and substitute *Scipione*.

Rolli had already published his libretto in London in 1726 as his own drama, although it was in fact based on an existing model which Handel must have given him. This was a *Publio Cornelio Scipione*, commissioned by Ferdinando de' Medici and performed at Livorno in the Carnival season of 1704. Although there is no mention of the name of either composer or poet in the libretto,[50] the signatories of the dedication – the 'Accademici Avvalorati' of Livorno – nevertheless commend the librettist to the patronage of Ferdinando. The person concerned was probably Ferdinando's Court-poet, Antonio Salvi. Rolli rewrote or replaced all the original arias, retaining only parts of the recitative but removing the buffo-scenes, among others.

There were at that time two other libretti on the subject of Scipio, both considerably more familiar and certainly known in London. The first of these was Apostolo Zeno's *Scipione nelle Spagne*, first performed at the court of Charles III at Barcelona (music by Caldara or possibly Chelleri) in 1710 and at Vienna in 1722, Venice and Rome 1724. The second was Agostino

Piovene's *Publio Cornelio Scipione*, (Venice 1712, Rome 1713, Milan 1718, Turin 1726). All three texts have the same contemporary reference – the Habsburg Charles III's Spanish campaign in the War of the Spanish Succession although this campaign never went further than the capture of Barcelona (1703) where Charles spent the next eight years. Handel had an opportunity to observe on the spot the effect of this war in Italy. The matter was of political interest to London audiences inasmuch as England actively supported Charles' campaign (thereby obtaining possession of Gibraltar). In these libretti Charles is represented by Scipio the Younger, whose capture of Carthago Nova established the Roman (or in this case Imperial) rule in Spain; and all three attempt to legitimise his action by emphasising his magnanimous and law-abiding behaviour towards the people he had conquered. In London this political reading of the text might in 1726 also be understood in reference to the first beginnings of the British Empire, in which case *Riccardo Primo* would not be Handel's and Rolli's first act of homage.

Alessandro (5 May 1726)

Paolo Rolli also wrote this libretto, which he published as his own drama in 1726, on an earlier existing model. Chrysander might have come upon this in *Mattheson's Verzeichnis Hamburgischer Opern von 1678–1728* where the mention of Handel's *Alessandro* (18 November 1726) makes reference to the Hamburg performance (in German) of Agostino Steffani's *La superbia d'Alessandro* (1695) (see Deutsch, pp. 197f). Both in 1695 and in 1726 the German title in Hamburg was *Der hochmüthige Alexander*.[51] In the 1726 Hamburg production all the arias were sung in Italian with Rolli's texts and Handel's music. Handel is named in the libretto, while the German recitatives correspond almost verbatim with those of 1695. Fiedeler had on that occasion made a German translation of the original Italian text set by Steffani (including the arias) and this followed the prosody of the Italian so exactly that Steffani's music could be used without any modifications.

In the Hamburg revival of 1726, it was possible to combine Handel's arias with Steffani's recitatives because the course of the action and the recitatives in Rolli's libretto kept fairly close to the Italian original: Ortensio Mauro's *La superbia d'Alessandro*, performed with Steffani's music at Hanover in 1690. (A slightly altered version was given there in 1691 with the title *Il zelo di Leonato*, but Rolli followed the original version.)[52]

The autograph of Steffani's opera (in the 1691 version), and a contemporary copy of it, are now in The British Library, London, both having come from the library of Georg Ludwig of Hanover and passing on his death in 1727 to Queen Caroline.[53] As a young man Georg Ludwig certainly had the opportunity to hear Steffani's opera, and Handel had both reason and opportunity to study Steffani's score. He could have seen the libretto in George I's library, if he did not in fact possess a copy of his own.

Handel's *Alessandro* was therefore a 'Hanoverian' opera from the start. Even the plot represents an act of homage to the reigning monarch, which Handel was able to employ Rolli to execute. George I was of course identified with Alexander the Great, as his father Ernst August had been before him, though with rather less emphasis on the trait of 'superbia'. In the plot Alexander suppresses a rebellion but has to renounce being revered as a god and of the two women whom he loves, wins only one as a wife. Rolli and his friends may well have been aware of the particulars of the work's history and may just about have accepted them.

Admeto (31 January 1727)

There are two studies of the libretto of this opera.[54] Abert gives a clear idea of not only the changing fashions in operatic subjects in that period but also the extent of their influence. In the case of this libretto of Handel's we should think of neither Euripides nor Gluck. Antonio Aureli's *L'Antigona delusa d'Alceste* – first performed, with music by P. A. Ziani, 1660 at the Teatro SS. Giovanni e Paolo in Venice – is an extremely Manneristic piece in which the classical story is almost entirely buried beneath amorous and burlesque elements.

After 1660 Ziani's opera was very often given on different Italian stages.[55] The existing model for Handel's text, however, did not come from Italy. The original version (Venice 1660) had been dedicated by Francesco Piva to Duke Georg Wilhelm von Braunschweig-Lüneburg and his brother Ernst August. It is to that, and a Venetian revival in 1670, that the dedication of a libretto entitled *L'Alceste* of 1679 refers. This belongs to a performance of the opera in Hanover given at the command of the Duchess Benedikta Henriette, one for which Ortensio Mauro had adapted Aureli's text and Mattia Trento had written new music. The opera was revived in Hanover only two years later with few alterations, which shows how highly it was rated by the new Duke Ernst August.[56] The basis of Handel's text is to be found in the libretto of the 1681 *Alceste*. The name of the London librettist has not survived, but the methods employed by whoever did the rewriting suggest Rolli rather than Haym, since Haym always changed the original less than is the case here, where only six aria texts and parts of the recitative have been left unaltered. The text of 'Mostratevi serene' (additional aria) comes from a libretto of Antonio Salvi's *Dionisio re di Portogallo*, which Handel later set as *Sosarme* (see p. 64).

A list of Hanover operas used by Chrysander and Georg Fischer, and edited by Philip Keppler, is said to have been initiated about 1698 by the then Electoral Prince.[57] The first opera entered is *Alceste* of 1679. This was the first Italian opera that Georg Ludwig had ever heard, and it was performed in February 1679 when Georg Ludwig, then nineteen, came from Osnabrück on a visit to Hanover with the rest of his father's (Ernst August) family.[58] All this may have been known to Handel from his contacts in court circles. His text had in any case links not only with the Hanoverian dynasty in general, but more particularly with King George I himself, who was to confirm Handel's naturalisation as an English citizen on 20 February 1727. It is probable that Handel's *Admeto* – with a king under the threat of death in the title-role – was the last opera seen by George I, who died unexpectedly on 11 June 1727 at Osnabrück, which he had left forty-eight years earlier to see *Alceste* in Hanover.

Riccardo Primo (11 November 1727)

Riccardo Primo formed part of the celebrations of the coronation of George II and was therefore related to an actual political event, but it also expressed – and far more clearly than Handel's earlier operas – a current political ideology. The new king is celebrated in the person of his famous predecessor Richard Lionheart and the old absolutist – or new imperialistic – conception of the British Empire is given an historical justification. The arranger of the text, Paolo Rolli, prefaces his libretto with a dedicatory sonnet to George II – 'Gran Re c'ai sommo e pronto in armi a un guardo/Su tutt' i mari e in tanti Regni impero/T'offre la Regia Scena il tuo guerriero/Predecessor, Cuor di Leon Riccardo/...' (Fassini, p. 80). Handel's only opera plot taken from English history must therefore be seen in connection with other 'commemorative–ceremonial–patriotic works' of the year 1727 (see Lang, pp. 218ff) and also with his own naturalisation at the beginning of the year.

Rolli, who spoke of the libretto as 'quasi tutto suo' (Fassini, p. 80), in fact made use of a preliminary model.[59] Handel's score was finished on 16 May 1727 when George I was still alive, and it stands to reason that alterations had to be made during the following months if the work was to be suitable as a coronation opera. Yet these alterations[60] have little to do with the political, ideological element in the work, which was present in the first version. On the other hand, the cast changes that took place before the opening of the 1727/8 season do not provide sufficient explanation, and in fact the musical revisions were on a larger scale than they had been in the cases of *Ottone*, *Tamerlano* and *Arianna* when the leading singers only arrived in London after the score had been completed. Both the early date of composition and the fact that a complete conducting score was already in preparation (see Clausen, pp. 206f) show that Handel intended the opera for the 1726/7 season. But in that case for whom was the homage expressed in the title-role intended? It would hardly have been suitable to compare the ageing George I with the youthful idealised figure of Richard Lionheart. It had furthermore been decided at the beginning of February by the Directors of the Academy, among whom support for Bononcini was strong (Deutsch, p. 200), that in the current season Handel's *Admeto* was to be followed first by an opera of Ariosti's and then by one of Bononcini's (Deutsch, pp. 201ff). This order of events was reversed. Bononcini's *Astianatte*, which he and Haym had prepared under the patronage of Henrietta, Duchess of Marlborough, was given on 6 May 1727, followed by Ariosti's *Teuzzone* on 21 October 1727 – and in June of that year Handel would have produced *Riccardo Primo* had the king not died in the meantime. Everything suggests that Handel's opera was conceived from the outset for the Prince of Wales. Although the Prince was not an out-and-out supporter of Handel's in the rivalry between the two operatic factions, the composer may well have thought it to be in his own interests to follow his *Admeto*, composed for George I, with an opera that paid homage to George's natural successor. The choice of libretto was in any case made by the opposition party. Although much of what occurred in the spring of 1727 remains unclear – and the quarrel about the prima donnas was an additional complication – everything points to a compromise of some sort. Either Henrietta – the old Duke of Marlborough's daughter – or one of her friends in the Academy, suggested the libretto after she had finally released the production of her own domestic composer Bononcini, *Astianatte*, for performance. On the other hand Handel was responsible for the original model of the text. The former plan was changed and Handel received his second commission in the season, while Ariosti's second opera (following *Lucio Vero* of January 1727) was postponed until October. The only possible dedicatee for the new opera was the heir to the throne, and it was simply a lucky chance for Handel that it was as the new king that he accepted the performance. Work remains to be done on both the artistic and the historical significance of the alterations made by Rolli and Handel, which in fact included the cutting of a number of Briani's still existing aria texts.

A projected opera – *Genserico* (early 1728)

Portions of an unfinished opera of Handel's on the subject of the Vandal king Genserich are preserved in a number of sources. Pages 29–36 in the autograph of *Siroe* (finished on 5 February 1728) (Squire, p. 81) contain scenes 5–9 of the project, though to which act they belong we do not know. They have been bound into the autograph so that the arias 'Chi è piu fedele' and 'Or mi perdo di speranza' can be included in the first act. In MS 258 of the autograph fragments in the Fitzwilliam Museum[61] pages 61–80 contain scenes 2–6 and 8–9 of what appears to be the first Act of the same project (in the catalogue these unfortunately appear under the misleading title of *Flavio Olibrio*). Furthermore, we can gather from the autograph of *Tolomeo* (Squire, p. 90) that Handel originally intended the overture for *Genserico*, as it is followed by the cancelled opening of Act I with corresponding stage-directions. Here again the fragment has no title.

The names of the characters and the voices required are preserved in the Fitzwilliam fragment, and if we take into account the comparative importance of each character in the text, we can guess at Handel's possible casting: Onorico–Senesino, Placidia and Eudossia–Cuzzoni and Faustina, Olibrio–Baldi, Genserico–Boschi, Elmige–Palmerini, Flacilla–Mrs Wright (who was partly at Handel's disposal in the season of 1727/28, see Deutsch, p. 213 on 30 September 1727). The libretto, which has nothing to do with Zeno, goes back to Nicolò Beregan's *Il Genserico* (Venice 1669): the libretto of this performance with music by Cesti (and Partenio?) is dedicated to the Duchess Benedikta Henriette of Braunschweig-Lüneburg.[62] The subject was therefore familiar in Hanover, from where Handel may well have known it. Postel's German arrangement, set by Conradi, was given at Hamburg in 1693 with the title *Der grosse König der Africanischen Wenden Gensericus*, and a new arrangement with music by Telemann was given in 1722 with the title *Der Sieg der Schönheit*.[63] Postel's version is rather closer than the Venetian original to Handel's version, and we may therefore suppose the existence of an intervening Italian model – between 1669 and 1693 – possibly in connection with the Hanover theatre.

In the fragments of *Genserico* the recitatives have not yet been composed, and perhaps no more than half of the arias (possibly up to Act II, scene 9), which means that the work had not yet been finally cast when Handel decided to set *Siroe* instead. This may have been in January 1728. The reasons for abandoning the project have not yet been discovered.

Siroe re di Persia (17 February 1728)

For this opera Haym used Metastasio's existing *dramma per musica* of the same name, which had its first performance (music by Leonardo Vinci) in the Carnival season of 1726 at the Teatro S. Giovanni Grisostomo in Venice. Handel's setting two years later was already the sixth setting of this libretto, the others being by Giovanni Porta (Florence, summer 1726 and Milan Carnival 1727), Nicolò Porpora (Rome Carnival 1727), Domenico Sarri (Naples Carnival 1727) and Antonio Vivaldi (Reggio, spring 1727). Metastasio's first two operas soon became widely known. As early as 3 October 1726 Giuseppe Riva wrote from London (letter to Muratori, Deutsch, p. 197, Fassini, p. 124) that it was regrettable that *Didone abbandonata* and *Siroe* had not been performed there. Interestingly enough it was Handel who fulfilled the wish of Riva and his friends by undertaking a corresponding task. Considering the unusual circumstances of the London seasons in 1725/6 and 1726/7 we can see that the beginning of 1728 was almost the earliest possible date for a production of *Siroe*. By that time the text used by Handel was just a year old: it is the version set by Sarri in 1727 for Naples and personally influenced by Metastasio, as was the version used by Vinci and Porpora; in fact it was this third, 'authentic' version that Metastasio later had published in the complete authorised edition of his works (Bettinelli, 1733ff Venice) and it was reproduced in all later complete editions. It appears that in addition to, or instead of, Sarri's libretto Handel used Sarri's score as a text-source. In any event he used an aria from this score ('Amico il fato') in his pasticcio *Ormisda* (see pp. 172f below), though this was a text that he had not used in his own setting of 1728.

Tolomeo re d'Egitto (30 April 1728)

Haym prepared his libretto from the following libretto-model:

TOLOMEO/ET/ ALESSANDRO,/OVERO /LA CORONA DISPREZZATA/ DRAMMA PER MUSICA/ Da rappresentarsi nel Teatro Dome-/ stico della Regina/MARIA CASIMIRA/ DI POLONIA./ COMPOSTO,E DEDICATO/ ALLA MAESTA' SUA / DA/ CARLO SIGISMONDO CAPECI,/ Tra gli Arcadi/ METISTO OLBIANO,/ E POSTO IN MUSICA/ DAL SIG.DOMENICO SCARLATTI./ IN ROMA MDCCXI.Nella Stamperia di An-/tonio de' Rossi alla Chiavica del Bufalo./ Con licenza de' Superiori./[64]

The performance took place on 19 January 1711 in the palace of the ex-queen, to whom Scarlatti was *maestro di cappella*; among the select public were Cardinal Pietro Ottoboni and Prince Ruspoli 'con tutti li loro musici'.[65]

Handel's relations with Capeci, Domenico Scarlatti, Ottoboni and Ruspoli had been close enough while he was in Italy for him to be able to keep in touch with them from London, either by letter or through third parties. But it was more likely that he received the libretto from two musicians who had attended the 1711 performance and had since come to London. These were Thomas Roseingrave, a pupil and loyal follower of Domenico Scarlatti during his Roman period, and Filippo Amadei, then Ottoboni's Kapellmeister (composing his opera *Teodosio il Giovane* for Ottoboni in 1711) and in 1728 a cellist in Handel's opera orchestra.

Later versions of the Capeci–Scarlatti opera (Fermo 1713; Rome 1724; Jesi 1727) do not qualify as source-texts for Haym's reworking. The alterations of the original made by Haym and Handel are quite considerable and include the cutting of one typically seventeenth-century role entirely – 'Dorisbe...sotto nome di Clori Giardiniera'. This part would perhaps have suited Mrs Wright, who may or may not have been available at the time of the first performance (see above). *Tolomeo et Alessandro* had been an exclusive work for the requirements of an exclusive society – almost the same society, in fact for which Handel had earlier produced his vocal chamber music and his first oratorios in Rome. Capeci's idea of a libretto was quite unlike that of other contemporary Arcadians (e.g. Zeno), with their attempts at reform, and this does not refer only to dramaturgy, but also to literary style and the delineation of character. Nature plays an unusual part in this libretto. Cyprus, the setting for the story, is represented as an island of Love, a fairytale Arcadian landscape. The fact that the whole action takes place out of doors, which imposed severe limitations on Juvarra's stage-sets, provided in this Carnival a cleverly calculated contrast in Maria Casimira's palace in comparison with those designed for Ottoboni and Ruspoli.[66] Although the text was considerably modernised for London, and an indoor scene added, the general pastoral setting was preserved. Indeed Nature, and the dialogue with Nature, were even given a thematic importance as is shown by the newly inserted aria texts:

I, 2 'Quell' onda che si frange'
3 'Mi volgo ad ogni fronda'
4 'Se talor miri un fior'
5 'Fonti amiche aure leggiere'
II, 1 'Voi dolci aurette al cor'
2 'Quanto è felice quell' augelletto'
3 'Aure portate al caro bene'
III, 3 'Senza il suo bene la tortorella'
4 'Tu pentirai crudele'
4 'Son qual rocca percossa dall'onde'

There is an increase not only in the number of so-called 'simile-arias' – to which Handel was not averse – but also of texts in which Nature is actually apostrophised. Handel was in fact trying to develop further that feature of Capeci's text which must have most impressed him.

Lotario (2 December 1729)

There is an account of the performance of this opera in Paolo Rolli's letter to Giuseppe Riva of 11 December 1729 (Fassini, pp. 86ff; Deutsch, p. 249). There we read among other things – 'Il libro fu recitato anno passato dalla F^a e dal Sen^o a Venezia intitolato *Adelaide*. Perfido!' Rolli calls Handel 'perfidious' for having composed his first opera after the departure of Faustina, and particularly Senesino, to a text that had meanwhile been performed by these two great virtuosi. Rolli was chiefly disappointed that Bernacchi had been engaged for the new Academy in Senesino's place.

The Florentine poet Antonio Salvi had written *Adelaide* in 1722 for the wedding of the Bavarian Electoral Prince Karl Albrecht and it was performed with Pietro Torri's music in Munich. Another later setting was made by G. M. Orlandini for the Venice Carnival of 1729. The performance at the Teatro S. Cassiano was close to being a failure, despite the presence of Bordoni in the cast, because Farinelli was making his first appearance in Venice at the same time, at the Teatro S. Giovanni Grisostomo.[67] Handel was in Venice during February and March of this year and would certainly have seen *Adelaide* as well as the two operas in which Farinelli was appearing. Later he certainly had a score of the opera in his possession or made occasional use of it.[68]

Salvi's drama presents the events of Otto I's Italian campaign and his marriage to the Princess Adelheid, who was held prisoner by the Margrave Berengar of Ivrea (951). As the widow of the Italian king Lothar, Adelheid could claim to be 'Queen of Italy'. Salvi makes these historical events a pretext for introducing the idea of Italian national unity; and in a second version made for Rome (1723) 'Italia' even appears at the end of the piece as a '*dea ex machina*'.[69] In what was once the Court library at Hanover there is still a score of an earlier *Adelaide* which Handel may have known – text by Bussani, music by Sartorio (Venice, 1672). It may possibly have been brought back from Venice by Duke Johann Friedrich of Hanover, to whom the text is dedicated.[70] In *Ottone* Handel had already taken over a libretto that had been written for a German court, and one in which a Saxon Crown Prince is compared to the Saxon Emperor Otto II (see p. 47); and it would have been even easier on this occasion to convert *Adelaide* into an act of homage to the Hanoverian dynasty. But strangely enough, while engaged in composing the second act he substituted the name Lotario for Ottone (Squire, p. 51ff), without any other alterations in the text and thus glossed over the historical references making it more difficult to identify the title-role of the opera with George II. It is not clear what Handel originally intended to call the opera, as 'Ottone' was now out of the question and 'Adelaide' might have been too clear a reference to the earlier Venetian model.

Handel got Giacomo Rossi to adapt the text, after he had become secretary of the Academy at Handel's wish in the summer of 1729. Orlandini's score may also have been drawn on as a text-source – Handel placed arias at two points where there were arias in Orlandini's score but not in the libretto; and he also used several of Orlandini's arias a year later in his pasticcio *Ormisda*.

An opera-libretto[71] entitled *Adelaide* was printed at Munich in 1730 and was dedicated to the Bavarian Electoral Prince Karl Albrecht by Michelangelo Boccardi (Deutsch, p. 257) with the date 1 June 1730. Here Boccardi – who was certainly hoping for a position or a fee from the Electoral Prince – gives Handel as the composer and the Haymarket Theatre as the place of performance. There can be no question, however, of Handel having even planned a second *Adelaide* as early as spring 1730, although Boccardi's plot differs in some particulars from *Lotario*. The list of singers in Boccardi's libretto makes it clear that he was not familiar with the situation in London at the time. Of the three titles that he claims for himself – 'Cavaliere', 'Pastore Arcade' and 'Compagno della R. Società di Londra' – the last, at all events, would be pure pretension.

Partenope (24 February 1730)

Silvio Stampiglia, who wrote his libretto La Partenope in 1699 for Naples, was the southern, Roman exponent of the 'Arcadian' aesthetics of opera, the counterpart of Apostolo Zeno further north, in Venice. La Partenope was Stampiglia's most successful opera text and one of the most popular of its day. This popularity may well have been in part due to interest in the political fate of Naples during the War of the Spanish Succession, the subject of the opera being the mythical foundation of the city.[72] One of the many settings was by Antonio Caldara, first for Mantua and then for Venice in the Carnival season of 1708;[73] and this version of the text was also the basis for Handel's opera. In the season of 1729/30, therefore, Handel produced in London precisely the two works that he must have seen in Venice. In any case the basic model for Lotario was just one year old, whereas Caldara's Partenope of 1708 may have represented one of Handel's first concrete contacts with the Venetian stage (Strohm 1974, p. 165). Handel knew a more recent version of the opera, also a Venetian one, namely Vinci's Rosmira fedele of 1725, on which he had also drawn in the same year for his pasticcio Elpidia (see pp. 167ff below). For his own setting, however, he preferred the older version of the text.

Poro (2 February 1731)

The text of Metastasio's Alessandro nell'Indie was the most recent libretto Handel had ever imported from Italy – a noteworthy choice coming immediately after Partenope. In 1729 Handel had collected in Italy a number of scores and libretti for London; but since the Metastasio–Vinci opera was only given at the Teatro delle Dame in Rome during the Carnival season of 1730, he must have had this forwarded to him in London; this is also true of the same authors' Artaserse, given at the same theatre a few weeks later and produced in 1734 by Handel as the pasticcio Arbace (see pp. 182ff below). His Poro is much closer to Metastasio's text than Porpora's Poro given at the same time (Turin Carnival 1731) and Hasse's Cleofide (Dresden, September 1731).[74] Winton Dean (1969, pp. 57–9) describes other alterations that Handel certainly arranged through Rossi, the most important being the cutting of two solo scenes and the resulting transpositions of other scenes owing to the fact that the bass Giovanni Commano (in the role of Timagene) was not allowed any arias. In the next season the outstandingly fine bass Montagnana was available for the revivals of Poro, and he was given three new arias, drawn not from Metastasio's libretto but from earlier operas of Handel's (Clausen, p. 201). Montagnana was a singing pupil of Porpora's and had sung the part of Timagene in Porpora's Poro.[75]

Metastasio's drama had a number of important features in common with Jean Racine's tragedy Alexandre le Grand (1665). We may take it for granted that both Handel and Metastasio were familiar with Racine's work (see pp. 232ff below).

A projected opera – *Titus l'Empereur* (1731–2)

Two autograph passages from an opera that Handel planned to write on the subject of Titus have been preserved. The first is the overture ('Ouverture pour l'Opéra Titus l'Empereur') and the opening of the first scene, which Handel, after abandoning the Titus idea, placed at the beginning of the autograph of *Ezio* in order to use it for this opera, just as he had used the *Genserico* overture for *Tolomeo* (see p. 57). The second is the immediate continuation of the first and continues as far as the third scene.[76] Whereas the *Genserico* project contained no recitatives, though the arias continue until the second act, most of the recitatives exist here. Handel, bearing in mind possible unforeseen cast changes, generally composed his recitatives later than his arias (in the first Act of *Poro* he even omits the recitative text entirely, see Clausen, pp. 68ff).

In the case of the projected *Titus*, therefore, the composition of the arias must have been far advanced and a large amount of the manuscript must be lost. It is unlikely that in this case Handel could have counted from the outset on a definite cast, since the *Titus* fragment that we possess demands a cast such as Handel had never yet had for any of his operas. It includes the roles of Tito (soprano), Berenice (soprano), Dalinda (alto), Antioco (alto), Paulino (tenor), Oldauro (tenor) and Arsete (bass?). The nearest to this is Handel's ensemble during the *Ezio* season (1731/2). The first four roles mentioned above could have been taken by Senesino, Strada, Bertolli and Bagnolesi, one of the two tenor roles by Pinacci and the 'confidente' by Montagnana. Only the second tenor role is unaccounted for, and for this Handel may have had in mind a singer like Thomas Mountier, Philip Rocchetti or Thomas Salway, who had been taking part in London performances of Handel's oratorios since 1731.[77] In any case we may date the *Titus* project as belonging to the beginning of the 1731/2 season, or at the earliest the end of 1730/1 season.

Hitherto we have had no information as to the libretto that could have served as basis for the text. Doubtless the basic literary source was Jean Racine's tragedy *Bérénice* of 1670. Racine's dramatis personae mentions 'Titus, empereur de Rome', 'Bérénice, reine de Palestine', 'Antiochus, roi de Comagène', 'Paulin, confident de Titus', 'Arsace, confident d'Antiochus', 'Phénice, confidente de Bérénice' and 'Rutile, Romain'. 'Arsace' was certainly Handel's 'Arsete', 'Phénice' and 'Rutile' probably 'Dalinda' and 'Oldauro'. There is nothing in Racine that corresponds to Handel's first scene, a typical operatic opening with a chorus of homage to the emperor and a programmatic aria for Titus himself. What follows, on the other hand, is very close in content to Racine's scenes 1–4. Indeed the parallel is so close that an actual libretto-model may not have been thought necessary.

Handel was in fact trying to establish a link with Racine not only in two of the oratorios of those years (*Esther* and *Athalia*), but also in operas; and this makes it all the more important to answer the question why he abandoned this plan. The lack of a second tenor can hardly have played an important part in his decision, and it seems more probable that there was some artistic reason. A possible hypothesis is that Handel wanted to adapt Racine's original text as an opera without any intervening model to work from, and the librettist (?Rossi) was simply not equal to the demands of such a task.

Ezio (15 January 1732)

Ezio was one of Metastasio's less famous pieces, though it deals with one of the most popular of *opera seria* themes – the conflict between a ruler and a subject and its consequences, which are in this instance considerable. It may be compared with Metastasio's later *Temistocle*, with which it also has in common the fact that it is the subject who gives his name to the piece, rather than the ruler (as opposed to *La Clemenza di Tito*, where the actual title reveals a quite different approach to the matter). In *Ezio* Metastasio borrowed features from Thomas Corneille's tragedy *Maximien*, but it also bears a similarity to earlier libretti of Handel's concerned with tyrants and conspirators – such as *Radamisto*, *Floridante* and *Alessandro*. Handel may well have chosen the text as much for its subject as for its author. We should also bear in mind that *Ezio* was taking the place of another work concerned with Imperial Rome and therefore demanded the same stage-sets.

Ezio was Handel's last Metastasio opera after *Siroe* and *Poro*: the poet's reputation was growing, even in London, but Handel began to look elsewhere for his texts. The relatively small success of *Ezio* with the London public cannot therefore be the explanation of this, nor was Handel's estimation of Metastasio as a librettist immediately affected, as he performed four more of his dramas during the following seasons, though – and this is a decisive consideration – with other men's music.[78] *Ezio* was a turning-point in Handel's relationship to Metastasio, as can be seen from his reshaping of the original text and his setting of it (see pp. 225–31 below). Handel's alterations to the text (cuts in the recitative, transferring and reduction in number of the arias, and a number of new lines) made by an assistant whose name we do not know, are fewer than in many of his other operas; purely numerically they are in fact less serious than those in the version of *Ezio* set by Porpora and Hasse.[79] But add to this the music and the artistic result in Handel's opera is a long way from the Metastasio ideal.

Handel would have procured the libretto – in the original form used at the first performance (Rome, Teatro delle Dame, Carnival 1729, music by Pietro Auletta)[80] – during his journey to Italy in 1729. He cannot have actually attended the Roman performance, as he only arrived in Rome after Carnival was over. There were other settings before Handel's by Nicolò Porpora (Venice, autumn 1728 – a reworking by Lalli, which deliberately anticipated the first performance in Rome), J. A. Hasse (Naples, autumn 1730), Riccardo Broschi (Turin Carnival 1731) and G. A. Predieri (Genoa 1731 and probably earlier in Milan 1730).

Sosarme (15 February 1732)

The text of Handel's *Sosarme* is controversial on account of what may kindly be termed its literary quality, and this makes it all the more important to be sure of both the author and the arranger. It can now be shown that the author was no other than Antonio Salvi, and W. Dean has recently suggested that the arranger was Paolo Rolli (Flower, p. 212; Dean 1975, p. 63). Handel's original libretto-model was Salvi's *Dionisio re di Portogallo* (music by G. A. Perti, performed at Pratolino near Florence on 30 September 1707).[81] Handel must have just arrived from Rome to prepare the Florence production of his *Rodrigo*, and may therefore actually have seen *Dionisio*. Both libretti have an Iberian historical interest, which was fashionable during the War of the Spanish Succession even at the Medici court. Salvi tells us in the introduction to his libretto that he took the subject of his *Dionisio* from a history of Portugal by Lequien de la Neufville.

In 1732, however, Handel changed the setting of the drama – which he had called *Fernando re di Castiglia*, after another leading role – after the second Act had already been written, placing the action in ancient Asia Minor instead of mediaeval Portugal and altering practically all the names (Squire, p. 83). He must actually have hesitated for some time about the new siting, as the names were at first omitted from the later acts in the conducting score, the first act of which was already written by this time (Clausen, p. 234). As there were no structural alterations in either the plot or the stage-sets and the new scene of the action was still undecided, the explanation of the changes can hardly be sought in technical problems of staging, e.g. the necessity, for economic reasons, of using existing sets rather than commissioning new scenery and costumes. W. Dean suggests political reasons for the change of setting, but connected with foreign rather than domestic matters, as the opera in its new setting still shows a son rebelling against his father, which was interpreted as a reference to George II and the Prince of Wales (and in any case ends with a general reconciliation).

Handel must have been responsible for the choice of a libretto-model borrowed from Ferdinando de' Medici's private performance at Pratolino.

Incidentally, it is noteworthy that Vittoria Tarquini 'detta la Bombace' probably had a leading part in *Dionisio re di Portogallo*.[82]

Orlando (17 January 1733)

We do not know for certain the names of the writers who adapted the texts of any of Handel's operas between *Sosarme* and *Deidamia*. Any suggestions are made doubly questionable by the glaring differences in style and – if judgements of this kind are in fact permissible – quality between texts after *Lotario*. About 1735/6 Giacomo Rossi was still employed by Handel in some capacity,[83] but this is very far from meaning that he is to be considered responsible for the intervening libretti. But who else is possible? If Paolo Rolli – who was unexceptionable as a writer – was the arranger of *Sosarme*, who else in London could claim the distinction of having provided Handel with a drama such as *Orlando*? The simplest answer is Handel himself. During the years of the so-called 'second' Academy he could, if he wanted, make an even more radical claim to the responsibility for his own opera texts than before; and thus differences such as those between *Sosarme* and *Orlando* are to be explained not so much by the different text arrangers as by the difference of original libretto-models, but most of all by the greater or lesser part played by Handel himself in shaping the text and the whole material of the drama.

Let us compare for a moment the production of *Orlando* with that of *Rinaldo*, which was in many ways its forerunner. For *Rinaldo* there was a poet (Aaron Hill), a composer (Handel) and a versifier (Giacomo Rossi) – who we may guess fulfilled the same function in 1732. Had Rossi ever been anything more for Handel than a versifier, we should know more about him today. Who then, if not Handel, took Aaron Hill's place?

Carlo Sigismondo Capeci is one of the many librettists (but perhaps the earliest one) who used Ariosto's and Boiardo's material for a 'dramma per musica'. Handel may have been acquainted with other elaborations on the same subject, but he chose as starting-point for his own drama the version made by the author of *La Resurrezione* (1708) and *Tolomeo et Alessandro* (1711). As far as the circumstances of performance go, Capeci's *Orlando* is a twin of *Tolomeo et Alessandro*: and it may have reached Handel in the same way. The title-page of the libretto[84] runs:

L'ORLANDO,/OVERO/LA GELOSA PAZZIA./DRAMMA/ Da rappresentarsi nel Teatro Domestico/ DELLA REGINA/MARIA CASIMIRA/DI POLLONIA. COMPOSTO, E DEDICATO/AL SERENISSIMO PRINCIPE/GIACOMO/DI POLLONIA/ DA CARLO SIGISMONDO CAPECI/Segretario di SUA MAESTA'/ Fra gli Arcadi METISTO OLBIANO,/E posto in musica/ DAL SIG.DOMENICO SCARLATTI,/Maestro di Cappella di SUA MAESTA'./IN ROMA, Per Antonio de' Rossi/alla Chiavica del Bufalo.1711./Con licenza de' Superiori./

The performance was during the Carnival of 1711. The stage-settings were again by Filippo Juvarra and were confined, as in the case of *Tolomeo et Alessandro*, to open-air scenes. But on this occasion in London the scenery was so notably elaborated by machines and allegorical decorations that Handel and his producer Heidegger seemed almost to be inviting comparison with the production of *Rinaldo*. Capeci's text was used more as raw material, which was not the case with *Tolomeo*. For instance the ariosos, accompagnatos and fragments of arias, so characteristic of *Orlando*, were hardly ever taken from the original. There the characters are Orlando, Angelica, Medoro, Dorinda and the couple Isabella–Zerbino, who do not appear in Handel. In their place is the figure of the magician Zoroastro (a part designed for Montagnana), whose presence introduces a new element all the more surprising because virtually unparalleled in libretti of the early eighteenth century.[85] Apart from the Zoroastro scenes the last Act in Handel's opera is shaped differently. Orlando's cure is brought about not by simply the touch of the magic ring (Capeci took this from Boiardo) but by Zoroastro's magic arts involving elaborate stage business; and Orlando experiences the cure of his madness as an individual, psychological breakdown involving remorse, grief and reconciliation. It is also significant that in his final chorus – which forms the trouble area of the drama, Capeci defends Love and attributes all hostile influences to Jealousy. In Handel's version of the text, and in his music, Love is not defended so unambiguously; in his rondo-finale he makes a refined emotion ('un diverso ardor') triumph over the passions.[86] In the preface to the London libretto we read 'likewise how a wise Man should be ever ready with his best Endeavours to re-conduct into the right way those who have been misguided from it by the Illusion of their Passions' (quoted from Dean 1969, p. 91).[87]

It seems necessary at this juncture to remember Aaron Hill's letter of 5 December 1732 to Handel, whom he wanted to see at the head of a new English operatic set-up. 'I am sure', he wrote, 'a species of dramatic opera might be invented, that, by reconciling reason and dignity with music and fine machinery, would charm the ear, and hold fast the heart, together' (Fassini, p. 92; Deutsch, p. 299). Handel's opera – the autograph of which was completed by 20 November 1732 – strikes one as being a positive and impressive response to Hill's wishes. Can we believe Hill when he maintains, in the same letter, that he is not acquainted with Handel's present projects, or had he in fact seen the autograph? Had there been discussions between him and Handel, and were these connected with the genesis of *Orlando*?

Arianna in Creta (26 January 1734)

The season of 1733/4 was Handel's last for the time being at the King's Theatre in the Haymarket and therefore still lies, economically speaking, in the creative period that began in the year 1729. It was also the first season of the 'Opera of the Nobility' – an organisation which by its very name reveals the fact that the problem of opera in London was a social one. The founders must have regarded the name as a pleonasm, since for them Italian opera was in any case a privilege of the nobility, who had in fact financed Handel and Heidegger even after 1729, both men being given freedom of activity only reluctantly. The 'Opera of the Nobility' was not to compete with Handel's operas, but to render them superfluous, at any rate from the moment when he ceased to be protected by the five-year contract drawn up in 1729.[88] The new enterprise was naturally joined not only by those aristocratic opera-lovers who, like Burlington, had no longer patronised Handel after 1720, but also by others who had still supported him after 1729.[89] The king's patronage of Handel, which could be set against that of the Prince of Wales, was possibly valued more realistically by the aristocracy than by Handel himself: and in fact the financial support became – after a year's delay – theirs.

The artists engaged by the 'Nobility' played no great part in this dispute, although Porpora and Rolli were concerned inasmuch as attempts were made to pre-empt the interest of the public by putting on operas with a similar subject-matter. These attempts seem to have been initiated by the 'Nobility', who were aware that Handel was working on an *Arianna* (completed on 5 October 1733), though Handel himself first put on pasticci by Vinci and Hasse, thus removing the area of competition to the musical and stylistic field. Porpora could have contributed a setting of his own (1727) of the libretto of Handel's *Arianna* without any fear of its being musically unsuitable. Instead, however, he found himself obliged to compose in haste quite a different *Arianna* libretto, possibly in order to give Rolli a more responsible part in the undertaking.

In any case Handel's *Arianna in Creta*, like the pasticci, is a pure castrato-opera in the Italian taste, which could have been popular with the aristocratic public. The chief parts were sung by the castrati Carestini and Scalzi, though difficulties arose after their (possibly belated) arrival, when it was discovered that the voices of both were now lower in pitch than when Handel had known them. A number of arias had therefore to be rewritten or transposed.

The text of *Arianna in Creta* has nothing to do with Francis Colman, who died at Pisa in 1733, and is rather a version of Pietro Pariati's *Arianna e Teseo*, which was performed during Carnival 1729 at the Teatro della Pace in Rome, with music by Leonardo Leo. It is not known who rewrote the text for this Roman performance, but the libretto is dedicated to a relation of Cardinal Colonna's. The texts of three of the arias were taken from the libretto of a pasticcio, *Arianna e Teseo* (Naples 1721), which Leo had arranged.[90] Handel may have met Leo himself, either during the 1729 Carnival in Venice – where he heard Leo's *Catone in Utica*, which he brought to London in 1732 – or immediately afterwards in Naples or Rome. Handel had also been interested in the castrati Carestini and Scalzi ever since his Italian journey of 1729.[91] It might well be worth comparing Leo's, Handel's and Porpora's different settings of Pariati's libretto.[92]

Oreste (18 December 1734)

This pasticcio, made by Handel from his own works, may have been an experiment from which the composer hoped to discover how much the choice of a classical-mythological subject would assist him in the present dispute with the 'Opera of the Nobility'. It may also have been no more than a stop-gap in the season's repertory. The original libretto-model for *Oreste* comes from a relatively unknown Roman opera, *L'Oreste*, by Giuseppe Barlocci (music by Benedetto Micheli, performed at the Teatro Capranica during the 1723 Carnival). The libretto is dedicated to Maria Isabella Cesi Ruspoli, the wife of Handel's one-time patron.[93] Handel may have received the libretto in Rome in 1729, though it may also have reached him through Carestini, who sang the part of Pilade in 1723 and now took over Handel's title-role.

Since Handel constructed the pasticcio entirely from earlier arias of his own (Clausen, pp. 181ff) and the only new music was that of the recitatives and ballets,[94] none of Barlocci's aria-texts were retained. Even so, Handel's text-arranger (?Rossi) had to make the texts of the original fit Handel's music and on a number of occasions to provide parody-texts that preserved the sense of Barocci's lines while observing the prosody of Handel's music. The following incipits are examples of this:

1   (Barlocci) Io sperai che gli occhi belli
     (Original text of Handel's aria) Io ti levo l'impero dell'armi
     (Parody-text) Io sperai di veder il tuo volto
2   (B) Pensa che re son io
     (H) Finchè lo strale – non giunge al segno
     (P) Pensa ch'io sono – un rege amante
3   (B) Dunque addio: parto, ne sò
     (H) Figlia mia non pianger, nò
     (P) Caro amico – a morte vò
4   (B) Qualor paga tu sei
     (H) Non chiedo o luci belle
     (P) Qualor tu paga sei
5   (B) Pianger' degg'io
     (H) Bacia per me la mano
     (P) Piango dolente il sposo

There are some other cases in which the arranger of the text spared himself this trouble and left the original aria texts if they at all fitted the action. The course of the drama (which is based on the story of *Iphigenia in Tauris*) and most of the recitative texts follow the original model.

Ariodante (8 January 1735)

The history of Antonio Salvi's libretto *Ginevra principessa di Scozia* has been described by Emilie Dahnk-Baroffio.[95] The alterations that Handel made to the text, which was twenty-six years old, were comparatively few in number, at least if we consider his innovations in stage-practice at Covent Garden. The use of English singers and the ballets at the end of each Act did necessitate changes that would not have been necessary at the time of *Rodelinda*, *Scipione* and *Sosarme*. But it was just in these matters that Salvi's original offered possibilities that interested Handel.

There was also an advantage for him in the fact that the great majority of his singers were British, since this gave him a freer hand with the subordinate roles, where he did not have to take into account the individual claims made by the Italian virtuosi. Of the Italians Strada and Maria Catterina Negri were entirely dependent on him artistically.

Salvi differed from other librettists of his day in that the hierarchy of his characters was very free. Although Ariodante is the central figure in the drama, he is given fewer arias and solo scenes than either Dalinda or even Polinesso. On the other hand even minor characters like Lurcanio and Odoardo are given solo scenes, which suggests that these roles too were sung by first-class virtuosi when the work was given at Pratolino in 1708. In 1735 it would be a matter of course that Handel should make the musical and the dramatic importance of these roles match. But the relative importance of the singers on this occasion could be adjusted comparatively easily to the original text because this in turn lent itself comparatively easily to such changes of emphasis. The same was true of Salvi's scene order which did not yet correspond to that of the so-called Reform librettists, who aimed at making the number of characters on stage increase and decrease only gradually. With Salvi, characters sometimes leave the stage in groups, while on other occasions he has no more than two characters on the stage for a whole series of scenes. This also turned out to be an advantage to Handel, and particularly in the circumstances of the present London season, during which a transparently simple plot and plenty of scenic effects were more important than the appearance of prominent singers in strict hierarchical order of precedence. The ballets at the end of the Acts play a much more important part with Handel than they did in the Italian opera of the day, which did not always even include them. This was made practically possible by the fact that Handel was obliged to pay far less attention to the claims of individual singers. He would never have been able to take such easy and substantial liberties with a libretto by Zeno or Metastasio as he took with Salvi's.

Ginevra principessa di Scozia was performed, with music by Perti, in autumn 1708 at the Villa di Pratolino. There are reasons to suppose that

Handel was present (Strohm 1974, p. 162). We may therefore wonder whether he retained any visual impressions of the Florence production, such as the garden scene in Act I or the moonlight scene in Act II, where Salvi's stage-direction says 'notte con lume di luna'. What Handel may have thought of Perti's music we do not know.

Alcina (16 April 1735)

Alcina is one of the libretti that Handel must have got to know during his visit to Italy in 1729. Once again we can see what a large part personal experience played in Handel's production of opera in London, and particularly experiences dating from his stays in Italy. Again, too, we are faced with a problem to which so far too little attention has been paid – namely the possibility of long-term planning in Handel's career as an operatic composer. We know that he hardly ever availed himself of the existing supply of libretti in London; but it is also unlikely that he casually, and at short notice, selected from his own (doubtless large) private collection of librettos pieces that seemed most suited to the circumstances of the moment. What seems more probable is that there was a close connection between Handel's becoming acquainted with an operatic text (possibly through attending a performance) and his decision to set it himself. The fact that he often waited until circumstances in the theatre seemed to favour some individual text tells rather in favour of the theory of continuous, long-term planning, except of course in cases where the initiative in choosing a libretto did not lie with him.

The original text-model for *Alcina* is the libretto *L'isola d'Alcina*, set by the Neapolitan composer Riccardo Broschi for the Teatro Capranica in Rome, Carnival 1728. The libretto was dedicated by the impresario to the widowed Grand Duchess of Tuscany and was printed in Florence. There was a later performance of the opera at Parma (Carnival 1729) with the title *Bradamante nell' isola d'Alcina*, again set by Broschi.[96] Handel most probably became acquainted with both librettos during his stay in Parma in May 1729. In any case he only made use of the Roman version, in which the part of Ruggiero was sung by Farinelli, who was a brother of the composer. The name of the author of the text is not known, but the dedication of the original version suggests that he was probably a Florentine.

Unusually few alterations to the original text were made for London, by whom we do not know. It must therefore have been very close to Handel's own conception of the drama, as there can be no question of his being in any way indifferent to the text, in this work particularly. This is not contradicted by the fact that in preparing the score he omitted the recitatives (Clausen, p. 69), as the casting of the work may not have been finally known until comparatively late and in this particular work the structure of the drama was determined once the arias were composed. For the only real freedom that Handel took with the original text consists of numerous transferrings of aria texts taken from the original, many of these being allotted to other characters. Handel's drama is constructed not on texts but on musical figures, as is shown by the single example of 'Verdi prati' which – as has been rightly observed – owes its effectiveness to its specific placing in the work as a whole. In the original text these lines are to be found in a context which is entirely different, both in content and in dramatic significance. Comparatively few changes were necessary in the text of the recitatives, if only because these were in any case scanty. In Act I, for instance, there are about 320 lines of recitative to twelve arias, whereas in Capeci's *Tolomeo et Alessandro* the proportion is about 400 to 15 and in Metastasio's *Ezio* about 530 to 11. Elsewhere most of Handel's text alterations are found at conclusions, but in this instance he could make use not only of the lines of the final chorus but also of the concluding ballet.

In a later phase Handel undertook alterations to *Alcina* which either did nothing to enhance his own conception of the work or actually militated against that conception. The cutting of 'Bramo di trionfar' (Clausen, p. 94) is musically speaking a loss; and the addition of the role of Oberto for the young William Savage is an expansion rather than an enrichment of the work. Oberto's intermezzo-like scene with the lion in Act III was added in 1735 as a sop to an audience hungry for spectacle. There is no hint of any such scene in the original, and the idea came not from the unknown librettist but either from John Rich or from the composer himself.

Atalanta (12 May 1736)

Handel's opera for the wedding of Frederick Prince of Wales to the Princess Augusta of Saxe-Gotha combines two interests that are otherwise rare among the subjects of his operas: myth and pastoral. *Admeto* and the pasticcio *Oreste* are both based on myth, but, apart from *Atalanta*, Handel's only 'dramma pastorale' was *Il Pastor fido*, which he revived in 1734. Also perhaps to be mentioned in this connection are *Jupiter in Argos* (1739) which has similar characteristics and was based on a 'festa teatrale' of 1717 also for wedding celebrations; and the wedding serenata *Il parnasso in festa* of 1734. We may still wonder whether Handel would have chosen *Atalanta* as the subject of an opera if there had been no external reason. From the theatrical point of view *Atalanta* fulfils the function of a court festival opera primarily by its final monologue, where the *deus ex machina*, Mercury, is given a *licenza* such as we find in Metastasio, and by the unusually brilliant stage-setting of the final scene, which is an apotheosis of the prince and princess (see descriptions in Deutsch, pp. 407ff). The stage-setting was in other respects modest. The suggestion for the opera may well have come

from the court (see Chrysander, vol. 2, p. 389), as did that for Rolli's and
Porpora's serenata *La festa d'Imeneo* (Haymarket, 4 May 1736). Handel had
not only to cater for the taste of the Prince of Wales – which probably
explains the engagement of the soprano Gioacchino Conti dello Gizziello –
but also to satisfy special wishes for the occasion including, as it seems, the
actual subject of his opera. The story of Atalanta had been used before on
occasions that suggested its present suitability and had long been popular,
especially at German courts. The most noteworthy example, after J. Kaspar
Kerll's *Atalanta* for Munich in 1667, was Ortensio Mauro's and Steffani's
Le rivali concordi (Hanover, 1693), which Handel certainly knew. A libretto
was in the possession of George I. A German version reached Hamburg
in 1695 and Stuttgart in 1699.[97] Bressand's German opera *Attalanta, oder
die verirrten Liebhaber* was performed at Brunswick in 1698, and another
opera on the same subject – originally entitled *La constanza in amor vince
l'inganno* – was first given at Parma in 1694 with music by G. Mazzoleni.[98]
It was soon given also in Hanover; and the libretto of a performance in
Salzthal (1702?) is dedicated to Sophie, widow of the Electoral Prince.[99] In
Italy the libretto was set by Caldara (1711 in Rome for Ruspoli, and
probably four years earlier for Mantua);[100] in Germany it was set by
Christoph Graupner (among others) for the court of Hesse-Darmstadt in
1715 and in 1719 as *La costanza vince l'inganno*.[101]

This detailed listing of occasions on which the Atalanta story had already
been used is to explain how the tradition of Italian opera in Germany, which
was so important for Handel, was partly associated with individual subjects
and reflects, by its very extent, the close cultural and dynastic ties that linked
the princely families of Germany and Italy.

Handel's immediate text-model was a relatively recent version – Belisario
Valeriani's *La caccia in Etolia* (Ferrara 1715), music by Fortunato Chelleri.[102]
This libretto also reached Germany, in fact by means of just such a dynastic
contact – Chelleri being in Florence from 1716 to 1719 as Kapellmeister to
Anna Luisa de' Medici, the widow of the Elector Palatine Johann Wilhelm,
with whom Handel was acquainted. Johann Wilhelm's brother and successor,
Carl Philipp, was also interested in music and had the opera performed on
4 November 1715 at Innsbruck, while he was still living there, and again
in 1722 at his residence in Heidelberg, in the Palatinate.[103] Carl Philipp was
Faustina Bordoni's first employer (from 1716 to 1725) and Handel had met
him at Innsbruck as early as 1710. It may be that Handel's contact with
the court of the Elector Palatine had never lapsed.

The wedding of Princess Augusta was celebrated in Gotha as well as in
London. Duke Friedrich III ordered a performance in the Friedenstein
theatre (April 1736) of a *dramma pastorale* (with music by his Hofkapellmeister G. H. Stölzel), and its title *L'amore vince l'inganno* conceals the
Atalanta version that goes back to Parma 1694.[104] This could mean that the

subject of the wedding celebration opera in London was suggested by Gotha, and that Handel used his private contacts to obtain a libretto better suited to his designs.

Arminio (12 January 1737)

In the autumn of 1736, when Handel composed Antonio Salvi's *Arminio*, the libretto he set was thirty-three years old. This is the more remarkable because it had in the meantime become a great favourite and already existed in many different versions that might have satisfied the more up-to-date claims even of the London stage. The original version dated from 1703 (a command performance of Ferdinando de' Medici at Pratolino, music by A. Scarlatti)[105] and this was followed by Caldara's setting for Genoa (1704),[106] a version for Düsseldorf (1707, with music by Steffani)[107] and performances in Naples in 1714, Florence in 1716 and 1725, Venice in 1722, Rome in 1722 and Milan in 1730. In London Haym had arranged a pasticcio on Salvi's libretto in 1714.[108] Handel, however, decided to take the original text of 1703 as the basis for his own.

Like *Ottone* and *Lotario*, the subject of *Arminio* is taken from Germanic history – or pre-history – and this no doubt explains its being chosen for performance at Düsseldorf in 1707. The first settings in Italian may well bear the political interpretation given by Ursula Kirkendale for Caldara's opera;[109] even in Tuscany there was sympathy in 1703 for the Duke of Mantua, who was threatened by the Emperor and Prince Eugene. There were no contemporary political feelings of this kind in London at the time, unless we count the German origin of the royal family and more particularly the Princess Augusta; but the individual action of the piece – the fates of the devoted couple Arminio and Tusnelda – must be understood as referring directly to the Prince of Wales and his wife.

Giustino (16 February 1737)

Giustino is an old Venetian libretto by Nicolò Beregan, based on events from early Byzantine history, and made famous by Legrenzi's music, with which it was first performed in 1683 at the Teatro S. Salvatore. In 1711 it was reworked by Pietro Pariati for Bologna (music by Albinoni) and in 1724 Vivaldi set a new version of Pariati's text for the Teatro Capranica in Rome.[110] This was the version used by Handel – for him, it was a Roman libretto, which he may have discovered when he was there in 1729. Vivaldi's setting obviously did not interest him if, indeed, he even knew it.

The majority of Handel's strophic verses are taken from the original, but he made considerable changes in their order, their distribution among the three Acts and in the characters to which they were assigned. Compared with some other operas, this gave Handel a lot of trouble (he was working on it from 14 August to 20 October 1736), but the fact that it was not performed until after *Arminio*, which was completed earlier, is probably to be explained by the casting difficulties of a work that needs eight singers. The bass-role of Amanzio was transferred to a woman, M. C. Negri, after the completion of the autograph (Clausen, p. 154). In *Giustino* the apparently historical basis of the drama is elaborately ornamented with the fairy-tale and magic elements that were traditional in Baroque opera. *Fortuna in machina* appears to Giustino in his sleep; Leocasta is rescued from a wild bear and Arianna from a sea-monster; the father's tomb begins to speak, etc. We must bear in mind that in the same season as *Giustino* the 'Opera of the Nobility' produced four Metastasio operas set by Hasse, Pescetti and others (the most successful of which was Pescetti's *Demetrio*), as well as intermezzi by Hasse and Orlandini. Handel's operatic ideas, however, were not quite so conservative as this might lead us to suppose. Sasse points out[111] that the story of Giustino could be taken to represent the interests of the middle class – a simple man reaching the pinnacle of social success by his own abilities. Admittedly, his rise is later 'legitimised' when he is revealed as the king's brother, thus making the privilege of birth once again turn the scales. This was a topos among libretti designed for the courts of absolute monarchs and one valued by Metastasio, who exploited it in his Viennese operas, notably *Demetrio*. There is a similar tendentiousness in the lines inserted in *Giustino* by Handel's librettist – 'Può ben nascere tra boschi' – and in Metastasio's 'Alma grande è nata al regno' in *Demetrio*, which was given at the Haymarket on 12 February 1737: both arias echo the belief, cherished by the supporters of absolutism, that the nobly born retain their dignity and their privileges even when in 'disguise'. There is a further, musical analogy between Handel and the 'Opera of the Nobility' in this season. By engaging the castrati Conti and Annibali, and retaining the arias composed for them, Handel made concessions to opera-goers whose tastes were modelled on those of the majority. This emphasises all the more how backward-looking he proved himself in his choice of text.

Berenice (18 May 1737)

Berenice is the fifth and last instance of Handel setting a libretto originally written by Antonio Salvi for Ferdinando de' Medici's theatre at Pratolino. When *Berenice regina d'Egitto*, with music by Perti, was performed there on 30 September 1709, Handel may well have been in the audience, since he stayed at Ferdinando's court that autumn.[112] As before, it was to Salvi's original version that Handel turned in London, despite the existence of more recent versions (e.g. Venice, 1711 and 1734 and Rome, 1718) and as before – and also in *Arminio* for that matter – he made less striking changes than other composers in the text. The fact that nothing new was added beyond three arias, speaks not so much for the quality of the text – as was the case with *Alcina* – as for the composer's lack of interest owing to severe illness. As in the case of the recently performed pasticcio *Didone* the suspicion arises that Handel was obliged to be economical in the matter of new lines (see p. 198 below), because he no longer had (or perhaps could no longer afford to pay) a trustworthy librettist. He needed no outside help with the only structural alteration that he made – transferring the important aria 'Chi t'intende' (see Dean 1969, pp. 167 and 187) from the subsidiary character Fabio to Berenice herself.

Faramondo (3 January 1738)

Handel started work on *Faramondo* on 15 November 1737 and completed it on 24 December 1737; but owing to the interruptions caused by the death of Queen Caroline on 20 November and the composition of the *Funeral Anthem* (finished on 12 December and performed on 17 December) he probably spent scarcely more than two weeks in composing Apostolo Zeno's libretto. This was Handel's only original setting of a Zeno text, though what he set had little in common with the original version composed for Venice in 1699 by C. F. Pollarolo.[113] Handel based his version on Francesco Gasparini's score (Rome, Teatro Alibert, 1720) both as regards text and music.[114]

Harold S. Powers, who has established the dependence of Handel's *Serse* on G. Bononcini's *Xerse* (Rome, 1694) (Powers, p. 77), has also found in the Bononcini score original models for one aria in *Giustino*, one in *Berenice* and one in *Faramondo*. He supposes rightly that there may be still further arias in the operas that Handel wrote in 1737/8 which are either borrowings or imitations. No score of Gasparini's opera has been preserved, but a collection of twenty-four independent pieces of Gasparini's makes it clear enough how Handel allowed himself to be guided by Gasparini's work, borrowing motifs not only in arias with similar texts but also where the text is different. For a discussion of his indebtedness to Gasparini, see pp. 80–92 below.

Alessandro Severo (25 February 1738)

In February 1738 Handel used earlier compositions of his own for the pasticcio *Alessandro Severo*, only the overture being newly composed (Clausen, pp. 99ff). In fact he took even less trouble with this opera than he did with *Faramondo* and *Serse* in the same season, when much of his music was inspired by that of other composers. This is not difficult to understand if we bear in mind that Heidegger was then paying Handel a fixed salary for his operas,[115] and that Handel had no longer the same immediate concern for their stage-success as he had generally had earlier. Heidegger's sole responsibility for the financial risks involved suggests that he may also have been responsible for the choice of libretti, and he had always had a much greater preference than Handel for Apostolo Zeno, the author of *Alessandro Severo*.

In the text, the original version of which was set in 1717 by Lotti for Venice, Zeno's aria texts had to be partly parodied in order to fit Handel's existing music: in fourteen other instances Handel's texts were simply used as they stood, though this meant modifying the text of the recitatives. Thanks to this, it is virtually impossible to establish which of the many versions of Zeno's text was used. The text-adapter – who had a lot to do in this case and may possibly have been a new librettist, Angelo Cori – still succeeded in fitting to Handel's music a text that had appeared in an earlier setting of *Alessandro Severo* by G. M. Orlandini (Milan 1723), 'Chi sa dirti o core amante'. This was an 'aria aggiunta' not printed in the 1723 libretto. It may therefore be Orlandini's score rather than the libretto that served as text-model.[116]

Serse (15 April 1738)

Of all Handel's operas *Serse* is closest to the operatic tradition of the seventeenth century, not only in the matter of the text but also musically. Whereas *Agrippina* departs from this tradition in matters of detail but in general employs traditional means of composition, *Serse* represents a conscious return to tradition, something only possible on a new level of composition which now includes this retrospection as an actual artistic means.

Harold S. Powers has discovered and analysed the connections between Handel's score and Giovanni Bononcini's *Xerse*, composed in 1694 for the Teatro Tordinona in Rome (Powers, p. 73ff). This original model, however, is – *pace* Powers – anything but a 'Venetian' work, unless 'Venetian' is used as a vague synonym for 'seventeenth century' rather than with the music-theatre of Venice in mind. The text of *Xerse* was written by the Roman Silvio Stampiglia for a Roman theatre and set by the Modenese Bononcini, who received his education in Modena, Bologna and Rome.[117] No important operatic composer of Handel's generation had so little to do with Venice as Bononcini who wrote nothing for that city. He worked in Modena, Bologna, Rome, Berlin, Vienna and London, where he mainly set works by the members of the Rome Arcadia, Stampiglia and Rolli. Stampiglia's *Xerse* is no doubt based on a libretto written by Nicolò Minato for Venice (1654), which it resembles in the action and in the order of scenes.

But it is not this 'external structure' (Powers), but the 'internal structure' – the actual layout of the scenes and placing of the arias – which is the musically deciding characteristic of Stampiglia's version, which follows the more modern operatic ideas of the Arcadia in these matters. It was these ideas that were decisive for Handel when he composed his *Serse*, not Minato's libretto; and, as far as the music is concerned, he follows Bononcini and not Francesco Cavalli. In the 1694 libretto one name stands out in the list of singers (none of them Venetians), 'Nicola Paris detto Nicolino', whom Handel may have met during his first stay in Italy.

Which score of Bononcini's did Handel use? Perhaps the one quoted by Powers and now in London (GB-Lbm add.22102). Handel may have got to know the work through Bononcini himself or during his stay in Rome from 1707 to 1709, but it was most probably through Nicola Haym who was active in Rome as a cellist in 1694 and died in 1729.[118] In any case Handel was in possession of the score before 1738. He modelled a movement on Bononcini in *Giustino*, another in *Berenice* and a third in *Faramondo* (see Powers, p. 77, n. 6).

Jupiter in Argos (1 May 1739)

The score of this opera (as Handel himself calls the work) was finished on 24 May 1739, shortly after the first performances of *Israel in Egypt*. Whereas Handel uses models of other composers in his big choral work (see Lang, 310ff), in the theatrical piece he makes use of his own earlier music, thus carefully distinguishing the reworking of other men's work – a more creatively demanding process – from the less demanding one of self-quotation. He had already made use of both techniques in *Faramondo* and *Serse*. Antonio Maria Lucchini's libretto of *Giove in Argo*, which Handel had got to know at Dresden in 1719 (with music by Lotti)[119] is entitled 'melodrama pastorale' and belongs to the genre of the *festa teatrale* rather than the *dramma per musica*. Comparable works of Handel's own are the serenata *Il Parnaso in festa* of 1734 and *Atalanta* (1736), the *dramma pastorale*. All three works were written for court weddings and based on mythological and pastoral subjects from the Greek and Roman classics. The pieces of his own which Handel uses in *Jupiter in Argos* are chosen preferably from such works as *Il Pastor fido* (1734), *Parnaso in festa*, *Atalanta* and the still unfinished *Imeneo*. But unlike most of these works and also its original model, *Jupiter in Argos* was not in fact composed for any court occasion. Handel must have chosen the form of the mythological 'festa teatrale' for its own sake – as a formal experiment that also had a bearing on the circumstances of the performance (see Deutsch 1955, p. 484). The case is parallel to that of another work planned at the same time, the serenata-like *Imeneo*.

Imeneo (22 November 1740)

Although Handel started composing *Imeneo* on 9 September 1738 and only finished it in autumn 1740, he did not of course spend all the intervening time on the work. In fact he only busied himself with it when there seemed to be a probability of its being performed, and that was in the autumn of 1738 and the autumn of 1740. Meanwhile the plan was probably even abandoned, as is suggested by the inclusion of two arias designed for *Imeneo* ('Se potessero i sospir miei' and 'Se ricordar t'en vuoi') in *Jupiter in Argos* (1739).[120] Important changes were also made when the work was performed in Dublin in 1742 as a 'serenata' (see especially Clausen, pp. 157–60). The original model of the libretto was itself not a real *dramma per musica* but a *componimento drammatico* in two parts, written by Silvio Stampiglia in 1723 on the occasion of a marriage in the family of a Neapolitan nobleman. The music was by Porpora, and we have a score-copy of the 1723 version. The work was performed again often, particularly in a more operatic, three-act version first given in Venice in 1726. But there was also another performance of the 'serenata' version in two parts, at Naples in 1732.[121] Handel used the original 1723 version as the basis of his text, and this is the furthest removed from the genre of *dramma per musica*. But whereas, as in the case of *Jupiter in Argos*, the particular form, or genre, of the original *Imeneo* was linked to a definite court occasion, in Handel's case the form seems to have been employed for its own sake. This 'serenata', which Londoners of the day referred to as 'operetta' (Deutsch, p. 507), is distinguished by its more chamber-music character from *Jupiter in Argos*, which is a mythological and pastoral *festa teatrale*. In fact Handel was searching in different directions for ways of escaping from the conventions of the traditional *dramma per musica*.

Deidamia (10 January 1741)

There is an ambivalent note of tragicomedy in this libretto of Paolo Rolli's, but it has no more to do with the *opera buffa* of the day than the text of Handel's *Serse*, and seems to belong rather to the traditions of seventeenth-century libretti. It must be admitted that Paolo Rolli showed himself a less authentic inheritor of the seventeenth-century opera's combination of the heroic and the high-spirited than Silvio Stampiglia in, for instance, his *Partenope* and *Xerse*. Rolli's literary taste, as seen in *Deidamia*, has most affinity with the lyrical and satirical veins that we find in the works of his later years in London, e.g. the epigrams in his collection entitled *Marziale in Albion*.[122]

A drama on the same subject, and one that Rolli must certainly have known, was written by Metastasio in 1736 for the wedding of Maria Theresa and entitled *Achille in Sciro*. The chief differences between the two works lie in Rolli's light-hearted treatment of Achilles' disguise and the soubrette-role of Nerea, whereas Metastasio's subsidiary characters (Teagene and Nearco) contribute nothing to the drama but noble sentiments and sage reflections. Both features of Rolli's version come from the libretti of the earlier Baroque age, and he may possibly have used as his model Ippolito Bentivoglio's *Achille in Sciro* (Ferrara 1663), in which there is a model for Nerea in the character of Cirene, Deidamia's sister.[123] There was no artistic relevance for either Rolli or Handel in the fact that the London *Deidamia* of 1741 was inevitably linked to the actual events of a war.[124] The nationalistic element is in any case far less prominent here than it had been in their *Riccardo Primo* of 1727. On that occasion both men had been able to combine an ostentatious support of British Imperialism with their own material interests.

Francesco Gasparini's later operas and Handel

F RANCESCO GASPARINI's mature career may be divided, albeit summarily, into three periods of roughly equal length: his life at Rome up to 1700, a stay at Venice from 1700 to 1713, and the final return to Rome from 1714 until his death in 1727. It is the last of these stages which is the subject of this essay. I believe that it can now definitely be stated, especially in the light of new documents presented during the conference 'Francesco Gasparini (1661–1727)'[1] that Gasparini lived at Rome for almost the whole of this period.

Apart from these details of the composer's biography and the bibliography of his works, various other problems have arisen, including those of stylistic development, local tastes and traditions, and Gasparini's position in history. The contribution which I hope to make here will be more like a series of notes and observations than a balanced historical judgement; and these notes themselves will be limited to Gasparini's output in the field of opera.

Until a few years ago, as far as students of Italian opera were concerned, Gasparini was a representative of the Venetian school. According to this view, however, 'Venetian' opera meant specifically that of the seventeenth century, since Venice was then the only centre of Italian opera in the period to be known about or studied. Gasparini was fitted into this scheme as a 'late Venetian', even from a stylistic point of view. Scholars from Kretzschmar to Abert, Lorenz and Gerber regularly attached labels describing regional origins to various stylistic details, and compiled a list of criteria defining style, chronology and local tradition. As a result, the concept of a 'Neapolitan school' in the stylistic sense developed, a school which was supposed to have taken over from the Venetian in the first third of the eighteenth century; and the term 'Neapolitan School' as used by Francesco Florimo[2] thus lost its innocent air of local patriotism. Non-Venetian opera composers of the seventeenth century, like their non-Neapolitan eighteenth-century counterparts, came to seem a little out of place. The chief victim of the rigidity of such constructs was Alessandro Scarlatti, who was shifted about from one school to another along with changing fashions in research.[3] The problem is no less complex in the case

80

of Gasparini. This prolific and versatile composer – a friend of none other
than Scarlatti – had a good deal to do with opera in the Venetian tradition,
especially that branch of it represented by the librettists Apostolo Zeno and
Francesco Silvani, in the early eighteenth century. But his career taken as
a whole shows him to have been much more closely connected with Rome
in the practice of his profession, and he himself, after all, was a Tuscan.

While at Venice Gasparini had been choirmaster at the Ospedale della
Pietà (and consequently Vivaldi's superior), and he seems to have left this
post in 1713, when he applied for six months' leave of absence from which
he failed to return. His operatic output in this transitional year seems to
confirm that he had decided not to go back to the Venetian Republic. For
the Carnival of 1713 he had written *La verità nell'inganno*, his last Venetian
opera for ten years, but in 1712 and 1713 various operas of his were already
beginning to appear on the stages of Florence (*L'amor tirannico*, 1712;
Merope, 1713), Milan (*Il comando non inteso ed ubbidito*, 1713), Genoa (the
same work, in the autumn of 1713), Reggio Emilia (*Eumene*, 1714) and, above
all, Rome, where he contributed to the opera-house owned by Cardinal
Ottoboni (for which he wrote the second act of *Eraclio*, 1712) and to the
Teatro Capranica (*Lucio Papirio*, 1714), which may already have come into
the hands of Prince Ruspoli. But it is not enough just to list titles. It would
be very interesting, from a biographical point of view, to know in exactly
which productions of his own operas Gasparini was involved in person, and
it is essential to distinguish these from the revisions of his scores undertaken
by other hands – a common practice which had begun to affect Gasparini's
work, without him being able to prevent it, long before 1713. If the original
libretti are compared with those of the various revivals, and the few
surviving scores from those years are consulted as well, it becomes possible
to identify the truly 'Gasparinian' productions: those which contain new
arias attributable to Gasparini himself, or whose texts differ less from their
originals than might be expected in the case of revision by another hand.
Using these criteria it is possible to work out when and where the composer
himself intervened in productions of his work. The following list covers only
the years 1712–14:

New material	Revision by Gasparini himself
1712 *Eraclio* (Act 2) (Ottoboni theatre) Score sent from Venice	*L'amor tirannico* (Florence, Carnival) The libretto is not dated *more fiorentino*
Merope (Venice, Carnival)	
1713 *La verità nell'inganno* (Venice, Carnival)	*Merope* (Florence, Carnival)?
Il comando non inteso ed ubbidito (Milan, Carnival)	*Il comando…*(Genoa, autumn)
	La principessa fedele (Genoa, autumn)
1714 *Lucio Papirio* (Rome, Capranica theatre, Carnival)	
Eumene (Reggio Emilia, May)	

This list is almost certainly incomplete and is presented here with all the diffidence proper to so unfamiliar a kind of research, albeit one which promises to lead towards a more exact chronology of Gasparini's work for the theatre.

Typical is the case of what is perhaps Gasparini's most famous opera, *Tamerlano*, written to a libretto by Count Agostino Piovene, for the Venetian Carnival of 1711 (though the libretto is dated, in the Venetian style, 1710). I do not believe that Gasparini had a hand in any of the numerous revisions of this work which took place in various towns during the following years, but it was certainly he who wrote an almost completely new version of it, under the title *Bajazet*, for the Este theatre at Reggio Emilia in 1719. The same is true of another *Bajazette*, performed at S. Samuele in Venice in the spring of 1723; and in both cases the composer's personal involvement can be deduced from evidence in the musical sources themselves. As I have shown elsewhere, I also believe that Gasparini stayed in Milan for the Carnival of 1722, and that while he was there he adapted two of his own works, *Flavio Anicio Olibrio* and *Astianatte*. A manuscript of the latter, partly in Gasparini's own hand and written for use in Milan, is still in existence (see pp. 106–21 below).

The years 1722–3 mark the end of Gasparini's career as a composer of opera. It seems strange that he should have written no genuine example of the genre after 1721 in Rome, where he was living. A possible explanation is that he lost some of his status and influence on the Roman scene around 1721–2, when his patron, Prince Borghese, went as viceroy to Naples. Gasparini was almost literally driven out of the Alibert, Capranica and even Pace theatres by the composers of the new generation, Porpora, Predieri and Vinci. He may well have taken refuge with one or other of the many patrons who had abounded in Roman cultural circles in the seventeenth century and were now sadly reduced; one such was the Portuguese ambassador, Andrea Mello di Castro, for whose palace Gasparini wrote two *favole pastorali* in 1723 and 1724. In doing so he found himself in friendly competition with Alessandro Scarlatti, who was also working for the ambassador in 1724, along with his son Domenico, who was at Rome that year in the Portuguese dignitary's service. Together they formed a small circle of conservatives who no longer had any influence on the development of a Roman opera now largely dominated by Neapolitans.

These facts accord neatly with evidence supplied by Gasparini himself as to contemporary developments in musical taste and, particularly, singing. As a singing-master and teacher of composition Gasparini had been a disciple of the famous Bolognese school (represented by Antonio Bernacchi, among others), which offered perhaps the staunchest conservative opposition to the new vocal virtuosity associated with the Neapolitans. Not only had Gasparini been displaced as a composer of operas for the Alibert theatre by Porpora and Predieri, even the singers he found congenial (especially the mezzo-sopranos and the tenors, Giovanni Ossi, Rapaccioli, Bartoluzzi and possibly Giovanni Paita) had been replaced by sopranos like Farinelli and Carestini, though this development was perhaps more important for Gasparini himself than for the stylistic history of composition. Then, in 1723, Pier Francesco Tosi published his *Opinioni de' cantori antichi e moderni*, in which he laid down the traditional standards of the Bolognese school, and sent a copy to Gasparini. Gasparini's reply was in the form of a letter (already published elsewhere),[4] a manuscript of which is preserved in the Civico Museo Bibliografico Musicale at Bologna, dated 'Rome, 11 March 1724'. Part of it runs:

I am already reading your most excellent book with enormous pleasure; indeed I think it must have been dictated to you by an angel... I sent at once for Sig. Rapaccioli, so that he could see your letter, and he said that he had written to you already; he added that he had only sold two copies of your book up to now, but had sent the rest to a bookseller, so as to put them on the market more easily... I myself have begun to talk about it whenever possible, and will become a very advertiser of it to the public. Believe me, though my compliments are worth little, when I say that it is one of the noblest and most splendid pieces of work ever to have emerged into the world as an aid and an adornment to the harmonious art. I pray God that it will be listened to and absorbed by those who, alas, have great need of it; and certainly it could have appeared at no more opportune time than the present. Although I naturally incline towards your view anyway, for the sake of our old friendship, I will observe your precepts with great care, in spite of the vile flattery of so-called 'modern' taste, and I shall be careful not to let my pupils fall in with such abuses at least as far as I am able. In particular, I shall prevent them from taking all those steps [i.e. 'florid passage-work'?] on which one is led by one's nose; and yet, I have some of this trouble in my employment.

Almost every single phrase of this extract has a special meaning in the context of the operatic situation of Rome in 1723–4, when Gasparini had withdrawn, probably against his will, from the stage altogether. Despite the mutual support Tosi and Gasparini offered each other, the latter's operas, which had been acclaimed throughout Italy and beyond, were beginning to disappear from the theatres even before his death.

It seems appropriate at this point to ask just what Gasparini, as a composer of opera, was able to hand down to later generations. Here I can give only one example, though it seems to be an important one: that of G. F. Handel.

It is my firm conviction that Handel's style as an operatic composer – and perhaps as a composer of instrumental music, for example – was formed, to a very large extent, on the models and experiences he encountered during his years in Italy (1706/7–10), the greater part of which he spent at Rome. His debt to Scarlatti and Corelli has already been underlined by other scholars, and here I should add that not only Handel's work but practically the whole of musical culture in the London of his day was modelled, as far as Italian precedent is concerned, on Roman examples of the seventeenth and eighteenth centuries. Evidence for this is provided by Haym, Rolli,

Geminiani, Thomas Roseingrave, Giovanni Bononcini and many others. Further, Handel, who had not seen opera performed at Rome and who may have met Francesco Gasparini in Venice itself in 1708, made some use of the scores of his operas. The chief example of this is mentioned by J. Merrill Knapp in his essay on Handel's *Tamerlano* (1970), and I also discuss this elsewhere (Strohm 1979; this volume pp. 49ff). Handel must, indeed, have studied Gasparini's two settings of this libretto (*Tamerlano*, 1711, and *Bajazet*, 1719) before writing his own *Tamerlano* for London in 1724. Very probably the 1719 score had been shown to him by the singer Francesco Borosini, a famous tenor in the service of His Imperial Majesty, who sang the part of Bajazet in both Gasparini's opera, at Reggio in 1719, and Handel's, in 1724. There is, in fact, no shortage of allusions to Gasparini as a model in Handel's score. They include the arias 'Forte e lieto a morte andrei', 'Sulla sponda del pigro Lete' and 'Padre amato in me riposa' (parts of which were deleted from the final version), as well as the opening accompanied number 'Lacci ferri' and, most obviously, the whole of Bajazet's last scene, an accompanied recitative never exceeded in tragic grandeur by anything in Gasparini or, perhaps, in Handel himself.

If this example of stylistic continuity still seems somewhat unconvincing, given that it involves an opera of Gasparini's which is not, properly speaking, Roman (as well as the fact that Handel seems rather to avoid, whenever possible, making direct allusions as such) there is another example which is more clear-cut musically.

At the beginning of the London season of 1737–8 the impresario J. J. Heidegger seems to have commissioned two (or perhaps three) musical dramas from Handel, for which the composer would receive a pre-arranged fee (Chrysander, vol. 2. p. 447). This suggests that Handel took little interest in their libretti, which may have been supplied by Heidegger, and that he was able to justify using the work of others as a model while writing the music (although his celebrated borrowings nearly always produced work which was itself original, or at least was an improvement on the models). One of the three operas which Handel wrote during that season (*Alessandro Severo*, text by Zeno) was a pasticcio made up of portions from his own works; a second was *Serse*, based on the score of the same name by Giovanni Bononcini, written for Rome in 1694 to a libretto by Stampiglia, as H. Powers has shown.[5] The first of these three pieces, *Faramondo* performed on 3 January 1738, has up to now been thought to be the only completely original work in this group. (Its libretto is also by Apostolo Zeno; Handel never set any text of his in any other season.) Handel's *Faramondo*, however, is another partly derivative work, drawing in this case on Francesco Gasparini's opera of the same name, performed at the Alibert theatre at Rome during the Carnival of 1720. All that has survived of the score is an anthology of twenty-three arias and one duet, put together at Rome shortly after 1720 (F-Pc D.4340). Yet it is obvious that Handel studied this music, that he absorbed it, and that he developed it, while respecting the spirit and the operatic aesthetic characteristic of Gasparini's later work.

In more than one aria Handel re-employs the melodic idea which Gasparini had created from the text, but he tends to modify and expand upon it. Examples of this method – common to many of his borrowings and yet mysteriously at odds with the creative spontaneity typical of Handel's work – include Clotilde's aria 'Conoscerò se brami', compared with Gasparini's setting of the same text, and Rosimonda's 'Sì, l'intendesti sì', which is derived from Gasparini's 'Del mio destin crudel' (Example 1):

Example 1
a. Gasparini, *Faramondo*, Act I scene 4

b. Handel

c. Gasparini, *Faramondo*, Act III scene 17

d. Handel

More often, Handel imitates a particular rhythm used by Gasparini, which, he feels, matches the words perfectly; and with it he reproduces the rhythmic and expressive characteristics of the whole aria (Example 2).

In these arias, as in some others, it should be noted how not only the opening motif, but also certain rhythmic figures of *coloratura* or accompaniment seem to be accepted by Handel as the exact expression of a specific emotion or concept mentioned in the text (Example 3).

In the last of these examples, the whole of Handel's aria is pervaded by the syncopated movement of quavers which represents the stormy sea;

Example 2
a. Gasparini, *Faramondo*, Act I scene 20

(Se   ben mi   lu - sin - ga   l'in - fi - da spe - ran - za...)

b. Handel

(Se ben mi lusinga . . .)

c. Gasparini, *Faramondo*, Act I scene 5

Van - ne,   van - ne,   che più ti mi - ro,   piu cre-sce il mio do - lor   più cre-sce il mio do - lor

d. Handel

Van-ne,   che più ti mi - ro,   più cre-sce il mio do-lor   più cre-sce il mio do-lor van-ne, van-ne

Example 3
a. Gasparini, 'Del mio destin'   b. Handel, 'Si l'intendesti'

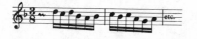   

                                        bar - - - - - - (baro)

c. Gasparini, 'Se ria tempesta', *Faramondo*, Act III scene 5

(Ritornello)

d. Handel, 'Se ria procella', *Faramondo*, Act I scene 9

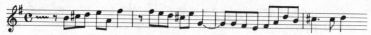

Gasparini only uses it in the instrumental continuations of the vocal line. But this goes further still. Gasparini's storm aria supplies a melodic motif and a characteristic rhythm which Handel seems to have shared between *two* arias: one in *Faramondo* and one in his *Giustino* of 1737, in which he had also used Giovanni Bononcini as a model:

Example 4
a. Gasparini, 'Se ria tempesta', *Faramondo*, Act III scene 5

b. Handel, 'Se ria procella', *Faramondo*, Act I scene 9

c. Handel, 'Un vostro sguardo', *Giustino*, Act I scene 2

It should be noted that in *Giustino*, where, if anything, the similarity of the melodies is even greater, Handel uses the model in the context of a completely different image. The musical sign, in itself, remains undefined and almost equivocal. That Handel had already studied Gasparini's score a year before he wrote *Faramondo* is also attested by two other quotations in *Giustino*, one of which is the opening phrase of the aria 'Del mio destin crudel' (Example 1c) in Giustino's aria 'Se parla nel mio cor'. The other involves Gasparini's aria-minuet 'Chi ben ama' (Example 5).

Example 5
a. Gasparini, *Faramondo*, Act I scene 5

b. Handel

c. Handel, *Giustino*, Act I scene 4

As far as *Giustino* is concerned, the aria's text is not to be found in the libretto which the London librettist used for his guidance; it is, in fact, a paraphrase in similar metre of an aria by Metastasio, 'Alma grande e nata al regno', which may perhaps have been adapted to Handel's already existing minuet. One might point out here that, in *Faramondo*, Handel reproduces precisely those rhythms and melodic phrases from his model which he had left out when writing *Giustino*. On the other hand, the similarities between all three melodies owe too much to their genre to be indisputably deliberate quotations: they are melodic 'types', which match types of dance.

In Handel's aria 'Chi ben ama' – whose motifs reappear several times in other parts of Gasparini's score (for example, the line-ends in ascending quavers, for which see 'Conoscerò' in example 1, or the amorous diction of bars 11–14) – the minuet serves to introduce a well-balanced, affectionate character of secondary importance, neither serious nor comic (Adolfo), while in the case of Giustino the dance represents the simplicity of his rustic life (the character makes his first appearance 'with a plough'). But Handel's *Faramondo* is rich in minuets to an even greater extent than *Giustino*. It is the only one of his operas not to contain a 'siciliano' or a mournful saraband. Rather, Handel reworks various types of aria, taking his cue from Gasparini, to conform to a taste for the 'cantabile' and the 'galant'; and he thus creates 'hybrid' combinations which nearly all have something of the minuet about them. There is a generic similarity between these arias by Handel and the models furnished by Gasparini, as well as a general tendency to expand on those models:

Example 6
a. Gasparini, *Faramondo*, Act I scene 13

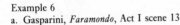

b. Handel

c. Gasparini, *Faramondo*, Act II scene 7

d. Gasparini, *Clotilde*, Act I scene 17

e. Handel

Example 6 (*cont.*)

f. Gasparini, *Rosimonda-Faramondo*, Act II scene 19

g. Handel

Finally, let us consider the only example of a gigue common to both scores. It is an amusing and highly interesting instance, since Handel seems to have chosen the wrong place for his reminiscence of Gasparini:

Example 7

a. Gasparini, *Faramondo*, Act II scene 2

Example 7 (*cont.*)

b. Handel, *Faramondo*, Act II scene 3

Non   in - gan-nar- mi, nò,   con - for - to del mio sen,   dol - ce,— dol - ce spe-ran- za

It will be apparent that the excerpt from Gasparini, characterised throughout by the rhythms of the gigue, has been taken up by Handel and applied to a different text, while the original text is set as a minuet, with a different allusion (see Example 1). But a glance at the texts is all that is required to explain the logic behind these relationships. Their metre and the words themselves, in their syntactical arrangement, serve as a 'tertium comparationis'. All four arias have this in common – Gasparini's 'Del mio destin crudel' and 'Sì l'intendesti, sì' as well as Handel's 'Sì, l'intendesti sì' and a 'Non ingannarmi, no'. The type of aria on a 'tronco' text (with the accent on the last syllable of each poetic line) takes the form of two dances in each of these scores, a minuet and a gigue. However, the expression of the dramatic circumstances described in the texts, and of the emotions they inspire, is conveyed not in the initial theme or the rhythm used, but in the manner of their treatment. Thus Gasparini accompanies the plaintive aria 'Del mio destin crudel' with a pair of recorders which play a third apart, while in Handel's 'Sì, l'intendesti' the devices used in the development of the tune – unison, octaves, suspensions, pauses – accord well with the aria's lively character, itself very similar to that of the aria-gigue to which Gasparini sets these words. For 'Non ingannarmi, no' Handel draws on precisely those elements in Gasparini's work which give it its sparkling good humour, in order to create a suitable atmosphere of hope and joy.

The fact that it is rhythmic types, types of dance, which form the point of contact between the two scores might seem to indicate a largely unthinking and impersonal relationship between the two composers. Certainly if one were to look for traces of Handel's personal style in this score, written to a strict deadline and perhaps with little enthusiasm, arias other than those quoted here would have to be considered, and the principal motifs themselves would be less important than the way in which they are treated. Furthermore, Gasparini's music, of which only fragments have survived, is itself richer and more varied than the few notes quoted here might suggest. But it was never the purpose of this comparison to show Handel's personal reliance on his predecessor. What is clear is a connection through adherence to a school, an affinity of attitude and general artistic approach. It is astonishing to see how far Handel is from his fellow-composers of opera in 1737, even in the use of minuets, with those precise and very simple rhythmic ideas. Nor had Gasparini been in complete agreement with the operatic composers of 1720 when he wrote his almost metallic melodies, so different from the turgid 'bel canto' style of Porpora or the abundant élan of the young Hasse. One thinks rather of the Giovanni Bononcini of the last years of the seventeenth century, with his *Xerse* or his *Trionfo di Camilla* (1696). Some trace of that Roman operatic style seems to have survived both in Gasparini's later work at Rome and in Handel's London. By 1737–8 Handel must already have been well aware of the successes of the 'moderns'; not only had he already written for Carestini and Caffarelli, not only was Farinelli enjoying great acclaim in London in the works of Porpora and Hasse, but he himself had conducted, for example, Vinci's *Didone abbandonata* in 1737, in a version supplemented with much music composed by Hasse. In his own works, however, Handel takes another line. His models are Gasparini, Bononcini and Stradella (*Israel in Egypt*, 1738), and his *Concerti Grossi* op.6 were intended as a memorial to Corelli. It should also be recalled that the libretto of his *Giustino* was an adaptation of the one which Antonio Vivaldi had written for the Capranica theatre at Rome in 1724, in the very weeks in which Gasparini wrote his letter, quoted above, to Tosi – perhaps with Vivaldi as an operatic composer in mind. But Vivaldi's music does not provide a model for Handel. Harold Powers ends his analysis of *Serse* with a fine image, describing that work as the last flower on the tree of the Venetian school. He should have said 'of the seventeenth century'. Not only because Giovanni Bononcini and his librettist Silvio Stampiglia are far from being Venetian artists, but also because of the evidence of his *Faramondo*, it is perhaps more accurate to say that Handel, at least in these years, shows himself attached to a musical tradition with a distinctively Roman basis.

Towards an understanding of the
opera seria

I F TODAY an operatic production appears to diverge from the author's intentions or from the printed 'work' (whatever it may be), it is not always because the producer or director, though fully understanding those intentions, has consciously developed a new conception. Cases in which the divergence is not deliberate may be quite as common, and there is a large range of possible reasons, as for example in the case of Handel's operas:

1. Circumstances in the modern theatre make it impossible from the outset to reproduce the original exactly (e.g. in the case of castrato-roles).
2. The theatrical practices of an earlier age have been replaced by a new theatrical tradition (e.g. the dragging, oratorio-like performance of *recitativo secco*, the changes of scene with the curtain down).
3. In the absence of thorough research it is not yet possible to be sure of understanding or reading the author's written instructions (there are cases for example of mistakes in the transcription and translation of Italian original texts, and also perhaps of insufficient understanding of the original instrumentation).
4. There are mistakes in stage-setting and production which could today be avoided by a conscientious study of the original source e.g. the performance of 'coro' passages by a chorus.

It is particularly early operas that suffer from misunderstandings and insufficiences of this kind, which should not be dignified with the name of producers' 'ideas'. Meanwhile we still tend to underestimate the difficulties that have to be overcome, particularly in the performance of Handel's operas. The chief problem, it seems to me, lies in the fact that these works belong to a genre – the *opera seria*, i.e. the *dramma per musica* – which has otherwise entirely disappeared from the theatre. The lack of all practical experience of *opera seria* common to producers, musicians and audiences alike is only matched by the conviction with which musical scholars have for generations been stating the same facile judgements. In the appreciation of Handel's position there are two specific dangers. First there is a tendency to apply a supposed knowledge of 'Baroque opera' in general to individual works and thus to distort the relationship between what is individual and what is characteristic of the genre; and secondly, in the aesthetic judgement

93

of Handel's works, respect for him as a great master comes not so much
from his actual personal achievement as from the wish to establish an easy
comparison between him and other masters such as Bach, Mozart and
Beethoven. It seems to be more necessary than ever to place Handel's operas
in the perspective of the genre to which they belong and from this angle
to throw new light on their aesthetic presuppositions, their conception of
the art-work and their practical realisation.[1] I should first like to suggest,
with the help of a utopian analogy, what separates us from the conception
of the *opera seria*.

In some 250 years time, against the background of a 'Handel renaissance',
Horst Zankl's recent Frankfurt production of *Giulio Cesare* will again be
discussed, edited according to the existing sources and performed in a newly
conceived production with its technical deficiencies rectified. It will be
recognised that video-tapes give only a partial idea of the actual production;
and it will be demonstrated that neither the public nor the experts of 1978/9
understood that the actual work of art is to be seen in Zankl's production,
not in Handel's score. This is exactly how we in 1979 think about Handel's
Giulio Cesare of 1724: what is to us the 'work' was 250 years ago only the
'production' – and G. F. Bussani's drama of *Giulio Cesare in Egitto*, which
Handel and his assistants performed with many alterations and conscious
artistic reshapings, is today as faded as a 'work of art' as Handel's music
will be in 250 years time. This seems to be historically inevitable and in
no way a matter for regret; live art develops, at whatever is the most recent
level, in the actual 'doing' – and only later becomes fixed as a 'work'.

This is perhaps a law that is valid for all musical theatre, but it applies
specially to the history of Handel's operas, which are in fact examples of
artistic 'revivals'. *Giulio Cesare in Egitto* returned to the London stage more
than half a century after its first performance, with music that was all
Handel's but drawn from a number of different scores. The reason given
for this was that the drama no longer satisfied the demands of the public
and that insertions and transferences were therefore essential.[2] The theatrical
practice of Handel's day had thus already become obsolete, while his music
still enjoyed a traditional respect. In 1821 neither Handel nor Bussani was
still being performed, but there was a *Giulio Cesare in Egitto* – composed
by Giovanni Pacini for the Teatro Argentina in Rome. Half a century later
still Friedrich Chrysander edited Handel's (!) *Giulio Cesare* (1875) from the
sources as part of the monumental complete edition, which occupies a
worthy place in Breitkopf und Härtel's great collected editions of German
composers. The music of *Giulio Cesare* has become an independent work,
represented in a musical score amalgamating written models and versions
varying in content and character. It is an individual work, but it also forms
part of a whole – the 'Complete Works' of G. F. Handel. At that time there
were no performances. These came some fifty years later, when Oskar Hagen

revived the Handel operas in the theatre with Expressionist sets and revised them musically and dramatically, with a great understanding of Baroque musical performance-practice (impossible without Max Schneider). This editing was naturally based on Chrysander's score. It was not, however, *Giulio Cesare* (Göttingen 1922), but the related opera *Rodelinda* (1920) that started the controversy between the director and practical musician Hagen and the Handel-scholar Rudolf Steglich – a controversy which involved almost all the important problems that we are still trying to solve.[3] Steglich disagreed with Hagen on the matter of cuts: Handel's carefully balanced key-structure which reveals a conscious shaping of the overall whole, must suffer if single arias are omitted. In order to make the necessary abbreviations it would be better to cut the middle sections and repeats in the arias. That cuts are necessary seems to have been agreed by Hagen and Steglich and apparently by all subsequent German producers. This theatrical tradition is now barely sixty years old. There were further points of agreement. Castrato roles must be sung by men's voices an octave lower (no other interval is ever considered); recitative-cadences are to be 'delayed';[4] and the language used must be German. All were agreed in their total rejection of Baroque theatrical practice – though Hagen reveals his ignorance of this when he maintains that he could easily have reconstructed 'the London stage-sets of 1725' at Göttingen;[5] Steglich recommended a more historicist solution. All were agreed in rejecting nineteenth-century reinstrumentation of the music. The decisions taken at this time, and the theatrical traditions established, had less to do with Handel than with Chrysander on the one hand and with the position in 1920 of German musicology and theatre-practice on the other. The majority of these decisions were not reconsidered or even questioned in 1978. Zankl's restoration of the original Italian is relatively insignificant compared to those elements he has in common with Hagen, and also those which his conductor Harnoncourt has in common with Chrysander (neither, for instance, are experts in theatrical matters). This appears logical – in theatrical matters there must be artistic freedom and contemporary ideas and contemporary audiences must be taken into account – but in musical matters fidelity to the work and historicism is all important. Both *opera seria* and Handel differ from more recent stages in the history of opera in which the theatrical element, the practical staging of a work may be out of date, but the musical element is 'still' binding. In the case of the *opera seria* the musical element has also perished and after being historistically 'revived' can never again 'age' naturally (as might occur if the music were re-composed).

If we compare the situation today with Italian operatic practice in the early eighteenth century, the first thing that strikes us is how little attention was paid in the theatre of the day to the individual 'work'. The continuity of planning, composing, rehearsing, performing and re-performing guaranteed artistic standards; even the most successful work could never be repeated unaltered in conditions that were perpetually changing – on the other hand, two different works created in similar conditions (at the same theatre in the same season, for instance) might resemble each other more closely than would be tolerated today. Individual works sharply distinguished in artistic character would have been uneconomic in the huge number of productions (more operas were given then, at any rate in Italy, than now) and with the quick turnover between production and consumption. In London there were some fifty operatic performances per annum, though these were attended by a comparatively small number of people, each of whom would see several performances of the same work. These performances would differ from each other at the very least by the changes freely introduced by the singers (in ornamentation, for example) or demanded by the composer, thus maintaining the interest of audiences. The fact that public interest was concentrated on apparently spontaneous variations of this kind from one performance to the next partly explains the mistaken impression often spread by foreign tourists that the Italians had no interest in the drama or the performance of the recitatives, but only in the arias. Of course the number of reasons for which people went to the opera other than out of artistic interest is very well known. Members of the audience were themselves active during a performance. Apparently theatres, even when 'sold out', generally had a number of unoccupied seats, so that it was possible to change one's seat, though there were no intervals between the acts.[6] Theatres did not permit the public to move all at the same time but many spectators came and went during the performance. The work being performed had to renew the interest of the audience as it were from one evening to another, and indeed from one number to the next: perfect balance and planning would have been largely lost on the audience.

The music composed for a drama was not distinguished by any name denoting its genre. 'Opera' is always the whole theatrical event, and also the institution and the building. The composition is considered as the musical garment in which the drama is presented; and in many libretto-prefaces the composer is praised for his art ('arte'), the notes with which he has adorned the drama ('rivestito di note'), not for his opera. The designation of the genre as *dramma per musica* (*opera seria* as the title of a genre does not appear before the later eighteenth century) always refers to the text; it appears not only on the title-page of the libretto, but also on the score itself – often followed in such a case by 'musica di...' or 'posto in musica da...' It was not Handel's *Giulio Cesare*, but the *dramma per musica* of that name with Handel's music.

Anyone wishing to produce an opera did not start 'from the score', as is sometimes expected nowadays. Rather, he had at his disposal an existing text, a drama. The drama alone was, in a sense, the self-contained *opus*, if only because the text was printed and could therefore be judged by the experts. The preparation of a drama in the theatrical circumstances of those days (which included its musical 'clothing') did not require a producer – much of the acting and stage design followed long-standing conventions – but a poet and a composer, creative artists in fact. This was true even for later performances of a work: the new production of an established and unchangeable score, one in which nobody could add new arias or transpose the recitative for a different type of voice, nobody could substitute new last lines for scenes that had been cut or write parody-texts, would have been something quite unthinkable. A modern operatic production has no need of either composer or librettist – they would in fact often only be in the way.

The fact that the drama came first determined the artistic demands. Any chance mistakes of the composer's, any rather free use of a colleague's ideas, could not possibly be detected by the general public. In the printed libretto, on the other hand, any educated man could observe any infelicitous expressions or metrical faults and also compare the work of a provincial littérateur with that of the famous Zeno, Stampiglia, Metastasio etc. Everything suggests that the librettist's chief aim was immaculate versification, an ambition that links a Metastasio to a Rolli; consequently the fault most to be guarded against in a singer was badly accented declamation or poor enunciation. The performance of a *dramma per musica* was regarded primarily as the music-dramatic recitation of poetry – and small wonder in Italy itself, which had virtually no literary form of theatre other than opera. It thus followed that, insofar as the stage realisation of a work was not implicit in the theatrical practice of the day and the text of the work concerned, it was the responsibility of the poet, who conducted the rehearsals. Nowadays producers, singers and even musical scholars and editors alike suffer from insufficient understanding of the literary components of the *dramma per musica* and an insufficient knowledge of the metres of Italian poetry and even of the language itself.

The production of an eighteenth-century opera is normally to be understood as a process that starts before the composition and ends after that is completed – if it is. The first consideration was the cast of singers available, and this could even play a part in deciding the choice of subject, whether this choice was made by the librettist or by the composer. The text would be altered in accordance with what happened at rehearsals, as would the music, insofar as it already existed: the first act might often be in rehearsal before the third was composed. The whole process was a swift one, and it might be a matter of weeks rather than months from the commissioning of a work to its first performance. The composer, who often had to conduct the first performances, generally had to be there beforehand, so that he could make any necessary adjustments and additions, and although scores were sometimes submitted, there is little evidence to show that the version submitted was then faithfully performed. Foreign composers received commissions both from the exclusive court-theatres and from those controlled by impresarios; but it should not be forgotten that hardly any composer could live by opera-writing; the steady income needed by most came, for court-composers, from their regular work of supplying the court chapel with music and, for others, from their posts as Kapellmeister at churches or conservatories. Virtuoso singers, too, were obliged to sing either in churches or in court performances of chamber music, though singers could specialise in opera more easily than composers, as is shown by comparing fees. A *primo uomo* (always a castrato) could and in fact had to earn his livelihood by opera-singing. In Italy between 1720 and 1740 these star-singers were paid, for a single role or for a season (both kinds of engagements were common), about three times as much as the composer, and up to ten times as much as the librettist or singers of the least important parts.[7] This can be explained not only by considerations of artistic priority and hierarchical rating of roles but also by the different amount of specialisation involved. The existence of these famous opera-singers was much more closely dependent on the theatre than that of any of the others involved, including the composer. The positive result of this was of course that they tried to dictate the character of the music and the production. It was on their personalities that the 'work' i.e. the actual theatrical event, had to be moulded. Not only individual roles, but whole works were conceived for individual singers – the actual drama of Metastasios's *Didone abbandonata*, for instance, for Marianna Bulgarelli, Zanelli's *Bajazet* (set by Gasparini, 1719) for Francesco Borosini,[8] Haym's and Handel's *Giulio Cesare* for Senesino. When the new London venture was initiated in 1728, Handel is said to have stipulated that new singers were to be engaged on each occasion so that new operas could be written for new performers;[9] this probably referred not only to vocal style, for which every opera-composer had in any case to take the individual singer's powers into account, but also to dramatic function, of the chief role in particular. What was clearly fixed and predetermined about any production in those days had so little to do with the score and so much to do with the presentation of the drama by a single, individual singer that a revival of an *opera seria* today should really concentrate less on what Handel or Hasse wrote than on what Senesino or Farinelli did with the chief role. The mere reconstruction of the stage-settings, costumes etc. (probably without the corresponding stage-technique) has no historical value. But if we had a Senesino, who had a deep understanding not only of singing but also of reciting Italian verse and not least of how to be an Emperor it might not matter so much that some of his arias were by Harnoncourt and not Handel. In fact they could even be by Penderecki: a conclusion that is only apparently absurd, since the claims of history in the matter of musical performance always collapse in cases where the performer has to become the creator.

In the revival of Handel's operas, however, it seems to be precisely this crystallisation of the score into a sacrosanct 'work' that has become an irreversible process. It began right back in the nineteenth century and is now complete, though perhaps not entirely since, in Germany at least, musical directors of Handel productions still cling to the red pencil as the last remaining tool of artistic freedom. (The process of crystallisation is in fact beginning to spread to the field of live production, i.e. the stage-settings, many of which are copied en bloc. In this case the most important factor seems to be the possibility of recording and comparing stage-sets by means of mechanical reproduction.) The fact that there is an audience for Handel's operas at all and that they are in practice revived with conscious historical intention clearly distinguishes Handel's from all the other Italian operas between Monteverdi/Cavalli and Gluck, with very few exceptions such as Pergolesi's *Serva Padrona*. This situation may well change in the future; but if it is true that we can still only assimilate early music in the form of crystallised 'works', the quick acceptance of Handel is easy to explain. It is in any case restricted to Anglo-German countries and may reflect what in Handel's own lifetime distinguished his operas from those of his Italian contemporaries. That – it must be said at once – has in my opinion very little to do with musical 'quality'. With regard to this I would like to mention at least four further points.

(1) Handel was composing in London for a public that did not understand Italian. The fact that English translations were printed in the libretti was of no great help. Riva in 1726 wrote, with a slight note of contempt, that 'what London wanted was a lot of arias and not much recitative'.[10] The original recitatives in Handel's source-texts were often cut almost to absurdity in his performing-versions – a technique in which Nicola Haym excelled and one which I suspect that Handel learned from him. (In modern performances the additional cuts in the recitative are often even more ludicrous.) Handel had to rely far more on the arias to present the drama, and this was achieved in the first place by making the aria texts, often contributed by Haym and Rolli, convey to the listener information that in Italian libretti was generally conveyed by the recitative, or – and this was the more frequent method – by Handel's actual setting of the arias taking over this function. A study of the source-libretti reworked by Handel's librettists will very often reveal the semantic origin of an aria-setting in a passage of recitative that was not performed in his production, but has been absorbed in the music.[11] Handel's settings, therefore, have less need of the informative dialogue surrounding them: they are full of musical symbols, 'speaking' motifs and nuances of feeling, and both more self-contained and more effective than Italian composers' arias, which are often 'superficial' because they are supported by the text. Handel's instrumentation is also more differentiated and individual: exploiting the semantic functions generally associated with solo instruments in the opera of the day. All this

may well have played a part in forming Handel's compositional technique. His works contain more purely instrumental music of descriptive illustration and more nature-scenes, whether these are purely instrumental or occur in arias or ariosos at the beginning of scenes – passages in which music is used to fill out not a text, but a visual image. It goes without saying that modern listeners are as grateful for such passages as were Handel's own non-Italian audiences – and it makes little difference whether the work is sung today in the vernacular or not.

(2) Another reason for Handel's London operas not having to satisfy any public demand for a literary form of theatre lies in the fact that London, unlike Italy, was well provided with a spoken drama of literary quality. Within a few moments walk of the Haymarket Opera were all the other theatres, where plays on the same, or similar, subjects were being given simultaneously and often in competition.[12] These were also attended by the aristocracy; and this facilitated comparisons and mutual comments or parodies, the *Beggar's Opera* being a particularly brash and hostile example. In a situation of this kind Handel must have felt challenged to exercise the same fascination in his music as other authors in their language. His audiences would be familiar with practically all the subjects of his operas. Many plays, French as well as English, were in fact printed in London; and purely musically London audiences had better opportunities for comparison and for educating their taste than the average Italian opera-goer. Members of the English aristocracy were collecting the capacious libraries which even today have only partially passed into public collections and become accessible to all. Music printers, John Walsh in particular, were more active, at least in terms of quantity, than most of those on the continent, with the possible exception of Amsterdam. We may conclude from this that Handel's public must have been musically active on a fairly wide scale. It was a public also familiar with the visual arts and with architecture, particularly that of the Italian (and more particularly the Roman) Baroque, either through imported Italian artists or by personal experience gained in Italy and elsewhere on those 'grand tours' that formed part of a gentleman's education. The determining influence among Handel's public consisted of the directors and subscribers of the Royal Academy, members of an aristocracy whose wide cultural horizon – in terms of genres, art-forms and national styles – resulted in the successful establishment of Italian opera in London and the importation of musicians like Handel and Bononcini, quite apart from Italian poets, singers and painters.[13] This whole question of importing art and artists, which often borders on a simple inclination for the exotic, must of course be viewed in the light of social and political factors that did not yet exist in the culture of the continental courts. In London the aristocracy had to demonstrate the superiority of their taste to that of a flourishing middle-class culture, first by means of the opera and later

within the opera itself. Both Handel and his colleagues and assistants were not only the objects but the practical allies of this need for self-assertion that in a way necessitated a higher standard of achievement than was necessary in the case of continental courts and impresarios. In Handel's London, analogies can be found with opera today, analogies that do not appear elsewhere until several generations later and may even help to account for the earlier acceptance of Handel by twentieth-century audiences.

(3) It was not only as an individual that Handel represented an exception in the field of *opera seria*: he also worked under exceptional conditions. In the Royal Academy period, and again between 1729 and 1734, he made a steady and comparatively good income,[14] and before 1728 the number of the works that he was expected to compose annually was apparently never specified. Thus he was not burdened, like the average Italian composer, with the continual search for new commissions, though he also lacked the security of employment enjoyed by a continental Court Kapellmeister. His ability to make his living from opera-writing depended on the success of the whole venture which meant, however, that he must perpetually seek to maintain public interest by every means at his disposal, and chiefly of course by his music. It was not that a single failure would mean disaster, inasmuch as the next production could make good any loss; but he was obliged to try to develop the taste of his audience in his own favour. (He succeeded in this for a longer period than might have been expected, given the economic conditions of the London opera.) He had the freedom, and in practice the authority, of an impresario or Court Intendant, but also carried the risk. His public still remained the same year after year, continually demanding something new and better. Not that each individual work had to be perfect, as was the case with the Italian composers, who were obliged to take full advantage of any particularly flattering commission. Handel was always judged by the standards which he himself had set, as is clear from contemporary, reactions to his works. The simple way out – re-using arias that had proved successful in operas performed elsewhere – was closed to him.

Handel's answer to these difficulties lay primarily in the amount of work that he expended on each opera. Hardly any contemporary opera composer (except Vivaldi) has left such extensive and varied autograph material, but we can conclude that Handel was exceptional in the amount of time and care with which he planned his works. Planning also included alterations: the different versions and stages of development that we can trace in his autographs often date not only from after the first performance but also from earlier.[15] This could be taken to show that in each case he worked, as it were with a file, in search of perfection, thus giving the versions performed at every first night that kind of 'work' character that had otherwise not been developed – something that can be traced, for instance, in the particularly delicate balancing of emotional states and tonalities, the particularly heightened presentation of character and situation. (This is how Steglich saw it.) But Handel would not have been clever had he shaped each work into an unrepeatable unity and given it a balance that any later change in details would have destroyed. Everything in the theatre of those days was incalculable – particularly anything to do with the singers – and this necessitated productions which could be changed easily and at short notice without damaging the effect of the whole; economy of effort and high costs demanded works that could be successfully repeated in later seasons. Since Handel on the other hand could never allow himself to use mere clichés (and only occasionally self-quotations) he gave each individual opera such a wealth of emotional moods, of internal musico-dramatic relationships and possibilities of interpretation that his scores survived the eroding effect of later revisions. It is of course possible to identify certain artistic symmetries and forms in a given version, as Steglich has done. The important point in Handel's case, however, is that there is always something that can be 'read into' every version. What he planned was not an 'unrepeatable' work but one that could very well be repeated. In operas of a later age it is often difficult to find where cuts can be made, but I personally find the exact opposite to be the case with, say, *Giulio Cesare*. Here, there are hardly any passages whose omission would spoil the work as a whole. The *accompagnato* 'Alma del gran Pompeo' is possibly such a passage. But take the preceding number, Tolomeo's E flat major aria 'L'empio, sleale, indegno', which is so closely related and contrasted with Cleopatra's preceding 'Non disperar chi sà' (E major). Handel first composed 'L'empio, sleale' for *Ottone*, then used it with a slightly altered text for a quite different dramatic situation in *Flavio*, and finally inserted it at the last moment in *Giulio Cesare* without making the necessary alterations in the text.[16] (The reason was Gaetano Berenstadt's taking over the role of Tolomeo from Alexander Gordon.) If this aria were cut, it would leave no lacuna – even if it seems to us to fit perfectly – because the contrast between Cleopatra's E major aria and Cesare's G minor *accompagnato* would once again be excellent. There are many examples of the same kind. Handel creates operas that are neither 'all of a piece' nor unalterable but can always be reshaped – at least by Handel himself – as though they were living organisms. At the same time it should be said that it does not devolve upon us to make cuts and transpositions in order to breathe some sort of new dramatic life into these 'works'; the time is long past for any such attempts at revivification. We should, and indeed may, retain Handel's own versions of his works.

(4) If we are to grasp Handel's unique position, we must face a question that has hitherto received very little attention – namely the historical origin of his operatic style. We can no longer be content with the old answer

'Venetian opera', because this rested on the mistaken belief that there was no other school in late seventeenth-century Italy but the Venetian, a tautological explanation borrowed even by Harold S. Powers.[17] As far as Handel's creative development is concerned, he (and in fact Giovanni Bononcini too) actually avoided the Venetian field of attraction despite the *Agrippina* that he composed in Rome as a commission for Cardinal Grimani. Nor was this his only work commissioned by a Roman cardinal. He worked in close connection with Corelli and Alessandro Scarlatti, chiefly for the court of Cardinal Pietro Ottoboni. The most important of his secular patrons in Italy were Prince Ruspoli in Rome and Ferdinando de' Medici of Tuscany. It was in Rome and Florence that Handel got most of his artistic experience, which included the spoken theatre as well as opera and oratorio, and there too that he encountered most of the original texts of the operas that he was later to set in London (see pp. 34–79 above). Ever since the days of Christina of Sweden musical and theatrical life in Rome has been in no way inferior to that of Venice; and between 1680 and 1700, when Rome was very busy with opera, French music and French classical tragedy were a particularly important influence. French tragedy was behind the theatrical movement initiated by the 'Reform'-librettists between Zeno and Metastasio; and one of Handel's favourite librettists, Antonio Salvi, converted French tragedies into libretti virtually by simple translation, while at the famous Collegio Clementino in Rome the Jesuit Filippo Merelli produced and performed Italian translations of these works, including (1709) Pradon's *Tamerlan*. Handel in fact was part of an eclectic and magnificent musical and theatrical life only to be repeated – on a more modest scale – in London. The circle was complete when Handel, his close colleague Nicola Haym before him, then Rolli and Bononcini after him, had all been engaged to London where Lord Burlington and other enthusiastic classicists tried to emulate Roman artistic exclusiveness and sublimity.

At the same time Handel remained a loyal servant of his Hanoverian masters. His first and most important sovereign was George I (Georg Ludwig of Braunschweig-Lüneburg), who before 1700 had made Hanover one of the most important centres of Italian opera in Germany. It was on the other hand a centre of French influence, which included both Lully's operas and instrumental music. Handel's relations with German courts were not confined to Hanover but seem to have been concentrated on those which showed greatest interest in opera (Düsseldorf and Innsbruck, Brunswick and Dresden), and everywhere he encountered the example of Steffani, although he only met him personally in Rome. Once again the original libretti used by Handel – which were for him only distillations of a much wider experience of the theatre – show that in London he was also continuing the tradition of Italian opera in Germany, a subsidiary tradition now twice removed from its source and in any case conservative.

This seems to be contradicted particularly by the case of *Giulio Cesare*, a drama that originated in Venice, where it had been set by Antonio Sartorio in 1677. Even Haym's and Handel's version shows traces of the loose dramatic structure and scenic variety of the old Venetian composers. Sartorio had been Kapellmeister at Hanover, and Bussani had even dedicated his drama to the daughter of an English diplomat; but apart from that it was a rather typical example of a Venetian opera. Against this, we should not overlook Haym's radical pruning of situations and characters and Handel's concentration of interest on the chief characters and their moving monologues. Why was it necessary to submit so old a drama to such laborious revision, which would not have been necessary in the case of modern librettists like Salvi and Stampiglia? Once again Handel appears to have started not with the ready-made drama but with a general conception of the chief character, Julius Caesar, as the embodiment of the absolute monarch who subdues the world and whose central blaze dims all merely local colouring. Thus Haym and Handel, unlike Bussani, range their scenes and their characters – Sesto and Tolomeo, Achilla and Nireno, Cleopatra and Cornelia – in a circle round the central point of the ruler. Caesar is the only character who embodies and presents not only all emotional states but all scenes from Nature (simile-arias and stage-sets and even direct addresses to Nature). The other characters merely fill out segments of this cosmos in different degrees and in different colours. (This explains why the tonalities associated with Cleopatra, Cornelia and Sesto are so clearly designed according to distinct areas of the circle of fifths.) Egypt, too, which is one of the segments of this cosmos, is related to Rome politically as London was artistically. It seems that Rome rather than Venice provided the inspiration for Handel's *Giulio Cesare*. There is a manuscript libretto, dated 1713, by Antonio Ottoboni, father of the cardinal, entitled *Giulio Cesare nell' Egitto*, with stage-sets by Filippo Juvarra and intended for performance. Mercedes Viale Ferrero,[18] who discovered it, believes it probable that Juvarra's sets were available in London; in fact two of them (or more, as I believe) can only be identifed in the 1713 and 1724 versions of this work which was set on many other occasions. Even if we do not know what sets were used for Handel's London performances, we can at least try to complete our idea of what took place in February 1724 by examining Juvarra's stage-designs with the sound of Handel's music in our ears. He may even have had them in front of him as he composed.

If the production of early operas today is, or is intended to be, art, then we can analyse it by uncovering the question to which it is an answer. The question answered by Zankl's production is, primarily, posed by Handel's score of *Giulio Cesare*. Handel's music itself, however, may be the answer to an earlier question which we are now challenged to uncover.

The Royal Academy balance-sheet – an attempted estimate

* = reconstruction according to figures proven for the years before 1720 and after 1729
** = directly proven figures (all the rest are estimated), based on *The London Stage*, Pt 2, vol. 1; Eisenschmidt; Deutsch.

Income

a. subscriptions – 1720–8 totalling about £25,000 (according to *The London Stage*). The number of subscribers varied between about 60 and about 160 (Eisenschmidt's figure of 500 is certainly wrong).

b. receipts: 1. tickets for non-subscribers mostly ½ guinea**
     2. gallery five shillings**
     3. public rehearsals one guinea** (rare)

With an average of fifty performances per season and two hundred tickets and one hundred and fifty in the gallery per performance, takings for the season would average £7,000–£7,500. Spreading the income from subscriptions over the eight and a half seasons would give, including takings, about £10,000–£10,500 as the figures available for a whole season.

Expenses for an average season (fifty performances)

Primo uomo	£2,000**
Primadonna	£2,000** (not 1720–2, but double 1725–8)
Remaining members of the cast, in all	£1,800*
Production	£1,200* (wages and material)
Orchestra	£750* (Eisenschmidt, for 1707)
Other staff	£750* (Eisenschmidt, for 1707)
	Total: £8,500

Consequently there was roughly £2,000 annually for librettists and composers. Handel had a fixed annual income, which has been estimated (Deutsch) at £800. In 1729–34 it was £1,000.

Nothing seems to be known about any lease of the theatre, which was the property of the king and was probably leased to the Academy for nothing.

The secretary of the Academy may well have also had a fixed annual income, certainly less than Handel's. Even so other composers can hardly have been paid more than an average of £200 for each work.

An opera autograph of Francesco Gasparini?

G OOD LIBRARY catalogues are of invaluable assistance – even when the information they provide is not wholly accurate. Additional manuscript 14233 in the British Library is described in A. Hughes-Hughes' *Catalogue*[1] as follows:

Paper; ff.155. Late 18th cent. Oblong folio. Portions of two anonymous Operas, with symphonies and accompaniments for oboes, strings, and other instruments mentioned below, in score. Acts 1 and 2 of an Opera (? 'Andromacca e Pirro'), apparently written by T.G. or G.T.(possibly Giacomo Tritto who wrote an opera of that name)... Characters: Ermione, Pilade, Andromacca, Pirro, Clearte, Oreste, and Astianatte...

(The volume contains in the second part a fragment of an unidentified *opera buffa* of the late eighteenth century.) Duncan Chisholm (London) kindly drew my attention to this manuscript and himself suggested that this might be an opera of Francesco Gasparini's. Comparison with the libretto confirmed this – it is Gasparini's *dramma per musica Astianatte*, performed in the Carnival season of 1722 at the Regio Ducal Teatro, Milan. Gasparini had originally composed the work in 1719 for the Teatro Alibert, Rome, and it was only from this version that some of the music was known, namely a collection of eighteen arias.[2] The London score, from which the third act is missing, contains 110 pages (28×21 cm) according to the new pencil-pagination, which is correct; there is no old paging, though there is a sheet-numbering (see below). The title-page and the sinfonia are missing, and the music begins on fol. 1r beneath the heading 'Atto primo, scena prima/Ermione, e Pilade/' with the text 'I dolci, e cari lumi'. At the end, fol. 110v, stands 'Fine del Atto Secondo', followed by the initials FG (or possibly TG).

All the music in the score appears to be written by a single hand (to be referred to as 'A') but four different hands can be distinguished in the text: A contributed some 30%, but the same hand is found on almost every page in the recitative sections and all aria texts are by A. B wrote most of the rest; C appears only on fol. 1r–2r, 30r and 80r. On fol. 36v–37r, a fourth hand, D, similar to C, may have written some lines. The identity of the music-copyist with A is automatically established by the handwriting of the

106

tempo and dynamic markings etc., which could only be properly inserted by the music-copyist himself.

Whereas the handwriting of A reminded me vaguely of Florentine or Roman (certainly not of Milanese) manuscripts and C suggested nothing to me, in B I immediately recognised the hand of a Milanese theatre-copyist who had worked on the scores composed during the years 1715-19 for Milan by Antonio Bononcini.[3] On that occasion he also copied some of the music, and he was therefore not a specialist in text-copying only.

The suggestion that the existing score was begun in Rome, where Gasparini was living in 1722, and completed in Milan before the performance involves a number of contradictions. In the first place A and B alternate with each other in every recitative, A very often writing only a few words at the beginning – sometimes also at the end – of a sentence, a page or a whole scene and B filling in all the rest. A also writes most of the names of the changing characters in any dialogue. C is also included in this: on fol. 30r we find all three hands – in the order A–B–C–A– alternating without regard to the coherence of the text. A strange kind of division of labour between theatre-copyists, whose fees were reckoned by the completed sheet! There is nothing comparable to this in Bononcini's Milanese scores mentioned above. Secondly – and almost more importantly – A has in some places corrected mistakes in B's copying, e.g. on fol. 4v at the word 'scherzai' (see Plate 1). On fol. 42v, B is corrected by A although no mistake is involved. Eight and a half lines are cancelled in the text entirely written by B ('Dopo tante ripulse[...] e mio trionfo./Che più?'), together with the music belonging to them. After this cancellation the text, in B's hand, continues 'De la tua prole/Volli far mio diletto' (stroke indicating end of line). The first of these two lines is metrically incomplete, since the two syllables 'che più' are cancelled – and A has therefore corrected it to 'della tua dolce prole'. What applies to the poetic metre also befits the musical harmony: A has also changed the music in both the voice and the continuo parts and thus made good the break caused by the cancellation. Such cancellations, or cuts, in the recitative were frequent, and often much needed, in the operatic practice of the time; but in order to make it easier for the audience the passages that were not sung were printed in the libretto and marked with inverted commas. This is the case on page 19 (Act I, scene 14) in the Milan libretto, where eight lines are marked with inverted commas but not the ninth beginning 'Che più?' since this, with a variant, was sung. Of course many cuts were not made until after the libretto was printed, after the first performance, for example. The lines concerned therefore appear in the libretto without any marks. This is the case in the present opera in two further passages in the same recitative, a very important but enormously long dialogue between the two protagonists. In the score four complete lines are cut after 'Tutte l'onte del fato' (fol. 43r/v) and six complete lines after

Plate 1 Possible autograph of Francesco Gasparini (1722). Text of the recitative by a Milan theatre copyist. London British Library, Add. 14233, fol. 4v.

'Così il mio cor' (fol. 44v); in each case the music has been altered by A to make it fit, but not the text, which in this case remains metrically complete and intelligible from the point of view of syntax. The cuts do not appear in the libretto. The text in C's hand has not been touched, although C – unlike B – makes serious verbal and writing mistakes. How can these have escaped A's keen sense of language?

Let us try to piece the facts together. A copied the music and prepared the text up to the point where B could complete it with the help of an existing text manuscript. The fragments of text in A's hand, which consist of individual page-beginnings and ends or scene- and sentence-openings are in fact 'cues' to ensure the correct underlay of the text by B; and the same is true of A's insertions of the characters' names at points in the dialogue where the speaker changes. Given a little knowledge of prosody, B could manage the text of the recitatives. B must have done his work before the libretto of 1722 was printed, as he does not take into account the first of the recitative cuts. A must have introduced this cut into the score before the first performance, and both the other cuts probably before one of the later performances. A did not correct C's mistakes because these were due to pressure of time at the last moment before the first performance (C was in any case only B's assistant) and because no musical changes were involved in the passages concerned. The text copied by B was ready earlier and A had more time to correct it. If A had not seen the score again until after the performance – for example, after the season, when it was back in Rome, his corrections would have included corrections of C's mistakes. Wherever A may have copied the score, he corrected it in Milan shortly before the first performance, or performances. In no other operatic scores in which B was engaged as copyist is there evidence of any other copyist to whom B was so clearly subordinate.

It is particularly noteworthy that on this occasion B, an experienced music-copyist, was not given a single note to copy. If A himself had copied from an existing manuscript, in which the music appeared in the same form, a more equitable division of labour between A and B – by sheets, as was the normal practice – would have been the obvious method. Copyist A, who was singly responsible for the music and also concerned with the text, not only produced a correct performing score (i.e. with recitative cuts) but must have previously established a version for which there was no complete existing model. The Roman score of the work (1719) would automatically have been at his disposal. Was this unsuitable as a model? Since there are no existing documents concerning the 1722 season in Milan, we can only reconstruct the origin of the score from internal evidence and from comparison with the libretti of 1719 and 1722 and the collection of arias (1719). These sources must of course be judged in the light of the general operatic practice of the day.

Like every *dramma per musica*' of the time, Gasparini's 1719 opera was commissioned for a specific theatre and a specific cast. 'Repertory operas' in the modern sense did not then exist in Italy. Since casts changed from season to season at each individual theatre, the repeating of a work in the season following its first performance usually meant a new production. If in addition to this, it was given in a different town, then sets and costumes, orchestra, stage-dimensions, price of tickets and of course 'public taste', i.e. primarily the wishes of the theatre's patrons, would all be different, not to mention the views of the censor when confronted with the newly printed libretto. Add to all this the vanity of a single *primadonna* anxious to make an impression with a favourite piece in her repertory or with a new aria composed especially for her, and it is hardly possible even to consider preserving the musical unity of the original score. The opera was in fact 'adapted', which meant replacing its component parts (recitatives, arias etc.), completely or in part, by new pieces until it might become little more than a pasticcio. It is useless to look for the unity of a Baroque opera in the score. The musical form given to any theatrical event was flexible, adaptable, even 'plagiarisable', and this was a presupposition for the new *theatrical* unity that had to be recreated on each occasion. If such a unity was not always achieved, the reason lay not in the fact that the score was recognised as subject to alteration but in the provincialism and lack of money that afflicted the many theatres in opera-obsessed Italy.

The Milan *Astianatte*, Acts I and II of which were copied by our copyist 'A', has thirty-one aria texts, one duet, one quartet and the final chorus in common with the Roman version of the text (1719, Teatro Aliberti, second opera of the Carnival season). Six arias were omitted and two new ones added, one of which replaces exactly one of those omitted, though the prosody of the text ('Fido amico a te sarò') is entirely different and will therefore not have been sung to the same music. The only divergence between the 1722 libretto and the score (except the two recitative-cuts already mentioned) is that one of the 1719 arias ('Da qual sì chiara stella') is lacking from the 1722 libretto, but present in the score though lacking the continuo part.

As stated earlier, eighteen arias from the Roman version have come down to us, and ten of these reappear in the Milan score, in which the third act is missing. In each case the music is the same, though the versions are not identical.

The recitative texts of 1719 and 1722 differ in only a few places – with the exceptions, that is to say, of points at which an aria has either been cut or replaced by a new one, thus affecting the transition from one scene to another. In Act II the recitatives are all identical, even at such points.

(* = music of 1719 preserved)

Scene	Character	Aria 1719	Aria 1722	Changes
I, 1	Pilade	Vezzosetta tra questi*	(missing)	Rec. end of I, 1 and beginning of I, 2 changed
I, 2	Ermione	Dissi talor per gioco	(libretto & score)	
I, 3	Pirro	Il vostro rigore	(libretto & score)	
I, 4	Andromaca	Amo e sdegno*	(libretto & score)	transposed up a third
I, 5	Clearte	(no aria)	Credilo a me	preceding rec. changed
I, 7	Pirro	Non è gloria	(libretto & score)	
I, 8	Pilade	Su quella fronte vaga	(libretto & score)	
I, 9	Oreste	Abbandona il caro lido*	(libretto & score)	transposed up a fourth, different instrumentation
I, 10	Pilade	Sono amico e sono amante	(missing)	
I, 11	Ermione	T'amerò se la mia gloria*	(libretto & score)	transposed down a fourth
I, 12	Oreste	Un'aura lusinghiera	(libretto & score)	text of lines 1–2 changed
I, 13	Clearte	Lascia d'esser tanto	(libretto & score)	
I, 14	Andromaca	Svenalo traditor*	(libretto & score)	transposed up a tone
I, 15	Pirro	Non si chiami pensiero	(libretto & score)	
I, 16	Oreste	Se da voi stesse nel cor	(libretto & score)	
II, 1	Pilade	Da qual sì chiara stella	(missing in libretto)	

Scene	Character	Aria 1719	Aria 1722	Changes
II, 2	Pirro	Vezzose pupille venite*	(libretto & score)	transposed down a fourth
II, 3	Ermione	Và prega e piangi*	(libretto & score)	changed but not transposed
II, 4	Clearte	Superbetta non chiedi	(libretto & score)	
II, 5	Pirro	Luci spietate	(libretto & score)	
II, 6	Andromaca	Il mio sposo tradirò*	(libretto & score)	transposed up a fourth
Iĩ, 7	Pilade	Compagna del suo fato	Fido amico a te sarò	
II, 8	Oreste	Un guardo mi negate	(libretto & score)	
II, 9	Ermione	Io sento una pietà*	(libretto & score)	transposed down a fourth
II, 10	Clearte	Infelice pargoletto	(libretto & score)	
II, 11	Andromaca	Viva ancor tra le mie ceneri*	(libretto & score)	changed but not transposed
II, 12	Oreste	Io non vi credo*	(libretto & score)	transposed up a fifth, different instrumentation
II, 15	Andromaca-Ermione	Le stelle s'armano (Duet)	(libretto & score)	
III, 2	Andromaca	Non ti sdegnar con me*	(libretto)	
III, 3	Clearte	Vide appena	(libretto)	
III, 4	Pirro	Se la Grecia s'armerà*	(libretto)	
III, 5	Pilade	Del mio del tuo fedele	(missing)	
III, 6	Ermione	Son come navicella*	(libretto)	
III, 9	Pilade	Combatte coi venti	(libretto)	
III, 10	Oreste	Del mio fato	(libretto)	
III, 11	Ermione	Tortorella che avvinta*	(libretto)	
III, 14	Andromaca	Difese mi giurasti*	(libretto)	
III, 15	Pirro	E vero che sdegnati*	(libretto)	
III, 16	Ermione	Vorrei pur che questo core	(missing)	
III, 19	Ermione-Pirro-Pilade-Andromaca	Caro–sposa–amico–figlio (quartet)	(libretto)	
III, 20	Coro	Prenda amor della pace	(libretto)	

It should be said at once that the encroachments on the 1719 arias that we find in the 1722 libretto are comparatively small by contemporary standards. On the other hand, the score shows that none of the 1719 pieces has remained exactly the same – another unusual feature of the case. The basic rule observed in adapting operas in the 1720s was to retain as much of the original as circumstances permitted, provided the music of the original is still of interest, and to introduce new or borrowed music if a singer or anyone else made any objections. This held good irrespective of whether the adaptation was made by the original composer or by someone else. The whole balancing of that theatrical unity was facilitated by this freedom to choose a suitable piece from the huge repertory, or to have a new piece composed, to occupy a definite position in the work's emotional scale and in the hierarchy of the dramatis personae, or to achieve some definite effect lacking in the original. Rewriting the score of the arias was more difficult, and even simple transposition could produce technical and musical problems.

All this seems to be contradicted by the Gasparini arrangement. Despite the small area of comparison provided by the music, the libretti alone reveal an intention largely to preserve the original music, even if this meant transposing and adapting. Even in the case of the arias not preserved the text generally remains the same, and not a single dramatic situation is changed.

The performances in 1722, however, were primarily concerned with quite another problem. A comparison of the libretti of 1719 and 1722 shows in fact that not a single one of the characters was sung by a singer with the same type of voice on the two occasions. It often happens, of course, that a cast consists of entirely new singers, but a complete change of the types of voices concerned is a disaster for the producer. It seems doubtful whether this can have been foreseen when *Astianatte* was chosen for performance in Milan.

The following provides a comparison of the two casts:

Rome, Teatro Aliberti Carnival, 1719		Milan, Regio Ducal Teatro Carnival, 1722
Giovanni Ossi (mezzosoprano)	Andromaca	Angela Augusti (soprano)
Francesco de Grandis (soprano)	Pirro	Diana Vico (contralto)
Giacinto Fontana (soprano)	Ermione	Antonia Maria Laurenti detta Coralli (contralto)
Francesco Santorini (tenor)	Oreste	Giovanni Battista Minelli (alto)
Gaetano Berenstadt (alto)	Pilade	Francesco Maria Venturini (bass)
Giuseppe Gallicani (alto)	Clearte	Camilla Zoboli (soprano)
	Astianatte (bambino che non parla)	

Of course far more is involved than voice-pitches. In eighteenth-century Rome women were not allowed on the stage and the three main roles were sung by male sopranos, only one part being sung by a natural voice. In Milan three of the roles were sung 'naturalistically'. The chief male part, Pirro, was given to the dramatic contralto Diana Vico; the confidant Clearte was taken by Camilla Zoboli and so, as a 'Hosenrolle', became a kind of page; Orestes (alto castrato as the pathetic lover) was a regular role-type that was to become frequent later in the century. This casting was in every sense more progressive in the manner of the later *opera seria*, though still not entirely naturalistic. The characters appear in the same order in both libretti, according to their importance in the drama. In Milan, however, this appears not to correspond with the reputations of the individual singers, i.e. the probable fees paid, and Angela Augusti must have had highly placed patrons to be allowed to appear on the same footing as Diana Vico. Even A. M. Laurenti had a number of successes to her credit, for example at Venice in 1720/1. Minelli, who was most in demand of all alto-castrato singers of the time, was – to say the least of it – dramatically under-cast. The above list of arias shows that there was no change in the *musical* importance of the main roles – and this meant an *over*-casting of the otherwise unknown Augusti, unless she may perhaps have been a pupil of Gasparini himself. In the Milan score she has three accompagnato recitatives. Gasparini had written the part for his pupil Giovanni Ossi.

In the four main roles the ten instances which can be checked show that the original music was adapted not by new music or by cutting arias, but by transposition and by changing the tessitura, combined in some cases with changes in the instrumental accompaniment (e.g. in Act I scene 9, where two flutes and viola were added to 'Abbandona'; Act I scene 4 and Act II scene 9, where the oboes are given a concertante part; Act II scene 11, where the viola is given an independent part in 'Viva ancor'; and in other places, too, where the violas are given their own line, which is missing in the Roman collection of arias, though this may have been simply an omission of the copyist's). This alone is unusual, and it is even more noteworthy that the transpositions are not always at the same interval. Andromaca's arias, for example, are transposed sometimes by a tone, sometimes by a third and sometimes by a fourth, and on one occasion left in the original key (E flat) which involved rewriting the vocal line, showing that the arranger did not work mechanically. Flexibility was perhaps intended to establish a new key-relationship between the arias. The arranger took equal trouble with the vocal range of each individual singer, of whom almost exactly the same is demanded in each of his or her arias. Thus the maximum range in Andromaca's arias is e'–a″, in Pirro's b–e″, in Ermione's a–d″, in Oreste's a–e″ (compared with Pilade's E–f′, Clearte's d′–g″). In the new version of the score most, if not all, of the recitatives, which should preferably lie in the favourable middle range, probably had to be rewritten.

The actual number of arias was only changed in the cases of the two subordinate roles. According to the libretti, Pilade lost five arias of his original seven and was given one other in return, while Clearte was given an additional aria beside his original four. *This* kind of arrangement, and not what we find in the case of main roles, was typical of the operatic practice of the day. It is clear from the score (see below) that things did not run altogether smoothly on this occasion.

How did it come about that for the Milan cast of 1722 they chose to perform an original that presented such problems from the point of view of vocal range and character? And how are we to explain the laborious and unrewarding method of arranging? Any Milan *maestro di cappella* who had to rearrange the music would have given himself less work and would also have added more of his own – which would have been alluded to in the libretto and thus increased his reputation. Can Gasparini himself have made the new arrangement? We must consider in this connection first the Milan theatre and then the importance of the composer.

The Regio Ducal Teatro[4] of the day could not compete with the main Italian theatres. After Milan became a Habsburg possession in the War of the Spanish Succession the province no longer had its own court orchestra and was overshadowed by Charles III's royal residences, first Barcelona and then Vienna. Although Caldara was working in Milan in 1711 and Giovanni Bononcini in 1713,[5] neither of them could be permanently engaged, and in the following years operas were commissioned by the impresarios mostly from the Modenese court composer Antonio Bononcini (in my opinion an excellent composer of the rather conservative kind) or from the Turin *maestro di cappella* Stefano Andrea Fiore. Other operas written specially for Milan are not of importance, though among local composers Giuseppe Vignati should be mentioned, of whose work almost nothing has been preserved. Antonio Vivaldi was in Milan in 1721/2, probably in search of a post: neither an opera, *La Silvia* (28 August 1721), nor an oratorio of his seems to have made any great impression, as no other stagework of his was given in Milan.

Francesco Gasparini's operas, however, form a thin red line in the programmes from season to season. From 1718 onwards we find an unbroken series of performances (always in Carnival time, which was the best): 1718 *Constantino* (as Gasparini is not mentioned in the libretto, this will have been someone else's arrangement), 1719 *Eumene* (libretto: 'La musica è dell' ammirabile Sig. Francesco Gasparini'), 1720 *La pace fra Seleuco e Tolomeo* (G. named), 1721 *Il più fedel tra vassalli* (G. not named, certainly someone else's arrangement), and in 1722 for the first time two works, with mention of his name in the libretto in both cases: *Astianatte* and *Flavio Anicio Olibrio*. Gasparini did not write any of these operas in the first place for Milan, but those performed in 1719 and 1720 were very probably – and *Flavio* certainly – rewritten by the composer himself. The music of *Flavio* reached Turin the same year, appeared in 1723 in a Florentine pasticcio of the same name, and was eventually heard in Hamburg.[6] It is worth noting that the Gasparini season of 1722 was the last in the series; people had now become fashion-conscious and begun to follow the style of the younger generation of composers. Giovanni Porta and Giuseppe Maria Orlandini made their first appearances as composers in 1723, Porpora in 1726, Giacomelli in 1728 and Hasse in 1730.

By that time Gasparini had already reached the end of a busy and enormously successful career. As early as 1689, at the latest, he was first harpsichordist under Corelli in Rome and producing his earliest operas. After 1700 he was in Venice, where he was choirmaster at the Ospedale della Pietà (with Vivaldi as his subordinate) and receiving in all more opera commissions even than Lotti and Pollarolo.[7] He was the teacher of

Benedetto Marcello and perhaps of Domenico Scarlatti, whom his father had sent – though he was already a fully trained composer – specifically to Gasparini. The first of the many editions of his *L'armonico pratico al cimbalo* dates from 1708. From about 1712 he must have been back in Rome, where he engaged in the well-known exchange of cantatas with A. Scarlatti, and after 1713 he composed a continuous stream of operas for the Teatro Capranica and the Teatro Alibert in addition to works for Naples, Florence, Bologna, Reggio, Mantua, Turin and Vienna as well as for Roman patrons. He was 'Virtuoso del Principe Ruspoli' (1717), 'Virtuoso del Principe Borghese' (1721), a teacher of singing, with Giovanni Ossi among his pupils, and of composition, including Giovanni Porta among his pupils (1716). Abroad his operas enjoyed more repeat-performances than those of any of his contemporaries, reaching as far afield as Prague, Brunswick, Hamburg and London. At the same time he was making a career for himself as a church composer. In 1722 Gasparini suddenly ceased composing for the Roman theatres, or even making arrangements for them, after having been in sole command of the opera-programmes of the Teatro Capranica in 1716 and 1717 and the Teatro Alibert in 1719 and 1720. His last important original works were *Il Bajazet* (Reggio 1719) and *Faramondo* (Teatro Alibert 1720), both of which were later to provide Handel with ideas and material. Handel must have become acquainted with Gasparini as early as 1708, in Venice, and he learned something from him as a composer. In 1723 Gasparini arranged two of his earlier works for Venice, but he wrote no further new works for the big operatic stage.

It is difficult not to seek an explanation for his sudden retiring from the Roman operatic scene in 1721/2 in external circumstances. One of these might well be found in the fact that in the immediately preceding years Alessandro Scarlatti had formed increasingly close ties with Prince Ruspoli, for whose Teatro Capranica he wrote his last two operas, *Griselda* (1720/1) and *Arminio* (1722). At some time between 1717 and 1721 Gasparini left the personal service of Prince Ruspoli and entered that of Prince Borghese. As a member of one of the most important families of the Roman nobility Marcantonio Borghese, Principe di Sulmona, was certainly a powerful patron, though he did not have close ties with a public theatre as Ruspoli had. On 21 April 1721 Borghese became Viceroy of Naples, then a Habsburg possession with an important Opera, which was at his disposal; and he was in fact one of Metastasio's first supporters.

In Naples, however, Scarlatti was the Hofkapellmeister; and Francesco Gasparini, who despite his successes had never occupied a comparable post, was left without a patron in Rome and without a chance in Naples. This was perhaps not the case in Milan, which was also under Habsburg control though under a governor rather than a viceroy. It was to this governor, Count Girolamo Colloredo, that the impresario dedicated the libretto of

Astianatte, in which Gasparini describes himself as 'Virtuoso del...Principe Borghese, Vicerè di Napoli'. Can he have been seeking a still closer link with Habsburg patronage in Milan? In that case the Regio Ducal Teatro missed the chance of a first-class *maestro di cappella* in 1722. It seems at least arguable that Gasparini, who produced nothing in Rome that year, spent the Carnival season of 1722 in Milan.

We do not know the details of that season, or even which of Gasparini's two operas was performed first; but it is almost certain that he himself arranged his *Flavio Anicio Olibrio* for Milan. This opera (to a text of Zeno's) had been written in 1707 for Venice, and that version may have formed the basis of the Milan arrangement, since we know of no intermediate version ascribed to Gasparini. Something like half of the aria texts in the libretto are different from those of 1707, which means that, in accordance with normal practice, at least the new aria texts, and probably some of those taken over from the original, were newly composed – something that would be taken for granted in the case of an opera composed fifteen years earlier. New aria texts were normally provided not for their own sake, but in connection with new music. We also have evidence that Gasparini himself, who is credited with the music in the libretto, was responsible for the new arrangement. This same opera was given again very soon afterwards, probably in the spring, at the Teatro Carignano in Turin, under the title *Il Ricimero*. On that occasion there is no mention of the composer in the libretto which, however, is signed by the 'compositore' in the 'protesta dell'autore', a quite unusual proceeding. Only eight of the aria texts are different from those of the Milan version, and three of these are identical with Gasparini's *Astianatte*, while some of the remaining texts may be parodies of texts in the same work. *Il Ricimero* was not in any case a new composition but based on the two Milan operas, though this was deliberately concealed by the change of title and the omission of the composer's name. The opera was in fact meant to be regarded as an original work, following the wishes of the Principe di Carignano; any other composer's name could have been cited in the libretto, but Gasparini's would have made the connection with Milan clear. Gasparini had in fact already worked for the Prince as early as 1718, when he was described in the libretto of his musical comedy *Democrito* as 'celebre maestro'. All these facts taken together constitute compelling reasons for believing that Gasparini himself arranged both operas for Milan between the end of 1721 and the beginning of 1722, and probably prepared *Il Ricimero* for Turin at the same time. It is hard to believe that he can have done all this while remaining in Rome.

There is not space here to describe the artistic content of Gasparini's *Astianatte*, which is the chief object of our historical investigations; but a few short comments on both the drama and the music may perhaps be permitted, without concealing the fact that the present study of sources is no more than the preparatory groundwork for a more thorough investigation.

Gasparini's earliest operatic activities coincide almost exactly, both chronologically and geographically, with the founding of the Accademia dell' Arcadia. During the next twenty years Gasparini's collaborations with Zeno and Silvani are unambiguous evidence of the trend towards classicistic tragedy in the opera, a trend inspired by the French tragedians of the seventeenth century. Gasparini's first close contact with Antonio Salvi, the poet of *Astianatte*, must have been in 1713, when he first began to work in Florence. Salvi's libretto of 1701, which is his earliest identifiable work, is an arrangement of Jean Racine's *Andromaque* (1667) and was also the first in a series of important and individual libretti based by Salvi on French tragedies. The plot of *Andromaque* goes back to Euripides and is one of the most tragic, even among Racine's works. Every character is involved in some guilt from which there is no escape, and Salvi faithfully preserved the fundamental pessimism of the drama and the nervous tension of Racine's dialogue. In spite of the 'happy ending' and the emphasis on the theme of maternal devotion, we are very far from Metastasio's sentiment. The character who gives the drama its name is Andromache's child Astyanax, who is exploited first by Pyrrhus, and then by Pylades (the archetype of the loyal friend!) for the purpose of sexual and political blackmail. Astyanax, who never opens his mouth, is in fact the only innocent character in the work. Salvi's libretto was not particularly popular;[8] but if we consider Gasparini's music here and in other tragedies composed by him we are confronted with an aesthetic problem that cannot be overlooked. Here, as in all his scores, we find skilful and pleasing melodies, dance rhythms, well-balanced proportions and thin, sketchy textures. Gasparini was very well acquainted with the taste of his public, which is certainly not our taste. But was it really possible to compose opera after opera without regard for the subject? It may be that the music simply reflects another aspect of precisely the same classicistic tendency. The Arcadian attitude to life was, in spite of everything, fundamentally optimistic, and perhaps there is a place for the catchword 'Enlightenment' in connection with this music.[9]

Let us now return to the manuscript. If the composer himself arranged the Roman score of 1719 for Milan – with the transpositions and smaller changes mentioned above – then his new manuscript would partly be a clean copy, and partly a composition autograph, albeit all in the same hand. This is precisely the character of the London score as far as the music is concerned. The manuscript was written over a period of time and reveals different speeds and levels of attention, and the use of different coloured inks; not all its sections were written in the same order as they now appear in the manuscript.

The recitatives are all smooth and uniform in character – composing recitatives would have been only a routine occupation for an opera composer like Gasparini; the text however was completed by hands B and C. There are a few irregularities in the music of the recitatives, beyond the cuts discussed above. Of the arias, some are clean copies without any mistakes, whereas the copying process in others was more complicated.

The score does not have an original foliation; but there is an original numbering of gatherings (usually consisting of two bifolios) in the top left corner, one series for each act.

Fascicle '1' has only three single folios. After the end of the recitative I,1 (text by hand C) on fol. 2v, fol. 3r is blank, followed by the recitative I,2 on fol. 3v (text by hands A and C), which is continued in fascicle '2' (fol. 4r) with text by hand B. This is all the result of the omission of Pilade's aria 'Vezzosetta' of 1719 at the end of I,1. Obviously, the fascicle '1' with the aria had already been copied before the omission was decided upon; the new version without the aria occupied less than even three single folios, which were substituted for the original fascicle '1'. Because of the omission of the aria, part of the recitative text had to be altered; it was therefore decided to recopy the entire recitative. Hand C was called in as an assistant, either because B was still busy copying later sections of the text or was no longer available.

Fascicle '2' is regularly numbered and written with the exception of the small correction at 'scherzai' (see Plate 1) and the aria 'Dissi talor' itself: here there are three distinct colours of ink. The clefs, the vocal part and the violin ritornelli are dark, the *colla parte* of the violins and the continuo are lighter, the text and the bass figures quite bright. It follows from this that the aria was not copied page by page, but part by part, so that the pages had to be turned for each part separately during the copying.[10]

In fascicle '3' in the aria 'Il vostro rigore', the vocal part and the continuo both have thicker strokes and note-heads than the accompaniment parts and the text. This is not familiar to me as a usage of contemporary copyists, though we find the same emphasising of the essential parts in opera autographs of Alessandro Scarlatti, for example in *Griselda* (1720/1).

Between fascicles '3' and '4' (the latter beginning with fol. 19r), there are several inserted folios, necessitated by the addition of the aria 'Credilo a me' for the role of Clearte. The original version without the aria is also preserved, but the pages fol. 15v and 16r have been glued together, and the recitatives of I,6 and I,7 were written out again, with adaptations to allow for the inserted aria. In doing this, hand A repeats a recitative passage on fol. 18v in a different version from what was originally on fol. 15v. The aria is written with some signs of haste and contains several corrected mistakes.

Pirro's aria 'Non è gloria' in fascicle '4' contains an interesting correction (see Plate 2) on fol. 22v: hand A corrects its own mistake in the voice part before the continuo part had been written. Throughout the aria the text is

Plate 2 Possible autograph of Francesco Gasparini, London, British Library. Add. 14233, fol. 22v.

written in a different (blue) ink from that of the music, except for the words
'si fa vasal-' at the beginning of the coloratura. It seems that these words
were 'cued in' before the rest of the text was copied.

Fascicles '5' (fol. 23–6) and '6' (fol. 27–30) contain the aria 'Abbandona
il caro lido', in which the instrumentation has been changed from that of
1719. It is evident that the aria was copied here after the surrounding
recitatives had been copied, whereby fol. 26r was left blank because the aria
required less space than expected. Fascicle 7 (without number) is a
replacement for the original fascicle: the original aria of Pilade 'Sono amico
e sono amante' must have been written out at first, probably transposed from
the alto to the bass register, i.e. from G major a seventh down to A major.
We can conclude this from an alteration of the preceding recitative at the
final cadence, which was brought from D major to E major by two additional
bars of music. Then, however, the aria was obviously dropped after all, and
the two additional recitative bars received no text underlay. In the present
substitute fascicle 7, there is no aria.

In the aria 'Un'aura lusinghiera' (fol. 36v–37r), the original text began
with 'La speme lusinghiera'. It seems that hand D (similar to C) inserted

an alternative text for the first three lines without cancelling the other text. The new text version was printed in the libretto of 1722.

In the second act, the arias 'Da qual sì chiara stella' (II,1; missing in the libretto of 1722) and 'La priega e piangi' (II,3) are not completely written out. In the first aria, we find only the voice part and that of the first violin in the ritornelli, whereas the staves for the continuo are blank. Possibly, the continuo had not even been composed (or, rather, transposed from 1719) when the aria was cut.

In the arias 'Vezzose pupille' (II,2) and 'Io sento una pietà' (II,9) different colours of ink can again be distinguished for the vocal and instrumental staves.

In several arias of the second act, the end is crowded on the page, whereas the beginning is widely spaced, for example in 'Un guardo mi negate' (II,8). Obviously, space had been left free by the copyist between the recitatives in order to insert these arias later on, but the calculation did not quite work out. On the other hand, most arias of the second act are copied quite smoothly. The largest number of (corrected) mistakes in this score occurs in 'Credilo a me' (I,6) which was newly composed for Milan.

Taken together, this is sufficient evidence to show that the arranger of the music himself is to be identified with hand A. If this person had copied from previously existing manuscripts, whether or not they were identical with the version of 1719, he would not have created as many unnecessary difficulties for himself. Especially significant is the writing out of the parts of an aria one by one, instead of copying all parts page by page: this involves more frequent page-turns (before which the ink had to be dried) for the copyist. The arranger of the music, however, might have had a reason to write out the parts successively. The same kind of evidence is provided by 'Da qual sì chiara stella' where the continuo was not yet written when the aria was cut.

Now we have adduced other evidence above to show that the arranger of the score for Milan – hand A – was not a Milanese *maestro di cappella* but Francesco Gasparini himself. The score and the way it was produced resemble very much the well-known conducting scores of Handel, with the sole difference that the autograph contribution of the composer is much larger here because so much had to be altered for the production in Milan in 1722. It is also clear that the initials at the end of the second act are, in fact, 'FG' and are Gasparini's own. Perhaps he signed the second act because the third was fully written out by copyists from more hastily written autographs. This may indeed be the reason why the score of the third act has not been preserved together with the rest of the manuscript: the third act remained with the Milan opera archive, whereas the first two were returned to the composer after the season.

It may seem dangerous to identify a composer's autograph on purely internal evidence as I have attempted here. Guesses of this kind have too often been proved wrong by the appearance of a genuine, accredited autograph.[11] What matters are the criteria applied in each individual case. Characteristics of the handwriting alone such as 'spontaneity' or corrections are rarely sufficient proof: it must be shown that they cannot stem from a copyist or an anonymous arranger of the music. This requires a careful assessment of copyists' habits within a particular area and genre, and some knowledge about how manuscript scores were actually produced. To use and to extend such knowledge was, therefore, the chief purpose of our discussion.

Postscript. It was only after finishing the above that I was informed of an accredited autograph of Francesco Gasparini. This is a letter written by him from Rome on 11 March 1724 to Francesco Tosi, thanking him in fulsome terms for sending him his new book (*Opinioni de' cantori...*).[12] The handwriting in this letter, which is signed by Gasparini, seems to me unquestionably the same as that of hand A in the score discussed above. The letter is in the Civico Museo Bibliografico Musicale of Bologna; I am indebted to Dr Oscar Mischiati for his swift preparation of a xeroxed copy.

Vivaldi's career as an opera producer

THE INCREASING appreciation of Vivaldi's operatic music in our day is largely a consequence of the privileged position which he holds, in the modern repertory, as an instrumental composer. By expanding our interest in Vivaldi to his operatic output, we enter a repertory which is otherwise virtually unknown to modern audiences: that of early eighteenth-century Italian opera. This context, which is so new to the performer, listener, and researcher today, formed an all too familiar musical environment for the composer himself, and his Italian public. Vivaldi's *drammi per musica*, particularly in Venice, were just drops in a sea of operatic music: many people must have appreciated them, who were perhaps neither interested in his instrumental production nor able to hear it. On the other hand, those same people will have known many operatic works by Vivaldi's immediate contemporaries and rivals, which are in turn unknown to us. To try to bridge the gap of perception between contemporary and modern audiences would do a necessary service to the composer Vivaldi, and to ourselves. To describe the general patterns of opera production at the time, is one such attempt; another is the investigation where and how the composer's own choices diverge from such patterns. The material presented here is supposed to serve the latter purpose, but only by making a first, even preliminary step: it is the investigation of where and when in his career Vivaldi was actually given a choice of how and for whom he composed.

The question 'for whom?' seems at the moment even more urgent than the question 'how?', because the purpose of communication will always determine the means, and particularly so in opera. The operatic composer knows this fact and reacts to it by trying to shape the purpose according to his means: success in opera depends very much on whether the composer has been able to find theatres, libretti, singers and audiences that are congenial to his own way of saying things. I believe that in Vivaldi's operatic career the search for this congenial context (and therefore, for success) is at least as important as his urge for self-expression, and, in the later stages of his career, even overshadows the composer's outstanding artistic personality.

122

I also believe that there is no such thing as an all-embracing convention of Italian Baroque opera. The 'general patterns' mentioned above are already a dangerous abstraction; they vary from place to place, and change with the years, so that we have a dynamic, rather than a static unity of procedures, whose details are marked by contradictions and, indeed, individual choices. When a composer's achievement is held against a grey-on-grey background of the so-called operatic convention (as has been done too often with Handel), no meaningful picture emerges. But when it is held against the organisational, dramatic, stylistic etc. options that were really open to the composer in a particular time and place, small steps in one or the other direction may become significant. Vivaldi's whole operatic output has little to commend him if we look for drastic departures from an all too widely drawn frame of conventions – but he emerges as a strong individuality if we ask what, in particular circumstances, he could have done differently.

One of the simplest questions concerning Vivaldi as a dramatic composer has not yet been answered satisfactorily: how many operas did he actually produce? How important is the share of operatic activity in his career as a whole? If his claim is correct that by the beginning of 1739 he had written ninety-four operas,[1] then he was almost primarily an opera composer by contemporary standards. But it seems now, as documentation increases, that in many of these works he acted rather as a producer and arranger than as a composer; many of them must be revivals of own works or arrangements of music by others, where his main creative task consisted in providing new recitatives for the particular cast, and in directing, perhaps, the first performance. Very often, he functioned as a kind of impresario ('franco intraprenditore' he calls himself late in his career),[2] and his amazing productivity divides into organising, directing, and composing operas. This is, in itself, a significant choice made by the man Antonio Vivaldi, as we know of no other musician of the time working in Italy who behaved quite like this. It also shows that he was perfectly able to sacrifice his own musical ideas for the sake of operatic success – an attitude which he had apparently never taken in the field of instrumental music. We must also consider that this choice was perhaps not completely free: would he have had to arrange works of others if he had received as many *scritture* for new scores of his own as did, for example, Hasse? His efforts as an impresario seem to make up, at least in later years, for some lack of success as a composer, if such success can at all be measured by *scritture*, i.e. commissions from outside. Furthermore, when Vivaldi produced his own operatic works, the decision to use his music may have been his own even if the initiative for the production came from somebody else, according to the often varying terms under which such commissions could be made. We have also to ask whether Vivaldi provided the score only (his own or an arrangement), or the singers, too, and whether he chose the time, place, and libretto of the production. Conversely, there are productions of Vivaldi's operatic music without the initiative, or even the knowledge, of the composer himself: here, we definitely cross the border between his own choices and those of others, but at the same time, we gain clues to his contemporary reputation and historical importance. It is often difficult to establish whether an operatic performance was assisted by the composer himself, and some doubtful cases for Vivaldi will be mentioned below. But at the present stage of documentation, performances of Vivaldi's operas without his assistance cannot be shown to amount to more than fifteen, against nearly fifty-five performances involving the composer himself (including new and rearranged works).[3] With at least three of his contemporaries (F. Gasparini, Vinci, Hasse), the former figure is higher than the latter, and there must be many other composers for whom the figures are about equal (C. F. Pollarolo, Orlandini, Porta, Porpora, Giacomelli etc.). But this evidence must be looked at from the reverse side, too: as Vivaldi sought financial success instead of living on *scritture*, he may have kept his scores to himself, and tried to deal personally with those theatres who wanted to use them. The fact that nearly all surviving complete scores of his operas are preserved in his personal collection, now in Turin, confirms this exactly. Therefore, Vivaldi has perhaps consciously restricted the distribution and thus, reputation, of his operatic music.

Assessing Vivaldi's activities as a whole, one may say that he spent even more time and effort on the production of his operas than on his instrumental oeuvre – only that the operas get a relatively smaller share of Vivaldi the composer. This particular combination – opera impresario plus concerto composer – is unique in his time, and perhaps in the whole of music history.

The qualitative side of Vivaldi's choices, again within the circumstances determining him, is more difficult to investigate. It might be argued that his artistic goals were as high in the dramatic as in the instrumental field, and that the more restricted distribution of the operas was due to a strongly individual style which fitted the average opera-house less well than the products of many of his rivals. (This could then be compared with the case of Alessandro Scarlatti, who, also by his own choice, became more and more stylistically isolated as an opera composer in the last twenty years of his life.) To what extent did Vivaldi conform to current practices or, simply, to the requirements of the theatre in question? The answer to this question is not as easy as it may appear, because it can be taken for granted that Vivaldi did not often risk the loss of a commission for purely artistic reasons, and if a performance came about (and was, perhaps, successful), a consensus between composer, theatre, singers, audience and patrons, librettist etc. must be assumed. The question is, how far and how often did the artistic result of such a consensus mirror Vivaldi's own intentions, and how far did it deviate from them? If the style – and, indeed, the quality – of his operatic output changes, how much does this have to do with the greater or lesser artistic control which he had over an individual production? It must be said that this kind of question has not really been asked with regard to any opera composer of the time, not even Handel. To help answer it for Vivaldi, I present in section 1 below a list of the known opera productions in which he was at all involved – but broken up into four columns indicating four different degrees of artistic control exerted by Vivaldi.[4]

The first column contains those productions where the composer was also the impresario or *direttore della musica* of the theatre at the time, and therefore must have been at least partly responsible for the choice of libretti, singers, and also of the other composers, if opera scores of other composers were used during a season. Normally opera seasons in a particular theatre were planned as a whole, and the contracts with the singers covered at least two Carnival operas, in Venice up to four or five operas from autumn to the end of Carnival. If Vivaldi was responsible for such a long season, notably at the S. Angelo, he must have had at least a rough plan of how many operas should be performed, who should prepare the libretti and the music, and who should sing. Sometimes the plans had to be changed, of course, during the season, and it may have happened that Vivaldi's plans were overturned by others (as, for example, perhaps in 1721). But normally his influence on the operatic style of that particular season must have been considerable, as so much money was involved, and the artistic choices concerning not only the texts and the music, but even stage machinery and orchestral forces, probably reflect Vivaldi's aesthetic most clearly.

The second column is of the same kind, except that the operatic season in question contains only one opera – it is the short one-opera season organised by many middle and small theatres at the Ascension fair or in the summer. When Vivaldi was commissioned to provide the opera for such a season, we can assume, in most cases, that he had a free hand also in the choice of singers, etc., since the financial risk as a whole was not so great. It seems that Vivaldi, in his later years, often provided such one-opera seasons for theatres outside Venice in a kind of wholesale arrangement. In both the first and second categories, the names of the principal singers mentioned in the table, and the librettists etc., represent Vivaldi's choice to a high degree.

The third column contains the commissions of operas from Vivaldi, in the manner of a regular *scrittura*: this normally meant that Vivaldi had to compose a score for singers not chosen by himself – as these had to sing also in other operas of the same season not composed by Vivaldi – and on a text which may or may not have been chosen by himself; often, the *scrittura* meant that the composer had to assist some of the rehearsals, and had to direct the first performance, but not necessarily the others. It also meant that a fair copy of the score remained in the possession of the theatre. Vivaldi can have influenced the choice of singers in these cases too, particularly if his contacts with the impresario, or the patrons, of that theatre were otherwise close enough. He may have been commissioned to write both operas of a full Carnival season (or to write one complete score and contribute to the other, as in Rome 1724), or he may have provided the only opera which was given during the Carnival in a smaller theatre (as in Verona 1735). In any case, he was not in full control of the theatre here.

The fourth column concerns the few remaining productions where Vivaldi cannot have had much influence on the *impresa* at all, but simply provided a score for which he was paid a certain sum. He may not even have visited the performances, but sent the score from Venice, whether a newly composed one or a rearranged one. In some of these cases, we are not sure that he had a hand in the production at all (as, for example, in Mantua 1725).

The remaining sections 2, 3 and 4 extract the names of singers, librettists and composers from section 1; they can now be assessed as being more or less closely connected with Vivaldi himself according to their appearance in his productions. It is striking that some of the most famous singers (Cuzzoni, Carestini) appear connected with Vivaldi only or mostly in columns III and IV, indicating that the choice in these cases was perhaps not his own. He has never composed, as far as we know, for Bordoni, Bernacchi, Farinelli, which sets him far apart from his major contemporaries. With the libretti, we have to distinguish between new texts and rearranged old ones; as can be expected, Vivaldi never enjoyed the privilege of collaborating directly with Zeno, Silvani, Piovene, or Metastasio on a new text, but the circle of poets writing directly for him is very circumscribed and interesting. Wherever Vivaldi seems to have had influence on the choice of an already existing libretto, he does seem to shun the great names among living librettists, with the exception of Metastasio in later years. Many productions are, of course, revivals of Vivaldi's own operas where the text was not a prime consideration – in a case such as *Siroe* (Metastasio) and *Farnace* (Lucchini), however, Vivaldi must have liked the libretto, otherwise he would have adapted his music for other texts if he wanted to re-use it. The list of singers and libretti most consciously preferred by Vivaldi himself has very much its own flavour, and is even uncharacteristic for the *dramma per musica* of the period. He excelled in the setting of libretti which nearly no one else ever chose (Braccioli's *Orlando finto pazzo*, Marchi's *La costanza*..., Palazzi's *La verità in cimento*), and in writing for singers whom he absolutely monopolised like the Girò, or who were not very successful with other composers' music. Moreover, it becomes clear that Vivaldi preferred the more old-fashioned type of mezzosoprano (in castrato and female voices) to the modern, high soprano tessitura as represented by

Farinelli – this was probably also a choice of economic character, as this type of voice was the most expensive one – and that he always preferred to have natural male voices in the cast, including basses. Vivaldi did write for some singers of the highest rank, notably the contralto Antonia Merighi and the tenor Antonio Barbieri, who owed to him some of their finest roles, but the Teatro S. Angelo could not often afford these virtuosi. We do not know whether Vivaldi ever trained opera singers himself, or even contributed to their artistic outlook (except with Anna Girò), but it seems that he was influential for the early career of some of them. As a whole, the choice of singers, libretti, and also of the music of other composers used in Vivaldi's productions, seems to undergo important changes in the latter part of his career. Starting out in Venice as a strong and self-confident individualist, he nearly became an eclectic in the 1730s, when he offered much music in the style of Hasse, Leo, Giacomelli, etc., and presented *drammi* by Metastasio and singers of a more modern type, in order to stay in business. The reasons for this change are to be sought in his experiences of the 1720s when he received most of his *scritture* for important theatres outside Venice (Rome, Florence), and made contact with styles and audiences slightly outside his original artistic world. During the same period, the younger composers from Naples started to appear in Venice, and the Venetian theatres all reacted favourably to them. It was probably impossible not to learn from their successes; unfortunately, we do not know how other Venetian composers reacted, as the only Venetian contemporary of Vivaldi who continued to write operas in the 1730s was Albinoni, whose later operas are not preserved – but this fact may speak for itself. One can say that Vivaldi accompanied truly Venetian opera on its decline from the splendour of the generation of Lotti, Pollarolo, Gasparini, to the almost total domination by composers from the south. But Vivaldi also had an important share in the expansion of Italian operatic practices into the German-speaking countries, which is one of the most interesting aspects of his career.

1 Vivaldi's opera productions

= arranged by; aut. = autumn; Car. = Carnival;
, = dedicator
 = libretto; M = music; spr. = spring; sum. = summer
= theatre; virt. = virtuoso

'ull opera seasons with control of heatre	II. One-opera seasons with control of theatre	III. *Scritture* with some control or influence	IV. *Scritture* without control

1713[1]
Ottone in villa
May, Vicenza
L: D. Lalli (ded.)

I. Full opera seasons with control of theatre	II. One-opera seasons with control of theatre	III. *Scritture* with some control or influence	IV. *Scritture* without control
1713[2] *Orlando furioso* aut., S. Ang. L: G. Braccioli (ded.) M: G. A. Ristori			
1714[1] *Rodomonte sdegnato* Car., S. Ang. L: G. Braccioli (Vivaldi ded.) M: M. A. Gasparini			
1714[2] *Orlando finto pazzo* aut., S. Ang. (10 Nov.) L: G. Braccioli (ded.)			
1714[3] *Orlando furioso* aut., S. Ang. (1 Dec.) L: G. Braccioli (new ded.) M: Ristori + Vivaldi			
1715[1] *Nerone fatto Cesare* Car., S. Ang. L: M. Noris (+ Braccioli?) M: pasticcio			
1715[2] *Lucio Papirio* Car., S. Ang. L: A. Salvi (Vivaldi ded.) M: L. A. Predieri			
		1716[1] *La costanza...* Car., S. Moisè L: A. Marchi (ded.)	
1716[2] *Arsilda regina di Ponto* aut., S. Ang. L: D. Lalli (anon. ded.!)			
1717[1] *Penelope la casta* Car., S. Ang. (opera 2ª) L: M. Noris – ? M: F. Chelleri			
1717[2] *L'incoronazione di Dario* Car., S. Ang. (opera 3ª) L: A. Morselli – ?			

I. Full opera seasons with control of theatre	II. One-opera seasons with control of theatre	III. *Scritture* with some control or influence	IV. *Scritture* without control
1717³ *Tieteberga* aut., S. Moisè L: A. Lucchini 1718¹ *Armida al campo d'Egitto* Car., S. Moisè (12 Jan.) L: G. Palazzi 1718² *Artabano re dei Parti* (= 1716¹) Car., S. Moisè L: A. Marchi (ded.)			
	1718³ *Armida al campo d'Egitto* (= 1718¹) spr., Mantua L: G. Palazzi (P. Ramponi ded.)		
			1718⁴ *Scanderbeg* sum., Pergola Florence L: A. Salvi
1719¹ *Teuzzone* Car., Mantua L: A. Zeno – ? (G. A. Mauro ded.) M: (with arias by Orlandini?) 1719² *Tito Manlio* Car., Mantua L: M. Noris (theatre architect ded.)			
	1719³ *Artabano...* (= 1718²) Car., Vicenza L: A. Marchi (impresario ded.)		
1720¹ *Alessandro cognominato Severo* Car., Mantua (opera 1ª) L: A. Zeno – ? (theatre architect ded.) M: pasticcio (F. Chelleri and others?)			

I. Full opera seasons with control of theatre	II. One-opera seasons with control of theatre	III. *Scritture* with some control or influence	IV. *Scritture* without control
			1720² *Tito Manlio* Car., Pace Roma (opera 1ᵃ) L: Noris – ? M: Boni + Giorgi + Vivaldi
1720³ *La Candace* Car., Mantua (opera 2ᵃ) L: D. Lalli – ? (anon. ded.)			
	1720⁴ *Gli inganni per vendetta* (= 1718¹) Car. (?), Vicenza T. Grazie (A. Cestari ded.) L: Palazzi		
1720⁵ *La verità in cimento* aut., S. Ang. L: G. Palazzi			
		1721¹ *Filippo re di Macedonia* Car., S. Ang. (opera 1ᵃ?) L: D. Lalli (ded.) M: G. Boniventi (I, II) + Vivaldi (III)	
	1721² *La Silvia* sum. (28 Aug.), Milan L: E. Bissarri – ?		
		1723¹ *Ercole sul Termodonte* Car., Capranica Rome (opera 2ᵃ) L: Bussani – ?	
		1724¹ *La virtù trionfante...* Car., Capranica (opera 2ᵃ) L: F. Silvani – ? (Capranica ded.) M: B. Micheli + Vivaldi + N. Romaldo	
		1724² *Giustino* Car., Capranica (opera 2ᵃ) L: N. Beregan – P. Pariati – ?	

I. Full opera seasons with control of theatre	II. One-opera seasons with control of theatre	III. *Scritture* with some control or influence	IV. *Scritture* without control
			1725[1] *L'Artabano* Car., Mantua L: Marchi .(S. Burigotti ded.)

1725[2]
L'inganno trionfante…
aut., S. Ang.
L: Noris – Ruggieri
(A. Biscione ded.)
M: pasticcio arr. Vivaldi?

1726[1]
Cunegonda
Car., S. Ang.
L: A. Piovene – ?
M: pasticcio arr. Vivaldi?

1726[2]
La fede tradita e vendicata
Car., S. Ang.
L: F. Silvani – ?
(A. Biscione ded.)

1726[3]
Dorilla in Tempe
aut., S. Ang. (9 Nov.)
L: A. M. Lucchini (ded.)

1727[1]
Medea e Giasone
Car., S. Ang.
(opera 1ª?)
L: G. Palazzi (ded.)
M: G. F. Brusa

1727[2]
Ipermestra
Car., Pergola Florence
(opera 2ª)
L: A. Salvi

1727[3]
Farnace
Car., S. Ang.
L: A. M. Lucchini

1727[4]
Siroe re di Persia
spr., Reggio E.
L: Metastasio
(impresarios ded.)

1727[5]
Farnace (= 1727[3])
., S. Ang.
Lucchini

I. Full opera seasons with control of theatre	II. One-opera seasons with control of theatre	III. *Scritture* with some control of influence	IV. *Scritture* without control
1727[6] *Orlando* aut., S. Ang. L: Braccioli – ?			
1728[1] *Rosilena ed Oronta* Car., S. Ang. L: G. Palazzi (impresario ded.)			
1728[2] *Gli odi delusi dal sangue* Car., S. Ang. (end of Carnival) L: A. M. Lucchini M: G. B. Pescetti + B. Galuppi			
		1729[1] *L'Atenaide* Car., Pergola Florence L: Zeno – ?	
			1730[1] *Farnace* (= 1727[5]) spr., T. Sporck, Prague L: Lucchini (perhaps without Vivaldi)
	1730[2] *Argippo* aut., T. Sporck, Prague L: Lalli – ?		
			1731[1] *Alvilda regina dei Goti* spr., T. Sporck, Prague L: Zeno – ? M: (without Vivaldi?)
	1731[2] *Farnace* (= 1727[5]) spr., T. Omodeo Pavia 4 May) L: Lucchini		
1732[1] *Semiramide* Car., Mantua (opera 1ª) L: F. Silvani – ? (impresario ded.)			
		1732[2] *La fida Ninfa* Car., Verona L: S. Maffei (from 1730)	

Full opera seasons with control of theatre	II. One-opera seasons with control of theatre	III. *Scritture* with some control or influence	IV. *Scritture* without control
732³ *arnace* (= 1727⁵) ar., Mantua pera 2ª) : Lucchini npresario ded.)			
			1732⁴ *Doriclea* (= 1716¹) Car., T. Sporck, Prague L: Marchi – ? (Denzio impresario)
			1732⁵ *Dorilla in Tempe* (= 1726³) spr., T. Sporck, Prague L: Lucchini
33¹ *otezuma* t., S. Ang. G. Giusti 34¹ *rilla in Tempe* 1726³) r., S. Ang. era 1ª?) Lucchini – ? ,4² *)limpiade* ., S. Ang. era 2ª?) Metastasio – ? 5¹ *nerlano* , Verona A. Piovene – ? aldi ded.) pasticcio arr. Vivaldi 5² *laide* , Verona . Salvi aldi ded.)			
	1735³ *Griselda* spr., S. Samuele L: Zeno – Goldoni (anon. ded.)		

I. Full opera seasons with control of theatre	II. One-opera seasons with control of theatre	III. *Scritture* with some control or influence	IV. *Scritture* without control
			1735[4] *Aristide* aut., S. Samuele L: Goldoni (Lalli ded.) M: not Vivaldi?
		1736[1] *Ginevra principessa di Scozia* Car., Pergola L: Salvi – ?	
			1737[1] *Demetrio* Car., Ferrara (opera 1ª) L: Metastasio – ? (anon. ded.) M: Hasse, arr. Vivaldi 1737[2] *Alessandro nell'Indie* Car., Ferrara (opera 2ª) L: Metastasio – ? M: Hasse, arr. Vivaldi (L: not found)
	1737[3] *Catone in Utica* spr., Verona L: Metastasio (anon. ded.)		
1738[1] *L'oracolo in Messenia* Car., S. Ang. (opera 1ª) L: Zeno – ? 1738[2] *Armida al campo d'Egitto* (= 1718[1]) Car., S. Ang. L: Palazzi (anon. ded.) M: pasticcio, arr. Vivaldi 1738[3] *Rosmira* Car., S. Ang. L: Stampiglia – ? (Vivaldi ded.) M: pasticcio, arr. Vivaldi			

I. Full opera seasons with control of theatre	II. One-opera seasons with control of theatre	III. *Scritture* with some control or influence	IV. *Scritture* without control
	1738[4] *Siroe re di Persia* (= 1727[4]) spr., Ancona L: Metastasio – ? (impresarios ded.) M: pasticcio, arr. Vivaldi?		
			1739[1] *Siroe re di Persia* (= 1727[4]) Car., Ferrara (opera 1[a]) L: Metastasio – ? (impresario ded.) 1739[2] *Farnace* (= 1727[5]) Car., Ferrara (opera 2[a]) L: Lucchini – ? Not performed; replaced by: *Attalo re di Bitinia* (M: Hasse)
		1739[3] *Feraspe* aut., S. Ang. L: F. Silvani – ? (G. F. Dini ded.)	

2 Vivaldi's singers: a selective list

Included are the names of most singers who worked for Vivaldi in more than one season, provided they were engaged at least once by the composer himself (categories I and II). The names are roughly classified according to voice types, although strict distinctions between these types cannot always be drawn. Taken as a whole, the list may give an idea of the composer's preferences for certain types of voice range and training. Full seasonal engagements are listed only once.

A. Male sopranos/mezzosopranos of conservative training (limited range)

GIROLAMO BARTOLUZZI detto il Reggiano, pupil of F. Gasparini (c. 1719–24): 1720[2], Capranica 1723 and 1724. Mainly female roles.

FRANCESCO NATALI detto il Perugino (c. 1713–21): S. Ang. 1714/15, S. Moisè 1717/18. Under Vivaldi secondary male roles, but elsewhere female roles, also in 1720[2].

GIOVANNI OSSI, pupil of F. Gasparini (c. 1716–31): Capranica 1723 and 1724. Famous virt. of the Borghese princes. Male and female roles.

B. Male sopranos of modern training (Milan, Naples: high range)

MARIANINO NICOLINI (c. 1731–8): Mantua Car. 1732, S. Ang. 1733/4. Virt. Armstat 1734.

GAETANO VALLETTA di Milano (c. 1726–40): 1729[1], 1735[3]. Virt. Cesareo in Milan 1727, virt. Gian Gastone di Toscana 1730. Mostly male heroic roles.

C. Male altos (mostly of conservative, mezzosoprano type)

GAETANO FRACASSINI di Padova (c. 1716–35): 1720[2], Mantua Car. 1725, 1731[2].

LUC'ANTONIO MENGONI (Mingoni) di Bologna (c. 1711–26): 1718[3], S. Ang. 1725/6. Very famous virt. Modena.

G. B. MINELLI di Bologna (c. 1711–34): S. Ang. 1713/14, 1721[2]. Mostly male heroic roles. Virt. Baviera 1724, virt. Armstat 1726.

GIACOMO ZAGHINI (c. 1737–39): 1737[3], S. Ang. Car. 1738, 1739[3]. Virt. of Wilhelmine of Brandenburg-Bayreuth.

D. Tenors

ANTONIO BARBIERI di Reggio (c. 1720–40): Mantua Car. 1720 (earliest known engagement), S. Ang. 1720/1, Capranica 1724, 1731[2] (as Farnace). A very famous singer, often *primo uomo* from c. 1729. Virt. Armstat 1724. Seems to have been 'discovered' by Vivaldi in Mantua; later, sang more often in S. Gio. Grisostomo, Rome, Naples. His wife, Livia Bassi Barbieri, also accompanied him to the *Farnace* of Pavia 1731.

ANTONIO DENZIO di Venezia (c. 1715–40): 1716[1], 1730[1], 1732[4]. The most important producer of Vivaldi's operas in Bohemia, partly as impresario; later also impresario in the Veneto. He created *Artabano* in 1716[1], repeated in 1732[4], and sang *Farnace*, *Orlando* (in his pasticcio 1738 in Bergamo and elsewhere). Perhaps related to Elisabetta Denzio, who sang for Vivaldi in S. Ang. 1713/14; husband of Teresa Peruzzi detta la Denzia (another singer of his Bohemian cast)?

ANNIBALE PIO FABRI di Bologna (c. 1716–48): S. Ang. 1716/17, 1718[3], 1721[2], 1727[2], 1729[1]. Perhaps the best known tenor of his time, who also sang under Handel in 1729/30; much later in Madrid, where he seems to have composed operas. Although he created *Dario* in 1717[2], he was not often *primo uomo*. Virt. Armstat 1721. His wife: Anna Maria Bombaciara Fabri (see below).

DOM. GIUS. GALLETTI di Cortona (c. 1723–31): Capranica 1723, S. Ang. 1726/27. Both times used as *secondo tenore*.

LORENZO MORETTI (c. 1724–1739): S. Ang. 1726/27, 1738[4]. First tenor. He was with Denzio in Prague 1724/25, and later joined the Mingotti troupe.

E. Basses

GIO. FRANCESCO BENEDETTI (c. 1719–20): Mantua Car. 1719; 1720[4]. Virt. Armstat.

ANTON FRANCESCO CARLI (c. 1706–1723): S. Ang. 1713/14 and 1714/15. Virt. of Ferdinando de' Medici and later Violante di Toscana, but mainly active in Venice, where he sang almost continuously in S. Gio. Grisostomo, interrupted by the S. Angelo engagements 1712–15. Fabulously low range.

FRANCESCO MARIA VENTURINI (c. 1711–31): 1725[1], 1732[2], Virt. Baviera.

ANGELO ZANNONI di Venezia (c. 1716–32): S. Ang. 1716/17, 1718. Virt. Armstat 1726. Vivaldi's discovery as a replacement for Carli?

F. Female sopranos/mezzosopranos of conservative training (limited range)

ROSA D'AMBREVILLE di Modena (c. 1715–30): 1716[1], 1718[3]. (Probably sister of Anna d'A.). Married the famous tenor F. Borosini in Vienna, c. 1725.

ANNA COSIMI di Roma (c. 1726–1743): 1727[4], 1730[1], 1732[4], 1739[1]. Virt. Modena. Travelled much with A. Denzio (Prague, later in the Veneto).

ANNA MARIA BOMBACIARA FABRI di Bologna (c. 1711–30): S. Ang. 1714/15 and 1716/17, 1721[2]. Vivaldi writes her parts with alto clef, other composers often with soprano clef. Her career seems to start under the influence of Vivaldi like that of her husband Annibale Pio Fabri. From c. 1716, the two sang often in the same productions, but apparently not in London under Handel, 1729/30.

MARGHERITA FACCIOLI detta la Vicentina (c. 1713–16): 1713[1], S. Ang. 1713/14.

MARGHERITA FLORA (c. 1730–1741): Although never directly engaged by Vivaldi, she sang much of his music under Denzio in Bohemia, as well as in *Orlando* in Brno, 1735, with Mingotti; later with the Mingottis in Graz, Klagenfurt etc.

ANNA GIRÒ (GIRAUD) detta la Mantovana: A list of her career is given by John W. Hill.[5] She seems to have begun 1723 in Treviso and sang in Venice for the first season 1724/5 at S. Moisè under the direction of the singer–impresario Cav. Antonio Gaspari (see below). Vivaldi was in contact with her and her sister in Mantua, 1718–20. Her career with Vivaldi from 1726[3] is characterised by the many *primadonna* parts in productions where the composer had some influence, and by the arias which she carried from one production to another. She performed very rarely in operas by other composers: during Vivaldi's absence 1730/1, and in Car. 1734 in Verona. After 1739[2], she went on tour with the Mingottis. That her well-known voice type and singing and acting style suited Vivaldi for so many different roles – only female roles, however – implies a self-imposed restriction of writing on his part. He preferred to give *primadonna* parts in her absence sometimes to contraltos. He writes her parts in the alto clef (like those of Anna Fabri), but her range was that of a mezzosoprano. Her 'forerunner' in Vivaldi's productions, in a stylistic sense, seems to have been Margherita Gualandi Campioli (see below).

MARIA GIUSTI detta la Romanina (c. 1709–25): 1713[1], S. Ang. 1713/14. She sang more often in S. Angelo, and 1724/5 with Denzio in Prague.

MARGHERITA GUALANDI CAMPIOLI di Bologna (c. 1709–38): S. Ang. 1714/5, Mantua Car. 1719, 1721[2], 1738[4] (?). No engagement known between 1726 and 1738; according to *New Grove*, she was then in Prague, but a confusion with an otherwise unknown Diamante Gualandi (in one libretto) is possible. It is also unknown whether Margherita was related to the Dresden court castrato Antonio Campioli (or A. Gualandi dettò il Campioli?), whose career seems to have started in Braunschweig and Hamburg (partly in productions with music by Vivaldi) c. 1720.

ANNA GUGLIELMINI di Bologna (c. 1717–28): 1718[4], Mantua Car. 1720, 1727[4]. Both female and male secondary roles, in productions of Vivaldi and others.

CHIARA ORLANDI detta la Mantovanina (c. 1717–32): S. Moisè 1717/18, Mantua. Car. 1720, S. Ang. 1720/1. Possibly quoted in the frontispiece of *Il teatro alla moda*, and certainly typical for the many Bolognese and Mantuan singers who then invaded Venice; connections with the Buini troupe. She sang in Venice almost exclusively at S. Moisè, mostly *seconda donna* roles. Like so many Vivaldi singers, she also worked with the Mingottis: 1735 in *Orlando*, Brno, as Bradamante.

ANTONIA PELLIZZARI di Venezia (c. 1710–22): S. Ang. 1716/17. Although engaged by Vivaldi in this season only, she was remarkable for her exclusive specialism in male roles of youthful character (*terzo uomo*), for which she was requested as far as Naples.

ROSA VENTURINI (c. 1717–31): S. Moisè 1717/18, 1718[3], 1718[4]. Helped exporting *Armida* to Mantua. Probably a very light style, *terza donna* or *terzo uomo*, also female roles in intermezzi. Virt. Parma 1717.

G. Female sopranos of modern training (Venice, Milan: high range)

ROSA MADDALENA CARDINA di Venezia, detta la Dolfinetta (c. 1730–37): 1731[2], 1737[1]. Possibly a pupil of Porpora (first engagement under him at S. Angelo 1730/1, including Getilde in Vivaldi's *L'odio vinto...*). Sang *primo uomo* (!) in 1737[1].

CATTERINA FUMAGALLI (c. 1738–1760's): 1738[4], S. Ang. 1739/40. This later very famous soprano met Vivaldi at the beginning of her career. In 1739/40 (after Girò's departure), she was *primadonna*.

MARIA GIOVANNA GASPERINI di Bologna (c. 1725–37): Mantua Car. 1725, 1732[2], 1737[3]. Also with Porpora, S. Ang. Car. 1731. Mostly *seconda donna*. Virt. Armstat 1727.

MARGHERITA GIACOMAZZI di Venezia (c. 1735–50s): 1735[1], 1735[3]. S. Ang. Car. 1738. Mostly *prima donna* in Venice, but under Vivaldi in 1738 she sang *primo uomo*!

ANNA MARIA STRADA DEL PÒ detta la Stradina (c. 1720–40s): S. Ang. Car. 1720/21, 1721[2]. Virt. Conte Colloredo, Milan 1720. Probably trained in Milan; always female roles. *Seconda donna* in Italy, then from 1729 regularly *primadonna* under Handel in London. Higher range than Bordoni and Cuzzoni (see *New Grove*).

H. Female contraltos (some of the conservative mezzosoprano type)

LUCREZIA BALDINI (c. 1726–31): 1727[3], S. Ang. 1727/28. Her contract for 1727[3], written and signed by Vivaldi, is preserved. Mostly female roles of secondary importance.

LUCIA LANCETTI di Venezia (c. 1722–37): 1727[2], 1727[5], 1727[6], 1728[2]. In 1728[1] replaced by Lucrezia Baldini. Specialist of male roles (*secondo uomo*), she sang the title roles of *Orlando* (1727) and *Farnace*. Virt. Toscana.

ANTONIA MARIA LAURENTI detta la Coralli (c. 1715–35): 1718[3], S. Ang. 1720/21. Well-known Bolognese singer, quoted in *Il teatro alla moda*. Although sometimes *primadonna* elsewhere, Vivaldi gave her only male roles. Virt. del Re di Polonia. Wife of the tenor Felice Novelli?

ANTONIA MARGHERITA MERIGHI di Bologna (c. 1714–40): S. Moisè 1717/18, 1718[3], S. Ang. 1720/21. Probably the best contralto Vivaldi ever had; she sang *primadonna* in many Italian theatres, also male protagonist roles. Her dark timbre and acting was famous – quite like that of her great rival, Vittoria Tesi. Employed by Handel and by the Opera of the Nobility in London in the 1730's. Partner, and possibly pupil, of Antonio Bernacchi. Virt. Toscana. She created Vivaldi's *Armida*, and took the role to Mantua, 1718.

ROSA MIGNATTI (MINIATI) di Bologna (c. 1715–28): 1716[1], S. Ang. Car. 1717. In 1716[2], she sang the female intermezzi part. Francesca Miniati di Bologna (S. Moisè 1715/16) was perhaps a relative.

ELISABETTA MORO di Venezia (c. 1723–41): S. Ang. 1725/6, 1729[1], 1737[3]. Although specialist in male roles, Vivaldi employed her in female roles 1725/6.

MARIA MADDALENA PIERI di Firenze (c. 1720–35): S. Ang. 1726/7, Mantua Car. 1732, Verona Car. 1735. She sang many male roles (although not exclusively), and created *Farnace* (1727[3]) and *Tamerlano* (1735[1]). Virt. Modena.

ANGIOLA ZANUCHI detta la Brescianina (c. 1722–40): Mantua Car. 1725, S. Ang. 1733/34, 1739[1]. Her voice range is not clear (high in *Olimpiade*). Male roles after c. 1730. Virt. Armstat 1725. Probably sister of Teresa Zanuchi, and perhaps Maria Maddalena Zanuchi (intermezzo singer).

Other notable singers, engaged only once by Vivaldi (the letter in brackets refers to the voice type):

GIOVANNI CARESTINI (B): Capranica 1723, 1727[4]
FRANCESCA CUZZONI SANDONI (F): 1718[4]
ANNA DOTTI (H): S. Ang. 1716/17
FILIPPO FINAZZI (A): S. Ang. 1726/7
Cav. ANTONIO GASPARI (A?): 1720[4]
ANDREA GUERRI (A): S. Ang. 1714/15
PIETRO MAURO DETTO IL VIVALDI (D): 1731[2]
MARIA CATTERINA NEGRI (H): S. Ang. 1727/8
ANDREA PACINI (C): S. Ang. 1714/15
GAETANO PINETTI (E): S. Ang. 1727/8
COSTANZA POSTERLA (H): S. Ang. 1725/6
PIETRO RAMPONI (C?): S. Ang. 1713/14
RAFFAELE SIGNORINI (A): 1727[2], 1727[4]
BENEDETTA SOROSINA (H): S. Ang. 1727/8
DIANA VICO (H): 1713[1]
MARGHERITA ZANI (F): Mantua Car. 1720

3 Vivaldi and the librettists

A. Poets who wrote new libretti for Vivaldi

DOMENICO LALLI: 1713[1], 1716[2] (but not acknowledged by Lalli), 1721[1] (but possibly not on Vivaldi's initiative)
GRAZIO BRACCIOLI: 1713[2], 1714[1] (both for Vivaldi as impresario), 1714[2]
ANTONIO MARCHI: 1716[1]
ANTONIO MARIA LUCCHINI: 1717[3], 1726[3], 1728[2]
GIOVANNI PALAZZI: 1718[1], 1720[5], 1728[1]
ANTONIO SALVI: 1718[4] (but only a *scrittura*)
GIROLAMO GIUSTI: 1733[1]
(CARLO GOLDONI: 1735[4], collaboration very doubtful)

B. Existing libretti, probably chosen on Vivaldi's initiative

MATTEO NORIS: 1715[1], 1717[1], 1719[2], 1725[2]
ANTONIO SALVI: 1715[2], 1735[2]
ADRIANO MORSELLI: 1717[2]
APOSTOLO ZENO: 1719[1], 1720[1], 1738[1] (1735[3] chosen by Lalli)
DOMENICO LALLI: 1720[3], 1730[2]
AGOSTINO PIOVENE: 1726[1], 1735[1]
FRANCESCO SILVANI: 1726[2], 1732[1]
SILVIO STAMPIGLIA: 1738[3]
PIETRO METASTASIO: 1734[2], 1737[3] (for Ferrara 1737 Vivaldi had originally proposed 1734[2] i.e. *Olimpiade*, and 1736[1] by Salvi)

C. Operas revived by Vivaldi, perhaps partly because of the libretto

GRAZIO BRACCIOLI, *Orlando furioso*: 1713[2], 1714[3], 1727[6]
ANTONIO MARCHI, *La costanza trionfante degli amori, e degli odii*: 1716[1], 1718[2], 1719[3], perhaps 1732[4]

GIOVANNI PALAZZI, *Armida al campo d'Egitto*: 1718[1], 1718[3], 1720[4], 1738[2]
ANTONIO MARIA LUCCHINI, *Dorilla in Tempe*: 1726[3], perhaps 1732[5], 1734[1]
ANTONIO MARIA LUCCHINI, *Farnace*: 1727[3], 1727[5], perhaps 1730[1], 1731[2], 1732[3], 1739[2]
PIETRO METASTASIO, *Siroe re di Persia*: 1727[4], 1738[4]

4 Vivaldi and other composers

A. Vivaldi produces works by other composers

1713[2]:   *Orlando furioso* (G. A. Ristori)
1714[1]:   *Rodomonte sdegnato* (M. A. Gasparini)
1714[3]:   *Orlando jurioso* (G. A. Ristori), arranged
1715[2]:   *Lucio Papirio* (L. A. Predieri)
1717[1]:   *Penelope la casta* (F. Chelleri)
(1721 End of Carnival: *Il pastor fido*, C. L. Pietra Grua, S. Ang., with Vivaldi's consent?)
1727[1]:   *Medea e Giasone* (G. Fr. Brusa)
1728[2]:   *Gli odì delusi dal sangue* (G. B. Pescetti + B. Galuppi)
1737[1]:   *Demetrio* (Hasse), arranged
1737[2]:   *Alessandro nell'Indie* (Hasse), arranged
(1739[2]: after the rejection of *Farnace* in Ferrara, did Vivaldi provide the score of Hasse's *Attalo*?)
(1740:   another revival of Hasse's *Demetrio* at S. Angelo?)

B. Vivaldi's pasticci

1715[1]:   *Nerone fatto Cesare* (arias by Orlandini, F. Gasparini, Perti et al.)
1719[1]:   *?Teuzzone* ('Ritorna a lusingarmi' by Orlandini: other arias?)
1720[1]:   *Alessandro cognominato Severo* (arrangement of a score by F. Chelleri?)
1725[2]:   *?L'inganno trionfante* [...]
1726[1]:   *?Cunegonda*
1734[1]:   *Dorilla in Tempe* (arias by Hasse, Giacomelli, Leo)
1735[1]:   *Tamerlano* (arias by Hasse, Giacomelli, R. Broschi)
(1737, May: Vivaldi offers a pasticcio, similar to *Catone in Utica*, to Ferrara)
1738[2]:   *Armida al campo d'Egitto* (arias by Leo)
1738[3]:   *Rosmira* (arias etc. by Hasse, Handel, Mazzoni, Micheli, Paganelli, Pampino, Pergolesi, Vinci)

C. Vivaldi sharing composition with others (third act is regarded as the best part)

1720[2]:   *Tito Manlio* (Gaetano Boni I, Giovanni Giorgi II, Vivaldi III)
1721[1]:   *Filippo re di Macedonia* (Giuseppe Boniventi I + II, Vivaldi III)
1724[1]:   *La virtù trionfante* [...] (Benedetto Micheli I, Vivaldi II, Nicola Romaldo III)

Comments on Vivaldi's opera productions in chronological order

1713[1]

Ottone in villa was an almost totally Venetian production for the *villeggiatura* outpost of Vicenza, where Venetian impresarios (most notably Giovanni Orsati) and composers (most notably C. F. Pollarolo) had regularly been active in the early years of the century. The spring season ('Fiera dell'Ascensione') was the typical production time for such opera houses; it avoided the competition of the Venetian Carnival season and, at the same time, enabled singers, composers, audiences to attend without missing the Carnival in Venice. Vivaldi's *villeggiatura* opera must have been planned from Venice, with Lalli as the poet – he had just started his Venetian career in 1710/11 – and with several singers who were then active for the Teatro S. Giovanni Grisostomo: the castrato Bartolomeo Bartoli, the very famous contralto Diana Vico, the tenor Gaetano Mossi (Mozi). To them were added Maria Giusti detta la Romanina, who had appeared in S. Angelo in 1709, and the local soprano Margherita Faccioli detta la Vicentina. The latter three, not the former singers, reappeared in later productions of Vivaldi. As for the choice of composer, the association of the Vicenza theatres with the champion of S. G. Grisostomo (C. F. Pollarolo) seems so close that Vivaldi may have received the *scrittura* by some coincidence; Pollarolo had composed the opera of the previous year for the inauguration of the new Teatro delle Grazie, *Peribea in Salamina*, and he is one of the composers of the Carnival production of 1713 (*more veneto* or not?) in that theatre, *La violenza d'amore*; Vivaldi's *Ottone* was produced in the Teatro Nuovo di Piazza in May 1713, not before. However, previous connections of Vivaldi with Vicenza are not impossible; there is a production of *La Silvia* (libretto by Conte Enrico Bissarri, set by Vivaldi for Milan in 1721) in the Teatro di Piazza in 1710, music anonymous. Direct comparison of Vivaldi's score with that of Pollarolo's *Peribea in Salamina* (Strohm 1976, vol. 2, p. 200) shows his perfect acquaintance with the operatic idiom then current in Venice, but also some independence of instrumentation and in the sweeping gestures of some aria themes ('Sole degli occhi miei', 'Gelosia'). Various alterations in the score are probably of 1713, and indicate some difficulties over the choice of arias. The last aria for Cleonilla ('Che bel contento') has the heading 'per la peruchiera', a nickname which does not seem to fit Maria Giusti – it is known only in connection with the much later singer Anna Maria Perruzzi of Bologna – and which might even point to a change in the cast, but when? The orchestra contained two oboes and two recorders (for the same players); the aria 'Guarda in quest'occhi' seems to have been performed with a violin cadenza. Two arias travelled abroad without Vivaldi's initiative: 'Io sembro appunto' appeared already in the London pasticcio *Arminio* (4 February 1714) staged by Heidegger, and was copied and printed in London, once wrongly attributed to A. Scarlatti; 'L'essere amante' appeared with different text in the Hamburg pasticcio *Die getreue Alceste*, 1719. Vivaldi himself used some of the arias in later productions.

1713²–1715²

Vivaldi says in his own dedication of the libretto of *Lucio Papirio*, S. Angelo, Carnival 1715, that he has served this theatre for two years. His 'service' for S. Angelo must therefore have started in autumn 1713 at the latest, and it is thus established that he was involved in the production of the *Orlando furioso* given in that theatre on 7 November 1713, the music of which is attributed to G. A. Ristori. Vivaldi certainly contributed much music to the revival of this successful opera on 1 December 1714 in S. Angelo (libretto anonymous): perhaps Ristori was the only name quoted in the libretto of 1713 because Vivaldi did not yet want to reveal his name as an opera composer, although he may already have composed some arias. Ristori was even less known to the Venetians than Vivaldi; his style in the preserved parts of the score of 1713 is quite indistinguishable from Vivaldi's. It may also be significant that Ristori's name is dropped from the libretto of 1714: have any of his pieces been retained in that performance?

M. A. Gasparini's *Rodomonte sdegnato*, the dedication of which is signed by Vivaldi on 20 January 1714, is identified in the preserved manuscript (arias only) in Dresden as 'opera seconda', which implies that another opera was performed at the beginning of Carnival. I suggest that the numeration refers to *Orlando furioso* of autumn 1713 as the first opera (as was in fact the usual way of counting the operas in Venice), which must then mean that this work was given well into the Carnival season: a splendid success (which is also alluded to by Braccioli in his new dedication of the revival 1714). We know very little of Michel Angelo Gasparini, except that he was probably not a relative of Francesco, and that he is traditionally identified as the teacher of Faustina Bordoni. He never worked together with Vivaldi again. But the librettist, Grazio Braccioli, seems to be a close ally. He had also just started his career, with two previous libretti for Ferrara and Bologna in 1710, one of which (*La costanza in cimento con la crudeltà*) was taken to the S. Angelo in Carnival, 1712: since then, he worked for several years faithfully for this theatre. The season 1712/13, however, saw the intrusion of a foreign composer, with two S. Angelo operas: Johann Heinichen of Dresden, whose successful *Calfurnia* (text by Braccioli) of Carnival, 1713, aroused some resentment among Venetians (Vivaldi included?) and may indeed have contributed to Vivaldi's delayed entrance on the Venetian stage. On the other hand, it is very likely that another Dresden musician, Pisendel, became friends with Vivaldi shortly later, and that, vice versa, Ristori left Venice in 1714 to take up an appointment at the Saxon court, where he remained. The singers of 1713/14 must reflect Vivaldi's preferences to a great extent; among them were Margherita Faccioli from *Ottone*, and Maria Giusti, but also the famous bass Anton Francesco Carli, and the alto castrato, G. B. Minelli. A figure worth investigating is Pietro Giacomo Ramponi, who seems to have been the composer of Braccioli's *La gloria trionfante d'amore*, S. Angelo autumn 1712, the singer of Astolfo in Ristori's *Orlando* 1713 – and the impresario of Vivaldi's *Armida* in Mantua 1718!

Vivaldi opens the season of 1714/15 as the composer of *Orlando finto pazzo* – almost symbolically, this was after he had presented himself to the Venetian public as an impresario, with *Rodomonte*. But the continuity with the previous season is very strict: the new Orlando opera was a follow-up to the success of the *Furioso*, and also *Rodomonte* had been an Ariostean subject. Two singers stayed on, Carli and Elisabetta Denzio, and the newly engaged ones were of a similar stature: Margherita Gualandi detta la Campioli was already a known S. Angelo performer from 1709 and 1712 (is there any connection between her and the castrato Antonio Campioli who later served the Dresden court?); Andrea Pacini replaced Minelli as alto castrato; at least Anna Maria Fabri and Francesco Natali were new for Venice. Excepting Carli, none of the famous singers of S. Gio. Grisostomo (D. Vico, D. Scarabelli, Santa Stella etc.) ever sang for Vivaldi, perhaps because he did not even try to hire them. Even the composer of the one opera of this season for which Vivaldi provided no music, Lucantonio Predieri of Bologna, was new for Venice. His setting of Salvi's *Lucio Papirio* seems to have been composed originally for the S. Angelo. With this text, we re-enter the sphere of Roman subjects, so popular in Venice, which the romantic Ariostean operas had interrupted. *Nerone fatto Cesare* was a pasticcio arrangement of the opera by Perti of the same title (of 1693, and then given in many theatres throughout Italy); just about this time, the production of pasticci was becoming rapidly more convenient for aesthetic as well as technical reasons: as the number of arias in each opera decreased, their length and dramatic weight increased and their orchestration with violins became more standardised, it was easier to exchange them; still, there had to be much alteration of the texts (parody: P. J. Martello referred to this practice in a significant way in his *Della tragedia antica e moderna* of 1714, see Strohm 1976, vol. 1, p. 253) but Vivaldi was also able to include several arias in *Nerone* without textual adjustment (those of Perti, A. Pollarolo, F. Gasparini, and probably Orlandini), which had been composed for other operas around 1710–14, except Perti's. All twelve of his own arias seem to be newly composed, but several of them have survived in later scores ('Ti seguirei', 'È troppo il bel diletto', 'Se lascio d'adorare'). Interestingly, the bass Antonfrancesco Carli composed an aria ('È la corte') for himself as Seneca. It was probably Predieri, not Vivaldi, who made later use of this pasticcio score: the Carnival season of 1716 in Brescia saw two operas, one of which was an exact repeat of the S. Angelo *Nerone*, the other a pasticcio *Griselda*, containing one aria (at least) by Predieri, and even one from Handel's *Agrippina* of 1710. Among the singers of this Brescia season were Margherita Albinoni, Andrea Guerri, Giovanni Ronzani, Margherita Faccioli, Gaetano Fracassini. Predieri's *Lucio Papirio* was less successful and is not connected with the opera of the same title given in Mantua, Carnival 1718 (probably F. Gasparini and Orlandini). The coherence of the two seasons of 1713/14 and 1714/15 is great: although some singers, and the scene painters changed (Antonio Mauro first, then Bernardo Canal), the continuity rests on the two personalities of Braccioli and Vivaldi, who together represent a new and independent aspect of Venetian opera. Their historical chance seems to have been, among other reasons, the gap left by the departure from Venice of Francesco Gasparini in the spring of 1713 and the subsequent closure of his opera-house, the S. Cassiano, for four years.

1716[1]

It may be due to the initiative of the impresario Orsati that, in the autumn of 1715, yet another theatre tried to fill the gap left by the S. Cassiano: the S. Moisè. Its season of 1715/16 comprised three (or four) operas, at least one of which was a mere revival (Gasparini's *La fede tradita*), but the main Carnival opera was by Vivaldi, probably a normal *scrittura: La costanza trionfante degli amori e degli odii*, newly written by Antonio Marchi on the famous subject of Tigrane, Re d'Armenia, also treated in 1715 by D. Lalli (music by A. Scarlatti, Naples 1715), but not directly related to Francesco Silvani's *Tigrane*, which Vivaldi encountered in Rome 1724. It is significant that Vivaldi's music was the real success of the reopened theatre, and had to be repeated in 1718. All singers were new to Vivaldi, but from then on he collaborated with several of them: the tenor Antonio Denzio (a relative of Elisabetta?), Rosa d'Ambreville (later Borosini) of Modena, sister of Anna d'Ambreville Perroni, and the (probable) sisters Francesca and Rosa Mignatti (Miniati), also of Bologna. There must be a significance to Vivaldi's connection with many members of singer families or even family troupes (the Miniatis also had contact with G. M. Buini's well-known family troupe Belisani-Buini), particularly as he engaged another couple in the following S. Angelo season: the Fabris, also from Bologna. But these years witnessed a wave of Bolognese singers flowing into Venice, anyway, of which the minor Venetian theatres such as S. Angelo and Moisè took more advantage than the S. Giovanni Grisostomo.

1716²–1717²

We do not know why Vivaldi abandoned the S. Angelo for the previous season, since he would have been able to combine the work for two theatres in one season – the gap in his activity really is the autumn of 1715. He tried to start again with the S. Angelo in the spring of 1716, but Domenico Lalli's new libretto of *Arsilda, regina di Ponto* was brought down by the censors refusing a *faccio fede*; when the opera was then given in the following autumn, Lalli took the extraordinary step of accusing not only the censors for that, but also the 'insufficienza del suo maestro che la compose', (i.e. 'l'opera') in the unsigned preface to the libretto, which he refused to recognise as his. This can only mean that a major row between Lalli and Vivaldi had taken place; the only time when the composer set one of his new texts again, was with the insignificant contribution to Lalli's *Filippo re di Macedonia* in 1721. But it is equally important that Lalli did not work again for the S. Angelo in 1717 – evidently because Vivaldi controlled the theatre. (Lalli had provided one Carnival libretto of 1716, for Albinoni.) The text choices at the S. Angelo in the Carnival of 1717 concern two very old libretti of the Seicento by Noris and Morselli, arranged by an unknown hand, certainly not Lalli's. By enlisting F. Chelleri for the new music of *Penelope la casta*, Vivaldi acknowledged this young composer's successes with Braccioli's *Alessandro fra le Amazzoni*, also of S. Angelo, Carnival 1716, and already in 1715 with the lovely score of *La caccia in Etolia*, for Ferrara. Vivaldi's singers in this season were actually a little less prominent than his previous ones, with the exception of Annibal Pio Fabri and his wife, Anna Maria. For the first time in his productions, *intermezzi comici* seem to have been played: *L'Alfier fanfarone*, sung by Rosa Mignatti and Lucrezia Borsari (a female couple for intermezzi is very rare), turns up again in Vicenza 1719, and in Vivaldi's own *Argippo* of Prague 1730; however, I am sure the music was not his, but came from the original performance of these intermezzi in F. Gasparini's *Eumene*, Reggio 1714. (Note also that a *Penelope la casta* was performed in Sporck's theatre in Prague, autumn 1730.)

1717³–1718²

There is perhaps a system in Vivaldi's changing back and forth between S. Angelo and S. Moisè in these years. As the librettists seem to stay more continuously with one theatre, except Lalli, it is probable that Vivaldi's negotiations were primarily made with the impresarios, Orsati and Modotto respectively, who may have tried to attract him by promising good singers. This does imply that Vivaldi was, at that time, sought after by the secondary theatres in Venice. This time at the S. Moisè, he again collaborates with two starting librettists, Giovanni Palazzi and Anton Maria Lucchini, both of whom were later to become very significant for him. He was also lucky as a discoverer of voices – Chiara Orlandi and Rosa Venturini were to turn out to be faithful Vivaldi singers, surpassed in importance only by Antonia Merighi. In spite of all her fame, she must have been immediately convinced by the role of Armida which Vivaldi wrote for her in her first Venetian season, because she took the role to Mantua in the following spring.

1718[3]

The Mantuan revival of *Armida al campo d'Egitto* was (together with the Venetian *Artabano* of 1718) probably the starting point for Vivaldi's operatic fame, not only outside Venice, but outside Italy. The distribution goes in two different directions: while *Artabano* was revived in Hamburg in 1719, where from then on other music by Vivaldi regularly occurred in pasticcio operas, the Prince of Hessen-Darmstadt must have provided Vivaldi with contacts to the Habsburg court in Vienna for which he ruled Mantua. Probably, Vivaldi had a choice of the opera with which he wanted to introduce himself in Mantua, and also a choice of the singers, as this concerned a one-opera season in the spring. This sheds a light on the opera itself, and on the singers Merighi, Zannoni, Rosa Venturini, A. P. Fabri (substituted for Ramondini), Rosa d'Ambreville – all known to Vivaldi in the seasons 1716/17 and 1717/18 – and the new choice of Luca Antonio Mengoni and Antonia Maria Laurenti detta Coralli. Pietro Ramponi of *Orlando* fame dedicated the libretto to the landgrave.

1718[4]

Scanderbeg was newly written by the famous court poet of the Medici, Antonio Şalvi, for the inauguration of the reopened Teatro della Pergola of ancient reputation. That the *scrittura* went to Vivaldi instead of the court maestro Orlandini, or perhaps somebody like Predieri, still needs an explanation, because he had no special protector in Florence. He must have influenced the choice of the singers (at least for Venturini, Mossi, and Agata Landi, who had sung for him before), and will certainly not have objected to writing for the court singers Francesca Cuzzoni and Antonio Ristorini. That three later *scritture* for Vivaldi from the Teatro degli Accademici Immobili followed at some distance in 1727, 1729, and 1736, may or may not confirm the success of *Scanderbeg*. Salvi's libretto was not set by any other composer, in strict contrast with his other dramas: this may be partly for political reasons, since the story of the 'Albanian Alexander' and his brave resistance to the Turks hit a period of reconciliation with the Ottoman Empire. Vivaldi did not revive his opera, perhaps for this reason, either.

1719¹–1720³

The service in Mantua required Vivaldi to provide some of the operas, but not all of them, as the spring operas in 1719 cannot be shown to be connected with him. However, he seems to have controlled both Carnival seasons, not as an impresario, but as a court composer (his title 'maestro di cappella di camera' was not uncommon with German princes of the time). There was a scheme in the two seasons: both started with libretti by Zeno – Habsburg court poet since 1718 – in the wake of a great revival of Zeno's works at the court theatres affiliated to the Habsburgs in Italy (Milan, Modena-Reggio, Naples), whereas the second Carnival operas, more splendidly staged than the first (as was usual), on both occasions reflected Vivaldi's own aesthetic better. It may be that *Teuzzone* of 1719 was not all by Vivaldi, since at least the aria 'Ritorna a lusingarmi' is attributed to Orlandini in a reliable manuscript,[6] and Vivaldi gave a different setting to the same text in his *Griselda* of 1735. *Alessandro cognominato Severo* is certainly a pasticcio, with many texts recurring in operas by Chelleri. *Tito Manlio* and *Candace*, the libretti of which attribute the music to Vivaldi, are very Venetian in text and music, although somewhat heroic in an old-fashioned sense. Among the singers, Vivaldi must have been pleased to be able to re-employ Margherita Gualandi (1719) and Anna Guglielmini (1720), but he also broke new ground with the young tenor Antonio Barbieri whom Vivaldi may have discovered in Mantua itself.

The Vicenza revivals of *Artabano* in 1719 (with intermezzi *L'alfier fanfarone*) and *Gl'inganni per vendetta* (= *Armida*) in 1720 were really only intermezzi for Vivaldi, who seems to have taken the opportunity to move into the Vicenza market, with the help of the impresario Attilio Cestari; the singers clearly came from Mantua (Chiara Orlandi) and Bologna (Cecilia Belisani, wife of Buini), hired by Vivaldi, and Francesco Benedetti was the bass singer of Landgrave Philip. The biography of one of the singers in 1720 deserves investigation: Cavaliere Antonio Gaspari, long established as a minor castrato on Venetian stages since 1712/13, who acted as impresario of S. Moisè in 1724/5, where he was the first to employ Anna Girò in Venice. At that time, Gaspari also was a virtuoso of Philip of Darmstadt. Anna Girò was perhaps of Venetian birth, but is identified in libretti as 'Mantovana'; it has sometimes been overlooked that Vivaldi says in his letter of 16 November 1737, that he was in Mantua with the sisters Girò during his three-year period of service.

It is doubtful whether Vivaldi had the time to go to Rome in the Carnival of 1720 for the sole purpose of supervising his third act for the *Tito Manlio* at the Teatro della Pace. If he did not – and therefore did not influence that performance – two things are remarkable: first, the choice of the libretto fitted Vivaldi extremely well for the re-use of some arias and, possibly, some of the recitative, of his Mantuan *Tito Manlio*, and second, he knew the castrato singer of the *primadonna* role quite well: Francesco Natali. Besides, Vivaldi has later claimed that he was in Rome to produce operas for three Carnivals, which is likely to refer to 1720, 1723, and 1724. The *impresa* of the Teatro della Pace is enigmatic; 1720 was the only year when they invited Northern composers (St. A. Fiorè composed *L'innocenza difesa* for that Carnival), but why Vivaldi should have shared his libretto with two musicians who never, before or after, composed an opera, can only be guessed: strikingly similar is the shared composition of *La virtù trionfante* in Rome 1724, which suggests that such an arrangement could have had to do with Vivaldi's own wishes.

1720⁵–1721¹

There is nothing strange about Vivaldi's departure from the 'actual servizio' at Mantua. Landgrave Philip may have wanted to save the expense of a full *maestro di cappella* – he did not in fact replace Vivaldi – and the composer himself must have preferred the freedom of the S. Angelo to the court service. But it is strange that Vivaldi did not provide the Teatro Arciducale with other operas, other than once, in 1732. (The question will be discussed in connection with 1725¹.) Vivaldi seems to have re-entered the Venetian scene with the plan of a full season 1720/1 at the S. Angelo. But the conditions had changed since 1718. Although Lotti had left Venice in 1718 for Dresden, and Albinoni and C. F. Pollarolo were not particularly active in these years, a whole group of composers of Vivaldi's own generation, or younger, began to dominate nearly all opera-houses: Giovanni Porta, the pupil of F. Gasparini, the earlier associates of Vivaldi, Michel Angelo Gasparini and Fortunato Chelleri, then Antonio Pollarolo, son of Carlo Francesco, and, most importantly, Giuseppe Maria Orlandini, who had a tremendous success with his classicist tragedies *Antigona* (S. Gio. Grisostomo, Carnival 1718, several times revived) and *Ifigenia in Tauride* (S. Gio. Grisostomo, Carnival 1719). Besides, the Bolognese Giuseppe Maria Buini with his family troupe (his wife, Cecilia Belisani, and her father Francesco, among others) actually controlled the S. Angelo in 1719/20, and the S. Moisè in 1720/1. In both these theatres, the public had become accustomed to expect the additional attraction of *intermezzi comici*, given either by the famous Florentine couple Antonio Ristorini – Rosa Ungarelli (at S. Angelo) or by the members of the Buini troupe, F. Belisani and Maria Maddalena Zanuchi (at S. Moisè). But even in the *dramma per musica*, a lighter and much more modern style characterised the scores of Orlandini, Porta, Chelleri, which are very similar to Vivaldi's own at the time. Some ingredients of this new style are the pre-eminence of the vocal tune, often accompanied *colla parte* for greater acoustic impact, the *al fresco* background of orchestral figuration with rapidly repeated chords, the simplification of the bass line into alberti figures or mere tremoli, the slower and more regular harmonic rhythm, the clear distinction between declamatory passages and long and difficult, often sequential, coloraturas, the pathetic unisono techniques, often involving voice and orchestra together, the bassetto passages (continuo played an octave higher by the violas or second violins alone), the abandonment of dance-types like gigue and sarabande in favour of the minuetto, and of neutral 'allegro' types in common time, the shift from passionate 'largo' and 'grave' movements to 'andante cantabile' or 'amoroso' for the more serious moments of the drama, the triadic and sequential melodic style as a whole. As can be seen, and as we know so well from his concertos, Vivaldi was one of the inventors of these things. With his instrumental achievements, he was more or less unrivalled in Venice; but in opera, he was only one of a larger group – quite different from the period of 1713–18, when he represented an alternative to the older composers like Pollarolo or Lotti.

I nevertheless regard *La verità in cimento* as the high point of this 'Venetian alternative': Vivaldi stands out by relying entirely on his own artistic resources. Soon after, he had to start learning from others in order to remain 'alla moda'. The opera is also aesthetically and culturally different from some by Orlandini, for example: with Giovanni Palazzi, the librettist of *Armida al campo d'Egitto*, Vivaldi provides a light and picturesque entertainment in oriental fashion, where amorous intrigue ranks higher than the aristocratic values of *onore* and *fortezza*, much to the delight of the increasing middle-class audience in the cheaper Venetian theatres. Vivaldi's effort to recapture this market is also evident in the insertion of intermezzi, although he did not compose them himself (*L'avaro*, which went with *La verità*, was almost certainly composed by F. Gasparini).

Benedetto Marcello's *Il teatro alla moda* strikes out against this type of theatre with uncanny precision. Everything he says about the musical practice is so exactly matched by the evidence of the scores, that we cannot help accepting his satirical descriptions of theatrical life in general as essentially true. He knew Venetian opera-houses inside out, and he has said more about the musical style than most modern interpreters of his little book have been able to grasp. Even if the allusions of the famous frontispiece were not so specific, we could gather from the contents that Marcello criticised almost everything that was going on at the theatres of S. Moisè and S. Angelo. This means not only Vivaldi, of course, but Chelleri, Fiorè, Buini, and all the Bolognese singers as well. The frontispiece itself, which may have been conceived a little later than the actual text, certainly specifies its targets as the people involved in the productions of both these theatres at the time of publication: late in 1720. They were the impresario Orsati, the composers Vivaldi, Porta and, perhaps, Orlandini (the latter two working for the

S. Gio. Grisostomo during this season), the poet Palazzi, the singers Caterina Canteli, Caterina Borghi, Cecilia Belisani Buini (S. Moisè 1720/1) and Anna Maria Strada, Antonia Laurenti detta Coralli, and Chiara Orlandi detta la Mantovanina (rather than the composer Orlandini), working for Vivaldi at the S. Angelo. Notable absences are all poets and singers active at S. Gio. Grisostomo and S. Samuele, and – Domenico Lalli. Pursuing this line, we now discover that the policy of the S. Angelo changed with the beginning of Carnival, 1721. Although the singers, on contract for the whole season, were staying (in addition to the three mentioned names, Vivaldi had procured Antonia Merighi, Antonio Barbieri, and Girolamo Albertini, altogether a formidable cast), the three Carnival operas were strikingly different from *La verità*: the pastoral *Il pastor fido*, a new libretto by B. Pasqualigo for the *maestro di coro* at the Pietà, Carlo Pietragrua, the heroic *Filippo re di Macedonia*, newly written by Lalli in which Vivaldi had only one act, and – probably last in the season – a revival of Pasqualigo's and Orlandini's *Antigona*, taken over from S. Gio. Grisostomo. The aesthetic change is a drastic one, also considering the outmoded style of Pietragrua's *Pastor fido*, the score of which is preserved. I feel it is unlikely that Vivaldi himself would have suggested works by Lalli, Pasqualigo, and particularly Orlandini, his biggest rival; it is far more likely that he lost control of the theatre. He ceased to write operas for Venice for more than four years – the longest interruption of this kind in his career. We cannot help ascribing this, at least partly, to the effect of Marcello's satire (see also Talbot 1978, pp. 69f).

1721[2]

Vivaldi's only operatic *scrittura* for Milan should not be considered just as an exception. Birthday operas (28 August) for the Empress Elisabeth were not the regular routine at the Regio Ducal Teatro, and carried some ceremonial weight. The pastoral libretto, celebrating probably Elisabeth herself as a shepherdess, may have been known to Vivaldi before, from Vicenza. He collaborated with some of his more faithful singers, the Fabri couple and Margherita Gualandi, but also with the virtuoso of the Milanese governor Colloredo, Strada, who had just sung in *La verità*. The cast was quite different from the Milanese Carnival productions on either side, and shows Vivaldi's hand. In the same period, he produced an oratorio for Milan – my conclusion is that he was looking for an appointment there, using his connections with Habsburg via Landgrave Philip, and perhaps other patrons. When this came to nothing, he apparently stopped producing operas for more than a year – perhaps the surest sign that Vivaldi had lost influence in Venice, and had no other connections with Italian opera-houses to fall back upon.

1723¹–1724²

In Rome, however, a *scrittura* for Vivaldi was due sooner or later. The policy of the two major theatres named after their owner–impresarios, the Capranica and the Alibert, was decidedly eclectic, dealing out *scritture* to composers all over Italy. With the almost simultaneous withdrawal from the stage of three or four major 'Roman' composers – A. Scarlatti, G. Bononcini (who had gone to London), and F. Gasparini – but also with the end of C. F. Pollarolo's active career in 1722, Rome now abounded with younger composers of Neapolitan and northern extraction; it was the turn of Antonio Pollarolo, Predieri, Orlandini, Porpora, and, in 1724, Leonardo Vinci. It is against these composers that Vivaldi's 2⅓ opera scores of 1723 and 1724 have to be measured, and plenty of their music survives. It was probably good for Vivaldi's success that his *Ercole sul Termodonte* – an old-fashioned Venetian libretto – had to be compared more directly with the first opera of the Carnival 1723 at the Teatro Capranica, Benedetto Micheli's *Oreste*, a weak drama set by an almost unknown composer (set again by Handel in 1734). We know that in Roman opera-houses in particular, the first Carnival opera often went to the less renowned composer, and was less expensively staged; some subscribers attended the second Carnival opera only. Vivaldi seems to have made some impact: Quantz reported that he had introduced the so-called *stile alla lombarda* in Rome, which refers surely to its written form (semiquaver – dotted quaver), not to the manner of performance in this rhythm, which was well-known to singers. A. Scarlatti, at least, had used this rhythm in his *Trionfo dell'onore* in 1718. Pier Leone Ghezzi, the famous portraitist, made a drawing not only of Vivaldi himself (reproduced in Talbot 1978, opp. p. 101), but also of the opera singer Farfallino in 1723 (20 January) to which he added the inscription 'Farfallino [...] che cantò nell'opera del prete rosso nel Teatro d'Aliberti': thus, he knew Vivaldi by his Venetian nickname. He confused the theatres, as Vivaldi's *Ercole* was then being performed at the Teatro Capranica, where G. Fontana (Farfallino) sang, not at the Alibert. The patrons of the Capranica, who included friends of Francesco Gasparini, must have liked Vivaldi's music, for they invited him again in 1724 for a bigger share of the Carnival. In the first opera, Vivaldi only had to compose the second act, however – the third would have been the more honourable commission. I know nothing about Nicola Romaldo who wrote the third act of *La virtù trionfante degli amori, e degl'odii*. *Giustino*, one of Vivaldi's best efforts of the 1720s (the score contains the rhythm *alla lombarda*), again uses a drama of the Seicento in the adapted form given to it by Pietro Pariati in 1711; Handel set Vivaldi's text in 1737, but no one else did in that period. It is probable that Vivaldi, who had already shown some preference for old Venetian libretti with *L'incoronazione di Dario* and *Tito Manlio*, may in these cases have influenced the text choice. But the singers included, in both Roman seasons, the pupils of F. Gasparini, Giovanni Ossi and Girolamo Bartoluzzi, who must have been advised by their mentor not to fall into the trap of the modern singing style, as Gasparini puts it in a letter to P. F. Tosi in 1723. It is therefore unlikely that Vivaldi had much influence on the singers, although one of them was Antonio Barbieri in 1724; Carestini (at the beginning of his career) sang in 1723. By some coincidence, at the same time as *Giustino*, the Teatro Alibert produced Leonardo Vinci's *Farnace* on the newly written libretto of the Venetian Anton Maria Lucchini, and it must be assumed that Vivaldi heard the opera. The text version is largely identical to the one set by Vivaldi in 1727, but the music is ahead of Vivaldi in the terse and powerful text setting, if not in its use of the instruments.

1725[1]

Between *Giustino* and *L'inganno trionfante*, Vivaldi seems to have missed another year and a half of opera productions. But our documentation may not be complete; it is still possible to find other Vivaldian productions by comparing the contents of the many anonymous libretti from provincial opera-houses in that period. Unlike other gaps in Vivaldi's operatic career, however, the one of 1724/5 coincides with the total absence of any documentation on his activities. A simple answer could be that he was just too busy composing concertos for the Pietà, and for his opus 8, which was to appear late in 1725. But this can hardly have filled all his time from March 1724; also, the cantata production and the serenatas (the performance of *RV 687* has been dated by M. Talbot as 12 September 1725, in Venice)[7] need not have occupied him in 1724. Of the various possibilities to be considered, we have to return first to Vivaldi's well-known assertion that he spent three Carnivals in Rome 'a fare Opera'. 1725 was an *anno santo*, and the Roman opera-houses were closed, and there was no autumn season at all in Rome at this time, which also rules out the end of 1724 for opera productions. But thinking back to Vivaldi's sojourn in Milan, we remember that he followed the production of *La Silvia* of 1721 with an oratorio in 1722 – and the Christmas and Lent periods in 1724/5 in Rome certainly required music for sacred dramatic works: Talbot has also shown that the Manchester violin sonatas were composed for Cardinal Pietro Ottoboni at a date after 1724, and close to 1726 – why not in Rome, early in 1725? (The surviving manuscript could nevertheless have been presented to Ottoboni somewhat later, during his visit to Venice in 1726.) It is quite possible that Vivaldi's statement in the letter of 16 November 1737 really combines two different things: he had produced operas for three Roman Carnival seasons, i.e. 1720, 1723, and 1724, but he had *been* in Rome for three other seasons, i.e. 1723, 1724, and 1725. Secondly, it has been suggested that Vivaldi was in Venice in 1724/5, and had his hand in the first appearances of Anna Girò at the S. Moisè in that season. As mentioned above, the musical director of that season seems to have been the Cavaliere Antonio Gaspari, surely known to Vivaldi, who also sang in these operas himself. The remaining cast was surprisingly 'Vivaldian' with Chiara Orlandi, Stella and Angelo Canteli, Felice Novelli. Of the four operas produced at S. Moisè in that season, three are ascribed to Albinoni, Porta, and G. M. Buini, respectively; only *Il nemico amante* (Carnival 1725) was presented anonymously and, therefore, arranged perhaps by Vivaldi. But it would be atypical for him to have so small a share in a Venetian season, with a cast of his liking, and a befriended impresario (Orsati? He presented the same opera, under its original title *La pace per amore*, and therefore – perhaps – with the original music of Buini and Chelleri, in Vicenza in 1724, according to T. Walker). The third possibility is, of course, that Vivaldi was in Mantua early in 1725, where his *Artabano* was given. The other Carnival opera was none other than an *Orlando furioso* on Braccioli's text, but with music by the shadowy Orazio Pollarolo. This fact seems to me to speak not for but against Vivaldi's personal participation in this season, as he would have preferred to present his own music for *Orlando*; furthermore, of the several aria texts which were new in *Artabano* only one ('Sì vo' abbracciar') reminds of a Vivaldi setting ('Sì vo a regnar') of those years. The Mantuan impresario, Santo Burigotti, chose some singers also known to Vivaldi (Gaetano Fracassini, Angiola Zanuchi, Giovanna Gasperini), and provided intermezzi. A fourth consideration concerns the patron of Vivaldi's opus 8, the Bohemian count Wenzel Morzin. In the dedication, the composer says that he has served the count for several years in Italy – but where? Is it possible that they never met personally, not even at the moment of a presentation of the manuscript of opus 8 to the count? Curiously enough, the years 1724–6 also witness the first known export of Vivaldi's opera music to Bohemia: this was due to the composer Antonio Bioni, a protégé of Count Franz Anton von Sporck, who may have included arias by Vivaldi in his productions of Braccioli's *Orlando furioso* 1724, autumn, in Prague, and 1725 in Breslau (but apparently not 1724 in Kuckusbad), and to the singer–impresario Antonio Denzio, a Venetian like Bioni, who sang in these performances, and later formed his own opera troupe; he presented *L'innocenza giustificata* in the Carnival of 1725 in Prague, and *La tirannia gastigata* in the following Carnival, both definitely with arias by Vivaldi. *L'innocenza giustificata* was an opera by St. A. Fiorè, first performed 1720 at the Teatro della Pace in Rome (together with *Tito Manlio*, see above), and largely altered by Bioni. The long story of Vivaldi exports to Bohemia/Moravia can only be touched on here: his *Orlando furioso* plays an important part in these, and it is still performed, with attribution to the composer, 1735 in Brno. But there was also an *Orlando furioso* 1727 as far away as Brussels, where many Venetian operas and intermezzi were produced in the latter 1720s. The most important thing about the 'Bohemian troupes' seems the choice of singers, including Anna Maria Giusti, Lorenzo Moretti, and Paolo Vida di Capo d'Istria in 1724/5, and none other than the Cavaliere Antonio Gaspari in 1726; from c. 1730, one would regularly encounter, apart from Denzio, Anna Cosimi, Margherita Flora, even Chiara Orlandi (all three together in Brno under Angelo Mingotti) – singers hired by Vivaldi himself at times when they were back in northern Italy. Even Margherita Gualandi Campioli is said to have been in Prague from 1728–35 (*New Grove*). The most extended activity of these singers and impresarios from Italy in the main Habsburg lands occurred in the later 1730s, when even Anna Girò joined a Mingotti troupe (see below). That Vivaldi was somehow in touch with these troupes is quite clear, but the true nature of the connections over the years has not yet been analysed. I believe that it was difficult to obtain a complete opera score from Vivaldi for anyone without paying him, and it must also be remembered that all these impresarios and singers regularly substituted arias in their productions with more modern pieces, particularly by Hasse.

1725^2–1728^2

The longest uninterrupted period of Vivaldi's activity at the S. Angelo starts hesitantly. He was certainly not the impresario of the theatre, but he styles himself 'direttore della musica' in the contract with Lucrezia Baldini of autumn 1726,[8] and the fact that he signed the contract does show him in control of the theatre's musical affairs. In 1725/6 however, the conditions were apparently different from the following two seasons. The dedications of two libretti are signed by Antonio Biscione, the third (*Cunegonda*) has no dedication. The singers of this season were not connected particularly with Vivaldi's productions in general, which may mean that Vivaldi was not present when the contracts were made in autumn 1725, or had little influence. For *L'inganno trionfante in amore*, both the attribution to Vivaldi and the (doubtful) assertion that Ruggieri arranged Noris' text, seem to derive from Bonlini. The libretto does not contain a single aria text known to have been set by Vivaldi elsewhere. He may yet be the arranger, but the work was surely a pasticcio. *Cunegonda* shows the same characteristics, and in addition several texts known to have been set by Porta, Vinci, and Porpora, which are not part of the original Piovene libretto. The foreword of the libretto admits that some arias had to be inserted in such a hurry that their texts could not be adapted; the immediate model of the opera came from Milan. It may well have been a version of the famous setting of F. Gasparini, which was also used in Mantua 1718. We are on much safer ground with *La fede tradita* [...] (a very popular Silvani libretto) which is ascribed to Vivaldi, and dedicated to his patron Count Schulemburg. Only two arias of this work seem to survive; one wonders why none of the three operas of this season has been preserved in Turin. There was, in fact, a fourth opera at the S. Angelo – Antonio Pollarolo's *Turia Lucrezia* on a text by Lalli (Carnival 1726); I suggest that, as in 1721, Vivaldi was no longer in control of the theatre at the time this opera was being prepared. The inclusion of the other three operas in the first category of section 1 must be taken as a tentative one.

In 1726/7 and 1727/8, however, Vivaldi behaved exactly as he did in his early S. Angelo seasons. He had a cast according to his wishes, for the first time with Anna Girò (who did not sing in 1725/6 in S. Angelo nor, it seems, anywhere else), and with tenors and basses (Galletti, Pinetti). In 1727/8, Lucia Lancetti, excellent in male roles, helped save the expense for a first-rank castrato. Lorenzo Moretti, a good tenor, was just back from Prague in 1726. The continuity between the seasons is further strengthened by the revival of *Farnace* in autumn 1727, and an overall 'Vivaldian' continuity by the adaptation of *Orlando furioso*. Moreover, the old associates Palazzi and Lucchini provided two new libretti each, and Lucchini also gave his *Farnace*, written for Vinci in 1724. For all these reasons, Vivaldi's choice of the other composers matters – the insignificant Brusa, and the two beginners Pescetti and Galuppi. It seems clear by now that Vivaldi preferred to be surrounded by minor rivals in his own house. The two *scritture* from Florence and Reggio Emilia in 1727 are of slightly different kinds: in Florence, Vivaldi was probably allowed to hire singers, including Lucia Lancetti (or did he get to know her there?), but not Anna Girò.[9] He was less influential on the Metastasio production at the court theatre in Reggio, but this was a more honourable task, not only because of poet and theatre, but also because of the rest of the cast with Carestini and Signorini as castrati: Anna Cosimi then became acquainted with Vivaldi, and she sang her role in *Siroe* again for him in Ferrara 1739, after many 'Bohemian years'. Anna Girò was not hired in Reggio. Vivaldi *may* have suggested the libretti, known to him from Venetian operas in 1724 (*Ipermestra* by Giacomelli) and 1726 (*Siroe* by Vinci), but only the fact that he imitated Vinci's music in one aria is certain; the rest of his own music for *Siroe* is not preserved. I see also an influence of Vinci, and perhaps even Porpora, in *Farnace* and *Orlando*, but referring only to some individual arias: what has changed since 1720, is Vivaldi's cautious look for stylistic idioms which the audiences might like beside his own, particularly in the 'cantabile' and 'singing allegro' types – not, however, in the dramatically more central items of the drama.

1729[1]

When Vivaldi continued his collaboration with the Accademici Immobili in Florence, it must be remembered that he was not their major composer: this was Vinci, four operas of whom were given at the Pergola between 1728 and 1730. But Vivaldi must have been eager to maintain this connection; in *Atenaide* (Zeno's libretto cannot have appealed to him very much), he was at last able to procure the post of a *seconda donna* for Anna Girò, second to the Florentine Giustina Turcotti.

1730[1]*–1731*[1]

The evidence for Vivaldi's travelling to Vienna and Bohemia in these years is circumstantial, but strong enough. Shortly after his father had asked for leave from S. Marco on 30 September 1729, they must have left – in time to be present at an operatic venture that might be staged in those lands. Vivaldi would have been unwise not to take his *Atenaide* score into Zeno's realm, and may have tried to have it performed in Vienna or elsewhere in the princely theatres of the area. The city opera-house of Vienna near the Kärntnertor was at that time busy with arrangements, mostly as pasticci, from Italian scores, whereas the court theatre was inaccessible for anyone not in Imperial employment; aria texts typical of Vivaldi in the Kärntnertor libretti are, however, rare before the later 1730s. The composer's relationships with Sporck's theatre in Prague are enigmatic. While we know about his links with the singers, and with Denzio himself, it does not appear that Vivaldi assisted in any of the performances about 1730–2 except for *Argippo*; but he must have delivered a great amount of music to Denzio, probably even complete scores, particularly of *Farnace*, *Dorilla in Tempe*, and *Doriclea* (performed 1732), which were then adapted by others. This was not Vivaldi's usual method; it seems that he had a special arrangement with Denzio who may have paid him well. We can exclude the possibility that Anna Girò went with him abroad: she sang in three operas by other composers in Milan and Venice early in 1730, but not in Prague in 1730/1. Had the two been together at any time during either period, we would have documentation of Girò singing a Vivaldi role. The adaptations made by others of Vivaldi's *Artabano* as *L'odio vinto dalla costanza*, and *Armida*, in Venice 1731, show his absence from Venice more conclusively than the Prague adaptations of 1730 and 1732 show it. No engagement of Girò is known for the season 1730/1: so much did she now depend on the composer.

1731²–1732³

Vivaldi was back in Italy by the spring of 1731 – but no evidence shows
him to be back in Venice before 1733. If he tried to re-enter the S. Angelo
business for the season of 1731/2, his failure would be conspicuous, as operas
by Pescetti and Porpora were performed then, with a cast rather
uncharacteristic for his tastes (three singers came from Florence, however).
But it seems that Vivaldi deliberately sought his fortunes elsewhere. The
libretto of the *Farnace* in Pavia, which corresponds closely to the score
Giordano 36, was first used by J. W. Hill, who describes some of the
arrangements made in it for Anna Girò;[10] among the other singers were
Antonio Barbieri and his wife, Livia Bassi, besides Gaetano Fracassini, and
two new singers who later worked for Vivaldi again, Rosa Cardina of Venice
and Pietro Mauro 'detto il Vivaldi', who even took over the title role in
the revival of this opera 1737 in Treviso, when Margherita Franchi, known
to us from Prague productions, sang the *primadonna* role and signed a
dedicatory sonnet. We have in Pavia a very closely knit group of earlier or
incipient Vivaldi supporters; as the libretto mentions the composer with
three titles, including the new one of a *maestro di cappella* of the Viennese
Prince of Liechtenstein, one has to imagine Vivaldi freshly back from
Vienna. How he established the connection with Pavia, is unclear; but the
libretto is dedicated to the Countess Delfina del Carretto Visconti, and the
soprano Rosa Cardina carried the nickname 'la Dolfinetta' (which could
refer, of course, to the Dolfin family of Venice). Cardina had sung in S.
Angelo in 1730/1, alongside Giovanna Gasperini, Giuseppe Alberti and
other singers somehow connected with Vivaldi. It seems that Vivaldi, before
his departure in 1729, had had a chance to influence the choice of singers
for the next S. Angelo seasons, and that these, besides performing his *L'odio
vinto* in the Carnival of 1731, helped him in turn when he came back. The
Mantua season of 1731/2, and even the *scrittura* for *La fida ninfa*, could
have been prepared from abroad: an aria collection in Dresden contains
settings of texts which belong to both these operas. Whereas the *Fida ninfa*
texts are original in Scipione Maffei's libretto, those of the Mantuan
Semiramide are probably substitute arias, and could have been intended for
a different work, before they were performed in Mantua. The Dresden
collection is possibly a set of pieces of the kind which Vivaldi sold to Denzio
or a similar impresario, in order to make an arrangement from them; it could
thus be dated c. 1731. The watermarks (not necessarily the copyist's hands)
may show whether the set was copied in Italy or not. The *Farnace* of Mantua
includes alterations first made for Pavia (substitute aria 'Eroi del Tebro').
The Mantuan cast includes intermezzi specialists; otherwise, many of the
singers in Mantua and Verona are those usually connected with Vivaldi;
Anna Girò did not sing in *La fida ninfa* however, which makes that

production a clear *scrittura*, unless one argues that she could not attend both Carnival productions at the same time.

1733¹–1734²

Similar to 1725/6, Vivaldi did not gain complete control over the whole S. Angelo season on his return. The three first operas, from the autumn, are certainly his – although *Dorilla* was a pasticcio – but a fourth opera (I do not know the order of the Carnival operas) was *La Candalide* by Albinoni. In this respect too the season is similar to 1725/6, as well as the similar gap of production from Carnival 1732 to autumn 1733. The interesting aspect is the departure of Anna Girò from the cast after the autumn opera; she was replaced by the good contralto Anna Caterina dalla Parte as *primadonna*. Such changes were very rare at the time, and this one suggests not only that the contract was broken, but possibly some problem between Vivaldi and his foremost singer. She sang, as *primadonna*, in Giacomelli's *Lucio Papirio dittatore* in Verona instead, precisely the place she could not go in 1732. But it was, perhaps, a result of her success there, that Vivaldi could actually run the next Verona Carnival, 1735, as impresario. The S. Angelo season of 1733/4 also saw other changes in cast: the German singer Giuseppa Pircher, 'virtuosa d'Armstadt', also departed after *Motezuma*, and in *Candalide* Rosa Cirili (Cirillo?) replaced Dalla Parte as *primadonna*. The new German bass, Massimiliano Miler, stayed, however, and also the two soprano castrati, Mariano Nicolini and Francesco Bilanzoni, both young and with modern training. The former had been used by Vivaldi in Mantua 1732; the latter was known in Venice since 1730, but came from Naples. Vivaldi seems to have wanted to go in new directions, which is also suggested by his choice of Metastasio's libretto; this was the third known performance of *L'Olimpiade*, and the second in Italy (after Genova). *Dorilla* contained at least ten arias not by Vivaldi, mostly by Hasse and Giacomelli; its libretto was printed by Bettinelli, who inserted an advertisement for his new edition of Metastasio's *Poesie drammatiche*, which by then already included *L'Olimpiade*, given special preference by the author.

1735¹–1735²

Such policies are clearly continued in the Verona Carnival 1735, where Vivaldi signed both libretti as impresario. He must have had a completely free hand in these productions, and even took the unusual step of recommending the second opera, *Adelaide*, to the audience as of particular patriotic interest: does it then shed a light on his own political views that this very opera text had originated in honour of a German prince (the Bavarian elector, in 1722), and actually celebrated German rule over Italy?

In artistic matters, it may be noted that Vivaldi left the *tragedia per musica Tamerlano* textually intact (the drama has a thinly disguised *lieto fine*), but also that it was a pasticcio with arias by modern composers such as Hasse and Giacomelli, the texts of which were adapted in the score by Vivaldi himself – on the other hand, the score contains an unusual number of the old-fashioned continuo arias, perhaps to save rehearsal time. The cast of the two operas is equally eclectic: besides Girò and the rather old contralto Pieri, there were the usual tenor and bass, a high female soprano (Giacomazzi) and two high soprano castrati – Pietro Morigi sang arias from Farinelli's repertoire, and Giovanni Manzuoli was one of the most brilliant high sopranos of decades to come; he cannot yet have been twenty. The distribution must have worked out very well in *Tamerlano*, where Pieri sang the male title role, while the tenor Mareschi sang Bajazet, the heroic loser of this plot so unforgettably shaped by Gasparini and by Handel. It is a strange coincidence that the distribution of voices is almost the same as that used by Handel in 1724. The Verona season included *balli*, which Vivaldi often preferred to intermezzi in his later years.

1735³

So much is known about this production that two remarks may suffice here. First, Vivaldi composed for a Grimani theatre for the first time, and that with the blessing of Lalli, who was – for him – certainly more important than Goldoni. But he must have needed a reconciliation, or new association, with the opera aesthetics of the Grimani theatres, and made good use of that later on when he sold two arranged Hasse scores to Ferrara, which came from Grimani. One should not therefore assume that he was particularly interested in Imer's and Goldoni's comedians and intermezzi at S. Samuele. Second, the style, and the working method of *Griselda* are eclectic and even pasticcio-like, although all the music is Vivaldi's own. He borrowed from himself; in some arias, the style is in a sense borrowed from Leo and Hasse. (Goldoni borrowed several lines from Metastasio's *Demofoonte*, when he extemporised Girò's aria text 'Ho il cor già lacero').[11] Goldoni's insertion of many 'simile' arias cannot be sufficiently explained with the requirements of Anna Girò; they are a true modernisation of Zeno's old libretto, and gave the composer his only chance to write modern orchestral pieces in his best concerto manner without reverting to the Hasse idiom.

1735⁴

The circumstances of this strange libretto need further investigation, which could help us to clarify the question of Vivaldi's supposed intermezzi of 1735/6, because the same *compagnia di comici* (of Giuseppe Imer) is involved. I suspect that Vivaldi had nothing to do with any of these works. If the only eight musical numbers of *Aristide* are by Vivaldi, then they may well be borrowed or bought from him; some are obviously parody texts anyway. In the form presented by the libretto, *Aristide* is more an intermezzo than an opera.

1736[1]

The rather old libretto by Salvi, first set by Perti for Pratolino in 1708, was perhaps thought fit for the Florentine audience who had seen the piece several times (as had the Venetians). Vivaldi had *balli*, but with the exception of Anna Girò an execrable cast (Natalizia Bisagi, for instance, had been tolerated by the Neapolitans as an intermezzo singer for only one month). But Vivaldi apparently liked Ariosto, and also the late Dottor Salvi; *Ginevra* could have represented a musical effort for him which he regarded suitable for a spring production in Lucca 1736, which was planned but not realised (according to a communication by M. Talbot); in the following Carnival, Vivaldi did offer the opera to Ferrara, and got it initially accepted.

1737[1]–1737[2]

This season, and the subsequent Ferrara productions of Vivaldi have recently been much discussed in the light of his own most instructive letters.[12] From them, we learn still more about the composer's own operatic practices, and also about those of his time in general. There is, for instance, the fact that Hasse's two scores were kept at 'Cà Grimani' by the owner of S. Gio. Grisostomo himself, Michele Grimani, that it was difficult and expensive to borrow them for copying, and also that different prices were due for copied, arranged, and newly written opera scores, to which Vivaldi adds the category of scores which can 'count as newly made', i.e. arranged! Although he points out his labour with the recitatives, all of which have to be changed because the voices in the original scores differed from those hired by the Ferrarese impresario – an important technicality indeed – and says that he has given 'moltissime arie mie' to the singers of *Demetrio*, there is no hint of envy about the preference given by the Ferrarese gentlemen to the famous music of Hasse. They knew, it seems, that they could get the Hasse scores through Vivaldi, who shows himself closely in touch with Michele Grimani: a very new situation in Venetian operatic politics. Vivaldi held three rehearsals (with the singers) in Venice for *Demetrio*, which was easy as Anna Girò, Rosa Cardina, and probably Elisabetta Moro were available there. The contact with his singers must have been much more continuous than the actual performance dates suggest, and very often he may have prepared his operas for theatres outside Venice in his own house. The cast of *Demetrio* (and, surely, *Alessandro nell'Indie*) has five women among six singers: the absence of castrati helped save expense as usual, but contrasts sharply with *Tamerlano*, for instance. Hasse may have known of the use of his scores; he lived then mostly in Venice and revised his *Alessandro nell'Indie* of 1736 again in 1738, both times for the S. Gio. Grisostomo. (I would like to point out that I recognised Hasse's authorship of both scores – before the attributed libretto of *Demetrio* was discovered – simply by *not* ignoring the major trends of the operatic world of those years, as also Vivaldi did not, but some Vivaldi scholars still do today.)

1737[3]

One of Vivaldi's letters (of 3 May 1737) reports the success of his *Catone in Utica*,[13] helped by the *balli* more than by the intermezzi, and offers a similar opera to Ferrara for the summer, when *ballerini* are cheaper. This similar opera should be composed 'peraltro in parte d'altre teste'. By implication, *Catone* was completely his own composition, unless one applies the expression 'simile opera' to *Catone* itself, which seems linguistically just possible. The music of this work is one of Vivaldi's major efforts although the cast was not much better than that of Ferrara 1737. He should not be criticised too much for having had the tragic ending altered, as many predecessors had tampered with this particular ending before, including Metastasio himself.

1738[1]–1738[3]

Vivaldi's last Carnival season at the S. Angelo: he was in charge of all three operas, but the production of autumn 1737, Lampugnani's *Ezio*, was under a different *impresa* and has a completely different cast! Difficult negotiations may have led to such an unusual arrangement, which had happened before only in the case of Albinoni's *Candalide* in 1734. Otherwise, Vivaldi's season follows some earlier patterns: one work seems completely his own (*L'oracolo*), the other two are pasticci, but have dedications, both to German patrons, the second (*Rosmira*), signed by Vivaldi, to the Margrave of Brandenburg-Bayreuth. One singer of the season, Giacomo Zaghini, was a virtuoso of the margravine, Wilhelmine, sister of Frederick the Great; she was a particular patron of opera, together with her husband (they favoured Hasse, of course), but she also wrote instrumental music in Vivaldi's style. The pasticcio score of *Rosmira* has been analysed by Ryom; Vivaldi's effort seems to become more and more perfunctory as he simply inserts aria copies wholesale, which could be had in copyist's fascicles on the open market. Again, the procedure has both aesthetic and economic relevance. *Rosmira* had *balli*, however, which was a considerable expense according to Vivaldi's letter of 3 May 1737 (see above), in Venice and during the Carnival season. That *Rosmira* includes an aria by Handel (from *Ezio*, 1732) is absolutely unique for Venetian productions of this decade. A glimpse at the surrounding events: Pergolesi's *Olimpiade* was given at S. Gio. Grisostomo in the autumn of 1738, in which Antonio Barbieri sang together with Faustina Bordoni. It is true that the best singers had left Vivaldi in recent years, although he could still enroll the good soprano Margherita Giacomazzi.

1738⁴–1739³

The last productions include the interesting *Siroe* of Ancona, almost certainly a pasticcio (aria texts come from *Olimpiade* and other Metastasian libretti), performed by Girò, by the later very famous Catterina Fumagalli, and by one of the 'Bohemian' singers, Lorenzo Moretti. It is possible that the Margherita Campioli of the title role was no other than former Margherita Gualandi Campioli. Also in the *Siroe* of Ferrara 1739, we find one of the 'Bohemians', Anna Cosimi. This production was quite different from the Ancona one; it has other substitute arias, though from similar sources, and Anna Girò, in particular, now almost never sang arias that were newly composed, but repeated her earlier successes. J. W. Hill has shown that she also sang in the opera *Attalo, re di Bitinia* by Hasse,[14] which was the 'opera 2ᵃ' of the Ferrarese Carnival 1739. The evidence of Vivaldi's letters, which prove that he was not allowed to go to Ferrara for his planned two productions, and the fact that his proposal for the second one, *Farnace*, was rejected, indicate that *Attalo* replaced *Farnace*. It is easy to conclude that Vivaldi provided this Hasse score, too, as he had in 1737. This work had been composed for Naples in 1728, and never been given since (although Handel exploited it for pasticci), but the only surviving copy in the Biblioteca Marciana is by a Venetian copyist. *Feraspe*, about which almost nothing is known, looks like a normal *scrittura* – the only one in this season. But there is another possibility: the *faccio fede* for *Tito Manlio* of 27 January 1739 may be dated *more veneto*, which would mean that Vivaldi attempted to provide operas for the whole 1740 season. The three that were performed were by Pescetti, Casali, and by Hasse – his *Demetrio* under the title of *Cleonice*. Hasse was in Dresden in this Carnival season, where he produced the same work on 8 February. He is also not likely to have worked for the S. Angelo then. Somebody revived his *Demetrio* in Venice – why not Vivaldi? The singers of this season (the same from autumn to Carnival) were young and cheap enough for a Vivaldi production, although including Caterina Fumagalli. The question must be left open; uncertainty arises from the fact that, at this stage of Vivaldi's career, any opera produced by him is quite likely to be composed by Hasse. For this same reason, we have to exclude, however, a few productions given in Austria since 1738 by the Mingotti troupe, which include a *Rosmira* and a *Catone*. All these are pasticci full of Hasse arias; a connection with Vivaldi is that he himself would have produced this kind of pasticcio then. One could say that the Mingottis of Venice had learned the technique partly from him. Vivaldi's influence on these opera troupes must have been enormous. They toured the Veneto with *Orlando furioso* and *Farnace*, and the Habsburg lands with Hasse pasticci (I am not sure who gave Hasse's *Alessandro nell'Indie* 1740 in Verona); the casts hired by the Mingottis look sometimes like those of a genuine Vivaldi production, for instance the *Rosmira* of Graz, autumn 1739: Marianna Pircher, Dorotea Loli, Giuseppe Alberti, Margherita Flora, and – Anna Girò. She had left Venice in 1739 in order to join these troupes, as several ageing Vivaldi prima donnas had done before her. Was it on an understanding with the composer? She certainly kept singing his arias, as J. W. Hill has shown. But none of these singers had good chances of further engagements in Venice at this time. It is only logical that the composer–arranger–impresario himself followed his singers to the North, when his chances expired, too. The opportunities for writing ceremonial serenatas for visiting princes in Venice, and even the successful trip to Amsterdam in 1738, apparently did nothing to distract him from his lifeline as an opera producer, nor from the realistic assessment that his last chance lay with Habsburg. I suggest he had watched the successes of the Mingotti troupe, but thought he could find an even better base at the Kärntnertortheater in Vienna, next to which he took residence in 1740 or early in 1741. The sudden death of the Emperor, and the outbreak of the war with Prussia, must have destroyed his hopes for a court position. But he must have initiated a performance of his *Oracolo in Messenia* which took place after his own death, in the Carnival of 1742. It was on a libretto by Zeno: Vivaldi's sense of purpose comes to light even posthumously.

Vivaldi never led an opera troupe. But he was not a *scrittura* composer either, nor for any length of time a court official. This distinguishes him from the histrionic sphere of the Buinis, Bionis, Denzios, Mingottis, on the one hand, but also from Hasse, Vinci, Giacomelli, Albinoni, Porpora, on the other. He relied on the impresario system, based in a central theatre, with a continuous rotation of contracts, scores and styles. This flexibility, or eclecticism, which he learned in the early 1720s and increased afterwards, is of a wider historical significance: it reflects the increasing disorientation of the Venetian opera composer under pressure from the south, but also the scruples of the older contemporary who could not produce the same modern idiom for any opera-house in the world as Hasse or Porpora could. And, his sense of independence pushed him to want to make profits with opera instead of waiting for salaries. This has certainly damaged the value of many of his later productions, but made him what he probably wanted to be: the best composer among the impresarios – the best impresario among the composers.

Handel's pasticci

THE ARTISTIC and scientific study of Handel's operas seems particularly relevant today. It is impossible at the present moment to foresee the place that these operas may yet come to occupy in our historical consciousness, but the more attention we devote to them the clearer it becomes just how remote we are from the operatic realities of that time.[1] One part of that reality is formed by Handel's pasticci: that is to say, the operas which he put together for the London stage from the works of Italian composers. Handel studies have hitherto paid small attention to these works, there being other more important problems to solve,[2] and the fact that the pasticcio is in itself a despised form provides a further explanation. Nevertheless the pasticcio form plays a by no means contemptible role not only in Handel but in the general history of Italian eighteenth-century opera.

The actual term *pasticcio* (literally pasty or pie) does not appear either on title-pages or in text-copies of Handel's day. What was meant was an opera or oratorio put together from the works of a number of different composers. It appears in this sense, and relating to the year 1725, in Quantz's autobiography.[3] Although it was probably in common use in Italy by that time, it must have struck the foreigner as strange. The concept is defined by two distinguishing features:

(1) The individual numbers (mostly arias) of the pasticcio are for the most part taken from their original contexts and put together to form a completely new entity. Pasticci are not to be confused with operas composed in the first place by several composers – generally a different one for each act – since in these 'shared' works all the numbers were originally designed for a single performance. In cases where an arranger modified an already existing opera by making additions that were exclusively his own, we should speak rather of an 'adaptation', since here again the numbers appear roughly in the same connection for which they were originally designed.

(2) The pasticcio includes music by a number of different composers. It often happened, even in the case of Handel, that a composer would introduce earlier arias of his own in a new context.[4] If these earlier pieces predominate, we may speak of a 'pasticcio of the composer's own works'.

164

The claim to single authorship, which can be made for such works, was important in the eyes of contemporaries.

We cannot discuss here the aesthetic problems connected with the whole concept of the pasticcio. It should simply be pointed out that there was no reason why a cleverly assembled pasticcio should be more lacking in musical or dramatic unity than a clumsily 'composed' opera.

In early eighteenth-century Italy, and in London too, no operatic performance was ever repeated exactly – on the same stage, by the same cast and for the same audience for which it was originally conceived. If, in other theatres, no composer capable of making a new arrangement could be found, recourse was taken either to rewriting or else to the practice of pasticcio. In provincial Italian theatres, and in London before Handel's time, local composers were commissioned to make a patchwork of arias by famous contemporaries rather than to contribute music of their own. Outstanding composers would arrange pasticci only under special conditions. Three such composers were Keiser, Vivaldi and Handel, and all three had a similar motive – the commercial success of a 'rewriting' or a pasticcio seemed as well guaranteed as that of a composition of their own, and the labour involved was noticeably less. Keiser and Vivaldi were both at times their own impresarios, and Handel, after 1729 at least, earned the same fee for an opera whether it was his own work or that of other composers (Deutsch, p. 235). In the years after 1729 he produced practically all his own pasticci; he provided one only for the (first) Royal Academy in 1725, and none at all before 1720.[5] The London tradition of pasticci, from which he had at first stood quite aloof, was actually continued by him when he was in sole command at the Haymarket Theatre.

The London operatic stage was, in its early days, provincial compared with, say, Rome, Venice or even Vienna, despite Handel – and certainly before his appearance. Until about 1720 the majority of operas performed in London were pasticci of Italian origin with contributions of varying dimensions by local musicians such as Clayton or Haym: before that date Handel had been the only composer to produce operas entirely his own. The music to which the London public was accustomed was pasticcio in character, the vernacular having been abandoned at the Haymarket at first partially and then, after 1710, completely. Obviously less attention was paid in London than elsewhere to understanding the actual plot of an opera and people were content not only to be ignorant of the language but even to tolerate arias with texts that were quite irrelevant to the actual situation.[6] It seems, however, that after about 1720, and under the influence not only of Handel but also of Bononcini and Rolli, an idea of the dramatic unity of an opera developed – something not necessarily incompatible with the form of the pasticcio – and even of musical balance and unity of style. In fact Giuseppe Riva, a friend first of Rolli and then of Metastasio, published in 1727 an English translation of his *Avviso ai compositori ed ai cantanti*, which surpasses even the Italian practice of the day in its ideas of musical and dramatic unity in opera (see Degrada). Between 1720 and 1728 the Royal Academy could command quite a number of composers capable of producing works entirely their own.

There was however one important reason for the popularity of the pasticcio form that remained quite unchanged, namely its perfect suitability as a vehicle for presenting new singers in favourite arias from their repertories; and the London public was always particularly ready to go half way to meet the wishes of Italian singers with big names. This certainly applied to Handel and the pasticci that he produced between 1730 and 1734. After that date he abandoned the pasticcio, with a single exception in 1737, whereas the Opera of the Nobility continued the tradition of importing Italian singers and putting on pasticci.

The present study is devoted to the nine pasticci of Handel's which answer, almost without exception, to the description given above. They are: *Elpidia* (1725), *Ormisda* (1730), *Venceslao* (1731), *Lucio Papirio Dittatore* (1732), *Catone* (1732), *Semiramide* (1733), *Caio Fabricio* (1733), *Arbace* (1734), and *Didone abbandonata* (1737). The scores of all nine have been preserved, as prepared either under his direction or in some cases with his own help. The majority of them are in the former Chrysander Collection of Handel conducting scores in Hamburg. Hans Dieter Clausen has presented a critical analysis of the collection.[7] This investigation of Handel's conducting scores – for this is what these so-called *Handexemplare* are – and the *Cembalopartituren*, or scores for the second harpsichordist, for the operas, pasticci and oratorios, has provided the most important evidence for the present essay. The chief weight of my arguments lies in the communication of the original settings used by Handel for his pasticci, and a catalogue of these will be found at the end of this article. The considerations immediately resulting from the bibliographical information fall roughly under three headings:

1. Biography. Handel produced pasticci in order to fill out his seasonal programmes with Italian operas designed to provide an additional attraction for his public. It may be possible to obtain more precise information on how he obtained original settings and on the part played in this by his agents in Italy and by London opera-collectors, as well as by the singers concerned.

2. Handel's general procedure in the matter of pasticci. The chief difference between this and his practice with regard to his own operas and also those of Italian and other London authors lies in the fact that, despite considerable irregularities, he made much less use of rewritings and additions of his own. In this matter the most important questions are still unanswered. Careful comparison of all these pasticci with their original models would still have to identify Handel's original contribution; and it would be necessary to compare his rewriting procedure with his treatment of his own works (a matter of great importance is the question of transpositions). There are many ways in which Handel's pasticcio procedure could be compared with that of, say, Keiser and Vivaldi; and we need to know much more about Handel's collaboration with his librettists.

3. *Handel's relation to the Italian opera of his day.* It is immediately clear that he had a preference for the music of Vinci, Hasse and Leo (in that order), while he chose his texts exclusively from Zeno (5), and Metastasio (4). It was Handel, and not the Opera of the Nobility, that was responsible for introducing to London the operas of the so-called 'Neapolitan School'. We still have much to learn, from the texts and scores known to have been familiar to Handel and used by him, about possible Italian stimuli for his own works; and a distinction must be drawn between works that he considered worth performing and those which actually stimulated his own compositions. Generally speaking it would seem that his objective esteem for Vinci and Hasse or Zeno and Metastasio was greater than the need he felt to adopt their manner himself.

Elpidia (1725)

L'Elpidia overo li rivali generosi had its first performance on 11 May 1725 at the Haymarket Theatre, and this was followed by eleven further performances before the end of the season (19 June 1725). The next season opened on 30 November 1725 with another performance, sung by a slightly different cast, and there were five performances between then and December 14.[8] The cast was as follows:

Belisario (bass): Giuseppe Maria Boschi
Olindo (mezzosoprano): Francesco Bernardi detto Senesino
Ormonte (alto): Andrea Pacini – later Antonio Baldi
Elpidia (soprano): Francesca Cuzzoni
Vitige (tenor): Francesco Borosini – later Luigi Antinori
Rosmilda (alto): Benedetta Sorosina[9] – later Anna Dotti.

Clausen has demonstrated that the score[10] belongs to the conducting scores and that *Elpidia* is thus one of the pasticci produced by Handel (Clausen, pp. 136ff).

The libretto of the first performance[11] gives Zeno as author of the text and 'Leonardo Vinci except some few songs by Signor Giuseppe Orlandini' as composer. The text is based on Zeno's *Rivali generosi* (first performed at Venice in 1697, with music by M. A. Ziani) in a much-adapted version. The adapter may have been Haym, who had also written three other texts that season after originals by Zeno and Salvi. The relatively precise naming of the composers in the libretto follows the practice of the (first) Royal Academy, whereas the composers' names are not given either in Handel's later pasticci or in his own works. As the conducting score lacks the Sinfonia and some cancelled arias, a number of printed aria collections of the time have to be used to fill in the gaps.[12] Handel and his adapter seem to have used not an earlier score of the *Rivali generosi* but Zeno's text, keeping only the dramatic skeleton, some of the recitatives and two duets, and dropping one character (Alarico) entirely. Handel may have newly composed the two duets and two accompanied recitatives from the original text, while the final duet (or quartet) and possibly the third accompanied recitative are taken from Vinci's *Ifigenia in Tauride* (1725). It also seems certain that Handel newly composed the *secco* recitatives. Even if he possessed the score of a previous setting, he could hardly have made use of it owing to the unusually drastic alterations in the text. In his later pasticci he rewrote the recitatives even when the text-alterations were less drastic, but by the standards of the day this hardly constituted a claim to authorship. It seems possible that Handel was also concerned in the sinfonia. The opening movement and a four-bar Adagio transitional passage come from Vinci's *Eraclea* (Naples, autumn 1724), but the final movement does not.[13] It is possible that the Sinfonia, in the form in which it has come down to us in *Elpidia*, is identical with the sinfonia in Vincis *Ifigenia*, which has not been preserved.

The text and music of most of the arias were taken by Handel from the latest and best-known operas given in the 1724/5 season at the Teatro S. Giovanni Grisostomo in Venice – Vinci's *Ifigenia* (seven arias and the final ensemble), Orlandini's *Berenice* (three arias) and Vinci's *Rosmira fedele* (six arias). These were distributed among the five singers Cuzzoni, Senesino, Pacini, Sorosina and Borosini in such a way that each had the arias of their Venetian counterparts with regard to voice-type and dramatic status. This had the double advantage of making transposition virtually unnecessary and also of satisfying each of the singers' ambition. Thus the rather mediocre contralto Sorosina could show her paces in two arias in which the famous Antonia Merighi had shone and, most important of all, Cuzzoni sang even in the first performance five arias that had been composed for her rival Faustina Bordoni. Haym managed to fit all these arias, virtually unchanged, to the text of Zeno's drama – Handel's later colleague, Giacomo Rossi, was obliged much more often to have recourse to parody – at the same time making the necessary adaptations in the text of the recitatives.

Even before the libretto was printed, an aria from *Berenice*, which Pacini was to have sung, was replaced by another that he had sung in 1724 in G. M. Capelli's *Venceslao*. He also introduced another aria from the same opera, though it had not been composed for him personally. After the publication of the libretto, three arias were added for the sixth member of the cast, the bass Boschi. Two of these are preserved in the score: they had originally been sung by Boschi in Lotti's *Teofane* (Dresden 1719).

A copy of the libretto in the British Library provides us with information about the remaining four unidentified arias, the composer's name having been added by hand above almost every number. Since in four out of seventeen cases these attributions are known to be wrong, the remainder are clearly not above suspicion.

When *Elpidia* opened the 1725/6 season, new singers took the place of Borosini (who returned to Vienna), Pacini and Sorosina. Only one of these, Anna Dotti, was already known to London audiences. It is significant that the new singers were not content simply to take over their predecessors' roles, but insisted on replacing a number of arias with others from their own repertory or that of more famous colleagues in order to introduce themselves to the public with renewed interest. Senesino and Cuzzoni each took the opportunity to sing an additional – not an alternative – aria. Cuzzoni's *aria aggiunta* was taken from Faustina's latest repertory and the score shows where the addition was made, whereas in Senesino's case we do not know the origin of the additional aria or where it was inserted.[14] There are two unusual points about *Elpidia* as a pasticcio. The first is the inclusion of the latest arias from Venice, with preference for Leonardo Vinci who was then quite unknown in London; and the second is the clear distinction between the basic text and the provenance of the musical settings which must have complicated the task of the arranger. In Handel's later pasticci it was no longer his practice to make use of favourite arias from different operas belonging to a single season, though *Ormisda* shows the same clear distinction between basic text and musical settings. Vinci, however, remained Handel's favourite in the later pasticci.

Handel had probably nothing to do with the pasticcio *Elisa* produced on 15 January 1726. Apart from the libretto six arias printed by Walsh survive, bearing the handwritten note 'Porpora', as do two anonymous bass-arias included in a collection consisting otherwise of bass-arias by Handel.[15] Judging by the music, these latter are certainly not Handel's work (nor was the collection in the handwriting of J. Chr. Smith, as Chrysander believed); on the other hand seventeen of the twenty-five aria- and duet-texts in *Elisa* can be traced to operas written by Porpora between 1719 and 1725, and in a number of cases this is also true of the music. Porpora never actually composed an opera on the subject of *Elisa*, which is reminiscent of Zeno's *Scipione nelle Spagne*; as the arias are drawn from at least eight of some of his less famous works, whoever arranged the music (Ariosti?) must have known the composer personally. It was Nicola Haym who arranged the text of *Elisa*, Handel collaborating with Rolli during this season. Since Handel's *Scipione* (performed on 12 March 1726), with text by Rolli, is based on a similar subject, what we have is something approaching undeclared warfare between Handel and Porpora, both providing operas with similar themes – a remarkable anticipation of the well-known events of the season of 1733–4.

Handel's travels 1729 and the pasticcio *Ormisda* (1730)

Between the provisional ending of the Royal Academy in June 1728 and the reopening of the theatre on 2 December 1729 Heidegger and Handel each made a journey to the continent. The only evidence for Heidegger's journey is a letter of Rolli's dated 21 December, no year given but certainly belonging to 1728 (Deutsch, pp. 229f); in it we learn that Heidegger is back from his travels, has heard Farinelli and is full of his praise, yet has re-engaged Cuzzoni, Faustina and Senesino. Farinelli was singing at Munich (in Torri's *Nicomede*) in October 1728, but may have been in Venice from December preparing for the Carnival season there. It is not known where Heidegger met him.

On 18 January 1729 Handel attended the meeting of the Academy at which a new contract was drawn up with him and Heidegger. Contrary to Chrysander's supposition this assured him the use of the Haymarket Theatre not only until 1733, but for five years, so that he could count in advance on five seasons, including that of 1733/4.[16] With this in mind he made his own, very well attested journey (Deutsch, pp. 236ff) and not only engaged singers for the 1729–30 season but also collected a number of scores for performance, and libretti for his own use.[17] He will then have been planning to produce one new work – not by himself – in each of the five seasons. He departed from this plan for the first time in the 1733/4 season when not only *Semiramide*, but also *Caio Fabricio* and *Arbace* were given, the second composed in 1732 and the third in 1730. Handel may have collected most of the material for the five other pasticci as early as 1729. In what follows I shall be mentioning a number of operas, the text and some of the music of which Handel collected in Italy for use in London, as well as the names of singers whom he engaged either immediately or later. These facts, taken in conjunction with the documents in our possession, enable us to identify the stages of Handel's visit to Italy. He made straight for Venice, where he met not only Senesino but also Farinelli, whom he was able to hear in Leo's *Catone in Utica* at the Teatro S. Giovanni Grisostomo. Farinelli's appearance raised problems for the rival theatres,[18] including S. Cassiano, where Orlandini's *Adelaide* was being given with Faustina Bordoni, Senesino and Domenico Annibali (who was engaged for London in 1736). Handel used some of the music of *Adelaide* in *Ormisda* (though not until 1730/1) and the text for his own *Lotario* (2 December 1729). Among scores and libretti of earlier productions, *Ezio* (Metastasio/Porpora), *Argeno* (Leo) and *Ormisda* (Cordans) of 1728 and *Orlando furioso* (Braccioli/Vivaldi) of 1727 may all have been available.[19]

A letter of Handel's dated 28 February (= 11 March) shows him still in Venice (Deutsch, p. 239), but he was planning a visit to Naples and also a further meeting with Senesino (on his return journey, in Siena),[20] though this last did not materialise. In Naples Handel witnessed a quarrel between Carestini on the one hand and Bernacchi and Merighi on the other, which resulted in the cancellation of an opera that had been planned for the spring season at S. Bartolomeo,[21] Carestini going off to Venice and Bernacchi to Parma. All three had been singing in Hasse's Carnival opera *Ulderica*, which Handel cannot have heard as Ash Wednesday fell that year on 9 March, though he may have met Hasse himself who in 1729 was living in Naples, not Venice. Also in Naples at the same time were the theatre architect Aurelio del Pò and his wife Anna Maria Strada, who before her marriage had appeared in Venice, Milan, Livorno, Lucca and Naples (1719–26), as well as the *buffo*-soprano Celeste Resse.[22] Among other Neapolitan operas that may have aroused Handel's interest were *Gerone* (Hasse, 1727), *Siroe* (Metastasio, Sarri, 1727), *Attalo* (Hasse) and *Flavio Anicio Olibrio* (Vinci) of 1728, as well as Hasse's new *Ulderica*. Mainwaring (p. 113) gives details of a visit of Handel's to Rome which may have taken place on his return journey from Naples, probably about the time of Holy Week. Carlo Scalzi had taken part in two Carnival operas, and Rome was also the home of Francesca Bertolli (we know of no engagement in 1729, but she had sung at Livorno and Bologna in 1728). Handel probably met her personally, as it was her appearance rather than her voice or her acting that would explain her being engaged for London.[23] Among Roman productions of recent years Handel was later to make use of the following: *Faramondo* (Gasparini, 1720), *Giustino* (Vivaldi, 1724), *Didone abbandonata* (Metastasio/Vinci, 1726), *Semiramide riconosciuta* (Metastasio/Vinci, 1729), *Arianna e Teseo* (Pariati/ Leo, 1729). In May 1729 Handel can hardly have missed visiting the only outstanding opera-house outside Venice – Parma – which was then producing a new work. This was Giacomelli's *Lucio Papirio Dittatore* – with Farinelli, Bernacchi and La Faustina – which Handel produced at the Haymarket on 23 May 1732, using a score that had been compiled in Parma on 15 May 1729 (see below). Bernacchi may have been engaged in Parma after Handel's last vain attempt to get Farinelli. It was not until early July that the rumour spread in Bologna, Bernacchi's native city, that he was to be paid 1500 louis d'or to go to England (Frati, p. 478). Rolli's letter of 16 May says nothing about Bernacchi's engagement, but speaks of the Fabri couple (the husband, Annibale Pio Fabri, was singing at the beginning of 1729 in the Teatro della Pergola, Florence) and of an Italian-German bass.[24] Could Handel have been in contact with Riemschneider earlier than May 1729? If so, he would have had no reason for visiting Hamburg.

Of the operas used by Handel, the following came from Parma – Capelli's *Venceslao* (1724), Vinci's *Medo* (1728) and R. Broschi's *Bradamante nell'isola d'Alcina* (Carnival 1729) which had in fact already been given in Rome as *L'isola d'Alcina* the year before (see also p. 70). Handel could not have gone from Rome to Parma without passing through Bologna and there, beside Bernacchi, lived the Fabri couple and the Pinacci-Bagnolesis, although of course Handel did not necessarily obtain Orlandini's famous *Ormisda* (Bologna, 1722) in its actual place of origin. We have no further information about the course of Handel's Italian travels based on evidence of this kind.

The pasticcio *Ormisda* was given at the Haymarket on 4 April 1730 with the following cast:

Arsenice (soprano): Anna Maria Strada
Ormisda (tenor): Annibale Pio Fabri
Arsace (contralto): Francesca Bertolli
Erismeno (bass): Riemschneider
Palmira (contralto): Antonia Merighi
Cosroe (mezzosoprano): Antonio Bernacchi; later Francesco Bernardi detto Senesino

Zeno's *Ormisda* had first been performed, with Caldara's music, on 4 November 1721 in Vienna. Handel probably used a second setting by Orlandini (Bologna, Teatro Malvezzi, May 1722) as his basic model. There is a mistaken belief that the pasticcio is based on B. Cordans' opera (Venice 1728), of which Handel may have seen the libretto, though he took nothing from it that he could not just as well have taken from Orlandini's version. The ascription to Francesco Conti is another error. Although the conducting score of *Ormisda* has no ascription, the harpsichord score[25] bears the heading: *Ouverture del S^r. Conti*. This can only refer to the overture and even that is not certain. The overture is in any case not the first that Handel intended for the work: a sinfonia copied into both scores, and then cancelled, is in fact by Vinci. The first movement can be traced to his *Gismondo* (Rome 1727), while the second appears in only one of his Neapolitan oratorios, which Handel can hardly have known.[26] The two together may have formed the Sinfonia (lost today) to Vinci's *Flavio Anicio Olibrio* (Naples, December 1728). Handel probably used the recitatives from Orlandini's setting, which are largely identical in text, though he took no more than four arias, at most. All these four occur in Bernacchi's part, and he had in fact sung them in 1722 when he played Cosroe. Although Orlandini's authorship is not confirmed by direct source-evidence in the case of all four arias (Handel's copies do not contain the music of 'Fia tuo sangue') it can be indirectly inferred. Handel took all the remaining arias from other operas. Both Fabri and Merighi, as well as Bernacchi, contributed arias from their own repertories. All three were confident and experienced singers who would certainly travel with copies – even in score – of the most important and popular arias in their repertories and might well urge these on Handel. Maria Strada was more dependent on Handel's own supply, though she had in fact sung the aria 'Se d'aquilon' in an opera of Porpora's in 1724. An English copy of this aria, however, bears not only her name but that of the opera *Siface*,[27] and we know that in Porpora's *Siface* in 1726 the aria had again been sung, but not by La Strada! Handel was in fact giving her back her own aria. The identification of the arias in *Ormisda* is partly based on ascriptions in London copies of these arias the majority of which are now in the Brussels Conservatoire.[28] There are no ascriptions in the score of the pasticcio itself, with the exception of the overture, although the composers of at least six of the arias were known in London. Handel may well have got to know them from individual copies that he found in London. *Ormisda* aroused great public interest and had fourteen performances in the first season, twice as many as Handel's own *Partenope*. Very soon after the first performance Walsh printed eleven *Favourite Songs* (Smith 1970, pp. 46f), but these did not include the alternative songs introduced into later performances of the pasticcio. Additions to the conducting score and the harpsichord-score make later exchanges clear. Even before the first performance Vinci's sinfonia was replaced by the one ascribed to Conti, a short sinfonia was added during the course of the first act as was Riemschneider's aria, which also appears in the libretto. Most of the later additions date from the benefit performance for La Strada, which took place on 21 April. On this occasion she was given, among other things, a new final aria, which appears as *The last song*. This practice was to become common in Handel's later pasticci which give the chief character a rousing *aria finale*, contrary to the normal Italian practice of the day. This final aria replaced the concluding *coro*. In the British Library copy of the libretto (11714 aa 20), the arias inserted later are printed by themselves, though not all of them date back to the performance on 21 April as is stated.[29] In fact three of the arias come from Orlandini's *Adelaide*, from which Handel had used nothing as early as the 1729/30 season; in *Adelaide* they were sung by Senesino and are here substituted for Bernacchi's. Doubtless *Senesino* had the arias included when he took over Bernacchi's part in the revival of *Ormisda*, which took place on 24 November 1730, and was followed by four more performances.

Partly at the singers' suggestion, Handel included in the version of *Ormisda* that dates back to 1722 thirteen arias from more recent works by Orlandini, Hasse, Vinci, Giacomelli, Sarri and Leo. This involved parody in a number of the aria-texts, as was not the case in *Elpidia*. Since 1729 Handel was able to call on Giacomo Rossi, author of the text of *Rinaldo* for work of this kind (Deutsch, p. 345).

Venceslao (1731)

The first performance of *Venceslao* took place at the Haymarket Theatre on 12 January 1731. As we learn from the *Opera Register*, the work was a failure[30] and taken off after the fourth performance on 23 January. (Handel's *Poro* did not take its place until 2 February.) We possess the conducting score, the harpsichord score and the libretto of *Venceslao*, and seven *Favourite Songs* published by Walsh.[31] We can reconstitute the cast, although it is not given in the libretto.

Venceslao (tenor): Annibale Pio Fabri
Lucinda (alto): Antonia Merighi
Casimiro (mezzosoprano): Francesco Bernardi detto Senesino
Erenice (soprano): Anna Maria Strada
Ernando (alto): Francesca Bertolli
Alessandro (bass): Giovanni Commano
Gismondo (bass): Giovanni Commano

Apostolo Zeno's drama *Venceslao*, on which the pasticcio is founded, has seven characters. As we learn from Handel's correspondence with his Italian agents during 1730, he had been looking for a replacement for Bernacchi since June of that year and was finally obliged, against his will, to re-engage Senesino (Deutsch, pp. 256–62). The original plan to engage an additional female singer capable of appearing in both men's and women's roles was now abandoned. To replace Riemschneider Handel himself had recruited the bass Commano in London, although he could not be entrusted with any arias. In *Venceslao*, therefore, he contented himself with five aria-singers, entrusting both the subsidiary roles of Alessandro and Gismondo (who have only recitatives to sing) to Commano – in fact Alessandro is murdered in the course of Zeno's first act. In Handel's version he makes his last appearance in scene seven and is replaced by Gismondo from scene ten onwards.

Zeno's libretto had been performed some ten times in Italy between 1720 and 1730, in different settings. There are five acts in the original version. Although the adaptation by Handel and his librettist Rossi is in three acts, it keeps relatively close to the libretto set by G. M. Capelli in 1724 for Parma. It is not certain whether Handel also had a copy of Capelli's score.[32] Only one aria in the conducting score is by Capelli and this ('Del caro sposo') could have been familiar in London as an isolated excerpt. Of two other arias by Capelli – 'Qual senza stella' and 'Vado costante a morte' – the former was probably planned and then dropped, and the latter seems to have been inserted at the last moment; both had already been included in *Elpidia* by the singer Pacini. Several other of Zeno's aria-texts, which Capelli had used, were given new music and parodied to a certain extent. Two arias with original texts ('Nel seren' and 'Balenar') and two accompagnato recitatives must come from another setting of *Venceslao*, most probably the pasticcio given in 1722 at the Teatro S. Giovanni Grisostomo in Venice, in which the five chief roles are given to the same voices as in Handel's version. It is also possible that Handel drew on the pasticcio *Venceslao* that was performed in London in 1717; although both text and music have disappeared, Handel's instrumentation of the accompagnato 'Correte a rivi', with bassoons, may point to an earlier London model. The origin of the sinfonia (though the final movement may be by Handel), the chorus and the secco recitatives is not clear – though Handel must have rewritten the recitatives in view of the considerable text-changes necessitated by the reduction of the drama from five acts to three. Proof of this is lacking, as in the cases of *Elpidia* and *Ormisda*, because both conducting score and harpsichord score are almost entirely the work of copyists. For the same reason it is not possible in either source to be certain what was added later. The two scores hardly differ from each other and were made at about the same time. There are almost no divergences in the libretto either, which was as usual printed only shortly before the performance. It is nevertheless possible more or less to reconstruct which arias must have been planned beforehand and which were only added during rehearsals. Thus Hasse's aria 'Lascia cadermi in volto' in the second act, for instance, was added later for Maria Strada,[33] while the aria that appears next, 'Del caro sposo' in G major, was transferred to the third act (the recitative-cadence has in fact been altered from the key of E to that of G). On the other hand 'Qual senza stella', which appears in Capelli's third act, may have been cut with its recitative, which had to be entirely rewritten. Only the first line of 'Del caro sposo' was retained, the rest of the text being parodied, since it appeared in a different context from Capelli's even in the first plan of the work. Restoring it to the third act made it possible to scrap the parody-text that appears in the conducting score and to go back to the original.

Generally speaking very little alteration was made to Handel's original conception of *Venceslao*. This is partly because suitable arias from operas by Vinci and Hasse were already provided for some of the singers, Merighi and Bertolli for instance, Merighi sang only arias that had been composed specially for her, three of which were from Hasse's *Attalo* (Naples 1728). In this particular case the singers' wishes may well have coincided with Handel's own ideas, as he borrowed from *Attalo* again in later pasticci and must have possessed a score of the work. On the other hand the arias of the tenor, Fabri, date back to Venice 1722 and remained unaltered. Musically speaking *Venceslao* is the least uniform of all Handel's pasticci. This is particularly true of the role of Casimiro, which was designed for Bernacchi, who in fact sang four of the six arias in Vinci's *Medo* (Parma 1728), which are characteristic examples of Bernacchi's very individual vocal style. Handel must therefore have had the performance of *Venceslao* in mind at least by May 1730 (after which time Bernacchi left London) and possibly even as early as 1729. When Senesino took over the part, he was given two additional arias from A. Lotti's *Alessandro Severo* of 1717, with which he may have become acquainted in Dresden 1718/9, when he was singing for Lotti. The first of the two was added at the last moment, as the transition from the recitative-cadence in B minor to the C major aria has not been corrected, at least in the conducting score. The second aria was cut again after the libretto had been printed. One of Bernacchi's arias ('Vado costante – della mia morte') seems to have been replaced for him by Capelli's original; at least the original text ('Vado costante a morte') appears again in the libretto. Bernacchi had in fact already sung Casimiro in Venice 1722, but none of the arias that he sang on that occasion found a place in the London *Venceslao*. La Strada, too, had already sung Erenice in Porta's setting (Naples 1726) but was either unwilling or unable to get any of the arias that she sang then included by Handel.

It is a remarkable feature of *Venceslao* that the actual text of many of the arias was not corrected – and thus fitted to the plot – until the last minute, or even written in later under the music. Handel himself may have been the author of one of these parody-texts that were added later, as he pencilled it into the score for the copyist ('Parto e mi sento'). The parody-text for the first aria of all ('Se già di Marte') arrived so late that it could not be included as a replacement for the original in the score and was only printed in the libretto. I have already mentioned the restoring of one text that was originally parodied.

Devising parody-texts was one of the chief tasks of anyone arranging a pasticcio. The commonest case in which parody was required was when an aria of the original opera was replaced by another though the dramatic situation remained unchanged; and the problem then was much the same as that which faces the translator of an operatic text. It was not enough to preserve the substance of the original dramatic content (i.e. of the text to be replaced); the parody must also follow the prosody model (i.e. the text of the new aria) so that it could be sung to the new music. We often find in the parody-texts used by Handel remarkably skilful compromises between dramatic faithfulness and perfect prosody. A comparison of the parody-text 'Parto e mi sento' with its two originals – whether done by Rossi or by Handel himself – provides an excellent example.

1. Dramatic model (Zeno's original text)	2. Prosody model (text of aria in Vinci's '*Medo*', by C. L. Frugoni)
Da te parto, e parto afflitto, o mio giudice, o mio re; dir volea: mio genitor,	Taci, o di morte non mi parlar, labbro vezzoso, se il mio riposo no vuoi turbar.
Ma poi tacqui il dolce nome, che più aggrava il mio delitto, e più accresce il tuo dolor.	Più lieta sorte fammi sperar, se il cor dubbioso, labbro amoroso, vuoi consolar.

3. Parody-text (Handel's underlay for Vinci's aria)

Parto, e mi sento	Il tuo tormento
mancar il cor,	mi fa penar;
perché sdegnato	sarò contento,
ti lascio, o amato	se il mio castigo
mio genitor.	ti può placar.

Lucio Papirio Dittatore (1732)

The deterioration of Handel's situation as operatic impresario first became clear in the season of 1731–2 from the greater frequency with which he was obliged to include new or newly produced operas in his programme. The first novelty on 15 January (after *Tamerlano*, *Poro* and *Admeto*) – was not a pasticcio as in the previous year, but Handel's own *Ezio* – and it had to be succeeded as early as 1 February by *Giulio Cesare*, which was followed by *Sosarme* (15 February), *Coriolano* (25 March) and *Flavio* (18 April). The first real success of the season was the oratorio *Esther* on 2 May, and this would have made further opera performances unnecessary. That Handel nevertheless produced *Lucio Papirio Dittatore* on 23 May is explained by the fact that this opera had been planned beforehand and possibly even rehearsed before the unexpected success of *Esther*. It was taken off after the fourth performance, which was on 6 June.

Lucio Papirio Dittatore was an adaptation of an original text of Apostolo Zeno's by the Court poet of Parma, Carlo Innocenzo Frugoni, and is not to be confused by A. Salvi's rival drama *Lucio Papirio*, from which Frugoni had nevertheless taken some of his recitatives. It was performed at the beginning of May 1729 at Parma, with music by Geminiano Giacomelli. Handel had probably heard the opera in Parma, and it is the only one of Handel's London productions that was a new work by an Italian with virtually no changes, at least as far as arias, choruses and sinfonia were concerned. It could therefore be called a revision rather than a pasticcio, strictly speaking.

Only one score of Giacomelli's opera is traceable today and that is at the Royal Academy of Music in London; it is the score that Handel must have used as his basic model. It was originally in the possession of a Sir John Buckworth,[34] whose name appears in 1726 in the list of directors of the Royal Academy and in January 1733 as one of the first directors of the Opera of the Nobility (Deutsch, pp. 199 and 304). Buckworth, whose relations with Handel would repay investigation, possessed several scores of Italian operas still in existence today. The manuscript of Giacomelli's opera is dated 'Parma a dì 15 maggio 1729' and is the work of a certain Francesco Faelli.[35] It is not known whether Handel or Buckworth commissioned the copy. The score still includes a fragment of an advertisement of the *Beggar's Opera*:

On MONDAY
WILL BE
The BEGGA
Capt.Macheath
Peachume by M
Lockit by Mr.D
Player   Mr.Anderson
Beggar   Mr.Bennet
Mat o' th' Mint by Mr.Baker
Ben Budge   Mr.Wignel

I have not been able to establish to what performance this leaflet refers; May 1732 would not be impossible.[36] Of course the leaflet could have been put into the score by any Londoner who owned it: but only Handel or his copyist would have had any reason for inserting it exactly where one of the only two arias added by Handel ('Alma tra miei timori') was to replace the original aria and where it would have served Handel or his copyist at least as a marker. The leaflet is torn in half, so it is tempting to think that the other (lost) half may have been used to mark the other aria that was to be replaced. Handel may possibly have borrowed the score from Buckworth and wished to treat it with respect, not making any pencil notes in the text.

No conducting score of the opera has been preserved, but we have the harpsichord score[37] and the libretto, which provides the names of the cast of the London production:

Lucio Papirio (tenor): Giambattista Pinacci
Marco Fabio (bass): Antonio Montagnana
Papiria (soprano): Anna Maria Strada
Rutilia (contralto): Francesca Bertoldi
Quinto Fabio (mezzosoprano): Francesco Bernardi detto Senesino
Servilio (contralto): Anna Bagnolesi Pinacci
Comino (mezzosoprano): Antonio Campioli

All the changes made in Giacomelli's opera by Handel were caused by the new casting; the work was rewritten almost exclusively in order to adapt the arias and recitatives to the different vocal ranges of the London singers. On the other hand the comparative importance of the roles in the original cast remained unchanged – whereas the opposite was the case in Handel's next pasticcio, presenting a problem which we shall have to discuss in more detail later. It was only in the case of the bass, Montagnana, that two arias from his personal repertory were introduced. Otherwise the pasticcio contains nothing but Giacomelli's original arias, though reduced in number from twenty-eight to twenty-one. The beginning of a twenty-second aria appears, but only in instrumental form, without any text: this is the aria

(Act I) with which Q. Fabio (Senesino) makes his entry as conqueror returning in triumph from the battlefield, and it is thus converted into a short, brilliant sinfonia. There was to have been a further aria for Papiria, but this was dropped before the libretto was printed. We learn something of Handel's general practice from the harpsichord score which must have been copied before the conducting score, contrary to his practice in *Ormisda* and *Venceslao*. It is particularly noteworthy that while he was content simply to transpose the arias, he altered the tessitura of most of the recitatives, and in fact rewrote them. The music of the arias plainly did not suffer by being transposed down a fourth or a fifth as, for instance, in the case of Senesino's arias, which Farinelli had sung at Parma; one aria of Senesino's was transferred from the part of M. Fabio, which was sung by Bernacchi whose vocal range was roughly the same, thus making transposition unnecessary. Bernacchi's role was transferred, by means of octave transposition, to Montagnana and all of La Faustina's arias were transposed up a tone or semitone for La Strada; there were further transpositions for Bertolli and Campioli, a mezzosoprano engaged from Dresden. There may have been other, external reasons for Handel interfering so little with the existing order of arias – it was late in the season and there may not have been time for more fundamental rewriting, and Montagnana was the only member of the cast who claimed his own, personal arias. Even so we must also suppose that Handel did not consider that, on aesthetic grounds, either text or music needed adaptation.

In the case of the recitatives Handel gave the copyist instructions to carry out the simple transpositions himself, partly by merely changing the clefs, as in the octave-transposition for Bernacchi–Montagnana, parts of the roles of Rutilia (Antonia Negri in the original), Cominio (Pacini), Servilio (Lucia Lancetti) and also the unaltered part of Lucio Papirio (Borosini). These he copied from the original into the harpsichord score of the more problematic recitatives. Only the text and continuo part were copied. Handel then pencilled in the new vocal lines, which the copyist simply inked over. Handel must have used a special copy of the original for instructions to the copyist about which recitative passages were to be copied as they stood and which not. This may have been a kind of basic conducting score or, more probably, a manuscript of the text, which in any case needed some adapting by Rossi. The arias were transposed by the copyist, Handel pencilling the new key into the harpsichord score ('ex C', 'ex F' etc.) and simply rewriting the necessary recitative-cadence.

Catone (1732)

Handel opened the season of 1732/3 with a pasticcio, *Catone*, which was an arrangement of Metastasio's second *tragedia per musica*, *Catone in Utica*, first performed in Rome in 1728. There were only four performances of this pasticcio, between 4 and 18 November, with the following cast:

Catone (mezzosoprano): Francesco Bernardi detto Senesino
Marzia (soprano): Anna Maria Strada
Emilia (soprano): Celeste Gismondi
Arbace (contralto): Francesca Bertolli
Cesare (bass): Antonio Montagnana

In Metastasio there is a sixth role, Fulvio, but the tenor to whom it might have been given, Pinacci, was no longer in Handel's company in 1732/3. The conducting score, which is now in Hamburg,[38] confirms Chrysander's supposition that the musical model was by Leonardo Leo (Chrysander, vol. 2, p. 252). Handel must have heard Leo's opera at the Venice Carnival of 1729, when it was given at the Teatro S. Giovanni Grisostomo, with Farinelli. As in the case of *Lucio Papirio*, the copy used by Handel still exists: it is the one belonging to the Royal Academy of Music[39] and contains Handel's own pencilled notes, which are concerned with the suppression of the character of Fulvio. Leo's score probably served the librettist as the original which he was called upon to adapt. John Buckworth is again the earliest known owner of the score. He must also have been at the Venice Carnival of 1729, as he is the dedicatee of the libretto of Porpora's *Semiramide*, which was the second opera given at S. Giovanni Grisostomo during that season. This opera is naturally also in Buckworth's collection.[40] Buckworth probably brought Leo's score back with him and lent it to Handel in 1732.

With *Catone* Handel wanted to introduce the work of a member of the younger generation of Italian composers, and one still unknown in London. At the same time he took the opportunity to stage yet another drama of Metastasio's after his own settings of *Siroe*, *Poro* and *Ezio*. In making up the score of the pasticcio he used Leo's sinfonia[41] and as much as possible of his recitatives, only pencilling into the conducting score – not the harpsichord score, as in the case of *Lucio Papirio* (we have no harpsichord score of *Catone*) – the recitative passages that needed altering. The copyists could be trusted to deal with the remaining recitatives and any simple transpositions by referring to the original. Handel's procedure with the arias was different on this occasion, and *Catone* became a genuine pasticcio if only because it was to open the season. The conducting score contains twenty-five complete or partly preserved arias (including those later replaced), only nine of which come from Leo's opera. The others are by Hasse (6), Porpora (4), Vivaldi (probably 3) and Vinci (1), and the authorship of two arias is as yet unknown. A comparatively large amount of aria-shuffling went on during the rehearsals of *Catone*. Before the printing of the libretto two of Emilia's arias (Gismondi) were replaced by others and Cesare's arias (Montagnana) were increased from three to four, while one of La Strada's (probably one of the original Leo arias) was cut. After the printing of the libretto, and therefore probably after the first performance, two further arias were exchanged for La Gismondi. As we saw in *Elpidia* and *Ormisda*, Handel was pretty generous in satisfying his singers' wishes in the matter of arias in pasticci, especially where new members of the cast were concerned.

We know from a letter from Lord Hervey (Deutsch, p. 296; see also p. 249 below) that Celeste ('Celestina') Gismondi (who became Mrs Hempson in London) was at Naples at the beginning of 1729, and she may have met Handel then, though it was not in fact she whom he engaged but Anna Maria Strada, who was also still a young woman. 'Celestina' appears to be identical with the buffa-soprano Celeste Resse, who sang regularly in intermezzi at the Teatro S. Bartolomeo between 1724 and 1732.

Handel's arrangement of Leo's *Catone* provides an instructive example of how he treated the problems of role-characterisation and of allotting to individual singers the right proportion of musical and dramatic responsibility. For a number of reasons he had needed to concern himself less with such matters when adapting *Lucio Papirio Dittatore*. But Metastasio's and Leo's *Catone* had to be arranged to meet quite different conditions of performance, and there were also other factors to be taken into account beside the purely artistic. The drastic shortening of Metastasio's recitatives is accounted for by the general theatrical tradition in London as described by Riva (Deutsch, p. 197; see also Streatfeild, p. 433ff and p. 99 above). The choice of arias was dictated specifically by the technique, the vocal range and the artistic personality of the newly engaged members of the cast but also by their individual ranking in the company as reflected in their different fees (see Deutsch, pp. 243 and 246), as well as by the comparative importance of their roles. According to long established operatic tradition the exterior and interior balance of a performance had to be assured by a number of conventions such as the distinction between *prima*, *seconda* and *terza parte*; the classification of arias according to affect and musical structure; and the number and position of each singer's arias. In this field, too, Handel fought against schematisation. We know directly from his letter to Colman of 19 June 1730 that he felt the need to observe this ranking of roles to be an intolerable restriction (Deutsch, p. 256). His chief concern was to have a free hand as director, whereas as an artist he was always ready to adapt. (He had already given evidence of a similar attitude in the quarrels between the rival singers Faustina and Cuzzoni in 1726–8.) In the case of *Catone* the alien conventions were in any case hardly possible to observe.

Montagnana, for instance, was quite exceptional as a bass, and Handel could not possibly expect him to accept the usual totally subsidiary role of, say, Fulvio. With Leo, even a singer like G. M. Boschi had had to be content with such a part. Montagnana sang the part of Caesar, which Leo had written for the soprano Gizzi, and was given important bass-arias from other operas. This meant inverting Metastasio's original intention, which had been to contrast the young, adventurous lover Caesar (a soprano) with the hero and austere father Cato (tenor). Even Leo, who was the second composer to set *Catone* (Vinci being the first) had given the part of Cato to a soprano as well and thus notably diminished the patriarchal character of the role. Grimaldi had entirely recreated the part which now perfectly fitted Senesino, who was in many ways Grimaldi's London successor and sang no arias but Leo's. Nor was there any problem involved in La Strada taking over the *primadonna* part from Lucia Facchinelli, Handel merely adding a 'last song' for her – Vinci's well known 'Vò solcando un mar crudele'. This new conclusion is of course a drastic solution to Metastasio's problematical *tragico fine*. Public criticism had already forced Metastasio to tone down the work's original, gloomy conclusion for Venice; but he had not altered the final accompagnato in which Caesar, though victor in the wars, found himself morally vanquished by Cato's suicide and threw his victor's laurel to the ground in vexation. The critical moral of the drama was preserved (in Leo's setting) in London, but weakened both dramatically and musically by the addition of a well-known popular aria. Handel is thus revealed not only as ready to make concessions to his singers and his public as far as the drama is concerned, but also as indifferent to the plot.

The role of Arbace, which Leo wrote for Farinelli, was so reduced in London that it was barely recognisable. Francesca Bertolli was neither able – nor permitted! – to sing a single one of Farinelli's arias. Celeste Gismondi would have been excellent as Leo's Emilia, as is shown by her arias in Handel's own operas. The changes in her part are to be explained rather by her personal ambition.

Catone was regarded in London by some as a work of Handel's and received, as such, a negative judgement (Deutsch, p. 296), though Walsh nevertheless printed six arias from the work in *Favourite Songs*.

Three pasticci in one season – *Semiramide riconosciuta, Caio Fabricio* and *Arbace* (1733–4)

In the summer of 1733 Handel was unexpectedly confronted by competition from the rival company of the Opera of the Nobility, for which all but one of his singers – La Strada – had deserted him, probably as early as June. This left him less time to make the necessary preparations than in former years, particularly if we take into account the oratorio performances at Oxford in July 1733. In spite of this he was able both to collect a complete company that included the well-known sopranos Carestini and Scalzi and also to prepare for performance three pasticci (rather than the customary one) of other men's music, as well as his own *Arianna*. This must be the reason for Hawkins' mistaken assumption that Handel made another journey to Italy in the summer of 1733[42]. Handel had in any case planned a season for 1733/4, since this would come within the five-year contract that he made with Heidegger in 1729. He may have got hold of at least the score of *Semiramide riconosciuta* (Metastasio/Vinci) during his visit to Italy in 1729, as it was performed in Rome that year (Carnival). Perhaps it was only the new pressure of competition that decided him to produce *Caio Fabricio* (Zeno/Hasse; Rome, Carnival 1732) and *Arbace* (= *Artaserse*, Metastasio/ Vinci; Rome, Carnival 1730). These very popular scores may well have been available in London. Carestini could have met Handel at Naples in 1729 though Handel's engaging of Bernacchi in 1729 excluded the possibility of his engaging Carestini.[43] When Bernacchi left him in 1730, Handel immediately thought of Carestini.[44] Scalzi had already played the leading part in Vinci's *Semiramide* (1729) and may have known Handel in Rome as early as 1729. Carestini also found himself again singing the leading part in *Arbace* as he had done in 1730.

The libretto of *Arianna in Creta* (which is by Pariati, not Colman) (see p. 67 above) is virtually identical with a version set by Leo, also for the Carnival season of 1729 in Rome. Nicolò Porpora had set Pariati's text in 1717 for Vienna and composed it again ten years later. Porpora was now chief conductor of the Opera of the Nobility and his setting of a new drama by Rolli on the subject of Ariadne (*Arianna in Nasso*) was a deliberate challenge to Handel, whose *Arianna* was already completed on 5 October 1733. The very fact of Handel's having anticipated him obliged Porpora to set a different Ariadne text, although a comparison of his two scores suggests that the music which he had written in 1727 would have done him more credit.[45]

For much the same reasons Handel was obliged to produce more new operas in 1733/4 than he had done in any previous season. But why did he increase the number of operas by other composers rather than of his own? He had opened the season long before his rivals with *Semiramide* (30 October 1733), new performances of his *Ottone* (13 November 1733) and with *Caio Fabricio* (4 December 1733). But his reply to Porpora's *Arianna in Nasso* (1 January 1734) was not his own *Arianna* – though this had long been completed – but Vinci's *Arbace* (5 January 1734): it was not his own work but the pasticci that were to provide the answer to his rivals. He wanted to confront Porpora with superior examples of Porpora's own kind of music. In spite of this, Handel's calculation does not seem to have been entirely successful, and it was only *Arbace* – which was then the most popular opera in Italy – that made some impact with eight performances, the two other pasticci only being given four performances each.[46]

Handel's rivals achieved a quite exceptional success during the season of 1734/5 with Farinelli in Hasse's *Artaserse*, due perhaps to Hasse's music and Metastasio's drama as well as to Farinelli. If so, this throws an interesting light on London audiences with whom two dramas of Metastasio's and an opera of Hasse's had proved virtual failures a year earlier under Handel's direction. Handel's strategical use of pasticci failed to take into account the polarisation of taste – his own supporters united in wanting only his compositions, while the public he hoped to attract by the works of more recent Italian composers were swayed by party-spirit and deserted the Haymarket Theatre for that reason.

From the opening of the 1733/4 season Handel's company included Strada, Carestini, Scalzi, Durastanti, the sisters Maria Catterina and Maria Rosa Negri and Gustavus Waltz. It is not clear from the conducting scores of the three pasticci whether these works had been designed originally for a cast which still included one of the singers who later deserted to the rival company. The part of Semiramide had in any case always been intended for Durastanti, since the arias transposed to suit her voice were among the first entered in the conducting score. If harpsichord scores of these works have ever existed, they may well have reflected an even earlier stage of preparation as was the case in *Lucio Papirio* and perhaps in *Catone*. Generally speaking it looks as though from about August Handel could count on a complete cast and that it was for them that he prepared the pasticci. The only evidence to the contrary is to be found in the satire *Harmony in an Uproar*, where we read that on the very day of the performance of a 'new opera' 'two very remarkable monsters' had been decoyed away, though replacements had immediately been found (Deutsch, p. 355). W. C. Smith was of the opinion that this must refer to the performance of *Ottone* on 13 November 1733, because a libretto of *Ottone* dating from 1733 still gives the Senesino–Montagnana–Bertolli casting and the new casting is only given on two additional pages that have been bound in.[47] In the first place, however, *Ottone* was not a 'new opera', and even more important is the fact that the new casting already appears in the libretto of *Semiramide* of 30 October 1733. Smith's libretto of *Ottone* was printed, according to Clausen, for a performance planned for March that year (Clausen, p. 189 n.6). The author of *Harmony in an Uproar* certainly gave a melodramatically exaggerated account of the singers' desertion and, even more certainly, grossly exaggerated Handel's plight.

Both the autograph of *Arianna* and the conducting scores of the first two pasticci were complete in their first form by October 1733 at the latest.[48] After that we can still see a large number of changes in the distribution of the roles as well as in individual arias. Although Waltz had been intended for all three operas, he could not – or was not supposed to – appear in either *Semiramide* or *Arbace*. He was replaced as Ircano in *Semiramide* by Caterina Negri, whose role of Sibari was taken over by her sister Rosa. In *Arbace* Durastanti replaced Waltz as Artabano, with Catterina Negri taking over

Durastanti's Semira and Rosa Negri replacing her sister as Megabise. These changes in *Arbace* took place while the conducting score was being compiled, so that the first five scenes have the old casting and from there onwards the recitative, which the copyist had already completed, is corrected by Handel; it is only after the end of the second act that both recitatives and arias appear in the keys in which they were actually sung. In the case of *Semiramide* this reshuffling of roles did not take place until even the recitatives had been completed, and these were not corrected, nor was the second of the three arias involved. In *Caio Fabricio* Durastanti and Catterina Negri exchanged roles while the conducting score was being compiled. This change involved questions of conventional ranking. Thus the character of Bircenna was given four instead of three arias when taken over by Durastanti, while Negri as Turio lost one of the role's three original arias. Not all the necessary transpositions were entered in the score; and the key-changes in the recitative cadences before transposed arias only appear in the conducting score when the copyist was in any case obliged to rewrite the whole aria with its introductory recitative. In fact there are many places in these pasticci where the conducting score differs at least in key from what was actually sung or played.

The final distribution of the roles in these three pasticci (we have only two of the libretti, *Semiramide* and *Caio Fabricio*) was as follows:

	Semiramide	*Caio Fabricio*	*Arbace*
Strada (soprano):	Tamiri	Sestia	Mandane
Carestini (soprano):	Scitalce	Pirro	Arbace
Scalzi (soprano):	Mirteo	Volusio	Artaserse
Durastanti (mezzosoprano):	Semiramide	Bircenna	Artabano
Cat. Negri (alto):	Ircano	Turio	Semira
Rosa Negri (soprano):	Sibari	Cinea	Megabise
G. Waltz (bass):	—	Caio Fabricio	—

The relationship between the original model and Handel's final version is vaguely similar in all three works. In each case he worked from one definite score which he modified in different degrees, though never altering the plot or even the order of the arias that he retained. His interference with the originals successively diminished, and this can be explained on two grounds. In the first place we can trace a line of development from *Catone*, in which he diverged even further from his original than in *Semiramide*, to the *Didone* of 1737, which is even closer than *Arbace* to its original. Secondly, as the season went on there was a diminishing need for arias in which new singers introduced themselves to the public. Even so there is a difference of principle between *Semiramide* and the two later pasticci. In Handel's basic design for *Semiramide* one third of the total number of arias came from other operas (parodied in some cases), while in the other two works all but one of the inserted arias – Carestini's 'last song' in *Caio Fabricio*, which had been planned earlier – were forced on Handel at a late stage in the proceedings, either by the rearrangement of roles or by the singers' special requests. Handel would certainly not have reckoned with the fact that Carestini – who must have arrived in London in October, like Scalzi – would want to enliven his performances by adding songs from his own repertory, not only in the first opera of the season and *Ottone*, but even in the pasticci that followed, despite the fact of his having created the title-role in *Arbace*. Both Strada and, to a lesser degree, Scalzi made similar demands. In Scalzi's case it turned out after his arrival that his voice had sunk so much in pitch since 1729 that he was no longer capable of singing his own part in *Semiramide*, and his arias were transposed down first a tone, then a minor third, and finally a major, third. In some cases it is no longer possible to be sure from the conducting score of the transpositions needed in *Caio Fabricio*; Scalzi was vocally equal to his part in *Arbace*.[49] Handel's different conception of *Semiramide*, which generally resembles that of his *Catone*, suggests that this first of the three pasticci was planned earlier than the others. This supposition is also supported by the fact that Handel used the sinfonia from Vinci's *Artaserse*, as though he had perhaps not yet thought of a performance of *Arbace* at the time when work was begun on the conducting score of *Semiramide*.

The recitatives of the three pasticci broadly follow those of the originals. In the case of *Arbace* Handel even had them copied directly from the score (or the vanished harpsichord score, which could then have been the direct copy). He only went on with the recitatives himself when changes in the cast made changes in the tessitura necessary. While doing this, however, he also made further alterations in a number of passages for reasons of vocal pitch. *Accompagnato* passages were mostly rewritten as *secco* recitatives. The texts of all three operas were cut successively at different times during preparations and the number of arias slightly reduced everywhere. A new feature of this season was the introduction of cuts actually within arias, and the whole production underwent a corresponding reduction. A short sinfonia disappeared from the second scene, first act, of *Semiramide*. In the second scene, second act of the original there is a chorus and a ballet, introduced in the recitative by the words 'ognuno/la mensa onori, e intanto/misto risuoni a liete danze il canto'. Handel corrected this in perfect Italian to ' ... e intanto/sciolga ognuno la lingua in dolce canto', thus making it possible to omit the ballet. Then, however, even the chorus proved too much and he cancelled his own correction by ending the recitative with the words ' ... la mensa onori'. He replaced this cut by a short sinfonia obviously of his own composition – so that all that remained of Metastasio's and Vinci's big ceremonial scene was this unpretentious instrumental piece played during the banquet.

Normally Handel left the musical substance of his models untouched.

Apart from the aria cuts mentioned above, which do not alter the character
of the work it has hitherto been possible to trace only two cases of rewriting
the music: 'Se vuoi ch'io mora' in the *Didone* of 1737 and 'Saper bramate'
in the *Semiramide* of 1733. Both versions of 'Saper bramate' are given on
pp. 187–95. Example 1 shows the aria from Vinci's *Semiramide* as it appears

Example 1 Leonardo Vinci, 'Saper bramate', *Semiramide riconosciuta*, 1729

Example 1 (*cont.*)

Example 1 (*cont.*)

Example 1 (*cont.*)

Example 1 (*cont.*)

Example 1 (*cont.*)

[Da Capo]

in a fragmentary score of the opera, copied in Dresden but reproducing Vinci's original version.[50] Example 2 shows it as rewritten. Although it is not in Handel's handwriting in the conducting score, the circumstances lead us to suppose that it is by Handel. The reason for this rewriting was the octave transposition from alto to bass necessitated by Gustavus Waltz's

Example 2 Leonardo Vinci, 'Saper bramate' in Handel's version, 1733

Example 2 (*cont.*)

co - re, sa - per bra - ma - te tut-to il _ mio co - re? Non vi _ sde - gna-te, _ lo _

spie - - ghe - rò, _ lo _ spie - ghe - rò. Mi dà di -

- let - to l'al-trui do - lo - re, per-ciò d'af - fet - to _ can - gian - do vò.

Violini

IRCANO (Violini colla parte)

Mi dà di - let - to l'al-trui do - lo - re, per-ciò d'af -

colla parte

forte

colla parte

Viola

- fet - to _ can - gian - do vò, can-gian - do vò.

Example 2 (*cont.*)

taking over the part of Ircano. This meant altering the continuo in a number of places; and the first violin part was also transposed down an octave, the second violin playing unisono with the first in vocal passages. The viola part could not continue *all'ottava col basso* in the new version and is simply omitted in the vocal passages. But Handel went much further than these necessary adjustments. He often changed the contour of the melody and the continuo, not simply in order to preserve the two-part texture but to obtain motivic unity (cf. bb. 10–16 and Vinci bb. 7–13) and replaces two major sections which in Vinci have their own motifs (bb. 23–7, 28–34) by repeating sections (bb. 26–31, 32–6). He enhances structurally the contrast between the first and second lines of the text, which Vinci leaves the performer to emphasise, by introducing the contrasting unison-group into the second vocal section as well (bb. 26–31). The fermata and the repetition of the final 'cangiando vò' (bb. 42–3), answered by bb. 52–3 in the ritornello, indicate professionally that the singer is here to be given the opportunity for a cadenza, and this is not found in Vinci (bb. 49–50). The final ritornello, which is entirely new, is remarkable for a *piano* passage (bb. 47–9) that contradicts musically Vinci's whole conception of the aria: chromatic harmonies, repeating pedal notes and tied-over dotted crotchets belong to the world of the siciliano aria, as we know it from other passages in Handel. Vinci, on the other hand, always avoided such unambiguous references to this rhythmic model, not only here but noticeably elsewhere in his music. Handel's middle section is also close to sicilianos in his own works. This is the point at which he diverges most from his model. We have the impression that his first idea was to make not much more than a transposed arrangement of the original but that, in the actual process of writing as it were, his own personality increasingly asserted itself. Like many composers of the time, he may well have found that, in practice, it was much more convenient for him to compose afresh than to make a scrupulous arrangement of another man's music.

We can judge the small success enjoyed by these three pasticci of 1733/4 by the fact that Walsh ventured no further than printing a volume of *Favourite Songs* from *Arbace* (Smith 1970, pp. 16f). Five arias from *Semiramide* also exist in a manuscript collection made by J. C. Smith senior (GB-Cfm 52 B1) probably copied from the conducting score. This collection includes among other things two arias from *Arbace* and many numbers from works produced by the Opera of the Nobility. Among these are six 'Songs in *Belmira*', pieces from a pasticcio produced in Lincoln's Inn Fields on 23 March 1734.[51]

Handel in Covent Garden and *Didone abbandonata* (1737)

In the first two years after the taking over of Covent Garden in the autumn of 1734 Handel pursued a new operatic strategy. He drew a number of conclusions from the comparative failure of the 1733/4 season, in which he had counted on Carestini and Scalzi and operas by Vinci and Hasse. He gave up engaging new Italian singers, but used choruses and introduced ballets and instrumental pieces (whereas in 1733 he had dropped the ballets and choruses from *Semiramide*); he offered more oratorio performances and, most importantly, made exclusive use of his own works. With the old strategy, he had been able to confront the competition of Senesino and Porpora, but this was no longer possible with Farinelli and Hasse, who could meanwhile be heard at the Haymarket Theatre. The new system is consistent in itself. The money spent on the ballets and the ballerina La Sallé had to be saved on the singers and, partly, on the stage-sets, and this forced Handel to engage English singers (such as Cecilia Young and John Beard) and to perform oratorios rather than opera, thus providing the public with something different in quality from his rivals, whom he was still trying in 1733/4 to beat at their own game.

In a sense, therefore, the ballet *Terpsicore* with La Sallé, which opened the first Covent Garden season (9 November 1734)[52] with *Pastor fido*, may be seen as a continuation of the pasticci, inasmuch as they were designed to present new performers. This is much less true of the pasticcio *Oreste*, composed from Handel's own music. *Oreste* contains instrumental suites and ballet-music; it was a make-weight in the season's programme, and there are therefore several reasons for not counting it with the pasticci of other composers' music, any more than the *Alessandro Severo* of 1738.

The new change of front in 1736, however, makes it clear that Handel's new strategies can hardly be regarded as marking new artistic ideals: they were dictated primarily by tactical considerations. The competition had lost Senesino, Farinelli's fascination had virtually ceased to work, and Handel had in the meantime acquired the personal protection of the Prince of Wales. He was basically returning to the dominant operatic style of the day, which was to satisfy the European public for some decades longer. The clearest sign of this return is his engagement of the castrati Gioacchino Conti detto Gizziello and Domenico Annibali and the performance of Metastasio's and Vinci's *Didone abbandonata*.

Both castrati had to be allowed arias from their own repertories in which to make their first appearance before the public; but a new feature on this occasion was the fact that these arias were not only sung in the pasticcio, but in Handel's own operas. Conti, for instance, sang seven new arias not by Handel in the revivals of *Ariodante* that took place on 5 and 7 May 1736 (Clausen, p. 116). In Handel's *Poro* on 8 December 1736 Annibali inserted three arias, two of which he had brought with him from Dresden – and another Dresden aria in *Didone*.[53] He may well have sung even more of these inserted arias during the season, as even the ones mentioned above appear only in part in the scores. The Metastasio–Vinci *Didone abbandonata* dates from 1726 (Teatro dell Dame, Rome, Carnival) (see also pp. 213–24, below). Handel wanted to perform it with as few changes as possible, including the *accompagnati*, which in other comparable cases he had replaced by simple recitatives. In fact the recitatives had to be partly rewritten and in some cases cut, and some of the arias were shortened (for instance by omitting the opening ritornello) and one aria was basically altered. This aria ('Se vuoi ch'io mora'), which in the conducting score diverges from the original, was in Handel's autograph in the harpsichord score, which no longer exists.[54] It was prepared first, as in other cases, the conducting score being a copy. The other changes in Vinci's music, which include the substitution of nine arias, were determined by the redistribution of the roles and the resulting shifts in precedence among the cast.[55] The following casting appears in the libretto:[56]

Didone (soprano): Anna Maria Strada
Enea (soprano): Gioacchino Conti detto Gizziello
Jarba (alto): Domenico Annibali
Selene (alto): Francesca Bertolli
Osmida (alto): Maria Catterina Negri
Araspe (tenor): John Beard.

Handel was very economical with the text as well as the music of Vinci's original. In three instances the new arias permitted to the new singers were simply sung to Vinci's original text, and this made parodies unnecessary. Handel dealt in much the same way with the problems of precedence that arose, which included a down-grading of Beard's part: he simply gave one of Araspe's aria-texts to Didone and another to Enea. One of these ('Sono intrepido') was, moreover, sung to other music, not of course without prejudicing the connection between text, music and dramatic situation. There is another noticeable example of this incongruity in 'Cadrà fra poco', the music for which Handel had used with a different parody-text in *Semiramide* and now reintroduced with a *Didone* text. The same happened with 'A trionfar', which had been heard with the original text in *Catone*. 'Tanto amor' from *Semiramide* was also at his disposal, but had not been used there. Handel was plainly having trouble not only with getting texts – perhaps he had lost Rossi as a collaborator – but it looks as though his supply of scores was also getting low.

The first performance of *Didone* took place on 13 April 1737. Owing to a stroke Handel was unable to conduct it himself. There were three more performances. Handel had again failed to succeed on the London stage with an opera universally admired in Italy. The rival company, though on the verge of bankruptcy, gave many more performances of Hasse's *Siroe* and Pescetti's *Demetrio*. In the meantime, however, Handel had attracted – not least with his oratorios – a new following unable to appreciate Vinci or Hasse, as he did. In fact the fundamental problem about Handel's pasticci lay in the fact that his own music, in his own theatre, presented too strong a rival attraction to any operas of Italian origin.

I append a detailed chronological list of the sinfonias and arias used in Handel's pasticci, in the order in which they appear in conducting score or libretto, including pieces that were either cut or inserted at a later date. The columns, read from left to right, show:

1. The name of the singer under Handel
2. Text of the aria in Handel, in parentheses if it does not appear in the conducting score.
3. Composer and title of the original opera.[57] The title is in parentheses if it is only inferred from the libretto or from secondary tradition; and also the name of the composer if this too is only inferred.
4. Original text of the aria, if parodied in Handel; otherwise 'id.'
5. Name of the singer of the original aria. The name is in italic if the same singer was employed by Handel. The horizontal lines in the two first columns indicate the separate acts.

Elpidia (11 May 1725)

	Sinfonia	Vinci, *Eraclea*, Naples 1724 (with new last movement)		
Senesino + Pacini	'Il valor – il vigor'	(ascribed to Vinci)*	id.	Bordoni
Cuzzoni	'Dea triforme'	Vinci, *Ifigenia in Tauride*, Venice 1725	id.	
Borosini	'Per serbarti'	Orlandini, *Berenice*, Venice 1725	id.	Barbieri
Sorosina replaced by:	'Si può ma sol'	Vinci, *Rosmira fedele*, Venice 1725	id.	Antonia Merighi
Dotti	'Sorge qual luccioletta'	Sarri, *Arsace*, Naples 1718	'Sì, sì, lasciatemi'	Benti Bulgarelli
Borosini replaced by:	'Se non trovo'	(ascribed to Peli)*		
Antinori	'Amor deh lasciami'	(Orlandini, *Lucio Papirio*, Bologna 1718)		G. Paita
Cuzzoni	'D'alma luce'	Vinci, *Ifigenia*	id.	Bordoni
Cuzzoni	'Amante tuo costante'	Vinci, *Rosmira*	'Amante ch'incostante'	Carlo Scalzi
Boschi	'Dopo il vento'	A. Lotti, *Teofane*, Dresden 1719	'Le profonde vie dell'onde'	*Boschi*
Pacini replaced by:	'Men superba'	Vinci, *Rosmira*	id.	Bernardi
Baldi	'Ahi nemico al nostro affetto'	(Giacomelli, *Ipermestra*, Venice 1724?)	'Dal tuo sdegno e dal tuo amore'	(*Baldi*)
Senesino	'Un vento lusinghier'	(ascribed to Sarri)* (*Merope*, Naples 1716)	id.	*Senesino*
Cuzzoni + Senesino	'Deh caro Olindo'	?		
Cuzzoni in libretto	'Parto bell'idol mio'	?		
Senesino	'Dimmi bell'idol mio'	(ascribed to Fiorè)*	id.	(Vittoria Tesi)
Pacini replaced by:	('Qual senza stella')	(Capelli, *Venceslao*, Parma 1724)	id.	
Baldi	'Parte il piè'	(Giacomelli, *Ipermestra*)	id.	Bernacchi
Cuzzoni	'Dolce orror'	Vinci, *Ifigenia*	id.	Bordoni
Borosini	'Al mio tesoro'	Vinci, *Rosmira*	id.	Barbieri
Senesino	'Addio dille'	Orlandini, *Berenice*	id.	Scalzi

Cuzzoni	'Pupillette'	Vinci, *Ifigenia* (ascribed to Vinci)*	id.		Bordoni
Senesino	'Di pur ch'io sono'				
Cuzzoni	'Bell'alma'	Vinci, *Ifigenia*	id.		Giovanni Ossi
Cuzzoni (inserted later)	'Più non sò dirti spera'	Vinci, *Trionfo di Camilla*, Parma 1725	'Più non sò finger sdegni'		Bordoni
Boschi	'Di quel crudel'	A. Lotti, *Teofane*, Dresden 1719	'Al minacciar dell'onde'		*Boschi*
Pacini	'Ad amar la tua beltade'	Orlandini, *Berenice*	'Ad amar varia beltade'		Bernardi
replaced by:					
Pacini	'Vado costante'	Capelli, *Venceslao*	id.		*Pacini*
Sorosina	'Già sente il core'	Vinci, *Ifigenia*	id.		Merighi
replaced by:					
Dotti	'Con nodi più tenaci?'	(Sarri, *Alessandro Severo*, Naples 1719)	id.		*Dotti*
Senesino	'Barbara mi schernisci?'	Vinci, *Rosmira*	id.		Scalzi
Cuzzoni	'Tortora ch'il sua' (unknown insertion)	Vinci, *Rosmira*	id.		Bordoni
Boschi	'Vanne e spera'	Vinci, *Rosmira*	id.		Barbieri
Borosini	'Stringi al sen'	Vinci, *Ifigenia*	id.		Bordoni + Scalzi
Cuzzoni + Senesino					
Ormisda	(4 April 1730) Sinfonia replaced by: Ouverture	Vinci (*Flavio An. Olibrio* Naples 1728?) (ascribed to Conti)			
Strada	'Pupillette vezzosette'	Hasse, *Tigrane*, Naples 1729 (Orlandini, *Ormisda*, Bologna 1722)	id.		Anna Maria Mazzoni
Bernacchi	'Sino alla goccia'		id.		*Bernacchi*
replaced by:					
Senesino	'Ricordati ch'è mio'	Orlandini, *Adelaide*, Venice 1729	id.		*Senesino*
Merighi	'Infelice'	Vinci (*F. A. Olibrio*)	'Tu m'offendi'		*Merighi*
Fabri	'Se non sa qual'	?			
Strada	'O caro mio tesoro'	Vinci, *Caduta dei Decemviri*, Naples 1727	'Del caro mio tesoro'		Carlo Scalzi
replaced by:	'Non ti confonder'	Hasse, *Sorella amante*, Naples 1729	id.		?

* Contemporary note in a libretto in the British Library (639.g.29)

Bertolli	'Tacerò se tu lo brami'	? (Text: *Didone abbandonata*)		
Fabri	'Se non pensi'	?		
replaced by:	'Non fulmina ancora'	(Orlandini, *Lucio Papirio*, Bologna 1718)	id.	G. Paita
Bernacchi	'Vede quel pastorello'	Orlandini (*Ormisda*)	id.	*(Bernacchi)*
replaced by:				
Senesino	'E quella la bella'	Orlandini, *Adelaide*	'Tiranna ma bella'	Senesino
Merighi	'Se quel cor con nobil vanto'	Hasse (*Ulderica*, Naples 1729)	'Pria di darmi un si bel vanto'	*(Merighi)*
Strada	'Se d'aquilon'	(Porpora, *Semiramide*, Naples 1724)	id.	*(Strada)*
replaced by unknown aria				
Bernacchi	'Leon feroce'	(Orlandini, *Ormisda*)	id.	*(Bernacchi)*
replaced by:	'Reo mi brami'	?		
Riemschneider inserted later	'Come l'onda furibonda'	Fioré (*Sesostri*, Turin 1717)	'Mira l'onda'	G. M. Boschi
Merighi	'La speranza'	Orlandini, *Antigona*, Bologna 1727	'Le pupille'	*Merighi*
later text underlay:	'Nel tuo amor'	Orlandini, *Antigona*, Bologna 1727	'Le pupille'	*Merighi*
Fabri	'Si si lasciatemi'	(Orlandini, *Lucio Papirio*, Bologna 1718) (cf. *Elpidia*)	id.	G. Paita
Bertolli	'Lasciami amico'	(ascribed to Porta)	id.	Elisabetta Uttini
replaced by:	'Tuona il ciel'	Leo, *Argeno*, Venice 1728	id.	*(Merighi)*
Merighi	'Timido pellegrin'	(Giay, *Publio Cornelio Scipione*, Turin 1726)		
Strada	'Sentirsi dire'	Vinci, *Semiramide*, Rome 1729	id.	Scalzi
Bernacchi	('Fia tuo sangue')	(Orlandini, *Ormisda*)	id.	*(Bernacchi)*
replaced by:				
Senesino	'Di mia costanza'	Orlandini, *Adelaide*	'Vedrò piu liete'	Senesino
Bertolli	'Io corro pietoso'	?		
Fabri	'Ti sento amor di padre'	? (Text: *Alessandro Severo*)		
replaced by:	'Speranze del mio cor'	Giacomelli, *Zidiana*, Milan 1728	id.	*Fabri*

Strada	'Passagier che in selva oscura'	Hasse, *Sesostrate*, Naples 1726	id.	Scalzi
Merighi	'Se mi toglie il tuo furore'	Hasse, *Attalo*, Naples 1728	'Tu svenasti il mio tesoro'	Merighi
Strada	'Amico il fato'	Sarri, *Siroe*, Naples 1727	id.	Maddalena Salvai
replaced by:	'Agitata dal vento'	?		
coro finale replaced by:	'D'applauso'	?		
	'Tutto rida'	?		

Venceslao (12 January 1731)

Sinfonia

Bertolli later parodied:	'Se a danni miei' ('Se già de Marte')	?	id.	Anna Bagnolesi
Fabri	'Se tu vuoi dar'	?		
Bernacchi, Senesino	'Quell'odio che in mente'	Vinci, *Medo*, Parma 1728 (Porpora, *Amare per regnare*, Naples 1723)	'Quel fiume che in monte'	Bernacchi
Merighi	'Lascia il lido'		id.	Merighi
Strada	'Io sento al cor'	Giacomelli, *Lucio Pap. Ditt.*, Parma 1729	'Tornate ancor'	Bordoni
Fabri	'Ecco l'alba'	?		
Merighi	'Per mia vendetta ingrato'	Orlandini, *Antigona*, Bologna 1727	'Se morir deggio ingrato'	Merighi
Strada	'Son belle in ciel le stelle'	Porta (*Ulisse*, Venice 1725)	id.	Carestini
Bernacchi, Senesino	'D'ira armato'	Vinci, *Medo*	'Vengo a voi'	Bernacchi
Fabri	'Nel seren'	(*Venceslao*, 1722?)	id.	Barbieri
Merighi	'Con bella speme'	Hasse, *Attalo*, Naples 1728	'Con dolce frode'	Merighi
Strada	'Lascia cadermi'	Hasse, *Artaserse*, Venice 1730	id.	Farinelli
Bernacchi, Senesino	'Parto, e mi sento'	Vinci, *Medo*	'Taci, o di morte'	Bernacchi
Merighi	'La vaga luccioletta'	Hasse, *Attalo*	id.	Merighi
Bertolli	'Vuo ritrar'	?		
Bernacchi	'Vado costante – della mia morte'	Vinci, *Medo*	'Nella foresta leone invitto'	Bernacchi

probably replaced by:

Singer	Aria	Source		Replaced by
Senesino	('Vado costante a morte')	?		
Strada	'Come nave in ria tempesta'	Porpora, *Semiramide*, Naples 1724	id.	Farinelli
Merighi	'Corro, volo'	Hasse, *Attalo*	id.	*Merighi*
Bertolli	'Spero alfin che il cielo irato'	Hasse, *Gerone*, Naples 1727	'Sappi poi che il cielo irato'	Bagnolesi
Senesino	'Da te se mi divide'	Lotti, *Aless. Severo*, Venice 1717	'Da te tu mi dividi'	Francesco de Grandis
Fabri	'Balenar'	(*Venceslao*, 1722?)	id.	Barbieri
Strada	'Del caro sposo'	Capelli, *Venceslao*, Parma 1724	id.	Bordoni
Senesino (cut)	'Fido amor non piu lamenti'	Lotti, *Aless. Severo*	'Fidi amori or sì dolenti'	Diana Vico

Lucio Papirio Dittatore (23 May 1732)

Sinfonia

Singer	Aria	Source		Replaced by
Pinacci	'Dall'alta tua'	Giacomelli, *Lucio Pap. Ditt.*, Parma 1729		
				Montagnana
Montagnana	'Chi del fato'	Giacomelli, *Lucio Pap. Ditt.*, Parma 1729		Bordoni
Strada	'Per dolce mio'	Porpora, *Siface*, Rome 1730		Pacini
Campioli	'Per te già forte'	Giacomelli, *L. Pap. Ditt.*		Lancetti
Bagnolesi	'Se ti ferisce'	Giacomelli, *L. Pap. Ditt.*		Negri
Bertolli	'Che follia pregar'	Giacomelli, *L. Pap. Ditt.*		Farinelli
Senesino	'Non ti chiedo'	Giacomelli, *L. Pap. Ditt.*		Bordoni
Strada	'Consigliando'	Giacomelli, *L. Pap. Ditt.*		
Bagnolesi	'Porto nel cuore'	Giacomelli, *L. Pap. Ditt.*		Lancetti
Montagnana	'Scostati nè più'	Giacomelli, *L. Pap. Ditt.*		Bernacchi
Strada	'Ti lascio m'involo'	Giacomelli, *L. Pap. Ditt.*		Bordoni
Bertolli	'Vanne e prega'	Giacomelli, *L. Pap. Ditt.*		Negri
Senesino	'Que' begli occhi'	Giacomelli, *L. Pap. Ditt.*		Farinelli
Strada	'Tornate amor'	Giacomelli, *L. Pap. Ditt.*		

				Bernacchi
Senesino	'Spera sì presago'	Giacomelli, *L. Pap. Ditt.*		
Bagnolesi	'Sorge dal monte'	Giacomelli, *L. Pap. Ditt.*		Lancetti
Bertolli	'Cor di viltà'	Giacomelli, *L. Pap. Ditt.*		Negri
Pinacci	'Sulla tomba coronata'	Giacomelli, *L. Pap. Ditt.*		Bordoni
Senesino	'Questa fronte'	Giacomelli, *L. Pap. Ditt.*		Farinelli
Montagnana	'Alma tra miei timori'	(Porpora, *Poro*, Turin 1731)		*Montagnana*
Strada	'Vengo a darti'	Giacomelli, *L. Pap. Ditt.*	'O sugli estivi ardori'	Bordoni

Catone (4 November 1732)

	Sinfonia	(not by Leo)		
Senesino	'Con sì bel nome'	Leo, *Catone*, Venice 1729	id.	Nicolino Grimaldi
Strada	'Non ti minaccio'	Leo, *Catone*	id.	Lucia Facchinelli
Bertolli	'Un raggio di speme'	(Hasse, *Dalisa*, Venice 1730)	'Un raggio di stella'	(Antonio Pasi)
Senesino	'Pensa di chi'	Leo, *Catone*	id.	Grimaldi
Montagnana	'Non paventa'	Porpora, *Siface*, Rome 1730	id.	*Montagnana*
Gismondi	'La cervetta timidetta'	Vivaldi, *Giustino*, Rome 1724	id.	Giacinto Fontana
replaced by:	'Priva del caro sposo'	Porpora, *Germanico*, Rome 1732	id.	Angelo Monticelli
Gismondi	'Vaghe labbra voi fingete'	(Hasse, *Ulderica*, Naples 1729)	'Vaghe labbra voi ridete'	(Carestini)
replaced by:	'Chi mi toglie'	Hasse, *Attalo*, Naples 1728	id.	Merighi
Strada	'È follia se nascondete'	Leo, *Catone*	id.	Facchinelli
Senesino	'Mi conosci'	Leo, *Catone*	id.	Grimaldi
Bertolli	'Vaghe luci, luci belle'	(Vivaldi, *Ipermestra*, Florence 1727)	id.	(Lucia Lancetti)
Montagnana	'Agitato da più venti'	(Vivaldi ?)		
Strada	('Di tenero affetto')	Leo, *Catone*	id.	Facchinelli
(cut)				
Gismondi	'Care faci'	?		
replaced by:	'Sento in riva'	Hasse, *Attalo*	id.	Merighi
Montagnana	'So che nascondi'	Vivaldi, *Orlando*, Venice 1727	'Benche nasconda'	Gaetano Pinetti
(inserted later)				

206

Singer	Aria	Source		Replacement
Senesino	'Dovea svenarti'	Leo, *Catone*	id.	Grimaldi
Strada	'Sò che godendo'	Leo, *Catone*	id.	Facchinelli
Gismondi	'Fra tanti pensieri'	Hasse, *Demetrio*, Venice 1732	id.	Bordoni
Strada	'Confusa, smarrita'	Leo, *Catone*	id.	Facchinelli
Bertolli	'Quando piomba'	Porpora (*Poro*, Turin 1731)	id.	(Anna Bagnolesi)
Montagnana	'È ver che all'amo'	(Porpora, *Poro*)	id.	(*Montagnana*)
Gismondi	(unknown aria)			
replaced by:	'Vede il nocchier la sponda'	Hasse, *Euristeo*, Venice 1732	id.	Caffarelli
Senesino	'Per darvi alcun'	Leo, *Catone*	id.	Grimaldi
Strada	'Soffre talor'	(Leo, *Catone*)	id.	Dom. Gizzi
replaced by:	'Vò solcando'	Vinci, *Artaserse*, Rome 1730	id.	Carestini

Semiramide riconosciuta (30 October 1733)

	Sinfonia	Vinci, *Artaserse*, Rome 1730		
Durastanti	'Non sò se più'	Vinci, *Semiramide*, Rome 1729	id.	Giacinto Fontana
Carestini	'Scherza il nocchier'	Fr. Corselli (remark in conducting score)		
Strada	'Che quel cor'	Vinci, *Semiramide*		
G. Waltz	('Maggior follia')	Vinci, *Semiramide*	id.	Gaetano Berenstadt
replaced by:				
Cat. Negri	'Trovo ch'è gran follia'	Hasse, *Caio Fabricio*, Rome 1732	'Non sempre oprar'	Domenico Annibali
Scalzi	'Bel piacer'	Vinci, *Semiramide*	id.	Scalzi
Rosa Negri	'Pensa ad amare'	?		
Carestini	(unknown aria)			
replaced by:				
Strada	'Dal labbro tuo'	Hasse (*Antigona*, Milan 1732)	id.	*Carestini*
Durastanti	'Ti credo a me pietoso'	Hasse (*Arminio*, Milan 1730)	'Potresti esser pietoso'	(*Bordoni*)
replaced by:	'Voi non sapete'	Vinci, *Semiramide*	id.	Fontana
	('Se colle vostre')	?		
Scalzi	'Rondinella'	Vinci, *Semiramide*	id.	*Scalzi*
Strada	'Mi disprezzi'	Hasse (*Arminio*)	'Dolce rieda'	(*Bordoni*)

Cat. Negri	'Saper bramate'	Vinci, *Semiramide*	id.	Berenstadt
Scalzi	'Sarà piacer'	Leo, *Demetrio*, Naples 1732	id.	Teresa Cotti
Cat. Negri replaced by:	(unknown aria)			
Rosa Negri	'D'amor trafitto sei'	Leo, *Argeno*, Venice 1728	'Mio cor tradito sei'	Farinelli
Scalzi	'Fiumicel'	Vinci, *Semiramide*	id.	*Scalzi*
Strada	'Tortorella'	Sarri, *Artemisia*, Naples 1731	id.	Cuzzoni
Durastanti	'Tradita, sprezzata'	Vinci, *Semiramide*	id.	Fontana
Carestini	'Passagier'	Vinci, *Semiramide*	id.	Barbieri
replaced by:	'Peregrin'	Hasse, *Attalo*, Naples 1728	id.	*Carestini*
G. Waltz replaced by:	(unknown aria)			
Cat. Negri	'Qual nocchier'	Feo, *Andromaca*, Rome 1730	id.	Annibali
Scalzi	'In braccio a mille'	Vinci, *Semiramide*	id.	*Scalzi*
Cat. Negri replaced by:	(unknown aria)			
Rosa Negri	'Avezzo alla catena'	Hasse, *Demetrio*, Venice 1732	'Non sembra ardito e fiero'	Appiani
Durastanti	'Fuggi dagli occhi'	Vinci, *Semiramide*	id.	Fontana
Carestini	'Se in campo'	Vinci, *Catone*, Rome 1728	id.	*Carestini*
Strada	'Per far che risplenda'	Hasse, *Tigrane*, Naples 1729	'Se brami che splenda'	Mazzoni
Carestini	'Un'aura placida di bella speme'	(Porta, *Gianguir*, Milan 1732)	id.	*Carestini*

Caio Fabricio (4 December 1733)

	Sinfonia	?		
Cat. Negri	'In così lieto'	Hasse, *Caio Fabricio*, Rome 1732	id.	Alessandro Veroni
Carestini	('Vedi l'amata figlia')	Hasse, *C. Fabricio*	id.	Caffarelli
replaced by:	'Fissa ne' sguardi'	Hasse, (*Ulderica*, Naples 1729)	id.	(Antonio Bernacchi)
Strada	'Il trono, il regno'	Hasse, *C. Fabricio*	id.	Angelo Monticelli

Cat. Negri	'Non ti ricuso'	Hasse, *C. Fabricio*	id.	Felice Salimbeni
replaced by:				
Durastanti	'Vezzi lusinghe'	Hasse, *Tigrane*, Naples 1729	id.	Teresa Pieri
	('Scherza talor')			A. Fontana
Scalzi	'Per amor se il cor'	Hasse, *C. Fabricio*	id.	Farinelli
replaced by:		Vinci, *Astianatte*, Naples 1725		
Carestini	'Reca la pace'	Hasse, *C. Fabricio*	id.	Caffarelli
replaced by:				
Durastanti	'Quando verrà'	?		
Strada	'Caro sposo'	Hasse, *C. Fabricio*	id.	Monticelli
Durastanti	'Amore a lei'	Hasse, *C. Fabricio*	id.	Salimbeni
Carestini	'Non ha più pace'	Hasse, *C. Fabricio*	id.	Caffarelli
Rosa Negri	'Giovani cori'	Hasse, *C. Fabricio*	id.	Felice Checacci
G. Waltz	'Non sempre oprar'	Hasse, *C. Fabricio*	id.	Dom. Annibali
cut: see *Semiramide*				
Scalzi	(unknown aria)	(Corselli, *Venere placata*, Venice 1731)	id.	(Pietro Murigi)
replaced by:	'Troppo fiere'			
Carestini	(unknown aria)	(Albinoni, *La fortezza al cimento*, Milan 1729)	id.	*Carestini*
replaced by:	'Al foco del mio amore'			
Strada	'Non mi chiamar'	Hasse, *C. Fabricio*	id.	Monticelli
Scalzi	'Nocchier che teme'	Hasse, *C. Fabricio*	id.	Fontana
Durastanti	('Sarà vezzosa')	Hasse, *C. Fabricio*	id.	Veroni
replaced by:				
Cat. Negri	'È grande e bella'	Anonymous, Naples c. 1725	'Non sempre torna'	
Durastanti	'Volgi a me'	Hasse, *C. Fabricio*	id.	Salimbeni
G. Waltz	'Quella è mia figlia'	Hasse, *C. Fabricio*	id.	Annibali
Carestini	'Vedrai morir'	Hasse, *C. Fabricio*	id.	Caffarelli
Strada	'Lo sposo va'	Hasse, *C. Fabricio*	id.	Monticelli
Scalzi	'Varcherò'	Hasse, *C. Fabricio*	id.	Fontana

				Teresa Cotti
Carestini	'Vorrei da lacci sciogliere'	Leo, *Demetrio*, Naples 1732	id.	
coro finale	'Con la pace'	(not by Hasse)		

Arbace (5 January 1734)

	Sinfonia	?		
Strada	'Conservati fedele'	Vinci, *Artaserse*, Rome 1730	id.	Giacinto Fontana
Carestini	'Fra cento affanni'	Vinci, *Artaserse*, Rome 1730	id.	*Carestini*
Scalzi	'Per pietà bell' idol mio	Vinci, *Artaserse*, Rome 1730	id.	Raffaele Signorini
Cat. Negri	'Bramar di perdere'	Vinci, *Artaserse*, Rome 1730	id.	Giuseppe Appiani
Scalzi	'Deh respirar'	Vinci, *Artaserse*, Rome 1730	id.	Signorini
Durastanti	'Non ti son padre'	Vinci, *Artaserse*, Rome 1730	id.	Francis Tolve
Strada	'Impallidisci ingrato'	Hasse, *Issipile*, Naples 1732	'Impallidisce in campo'	Lucia Fachinelli
Carestini	'Vò solcando'	Vinci, *Artaserse*	id.	*Carestini*
cf. *Catone*; replaced by:	'Son qual nave ch'agitata'	(Hasse, *Artaserse*, Lucca 1730)	id.	(Farinelli)
Scalzi	'Rendimi il caro'	Vinci, *Artaserse*	id.	Signorini
Carestini	'Mi scacci sdegnato'	Vinci, *Artaserse*	id.	*Carestini*
replaced by:	'Caro padre ah forse è questo'	Porta, *Lucio Papirio*, Rome 1732	id.	*Carestini*
Rosa Negri	'Non temer ch'io'	Vinci, *Artaserse*	id.	Giovanni Ossi
Strada	'Se d'un amor'	Vinci, *Artaserse*	id.	Fontana
Carestini	'Per quel paterno'	Vinci, *Artaserse*	id.	*Carestini*
Scalzi	'Potessi al mio diletto'	Hasse, *Dalisa*, Venice 1730	'Se fosse il mio diletto'	Bordoni
Durastanti	'Così stupisce'	Vinci, *Artaserse*	id.	Tolve
Carestini	'Perche tarda è mai'	Vinci, *Artaserse*	id.	*Carestini*
Scalzi	('Nuvoletta')	Vinci, *Artaserse*	id.	Signorini
replaced by:	'Se l'amor tuo mi rendi'	Hasse, *Siroe*, Bologna 1733	id.	Farinelli
Carestini	'L'onda dal mar'	Vinci, *Artaserse*	id.	*Carestini*
Durastanti	'Figlio se piu'	Vinci, *Artaserse*	id.	Tolve
Strada	'Mi credi spietata'	Vinci, *Artaserse*	id.	Fontana
Strada + Carestini	'Tu vuoi ch'io viva'	Vinci, *Artaserse*	id.	Fontana + *Carestini*

coro finale replaced by:

				Carestini
Carestini	'Di te degno non sarei'		id.	Carestini

Didone abbandonata (13 April 1737)

		Porta, *L. Papirio*		*Carestini*
Sinfonia				Carestini
Conti	'Ahi lasso vorrei'	Vinci, *Didone*, Rome 1726	id.	Finazzi
Bertolli	'Dirò che fida sei'	?	id.	Fontana
Strada	'Son regina e sono amante'	Vinci, *Didone*	id.	Franchi
Cat. Negri	'Grato rende'	Vinci, *Didone*	id.	Berenstadt
Annibali	'Fra lo splendor'	Vinci, *Didone*	id.	Domenico Gizzi
Beard	'Se dalle stelle'	Vinci, *Didone*	id.	Antonio Barbieri
Conti	'Quando saprai'	Vinci, *Didone*	id.	Gaetano Berenstadt
Annibali	'Son quel fiume'	Vinci, *Didone*	id.	Fontana
Strada	'Non ha ragione'	Vinci, *Didone*	id.	
Conti	'Tra fieri opposti'	?	id.	
Annibali	'Leon ch'errando vada'	Vinci, *Didone*	id.	Berenstadt
Bertolli	'Tanto amor si bella fede'	Vinci, *Semiramide*, Rome 1729	'Ei d'amor quasi delira'	Pietro Murigi
Beard	'Amor che nasce'	Vinci, *Didone*	id.	Gizzi
Strada	'Se vuoi ch'io mora'	Vinci, *Didone*	id.	Fontana
Conti	'Vedi nel mio'	Vinci, *Didone*	id.	Barbieri
Conti	'Sono intrepido nell'alma'	Giacomelli, *Annibale*, Rome 1731	'Per te perdo il mio contento'	Angelo Monticelli
Annibali	'Chiamami pur cosi'	Vinci, *Didone*	id.	Berenstadt
Strada	'Ritorna a lusingarmi'	Vivaldi, *Griselda*, Venice 1735	id.	Margherita Giacomazzi
Annibali (insertion lost)	('Quel pastor')	Ristori		(*Annibali*?)
Conti	'Mi tradì l'infida'	?	id.	
Cat. Negri	'Quando l'onda'	Vinci, *Didone*	id.	Franchi
Conti	'A trionfar mi chiama'	Hasse, *Euristeo*, Venice 1732 (cf. *Catone*)	'Vede il nocchier la sponda'	Caffarelli

Bertolli	'Ch'io resti! Ch'io viva! Ma come?'	Hasse, *Issipile*, Naples 1732	'Ch'io speri! Ma come?'	Lucia Fachinelli
Strada	'Va crescendo'	Vinci, *Didone*	id.	Fontana
Strada	'Già si desta'	Vinci, *Didone*	id.	Gizzi
Annibali	'Cadrà fra poco in cenere'	Hasse, *C. Fabricio*, Rome 1732, cf. *Semiramide, C. Fabricio*	'Non sempre oprar da forte'	*Annibali*
Strada (Final *accompagnato*)	'Vado ma dove'	Vinci, *Didone*	id.	Fontana

Leonardo Vinci's *Didone abbandonata* (Rome 1726)

L EONARDO VINCI (1696–1730) had enormous success as an opera-composer during his life, and posterity has, for once, confirmed rather than denied this success. His works were more frequently performed after his death than was usual for the time, and they were much studied. Among the many who praised them we find Metastasio, Algarotti, Burney, and Grétry. Grétry, although he also criticised his work and compared it unfavourably with that of Pergolesi, still allowed that Vinci was a 'genius'.[1] Grétry's generation knew only Vinci's *drammi per musica*, the very first of which (*Publio Cornelio Scipione*, 1722) had been a huge popular success in Naples, while his last work (*Artaserse*, with libretto by Metastasio, Rome 1730) must have had a bigger European reputation than any single work by Hasse or Pergolesi, with the exception of *La Serva Padrona*. Vinci died young, but he was regarded in retrospect as one of the first important representatives of the Neapolitan operatic tradition which liberated the aria from the shackles of counterpoint (as Burney says) and, with the help of Metastasio's libretti, produced the first examples of good declamation and orchestral colour. Taken with a grain of salt, these judgements still stand. Of course Vinci was also credited personally with merits which he cannot claim – the 'invention', for instance, of obbligato accompaniments for the second violin (actually an innovation introduced about 1720) and even of accompagnato recitative, which existed a hundred years earlier. In fact memories of him combine truth and legend only slightly less remarkably than in the case of Pergolesi. This proves, in spite of the naïveté of early historians of opera, the lasting fascination exercised by these two remarkable artists, who had much in common with each other. Pergolesi was in fact a pupil of Vinci during his short spell as Kapellmeister of the 'Poveri di Gesù Cristo' in Naples (1728). During the eighteenth century, the four Naples conservatories were the most influential educational institutions in Italy for both singers and composers.[2] It was there that young musicians, often of very humble social origin, must have conceived ambitions to become Kapellmeister or famous opera-composers; there too that the arduous education began of those boys to whom castration had denied all but a single

213

path to professional success. Before Vinci's day these conservatories had numbered Nicola Porpora, Francesco Feo and Leonardo Leo among their students and professors, these being only the best known of a long list of musicians educated at these conservatories and then left to earn their livelihood as best they could. Only a few of them could be absorbed by the other musical institutions in Naples, chief among which were the vice-regal and municipal chapel. Naples was an overcrowded city, commercially weak and impaired from the cultural point of view by the War of the Spanish Succession, which had robbed many potential patrons among the aristocracy of their possessions and many musicians of their livelihood. This was the cause of many artists, not only musicians, emigrating – a movement that began about 1710 and accounts for the spread of Neapolitan music first over Italy and then over the whole of Europe, thus creating the collective Neapolitan reputation for musical talent. There is a parallel instance in the emigration of Bohemian musicians to Western Europe about the middle of the century.

Leonardo Vinci was a typical example of this group of composers, although Naples always remained his home. His first major successes were in Rome (from 1724 onwards) and Venice (from 1725) and he won them not with his *commedie per musica*, which were only appreciated in Naples, but with his *drammi per musica*.[3] *Opera seria* was the fashion of the day, attracting the interest (and money) of the princes of the church in Rome, the patrician families of Venice and the courts of northern Italy and the rest of Europe. Any Neapolitan composer unable to earn enough by regular employment (if he could find it) in that city was obliged to look for individual operatic commissions (*scritture*) from theatres in the north and to learn to conform with the public taste and the theatrical organisation in all the different centres. Similarly, the singers trained in Naples (for example, by Porpora), for the most part castrati, had from the start to plan their careers on inter-regional and international lines.

In fact nothing contributed more to unify the technical and stylistic means of operatic composition and singing. Unlike the court composers with fixed posts at royal or aristocratic residences who were seldom given leave of absence, musicians who depended on obtaining individual commissions could broaden their experience by contact with foreign conditions of performance, foreign music and foreign audiences, insofar as they had to travel to carry out their commissions on the spot. This soon became the normal practice for composers.

Besides, music itself was kept perpetually 'on the move', either by the singers who travelled from one place to another inserting their most successful arias in the numerous pasticcio operas of those days or by scores being copied and reperformed in different places. Moreover the public itself began to become more mobile during these years. Not only German princes with their retinues, but rich and cultured individual members of the aristocracy and the grande bourgeoisie of Italy and the rest of Europe began to travel in Italy and visit its opera-houses, collecting impressions and acquaintances, antiques, relics and objets d'art. These might also include manuscript music, mostly operatic arias which were at the time copied individually and sold to the public in large quantities. Italian souvenirs of this kind would be used for private performance or further adapted. These foreign visitors very often recorded their impressions in literary form, and their travel-diaries, letters and more novelistic descriptions became a characteristic eighteenth-century literary genre. Many of these descriptions deal with operatic music, and the most professional of them are those of Charles De Brosses, who was in Italy in 1739–4,[4] and Charles Burney.[5] Apart from spreading the fame of Italian operatic music, such writers as these obviously prepared its reception by the public in their respective countries.

This increase in circulation and the unification of taste first benefited the Neapolitan composers round Porpora, Vinci and eventually Hasse. For this reason it is virtually impossible to decide after the event whether the influence of 'the Neapolitan School' on European eighteenth-century music in general was due to its artistic superiority and its 'advanced' character or whether the reverse is true – that the universal influence of this music shaped the actual aesthetic standards of the two succeeding generations. The beginning of musical historicism, which also put an end to musical provincialism of many areas, attributed to the operas of Vinci a quite different actuality than to the works of, for example, Alessandro Scarlatti, despite his fame. The reawakening of interest in Scarlatti's use of the ecclesiastical style and of counterpoint is largely explained by the fact that these had become alien to later generations. But Vinci's operas had become universally familiar so soon that they were linked with more recent music by a network of traditions impossible to unravel. The reformer Algarotti refers, 1755, to the final scenes of *Didone abbandonata* as representing an as yet unsurpassed example of music-dramatic reality;[6] and Grétry, for all his criticism of Vinci, applies the same standards to an aria from *Artaserse* as he applied to the music of his own contemporaries.

Pietro Metastasio must be considered against the same background since his career began in similar circumstances. He was the exact opposite of the aristocratic reform-librettists of northern Italy, the men around Zeno, in that he was dependent from the start on the extended success of his pieces. On the other hand, in spite of friendly patronage from aristocratic circles in Naples, he did not have the fixed post that would have imposed on him the individual taste of a prince (and perhaps of his courtiers). He depended simply on a successful performance that might arouse the interest of some foreign patron or impresario and lead to a commission. The dramas that he wrote up to 1730, when he was officially appointed to Vienna, had to be constructed in quite a different way from those of, say, Zeno. They were written from start to finish in close collaboration with musicians, with the singers on whom the success of a work depended and by whom – as in the case of Marianna Benti-Bulgarelli, who sang the title role in *Didone abbandonata* – the success was in fact achieved. A close personal and artistic association of this kind between author and *primadonna* would have been unthinkable in Zeno's case, but it became common form in the eighteenth century – we have only to think of Vivaldi and Anna Giró, Hasse and Faustina Bordoni, Traetta and Caterina Gabrielli and indeed, in a sense, of Metastasio's own close friendship with Farinelli. The professional life and the private life of the eighteenth-century artist were closely linked because his material existence depended on his art. This was certainly true of Metastasio's life in Rome and Naples, where he wrote a number of the libretti that had most influence on the genre, before becoming Imperial Court Poet in Vienna in 1730.

It was Metastasio's earliest works that most quickly became popular. The earliest 'collected edition' of his works was published (by Bettinelli in Venice) from as early as 1733, and London was already complaining in 1726 that there had been no Haymarket performances of the two of his works (*Didone* and *Siroe*) already in existence. (See Deutsch, p. 197.)

The receptiveness of the operatic public during the 1720s and 1730s not only ensured the artists working in Naples the success that they needed, it also did much to determine their ideas in advance. These ideas had nothing whatever to do with operatic 'reform'. All the artistic resources of the day were concentrated on the *dramma per musica*, and not on the intermezzo or, still less, on the *commedia per musica*, which still had no more than a restricted, provincial appeal. Nobody wanted to risk yet another revolution in dramatic ideas. Greater musical demands were made on the orchestra, it is true, but these consisted of fuller, more intensive use of existing instruments rather than recruiting new instrumental forces. Both text and music of the arias are totally identified with the singers and their acting, and more particularly with those singers of whom audiences expected most. The importance of stage sets and machinery, of crowd scenes, stage fights ('abbattimenti') and ballets diminished because attractions of this kind needed complicated preparation and were difficult to transport from one theatre to another, thus prejudicing the popularising of a work. Large theatres still continued to offer such attractions as were within their powers, but they are only rarely incorporated in libretto or score. The same is true of the chorus, whose role certainly does not increase during these years.

We must not of course confuse the skill with which Metastasio and his fellow-composers exploited the historical situation with their real contribution to the genre of the *dramma per musica*. To assess that contribution, let us try to understand the situation in the year 1725 when Metastasio and Vinci began their collaboration, and consider for a moment the artistic solutions which seemed correct to them at that time and to promise well for the future with the public.

Some time in the autumn of 1725 the two of them received corresponding commissions from outside Naples. Metastasio, whose *Didone abbandonata* had been given in Venice during that year's Carnival, was now to write a new drama for the Teatro S. Giovanni Grisostomo. Conte Antonio d'Alibert's theatre in Rome commissioned a new version of his *Didone*. (This theatre, founded in 1717, had just passed from the possession of Alibert to the Knights of Malta and was renamed 'Teatro delle Dame' after its enlargement in 1725.)[7] Vinci was chosen to set both of these works. It seems improbable that he picked on the librettist or that Metastasio actually chose him as his collaborator. It is more likely that the collaboration was arranged by the impresarios. The work for Venice was *Siroe re di Persia* and Metastasio was present at the performance in February 1726, when he gave an enthusiastic account of its success.[8] *Didone abbandonata* had its first performance on 14 January 1726 in Rome and on 31 January Metastasio received a gift worth 65 scudi as fee for his adaptation of the text.[9] This must have been about a quarter of the fee paid to the composer and about a tenth of that paid to the best singers. For ostensibly moral reasons only male singers were employed in Roman theatres during the eighteenth century, that is to say castrati and tenors. In this particular case the cast consisted of three sopranos (two of them in women's roles), two altos and one tenor. It is very possible that Metastasio, who was working in Rome for the first time, assisted at rehearsals, possibly with Marianna Bulgarelli (who sang Didone at the first performance of the work in 1724 at Naples), as we have evidence that this was so in the corresponding case of the opera in the following year. The giving of such an all-important woman's role to a castrato seem to have presented no problems of dramatic presentation; and indeed audiences do not appear in general to have wanted 'naturalistic' casting in the *dramma per musica* of the day.[10] In a later letter Metastasio spoke highly of the feminine grace of the castrato Giacinto Fontana's acting – he was in fact nicknamed 'Farfallino' (little butterfly)! – who sang the part of Didone in 1726. Male sopranos specialising in women's roles were almost only to be found in Rome, where acting in general was not judged by naturalistic standards. There, as elsewhere, the decisive factor was the virtuoso singing, with its extraordinary – and as it were sexually neutral – power of conviction. Not that this meant dull acting. According to the account of the 1726 performance Didone's first aria ('Son regina e sono amante') was greeted with a storm of applause which 'appeared to shake the theatre to its foundations'.[11] Such comments demand an explanation, which should take into account both the acting and the music.[12]

If Metastasio, as the poet, was concerned with rehearsing the opera from the textual (and perhaps also the stage) point of view, he had in the first place to come to a complete understanding with the composer. The overriding concern of both was to make the greatest possible use of the stage and of the singers' powers. Therein lay the simple secret of the success of Metastasio's early libretti, which did not make their way purely by their literary quality but benefited from the author's further assistance. For this Roman performance Metastasio provided no less than eight new arias (one of which he had already used in an early serenata). These are not referred to in any of the editions. An even greater number of the arias in the original version, however, were dropped, and the distribution of arias among the different characters was slightly changed – both Enea and Jarba, for instance, lost an aria while Araspe gained one. Even so the changes of this kind were, by the standards of the day, small: it was not only a matter of the singers' claims, the composer's wishes played in fact a more important part. In seven cases Vinci made use of music that he had already composed for other operas, either earlier or contemporaneously – *Ifigenia in Tauride* (Venice, Carnival 1725), *Astianatte* (Naples, December 1725) and even *Siroe re di Persia* (February 1726). In some cases Metastasio had to write parodies of texts that had already been set, bearing in mind of course the character of the music. In other cases Vinci seems to have composed arias which could be used with one text in *Didone* and another in *Siroe*. The aria with which Didone concludes the second act ('Prende ardire e si conforta') appears also at the end of the second act of *Siroe* with Metastasio's text 'Non vi piacque ingiusti dei', and is marked in the score 'un poco ardito'. The music of the arias 'Ardi per me fedele' and 'L'augelletto in lacci stretto' appears with different text in *Astianatte*. Since Metastasio's texts had been in existence since 1724 and Vinci's music suits them very well, this music seems originally to have been written for *Didone*, which would make the date of composition before December 1725. On the other hand the music of 'Se ti lagni sventurato' seems to have belonged originally to *Astianatte*, which has independent links with *Siroe*. Vinci obviously worked, with Metastasio's help, on all three works at more or less the same time. The sinfonias of *Didone* and *Astianatte* are identical and share a third section with the sinfonia of *Siroe*.

It is unfortunately impossible to go more thoroughly into the whole question of 'borrowings', since not all pieces concerned have been published. It must however be borne in mind that the emotional contents of a text often played no part in Vinci's decision to use the existing music of an aria with another text. It is worth noting that, even in the case of *Didone abbandonata*, Metastasio completely rewrote or substituted some aria texts in 1725, although the old text would have fitted both scenically and dramatically. This is the case with 'Grato rende il fiumicello', three lines of which are identical with the original 'Tu mi scorgi al gran disegno', 'Amor che nasce', 'Se vuoi che mora', 'Prende ardire' and 'Cadra frà poco in cenere'. There are quite a number of other instances in which it was not the content of the text that gave rise to alterations and reassignments of arias but rather the reverse, e.g. the parody of already existing arias was the cause, the alteration of the emotion expressed the result.

Thus the collaboration between Metastasio and Vinci was aimed not so much at a revision of the drama as at the perfect agreement between the structure of the text and the singing. Only one of Metastasio's parody texts seems to fit Vinci's melody poorly ('Sono intrepido nell'alma'), and it is interesting that in this case the original text ('Dolce horror che vezzeggiando' from *Ifigenia in Tauride*) was also a poor fit: a strange exception that proves the rule. The rule in Vinci's case, however, is the priority of declamation, and this establishes at the same time the priority of the speaking and acting stage-character over the atmospheric, non-verbal concept of 'affect'. This does not mean, of course, that Vinci did not also have inspired moments when it came to expressing an emotion, or a picture, without words – but those expressions are most often mediated by the speaking character on stage. Neither does the priority of speech imply that the speech in the arias was of a naturalistic kind – this would have been made impossible by Metastasio's artful poetry, which Vinci translates into musical formulae.

The first da capo aria of the opera is Selene's 'Dirò che fida sei' (Example 1). Selene promises to convey her sister Didone's love and fidelity to Enea,

Example 1

whom she herself secretly loves. Against this emotional background the music seems rather cool, and the opening theme even frivolous, its metrical and melodic symmetry being an abstract musical idea. The two-part structure, which is capable of forming the basis of an eight-bar period, is distilled from the very first line above – a self-sufficient statement on which the following lines comment. The accented words 'dirò', 'sei', 'fida' are emphasised by rhythm and interval – 'dirò' by the leap of a fifth, 'sei' by extreme melodic positions and 'fida' by repetitions. 'Dirò', which is not repeated, is also isolated by the unusual interval, which at the same time accentuates the sonorous difference between the two syllables – whereas the linking of the two vowels in 'se-i' is perfectly smooth. The repetition of notes in the first half is matched by the repetition of words and motifs in the second, just as the firmness of Selene's promise matches the firmness of Didone's fidelity. If we first familiarise ourselves with the phrase, we can experiment with possible alterations of it. If, for instance, the second half were declaimed to a strict repetition of the whole line, the repetitions of the motif 'fida' would lose their meaning, i.e. their reference to Didone's fidelity. If we imagine a falling instead of a rising fifth at the opening, we would replace the imaginary colon by a full stop. Vinci's phrase is subtly balanced with the verse-line, without which it makes a primitive impression. Musical simplicity was sought for its own sake by other composers – Vivaldi, for instance – before Vinci. They, however, showed themselves indifferent to the verses.

The motivic material of the aria is strictly divided between the different lines, not because Vinci works in a 'schematic' way, but because Metastasio strictly divides the different contents of the lines. The addition of emotional expression remains, as it were, optional when the line 'sarò per te pietosa' is provided with plangent chromaticisms only at its second appearance in the aria. This motif in fact anticipates the opening of the aria 'Se vuoi ch'io mora', where Didone herself begs for sympathy. The motif 'per me sarò crudel' (the rearrangement of the text here is an improvement on the line which, in the libretto, runs 'per me crudel sarò') returns in Selene's own aria 'Ardi per me fedele' to the words 'se poi non hai mercè', where she must herself now treat Araspe without pity.[13] What is remarkable here is not the thematic connection as such, since in this work Vinci employs a fairly rigid repertory of formulae, but the way in which it corresponds to the mutual relationships of the characters: the repetition of the theme of unrequited love and fidelity ('pietà–crudeltà') on three different planes, Didone–Enea, Selene–Didone and Araspe–Selene.

In Didone's first aria 'Son regina e sono amante' she presents herself in the full glare of the footlights: it is a self-portrait in words. After fierce exchanges with Jarba in which each party firmly establishes its own arguments, Didone (now rising to her full height) finally concludes the game of thrust and counter-thrust with an aria to which there is absolutely no reply. She 'alone' sacrifices her heart as well as her kingdom, and this is expressed in stage-terms by her physical isolation as she sings her aria. The conflict becomes wholly personal and centres around her twin identities as both 'regina' and 'amante' (Example 2). We move from the visual perception of the stage in general to the portrait. The listener, who has already identified himself with the singer of the role but has been obliged to listen to the display of the wicked Jarba, is now released from tension – wild applause denotes his sense of liberation. The music of the aria is correspondingly less differentiated than that of Selene's preceding music, and the imperious repetitions of downbeat motifs give the aria an almost aggressive

Example 2

character. A less accomplished dramatist than Vinci would have made a strong musical contrast between 'regina' and 'amante' (with some kind of sentimental motif), thus touching the queen, as it were, too closely: the fact that she is in love does not as yet concern anyone but herself. Vinci does not musically interpret her personality, but first allows her to present herself fully in theatrical terms. La Bulgarelli must have regretted that she did not have the chance to sing this setting.

The chief male characters of the work are also given similar opportunities for self-portrayal. When Enea sings 'Quando saprai chi sono' (Act I scene 10) he is still incognito, and the music is content to refer to his hereditary kingship by means of the traditional ciacona-pattern and the strict dotted rhythms of the French overture, historically associated with 'le Roi Soleil'. In 'Vedi nel mio perdono' (Act II scene 8) he reveals himself to the inferior African princes in the full glory of his magnanimity and 'virtù' (Example 3). Here the dotted rhythms occur also in the vocal line, while the violins are given aggressive demi-semi-quaver figures. At the opening of the middle section there is a really magnificent change of manner in the switch from

Example 3

Example 3 (*cont.*)

'vedilo' – which is a quotation from the beginning of the aria – to 'e dimmi poi'. 'Vivi superbo e regna' (Act III scene 2) sets the musical seal on the parity between Enea and Didone as royal personages. The words in a situation similar to that in 'Vedi nel mio perdono' are addressed to Jarba, but Vinci rightly refers the words 'superbo' and 'regna' to Enea rather than to him. Among the motifs recalling 'Son regina e sono amante' should be mentioned the unison-cadences of the voice on the notes of the triad, which introduce the aria as an instrumental motif. Bass-like cadences ('bassierende Klauseln', Heinichen) of this and similar kinds in the voice part militate against the contrapuntal thinking of the day (formulated, for example, in Marcello's *Teatro all moda*), and may also appear primitive to us. They are in any case the reverse of 'bel canto'. But Vinci's unison technique in heroic passages becomes something approaching a symbol of absolutism – the absolute domination of the many by the one, whether applied to human beings or to notes. Complementary in spirit is the technical idea of the busy accompaniment-figure, the 'accompagnato obbligato' of the second violins. Whereas Aeneas' kingship lived on in an empire to which the clergy in the boxes of the Teatro delle Dame still reckoned themselves as belonging, Dido's palace and Dido's empire disappeared. The evil Moorish king Jarba prophesied this in his 'Cadrà fra poco in cenere' (Act III scene 3), where once again Vinci isolates a single word – 'cadrà' which says all. The rest is, as it were, figurative presentation of the words of the text (for instance, the snaking melismatic lines suggesting the path of the errant wanderer) and is also concerned with establishing their most convincing declamation. Jarba does not speak emotionally, from a vague desire for vengeance: the very words of his curse give him the grandeur of a mythical figure. Musical formation must have been regarded by Vinci not as a matter of emotional interpretation but as a sculpting of words to which music lent, as it were, substance. There is therefore something crystalline about his forms. His music is so closely identified with the words that the listener is still aware of them as living speech, Metastasio's lines being converted into musical sound and only thus perfectly achieving their identity. We shall be on the right track if we study Jarba's words, 'E se all'età futura non rimanesse oscura' (Example 4), where Vinci's music is so perfectly natural that we are

Example 4

hardly aware of its existence: it has 'nothing to add'. Metastasio in fact later replaced the text of this aria by a two-line cavatina – 'la caduta d'un regnante/ tutto un regno opprimerà'. This is a paraphrase of the last line of the original recitative – 'opprimerà la mia caduta un regno'. Here in fact we have a 'Cavata' in which the text of an aria is 'hollowed' (cavato) out of a recitative. The cavatina of the eighteenth century is only a development of this procedure, its defining characteristics being merely brevity and uniformity.[14]

Didone has two such 'cavatinas' (as thus defined) in the final scenes of the opera. In the first, 'Và crescendo il mio tormento' (Example 5), she

Example 5

appears calm, though already anxious. The stage situation anticipates that of Mozart's Countess in *Figaro* – a solitary woman worrying about her future and appealing to heaven, but never losing her external calm or her clarity of mind. This is not so much a literary idea or a composer's imagination as a stage picture which, in this particular instance, we owe to the originality of a great actress, Marianna Bulgarelli. Metastasio and Vinci did no more than express her vision of the scene in words and music. Notice the growing intensity, the crescendo, of expression from the uneasy questioning of 'io lo sento – e non l'intendo' to the violent outburst of 'giusti dei' which dies away into the despairing 'che mai sarà?' (fermata). The repetition of that final question is taken back again, as she awaits the mysterious future with beating heart.

With 'I miei casi infelici' the orchestral recitatives begin, long before the final scene. As in Gasparini's *Bajazet* the whole final tragedy is enveloped in instrumental music (see Strohm 1979, p. 110). The broken or dotted violin figures, which are not continuous but reappear at unexpected intervals, have a threatening life of their own. Algarotti speaks of this sequence of recitatives as 'animata e terribile' – a description that applies in fact to the orchestra. The most astonishing feature, if we compare this with the tragic climaxes in other operas, is the economy of Vinci's means. He does not need to overwhelm his audience with sheer dynamic power, because his music is only the surface of an interior drama which is itself terrible. The end is prepared long beforehand. In the second cavatina, 'Vado...ma dove', Metastasio refers back to Enea's very first arioso, 'Dovrei...ma no', in the metre, the verbal style and even the assonances of the text, but makes the final line rhyme with the end of Didone's first cavatina. These dramatic references in the text explain Vinci's music, which is determined by words, rhymes and phrase-shapes. In his setting of this final scene the catastrophe is actually expressed by the extinguishing of the language – which is the life of the whole – by the orchestra, just as Dido's voice is extinguished by the flames. If the orchestra had played a noisily insistent part, it would not now have the same mysterious power. And if language had not reigned supreme over the whole work, its final extinction would not now be the symbol of total destruction.

Handel's *Ezio*

WHEN HANDEL wrote his London operas, he was looking back to his early years in Italy, that is to say before 1710. Their style is in fact so rooted in those youthful experiences and early models that already by 1720 his works had ceased to appeal to Italian audiences. Handel himself was of course well aware of the reasons why he did not adopt certain technical features more recently developed by Italian composers: he was certainly well acquainted with those idioms and showed, in exceptional cases, that he had fully mastered them. He was guided to a large degree in this matter by the specific nature of Italian opera in London, by the demands of audiences and of those who commissioned new works. It is not that his development as a composer had in any way come to a halt: he was searching for answers to Italian innovations, and searching in tradition, and many of his answers are unique in the history of opera. His shrewd appreciation of Italian developments can be seen, among other places, in the pasticcio operas that he arranged from the music of other composers. As early as 1725 he was the first to perform Leonardo Vinci's music outside Italy – that was in the pasticcio *Elpidia* (see pp. 167–9 above). His own *Ezio* (1732) was the third, and revealingly enough the last occasion on which he concerned himself with one of Metastasio's dramas.

Let me give a short sketch of the features which lead me to speak of Handel's technique of composition in 1732 as 'backward-looking'. There is, in the first place, the rhythmic character of the arias, in which there is a preponderance of the sarabands, gigues and gavottes that Italian composers had almost completely ceased to use. The siciliano becomes if anything increasingly important, while the minuet is not stylised but retains its geometrically precise proportions. In the second place voice and orchestra retain equal rights in the matter of counterpoint, and the rich accompaniment figures used by Porpora, for instance, appear only in exceptional cases and then as a special means of expression, not as a musical principle. Handel is very careful with his use of 'colla parte' (unison or octave doubling of the vocal line by the violins), which he frequently conceals in a middle voice, whereas Italian composers are happy to allow it to occupy the top line of

225

the orchestral part. In the aria 'Se fedele mi brama il regnante' (HG, p. 34), for example, the melody of the voice is almost always covered by a higher-lying violin part often in contrary motion, and the 'colla parte' is divided between different instruments. It is even more common, however, for the violins to be given a concertante line that imitates and rivals that of the voice, something that had been developed by such composers as G. Bononcini (*Trionfo di Camilla*) and A. Scarlatti before 'colla parte' became common. Handel's basses, in particular, refuse to give up their dominant or at least independent position. Whereas a composer like Hasse often gives them no more than a simple, subordinate role supporting the voice, with Handel the bass-line is almost always mobile, with important intervals and figures that give it a share in the motivic expression. Harmonic rhythm remains short-paced, and long stretches of static harmony are only used at individual points for the sake of contrast, not – as so noticeably in Vivaldi – as foundations of the harmonic articulation. When Handel wants to give the vocal line unquestioned prominence, he leaves it – as Scarlatti does – unaccompanied, whereas Vinci and Pergolesi in such cases give the voice grand gestures and wide leaps against a vibrant orchestral background. Orchestral differentiation itself is very seldom so marked as, for example, in the obbligato accompaniments that Vinci gives to the second violin.

The orchestra in general assumes descriptive functions quite apart from the voice and the words. The ritornelli of the arias are constructed with increasing mastery and maintain, for all their relative brevity, a kind of formal independence. In purely orchestral passages – which Italian composers of the day neglected – and in the accompanied recitatives the instruments claim the listener's concentrated attention (see Fulvia's *accompagnato*, HG, p. 52, where the orchestral introduction is full of expressive power and is followed by the independent gestures of the violins, which then as it were die away). Work still remains to be done to discover why Handel always begins his operas with an overture rather than a sinfonia, bearing in mind the function of these pieces for patrons and public.

Technical musical reasons will not of course explain why Handel, who generally chose his own libretti, so seldom chose Metastasio. There is a real problem here. We know that as early as the 1720s, the poetry of the great Arcadian was sought after in London and that Handel's setting of Metastasio's *Siroe re di Persia* in 1728 fulfilled a universal wish that had been expressed long before (see Deutsch, p. 197). After 1732, however, when Metastasio had become a kind of European institution, Handel set no more of his works. On the other hand he used Metastasio texts for four of his nine pasticcio operas with music of different composers in the years 1732–7 (see pp. 179–99, above). The other five had libretti by Zeno, only two of whose dramas Handel himself had set – both in 1738 and probably at Heidegger's instigation rather than by his own choice. As operatic producer, therefore, Handel seems to have followed public taste rather than his own ideals as a composer. A factor that probably contributed to Handel's choice of *Ezio* in 1732 was the foundation of the libretto on the *Britannicus* of Jean Racine, in whom he seems to have been particularly interested at this period.[1]

The first performance of Metastasio's *Ezio* was in Rome (Carnival 1729) with music by Pietro Auletta, since when it had also been set by Porpora, Predieri and Hasse. In each of these cases the text had been 'arranged', i.e. provided with new aria-texts and slightly cut, as was common practice at that time, though the recitatives had been little altered. Handel's procedure was quite different – no new aria-texts, hardly a line changed even in the recitative, stage-settings and stage directions scrupulously observed, but the total length of the recitative reduced by a third, though the dramatic action remains exactly the same. Whoever rewrote the text for Handel – we do not know his identity – had the difficult task of reducing Metastasio's fluent and prolix dialogue to the minimum demanded by the drama: and this was doubtless because, despite the translation printed in the libretto, the London public did not understand the text of the recitatives well enough to appreciate its literary quality. Many scenes consisting entirely of recitative were simply cut (for example, the opening scene, which is a kind of prologue) and even scenes ending with an aria. Other than this, however, the first and last lines of scenes, marking entrances or exits, were retained so that the characters still observe, as it were, the choreography of Metastasio's original. The balance between poetry and music is of course shifted. What is lost is the dialogue in which Metastasio characterises his figures by their words; what is added is Handel's art, which characterises them by their singing. In spite of that art, there is a real loss – chiefly in the comments which the characters make on each other's actions, either directly or to a third person. The result of this is that characters stand out by their actions and no longer by the way they speak, that no light is thrown on an individual's action by the comments of others and that they all make a more confident and less reflective impression than they do in Metastasio. This is particularly true of Fulvia and Ezio. Fulvia no longer has the intelligence or the inclination to reflect and to question which make her heroism all the more admirable, whereas Ezio is no longer obliged to expose his funda- mental simplicity and self-conceit to the comments of the other characters. The motivations of the villainous Massimo virtually disappear, as does the real malice of his slandering, e.g. Ezio to Onoria in Act II scene 9 and to Valentinian in Act II scene 11.

Metastasio's art of psychological characterisation, however, reckoned without Handel's music which, on some occasions at least, conveys by means of an aria's music what was lost by the cutting of the recitative. Massimo has a longish monologue in Act I scene 5, where he carefully weighs up his

chances and comes to the conclusion that he can only rely on luck. In Handel
the recitative speaks only of swift courage to act, but the aria that follows
makes it clear by musical means that confidence may be deceptive and there
can be no hope of certainty. The aria thus adds something new to what the
words convey to the listener. This may of course sometimes result in
unintended surprises. In Act II scene 7 Fulvia has no opportunity to express
her scruples about Varo's suggestion that she should pretend to return
Valentinian's love. Her answer is to be found rather in the fourth line of
the aria where she can for the first time express how distasteful she finds
it to practise deception. This is important, because it also explains why, in
the great scene with Valentinian and Ezio (Act II scene 12), she hardly
manages to express her agony of mind in words, so that the listener must
recall the aria if he is to understand her violent rejection of the odious role
she has been made to play. The conversation between Varo and Onoria in
Act I scene 5 is less subtle and is, in fact, a failure from the dramatic point
of view. In Handel Onoria replies to Varo's suggestions with the aria
'Quanto mai felici siete, innocenti pastorelle', which must puzzle not only
him but the listener, who wonders why she should suddenly think about
shepherdesses, until the middle section of the aria finally explains why – and
by that time there has already been a great deal of pretty rococo music, for
no apparent reason. In the next scene Varo is alone and his aria is full of
expostulations to Onoria, who has meanwhile left the stage. In Metastasio
the arias occur in reverse order, which is the only logical one, chiefly because
Onoria remains on the stage and explains her thoughts (her longing for the
'libertà d'un ineguale amore', in fact) before the pastoral music begins.
Varo's aria was probably placed at the end of the scene for the benefit of
the bass Montagnana. This is theatrically more effective: Onoria cannot of
course reveal to a vassal what, in Metastasio, she reveals to the audience.
Even so, Metastasio leaves us more than once with the problem of the
simile-aria that opens with an unexplained nature-picture, for example at
the end of Act I, where Fulvia first denounces the cruelty of fate and then
starts singing about a sweet zephyr-breeze. Flights of fancy of this kind are
of course expected at the end of an act. The most disruptive of Handel's
transpositions comes at the end of Act II and was made in order to give
Senesino the effective final aria. In Metastasio Ezio's aria 'Ecco alle mie
catene' is his immediate reaction to the disaster which has just occurred
(scene 12), and he uses the universal consternation as an occasion for an
heroic self-portrait, with a glance of tender gratitude to Fulvia. Handel has
first to find room for La Strada's aria, which follows logically enough from
what goes before but leaves the two fighting-cocks Valentinian and Ezio
standing about with nothing to do, though these were previously the two
men who would not let her speak. In Handel it is only the music that makes
La Strada an acceptable partner in the dialogue (she is said in fact to have

Handel's *Ezio* 229

been a plain woman). Valentinian and Massimo have then to disappear abruptly and the castrato is left alone for his curtain-aria. In this aria the lines addressed to Fulvia have melodic phrases that he has already used in addressing her (in 'Pensa a serbarmi, o cara') and the whole siciliano both recalls and anticipates other passages in Handel's opera (e.g. 'Ah non son io che parlo'). By purely musical means Handel achieves a dramatic logic at a higher level, a level at which the theatrical coherence of Metastasio's text had to be destroyed. He had the emperor standing alone on the stage at the end of the act, thus symbolising his inner loneliness.

Purely technical features do still help to explain why Handel's music is capable of expressing more than what happens on the stage or stands in the text. A continuo part that demands attention by its interest and violin parts that are never quite subordinated to the vocal line communicate to the listener information that is only incidental in the text or may even contradict it. Valentiniano's aria 'Vi fida lo sposo' (Act II scene 3) does not express simply confidence – there is also a note of anxiety in the threatening rise of the bass line. Fulvia's despairing aria 'Ah non son io che parlo' (HG, p. 123) is dominated by a marvellous ostinato motif that makes only occasional appearances in the voice-part (on the word 'delirar') but it is not tailored to any individual words. This motif, which recalls Schubert, does not really belong to Fulvia's own language: it is the voice of fate. In fact the middle section of this aria acts as a kind of relief because the actual meaning of the words is more important here. The ostinato bass has become the perpetuum mobile of a storm repeatedly pierced by the lightning flashes (mentioned in the text and imitated in the vocal line) of the violin figures. Fulvia has then to return, with the Da Capo, to the previous darkness, a prey to the threatening gestures of the bass-line. Handel's music is so deeply rooted in counterpoint and in the initiatives of the individual voices that his technique itself becomes a symbol. His is of course the Baroque conception of allegory as an idea embodied in an actual figure. This may occur in Handel on a quite unsophisticated level as for example in the gnomic wisdom of the subordinate character Varo 'Nasce al bosco in rozza cuna': the rise and fall of Fortuna's ethereal wings, the climb of the single individual (a single sustained note!) to the topmost peaks and to dominion over the world, followed of course by his inexorable fall. We can hardly speak of this as tone-painting, since it is abstract ideas rather than actual objects that are represented. The latter appears in almost every aria, though they may not be immediately recognised by the modern listener, for example the 'tears' (violin staccati) in 'Tergi le ingiuste lagrime' Act III scene 11. But what is Handel expressing at the opening of Ezio's 'Recagli quel acciaro' (HG, p. 54), where he for once makes use of a strict 'colla parte' i.e. unison? A unison tutti need not simply mean an overall emphasis, as it so often does with the Italians. Ezio is after all speaking quite calmly and without hesitation. I can provide no explanation, but I suspect that there is some quite concrete answer. It may be that Ezio is pretending that he is perfectly self-possessed or that he is not dependent on others helping him. (The middle section is unproblematic, on the other hand, and we can confidently explain the change from E flat major to C major by the words 'serena il ciglio').

In Act III scene 6 the hero after his unexpected release sings a hymn of gratitude to the emperor. Not only he, but all nations from the cold Scythians to the scorched Ethiopians (to use Metastasio's words) pay homage to the monarch. The instrumentation of this aria is exceptional – two horns and two flutes added to the orchestra – but it is typical of Handel that his object is not simply greater brilliance or local colour. (Or perhaps I am wrong, and we should regard the horns as northern, and the flutes as southern instruments?) Handel makes the instrumental groups of the concerto grosso movement physically appear from different sides and with clearly differentiated features, and they unite to pay homage to the monarch to whom they are all subject (falling figurations). Thereupon we hear festal music – the obligatory fanfares are executed by the violins. The text can be transformed directly into musical scenery, because the instruments of Handel's orchestra are not parts of an acoustic machine but belong to the human beings who hold them and play them.

This aria also shows how well Handel understood Metastasio. Although there is no predicate in the first four lines, all the components of the picture are mentioned; and the lines themselves are as loosely juxtaposed in the music as in the poetry, but also with the same static symmetry. Handel must have been struck by Metastasio's crystalline symmetry and lapidary economy. His use of asyndeton in 'Sò chi t'accese' (HG, p. 31), where the four dictatorial main clauses resemble so many hammer-blows, is even more powerful in Handel's music. Everything is broken up into single bars; a single, unchanging instrumental motif interrupts the phrases of the text like an arrogant ostinato, while the vocal phrases themselves change from one instance to the next and equal each other only in length. In Metastasio the repetitions are syntactically speaking the same, though their sense is expressed in different words; this is translated into purely musical terms by Handel – he accentuates similarity (the metre, the ostinato-motif) and difference (melodic content and degrees of the scale), introducing an instrumental partner to make the situation clear. Any less observant composer would almost certainly have repeated the same sequence of notes where words are equivalent.

Once again Handel makes use of conservative means (ostinato), but the way he applies them to a typical Metastasio strophe is something entirely new. We ask ourselves why, if he was capable of interpreting Metastasio texts so well, he did not feel drawn by the idea of setting more of them.

The fact of *Ezio*'s failure with the public – it had only five performances – must be part of the reason, but itself needs explaining. It is a well-known fact that London audiences in Handel's time – as today – did not understand enough Italian to be able to follow the recitatives, and that the solution of this problem was found in giving them many arias and only a little recitative. This meant laborious rearrangements of the text and, for the composer, the necessity of expressing in music what was conveyed to Italian audiences in dialogue: this is probably the chief reason for the complexity and density of expression of Handel's arias. Yet in the case of Metastasio's libretti his efforts in this direction seem somehow not to have succeeded. We may even doubt whether Handel himself was content with the artistic result in *Ezio*. He perhaps felt that his art was not compatible with libretti of the highest literary quality. Zeno was the librettist who attracted him least and Zeno, like Metastasio, regarded his poetical texts as independent dramas. Such texts as these could be combined with the music of Vinci, Hasse and Leo – all of whom Handel admired and performed – in a less complicated way.

Metastasio's *Alessandro nell' Indie* and its earliest settings

I T WAS often Handel's practice, particularly in his dramatic works, to start with a model, taking its basic idea rather than its definitive form and developing that idea in new ways and with added significance. His Italian operas are almost without exception settings of libretti that were already in existence and were not specially written for him. There were a number of external reasons for this, not least the rarity in London of Italian poets with real dramatic gifts; but there is also a literary and dramatic parallel with Handel's practice of borrowing. What he did was to make whoever might be his literary collaborator at the time adapt an existing libretto in such a way that it provided the basis for him to develop his own musico-dramatic ideas. A study of the nature of these adaptations and why Handel felt them necessary could take us to the very heart of the composer's attitude to the drama and help us to understand his relations with the public. In attempting such a study we must also undertake a more systematic comparison between Handel and contemporary Italian opera composers. It is not a question of simply comparing the respective end-products, but the cultural backgrounds, what each assumes and what each attempts to achieve.

Handel's settings of Metastasio libretti (*Siroe* 1728, *Poro* 1731, *Ezio* 1732) are borderline cases in a study of this kind, for in them we have apparently complete and acknowledged literary works to which only musical notes had to be added. That appearance, however, is deceptive; for although there was little interference with Metastasio's verses in these London versions, Handel's conception of the drama – his 'dramaturgy' – differed in a number of ways from Metastasio's. Once again we can learn something by a comparison with Italian contemporary composers; and it is particularly true in the case of *Alessandro nell' Indie* that Handel's contemporaries often diverged even further from the text itself than he did, but much less from the spirit of Metastasio. Metastasio's dramas were in no way regarded as sacrosanct even in Italy at that time, nor indeed by the author himself, who made important alterations to his three earliest *drammi per musica* (*Didone abbandonata* 1724, *Siroe re di Persia* 1726, *Catone in Utica* 1728) for later performances at other theatres. He took it for granted that a librettist was

232

obliged to take into consideration the actual circumstances at any given theatre and in any given season, regardless of whether it was the actual author or another librettist that made the necessary modifications. The same kind of considerations that had determined the original production – from the choice of subject to the actual performance – had freshly to be observed when the work was revived or set by another composer. Thus in the case of *Alessandro nell' Indie*, which was first set by Leonardo Vinci (Teatro delle Dame, Rome 1730, first opera of the Carnival season), the immediately succeeding composers of the work – Porpora, Predieri, Hasse and Handel himself, not to mention the dozens of composers who followed them – were entirely justified, and indeed invited, to let their librettists make any cuts or transpositions they found necessary in the libretto. What distinguishes Handel's setting from that of any of his contemporaries is therefore not simply a matter of fidelity to the original text. Nor indeed does it lie simply in the different quality of the music, but in a fundamental difference in the kind of communication between composer and public – a difference which is in fact still characteristic of the way in which the modern public accepts his works, their actual survival. We have only to compare the fact of the Handel revival, which is virtually confined to northern and central Europe, with the absence of any Italian revival of interest in the works of Vinci or Hasse.

In Handel's day there was certainly a clear understanding between the public and those concerned with producing operas that the music was the most important thing; and this was as true in London as in Italy. But this does not amount to very much, since music is inevitably the façade that cannot fail to attract notice. We must also examine the opposite end of the spectrum, the origin of all the impressions made on an audience, namely the dramatic subject. It is for this that people go to the theatre wherever theatres exist, though it is not quite the same thing as the 'dramatic action'. The subject of an opera was in most cases familiar to the audiences of those days – certainly true of Alexander the Great – and was articulated in their consciousnesses in the form of certain historical (or mythical or literary) characters and events. (In this they enjoyed an unquestionable advantage over opera-goers today.) The fundamental difference between opera in Italy and opera in London lay in the fact that in Italy these characters and events were given life by the *literary text* but in London directly by Handel's *music*. The English listener did not appreciate the literary niceties of a language that was foreign to him; and he followed the action in so far as it could be articulated in music, vocal and instrumental, and communicated visually, particularly of course by the stage-setting. Italians on the other hand experienced the action, i.e. the realisation of the story, as the recitation of poetry, and thus primarily through the singing. While the task of Vinci or Porpora consisted primarily in making it possible for the singers to recite

Metastasio effectively, Handel had to communicate the story directly to his audience, with the help of singers – but also of instruments. Handel's singers, therefore, were more closely identified with the historical characters whom they represented (their roles were more personally characterised), whereas the Italian public regarded the singer more as a kind of acoustic instrument for reciting poetry, distinct from his or her role. Perhaps the two different approaches can be best distinguished by a diagram (Fig. 1):

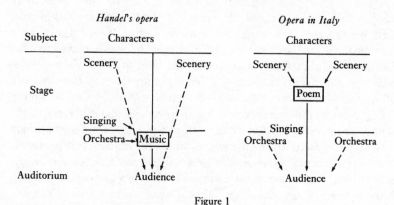

Figure 1

Apart from the decisive relationship between subject and music (and/or poetry) and audience, the stage-sets and stage-action (in so far as there is any) are not so much actual sources of communication as factors that serve to clarify and enhance the experience. But in Handel's operas these too were articulated by the music, as in the instrumental introductions to a new stage set at the beginning of a new act. In Italian theatres, on the other hand, the poet was responsible for these, and we know, for example, that librettists often directed the rehearsals of an opera, as Metastasio did at the Teatro della Dame in Rome, where *Alessandro nell'Indie* had its first performance. And Metastasio's descriptions of stage-sets are most explicit; they are part of his poem.

Let us now shortly examine Metastasio's attitude to the subject-matter of his dramas, and we may then hope to understand better the different attitudes of the Italian composers and of Handel to his drama. In the case of a well-known subject, where at least the outlines were historically determined and familiar to all educated people, Metastasio could add less than in a freely invented plot, such as that of *Siroe*. Even so, it was he who chose his subjects thereby imposing his own restrictions. His choice in this case was in keeping with the tendency to historical truth that was a feature of the 'reform' libretti of the early eighteenth century, a tendency closely connected with the flowering of antiquarian studies. Witness of this is the emphasis laid by Zeno and Metastasio, amongst others, in their libretto prefaces, on ancient sources. In his choice of Alexander, Metastasio was also choosing a subject that had often been treated by seventeenth- century authors (though he did not point this out), and one that may have been familiar to many spectators not only from historical sources, but quite possibly from some existing dramatisation. If we examine these earlier dramatisations, we shall see that Metastasio borrowed from a number of them. How could he have failed, for example, to take into account Jean Racine's famous tragedy of *Alexandre le Grand* (1666), knowing as he must have done that many of his cultivated listeners would at least have read it? How could he have avoided the influence of Domenico David's libretto *L'amante eroe* (1693), David being the first member of the Arcadian movement to make a name for himself, and his *La forza della virtù* having served Metastasio as a model for his first opera libretto, *Siface*? If we compare the different dramatisations of the subject prior to Metastasio's, we shall also discover connecting links between them. These are not so much stylistic, or concerned with the tragic, galant, or even comic, handling of the subject as to do with the working out of basic features – the historical conflict between the most successful of all conquerors and the heroic defender of his country, between the victorious youth relying solely on his own powers and the true king of his people dependent upon native traditions. It seems to be characteristic of the Baroque theatre that this conflict is brought to its climax at the end of these pieces in what was thought to have been a *historic* dialogue between Alexander and the twice defeated Poros, now his prisoner. How, asks Alexander, does he now wish to be treated? Poros, who expects nothing but death, answers, 'Like a king', whereupon Alexander grants him his life and restores him to his kingdom. The age of Absolutism admired Poros' attitude because it exemplified the unshaken belief in the idea of monarchy even in a moment of total disaster, as well as heroic personal courage and self-confidence. Alexander, on the other hand, was allowed the moral victory by virtue of his restraint and generosity towards a conquered enemy. Racine himself commented on this fundamental feature of his tragedy; replying to critics of the first performance he pointed out in his preface to the printed edition that Poros was only superficially greater than Alexander. It was easier for Poros because all the sympathy of the audience was concentrated on him: Alexander remained in the last resort the greater of the two because he was both victorious in the war *and* magnanimous to his defeated enemy. He (and in fact his general, Ephestion, also) could do something that was not in Poros's power – acknowledge his enemy. The criticisms of Racine's piece, and his answer to them, reveal that the society of that day found it hard to allow any questioning of Alexander's superiority: Poros, said the critics, had been represented as 'too great'.

Racine's Poros is in fact a better-matched opponent for Alexander than Metastasio's, in that Racine's Poros shows no evasiveness and no desire for vengeance either on Alexander or the queen Axiane, whom he loves with a total devotion, neither suspecting her of disloyalty nor wishing to kill her for it. Poros, it is true, kills his rival Taxile in a duel because he has collaborated with the enemy, but he does this when he is himself a prisoner and can only expect punishment. The attitude of Poros' beloved, Axiane, is correspondingly noble. She wishes to take her own life when she believes Poros to be dead and openly resists Alexander even when she is in his power, refusing either to come to terms with him or to arouse Poros' jealousy. Metastasio borrowed traits from Axiane for his Cleofide, while at the same time diminishing her personality. In the same way his Timagene is a diminished version of Racine's Ephestion, who does *not* betray Alexander. Even the collaborators, Taxile and his sister Cleofide, at least arouse the sympathy of the audience in that they act in good faith for the best interests of their people. In accordance with another tradition – said to be an historical fact – which runs through all these pieces, Cleofide is Alexander's mistress and suffers from the resulting conflict without being able to help it. The conflict is not between good and evil, but between strength and weakness. It is also now clear that Metastasio combined Racine's Axiane and Cleofide in a single person (thereby inevitably making her a leading character in the drama!), transferring the struggle between personalities and nations on to the spiritual plane of the individual's conscience. This is unquestionably of greater interest and perhaps reveals a more humane attitude, but it introduces a love-interest that is absent in Racine – the mutual exchanges of the lovers, especially in the duet 'Se mai turbo il tuo riposo', lead to characteristically operatic effects of emotional tension. In portraying Poros, Metastasio went back to an older and much less admirable dramatic source, Claude Boyer's tragi-comedy *Porus, ou la générosité d'Alexandre* (1648). The title itself betrays uncertainty or indifference as to the relative importance of the two. This piece was revived at almost the same time as Racine's tragedy appeared, and reprinted with the title *Le Grand Alexandre, ou Porus*. This led to a famous controversy, which in fact caused the break between Racine and Molière. In Boyer Porus is married to Argire but a prey to jealousy and determined to kill her despite the efforts of his trusty companion Arsacide (Gandarte!) to dissuade him. Alexander is betrayed, chiefly of course by Porus himself, who is protected by the good Arsacide; Argire's presence as a prisoner in Alexander's camp is exploited to erotic effect, and a further amorous intrigue among the subsidiary characters adds a note of comedy. Metastasio's ability to transform such a worthless plot into high tragedy does deserve our admiration; he undertakes the same role, reforming and ennobling a mediocre work, in his handling of Domenico David's *L'amante eroe*. The libretto of this, at least as far as the relationship between the characters goes, was clearly based on Racine: but the tradition of the Venetian opera seems to be responsible for concealing the fundamental lines of the plot behind a façade of fairground theatre. Poros and his wife Berenice escape through an underground passage, and it is there that he tries to kill her. Poros appears before Alexander disguised as one of his own servants (as in Metastasio), so well disguised in fact that not even his own wife recognises him; she even receives news of her husband's supposed death from his own lips – which finally provides the opportunity for a touching recognition scene. Berenice is the victim of an attempted rape by Tassilo; Efestione falls in love with Cleofile, who, being herself in love with Alexander, makes fun of him (here we have the Timagene–Erissena relationship). Most important of all, Alexander himself is in love with Berenice but decides to ennoble this love by heroism, that is to say renunciation. Metastasio could not omit this trivial detail: it provided him with another emotional conflict (as in the aria 'Se amore a questo petto non fosse ignoto affetto') and also a further 'proof' of Alexander's greatness, which has something of the 'greatness' of a famous castrato. It is not so much a question of Metastasio, as a man of the theatre, borrowing from his predecessors anything that he finds theatrically effective (as he was quite entitled to do) but of his refusing to adopt the moral precepts of their characters, whether these were noble (as with Racine), mean (as with Boyer) or simply trivial (as with David). He makes love, and particularly jealousy, a raison d'être of these historical characters and thus completely reinterprets the subject – the personal, erotic conflict between Poros and Cleofide threatens to outweigh the objective, political conflict between Poros and Alexander. Metastasio achieves this reinterpretation, over and above all the borrowed themes, by means of a poetic synthesis which, at least in language, is not too far from Racine's own in subtlety. This frees him to follow Racine almost exactly in his treatment of the most delicate political theme, the criticism of Alexander's imperialist policies. The objections which both Axiane and Poros make to Alexander (each on their own account, but in agreement with each other) Metastasio sums up in Poros' short but indicative speech:

Alexander: And what insults have you received at my hands?
Poros: The same as the rest of the world. What is it that brings Alexander to the countries of the East, to disturb their peaceful existence? Are the children of Zeus so inhuman? To defend itself against your lust to conquer, Asia has in vain sacrificed its riches, Africa opposed its wild animals; it is of no help to us that we are unknown to the rest of mankind. You have already made the whole world your tributary, and the whole world is still too little for your appetite.

Here we have the essence of the political criticism of Alexander, summed up as succinctly as is his moral triumph at the end of the work in his dialogue with Poros. These lines are recitative and not even conceived as *accompagnato*, and therefore not left to the composer to 'interpret'. They remain the statement of Metastasio's personal attitude, regardless of the music to which they are sung. He drew the action and the visual setting of his drama from the most diverse sources, recombining the facts in his own way and giving both the characters and the plot a new moral interpretation; in the same way he ensures it by his language against any reinterpretation or misinterpretation of the problematical features of the story. He is master of that story and, as far as *opera seria* is concerned, his interpretation remained for generations the only one acceptable. In Italy, moreover, his libretto largely replaced Racine's tragedy with the reading public, while in the opera house he remained the supreme librettist uniquely responsible for presenting the story to the public and thus interposing his poem between the subject and the spectator (see Fig. 1).

As a result, the many adaptations of this libretto which continued to appear in the Italian opera from one season and theatre to another had to be mere derivatives. They are clumsy and superficial, with ruthless cuts, substitutions of arias, transferring of scenes, occasional additions of lines – always in aria-texts. But there are no alterations of the text, even in the recitatives, with the object of adding new points of emphasis or altering Metastasio's interpretation of the story. This is true up to about 1750, a period of some twenty years during which there was a decline in the number of reworkings of the drama though the number of settings steadily increased – Metastasio became increasingly sacrosanct. It is only after the middle of the century that we begin to meet with a change in critical attitudes towards his work. He himself was responsible for the only early reinterpretation – and in fact a political reinterpretation – of one of his works. This was the second version of his *Catone in Utica* (1728) made the following year. Here the hero's suicide on stage has disappeared and the emphasis of the work shifted in favour of his opponent Caesar.

In the early years by far the most common method of adapting Metastasio was by cutting the text of the recitatives. This was not done with any wish to influence the argument of the piece but simply changed – and often complicated – its logical unfolding to the audience. The chief responsibility for these adaptations lay with the singers, who wanted as many arias as possible and the minimum of recitative (difficult to memorise). In addition, composers could show their paces to the public better in arias and would often substitute earlier arias of their own for those in the libretto, to the point of creating a pasticcio. Perpetual changes of cast involved changes of precedence among the singers with the result that, for example, different arias had to be placed at the end of acts so that the better singers could be assured of greater applause. This did not compromise Metastasio's characterisation, concentrated in the arias, so much as destroy the intelligibility of the recitatives, which were often thus left virtually irrelevant between the arias (there is even an example of this in Handel's *Ezio*). In the case of *Alessandro nell' Indie*, one of the first sacrifices made when the opera was cut was precisely the political criticism of Alexander by Poros. In fact there are many libretti in which the passage quoted above simply does not appear, and even in Handel all that remains is 'The same as the rest of the world, which is devastated by your lust to conquer'. In other versions the passage was cut differently. Metastasio's own much later suppression of the whole speech in the collected edition of his works seems to suggest a new, more conservative, interpretation, which it was certainly not in other adaptations of the libretto, where the only reason for cuts was to gain more time for the arias.

The tables in Appendices 1 and 2 (pp. 245 and 247) show from another angle how the poet, and not the composer, claimed responsibility for Alexander and Poros. During the period mentioned this single literary presentation of the story was set by some fifteen to twenty different composers, though hardly one of these was given more than six or seven productions, and that was generally only in the case of the famous composers Vinci and Hasse. (The statistics show that Hasse was involved in three different versions, all made by himself; the second and third of these, which were made for Italy, stick much closer to the original text than the first, which was in fact never given in Italy.) The conclusion to be drawn from these statistics seems to be that the impresarios, the singers and the audiences wished to use Metastasio's libretto, rather than any particular setting of it. As far as I have been able to discover no single successful opera on the subject by any other librettist was given during these years; even Vinci's comparatively successful setting had so many rivals that it was never repeated either in his native Naples or in Venice, where standards were high. The statistics are even more surprising in the case of singers, many of whom specialised in individual roles – often depending on their artistic reputation and the degree of precedence that they could claim – and they were more or less indifferent to whose music they sang. What remained constant for them was their lines, and particularly the texts of the arias; they regarded the music to which they sang these texts as a kind of garment, rather like the costumes which they liked to be different in each theatre where they appeared. Some singers who appeared frequently, changed their roles from one theatre to another; this probably had much to do with their rise in the profession. Are we to suppose that they ever gave a thought to the historical Poros or the historical Cleofide, as a few singers might do nowadays? That seems most improbable: Metastasio had done it all for them.

It would be possible, though irrelevant to our present purpose, to draw up a third table showing how much of the original text was omitted or changed in the different adaptations of the libretto. Porpora, Predieri and

Mancini, for instance, have respectively eight, nine and six new aria texts replacing the original, and each makes drastic cuts in the recitatives. Moreover it is almost certain that Porpora, for instance, followed his usual practice of introducing earlier arias of his own, to which Metastasio's texts were simply 'fitted'. In fact only Hasse's attitude deserves individual comment. His libretto was adapted for Dresden by an Italian, Michelangelo Boccardi, and there is no evidence to show that the Dresden Court in 1731 expected anything from Boccardi, Hasse or Faustina Bordoni other than a typical Italian opera. Hasse simply seized upon the fact that his earlier Italian arias (many of them excellent) were not known to the Dresden public and he therefore introduced plenty of them into his opera with parody texts when necessary. This produced a kind of 'pasticcio of his own works', in which only fifteen of the original aria- or duet-texts remained, the other fourteen texts either being taken from entirely different libretti or else being parodies. More than fourteen of the settings used had originally nothing to do with *Alessandro nell'Indie*. This means that even Hasse at least tolerated, perhaps even approved, the new underlaying of one of his arias from an earlier opera with Metastasio's text in order to fit into the Dresden *Cleofide*. Such is the case with Poros' 'Se possono tanto due luci vezzose'. In Hasse's *Attalo* (1728) this had been thundered out by an enraged *primadonna* with the following words, 'Del nobile vanto indegni voi siete! Superbi, tacete! Nol posso soffrire...', and the music matched it! (see Example 1). With Metastasio's text all that remains to be expressed by the youthful élan of this typical Hasse aria is the external linguistic pattern of the lines: their dramatic content has vanished.

In fact it was the vocal mechanisms of all this music that provided the common denominator on which Italian composers, including the Italianised Hasse, could always rely. Metastasio would certainly not have made any objection. We can gather how he wished Poros to sing this passage from the way in which it was set by Vinci, his collaborator in Rome in 1730 and a composer whom he particularly respected. Vinci's setting is a tender A major aria in 'tempo giusto' with syncopations and slurred rising triplet-figures, galant but somewhat meditative. When Hasse set the libretto for Venice in 1736, replacing all the substitute arias of *Cleofide* by new settings of Metastasio's original words, he also wrote an A major aria, 'poco lento', with syncopations and slurred descending figures.

On the other hand Handel's setting of this text is so serious that Poros quite forgets Cleofide's fascinating eyes. When the work was given at Halle in 1981 the German text, which was both singable and had literary quality – 'Wer einmal vom Dämon der Liebe verwundet...' – did not translate Metastasio's lines but followed Handel's interpretation of them. It was in fact the verbal expression of what the music alone could express almost without the help of words.

Example 1 J. A. Hasse, *Attalo re di Bitinia* (Naples 1728)

In the cases of Vinci and Hasse a more literal translation would be
better – something like 'Wenn soviel vermögen zwei reizende Augen' –
because their music is much more closely modelled on the external features
of the text. Handel is able to penetrate beyond the actual words and
expresses Poros' personality, disregarding the galant symbol of 'luci
vezzose' and deliberately creating a tension between Poros' words and what
the music tells the listener – a tension, of course, that disappears in the Halle
translation. For Handel the galant commonplace has nothing to do with what
Poros is feeling, but he is pained by the fact of his being so completely
mastered by jealousy. Only the highly stylised minuet-rhythm of the aria
remains as a reminder of the conventional nature of the whole conception.
Handel's development of Poros' situation is something new and his music
realises – partly by the falterings in the vocal line – the sense of irony and
the bitterness of a jealous man. It was Metastasio's intention that all this
should be completely expressed in his text, the composer being regarded
as essentially an assistant. In this way Handel may be regarded as the rival
not of Vinci or Hasse, but of Metastasio himself.

Today it seems natural to us that Handel when composing should go
straight to the feelings of his characters, and thus penetrate to the heart of
the drama with all its personal tensions; this has become, at least since Gluck

and Mozart, the opera-composer's most important task. But in the operatic
world of his day Handel was an 'outsider': the normal attitude was that
of Vinci and Hasse, which we now find too difficult to appreciate. It was
not simply that they composed more thoughtlessly: their actual aim was
slightly different.

Whereas the jealous pangs of Poros are the subject of Metastasio's 'Se
possono tanto', Cleofide's aria 'Digli ch'io son fedele' is concerned both
with a person – the faithful lover Cleofide – and with a stage situation, the
secret declaration of love to Poros who is actually present, though in
disguise. Cleofide is speaking to Timagene, entrusting him with a lover's
message, but addressing herself to Poros, who is in fact present (and
exclaims, moved with admiration, in an aside 'what ingenious tenderness!').
There are many instances in Metastasio of clever stage-devices of this kind,
inherited from Venetian opera and in this particular case from Domenico
David. The topos of the lover's message also appears in Neapolitan
folk-versions, and it was common in the Neapolitan *commedia per musica*
with which Metastasio was familiar. In this aria the poet is particularly
concerned with Cleofide's insistence, her total devotion and her desire to
convince Poros that she respects and loves him and that he should not
despair. She repeats the words 'tell him' as though she particularly wishes
to be quite sure of Timagene's reliability as messenger – though in fact this
repeated 'tell him' is simply 'I am telling you' addressed to Poros – an
example of Metastasio's subtle use of irony. *Vinci* was very aware of this
and he therefore gives these words the same insistent character as they would
be given if spoken. His 'Digli' is a characteristic descending word-gesture,
but the other words that are so important to Cleofide are also given their
own special emphasis – 'son' is broadly reassuring and 'fedele' is given a
tender chromatic inflexion. The repetitions are left entirely to the singer,
interrupted by pauses, as if to say 'let me say it again'. The instruments
remain unconcerned, simply reflecting the notes of the voice (Example 2).
Hasse discovered a further point in Metastasio's presentation of the

Example 2 L. Vinci, *Alessandro nell'Indie* (Rome 1730)

Example 2 (*cont.*)

- so - ro, ch'è il—mio— te - - so - ro, che m'a - mi, ch'io l'a - - do - ro,

Violini unis.

Viola

che non di - spe - ri an - cor, non di - spe - ri an - cor.

Violini unis.

Di - gli che m'a - - mi, ch'io son— fe - - de - le,

situation – something secret, a hidden warmth, an all-embracing tenderness – and this atmosphere is evoked in the touching melody of his E major aria, expressing an emotion that he read between Metastasio's lines. The coloratura passages are more than mere surface embellishment: they are a further development of the feelings expressed in the words (Example 3). Here, as in Vinci, the invention lies in the vocal line and the orchestra provides no more than a sympathetic framework.

Example 3 J. A. Hasse, *Cleofide* (Dresden 1731)

Handel, on the other hand, transforms the stage situation into a musical one. He 'composes' not only the words or the general emotion of the scene, but the event itself, the actual giving of the message. His declamation alone is intense, with its suggestion of gesture in the prolonged, expectant semitone interval on 'Digli' ('Sag' ihm' is a good translation), but for Handel this is not enough. The instruments come to Cleofide's assistance and add their voices to hers, in imitation. They have their own motifs too, the quavers which communicate something different to the listener, something not communicated by the words – tension and secret fear. In this way Handel fills his whole score with something which, in Metastasio, is concentrated in the narrowest space. Something is lost in Handel, it is true, for Metastasio's repetitions only make their full effect when they are not overshadowed by too many repetitions in the music. With Handel it is impossible to know how many repetitions of 'Digli' there are in Metastasio's original text, though this can still be sensed in the simpler and clearer aria-forms of Vinci and Hasse. This is of no importance, of course, to listeners for whom Italian is a foreign language. Handel concentrates entirely on communicating the message to his listeners, and it is his music which assumes responsibility for this communication. Vinci and Hasse set to music simply what *is* on the stage – the words, or even simply the sound of the words or, in Hasse's case, the overall atmosphere.

We do not know why Handel chose to set *Alessandro nell' Indie*. The greater success of his opera, and the real superiority of this score to those of *Ezio* and *Siroe* suggest that he was surer here of his ability to communicate with his audience. Here he could start directly with Alexander, Poros and Cleofide and employ his music to fill the gap between story and listener, supported by his knowledge of Racine's drama, which was certainly shared by his listeners. He looked beyond Metastasio to the long tradition of the subject itself, tactfully sidestepping the poet. Vinci and Hasse owed virtually everything to Metastasio. Audiences today, to whom Metastasio has become no more than a name, owe Handel more.

APPENDIX 1

Performances of *Alessandro nell' Indie* (*Poro, Cleofide*) from 1730 to 1745

Characters: Poro (P); Cleofide (C); Alessandro (A); Erissena (E); Gandarte (G); Timagene (T)

Year	Theatre	Composer	Notes
1730	T. delle Dame, Rome	L. Vinci	With *balli*. Carestini (P)
1731	T. Regio, Turin	N. Porpora	With *balli*. Farinelli (P); Faustina (C); A. Girò (E); A. Amorevoli (A); A. Montagnana (T)

Year	Theatre	Composer	Notes
	Haymarket, London	G. F. Handel	A. P. Fabbri (A)
	Regio Ducal T., Milan	L. A. Predieri	With *balli*. Carestini (P); V. Tesi (C); A. Peruzzi (E)
	S. Sebastiano, Livorno	(Vinci?)	(Pasticcio). G. Valletta (P); C. Pusterla (C); L. Antinori (G)
	Kärntnertor, Vienna	(Porpora?)	Pasticcio
	Hoftheater, Dresden	J. A. Hasse	Version reworked by M. A. Boccardi. With *balli*. Faustina (C); D. Annibali (A); A. Campioli (P)
	Haymarket, London	G. F. Handel	Revival with A. Montagnana (T) and A. Campioli (G)
1732	S. Angelo, Venice	G. B. Pescetti	G. Valletta (P); G. Turcotti (C); F. F (A); A. Peruzzi (E)
	S. Bartolomeo, Naples	F. Mancini	With *intermezzi comici*. Teresa Cotti (P); Conti 'Gizziello' (A)
	T. Cocomero, Florence	(Vinci?)	(Pasticcio)
	T. Pubblico, Reggio Emilia	L. Vinci	G. Turcotti (C); L. Antinori (G)
	Gänsemarkt, Hamburg	G. F. Handel	Reworked by Telemann
	Hoftheater, Brunswick	G. F. Handel	
	T. del Falcone, Genoa	(Predieri?)	
1733	Accademia, Brescia	(Vinci?)	F. Finazzi (A), was also impresario
1734	T. Formagliari, Bologna	G. M. Schiassi	F. Finazzi (P); A. Peruzzi (C); A. P. Fabbri (A)
	Breslau	A. Bioni	
	Kleinseite, Prague	M. Lucchini	
1735	Hoftheater, Munich	L. Vinci	Reworked by G. Ferrandini (Pasticci
	T. Pubblico, Pisa	?	
1736	T. Ducale, Parma	L. Vinci	With *balli*.
	T. S. G. Grisostomo, Venice	J. A. Hasse	Largely reset, with *balli*. V. Tesi (C) A. Amorevoli (A); M. Giacomazzi (I
	T. Pubblico, Prato	(E. R. Duni?)	With *intermezzi comici*
	Accademia, Lisbon	G. M. Schiassi	G. Valletta (P)
	S. Bartolomeo, Naples	J. A. Hasse	Version 1736 reworked by G. Di Ma With prologue and *balli*, Carestini (P V. Tesi (C); A. Amorevoli (A); M. Giacomazzi (E)
	Covent Garden, London	G. F. Handel	With arias by Ristori and Vinci. D. Annibali (P)
1737	T. Obizzi, Padua	G. A. Pampani	
	T. Bonacossi, Ferrara	J. A. Hasse	Reworked by Vivaldi; possibly not performed
1738	T. del Buon Ritiro, Madrid	F. Corselli	A. P. Fabbri (A)
	Accademia, Mantua	B. Galuppi	With *balli*. M. Camati (C)
	T. S. G. Grisostomo, Venice	J. A. Hasse	With *balli*. With alterations by Hass
	Tummelplatz, Graz	J. A. Hasse	Company Mingotti
	T. Pubblico, Rimini	?	
1739	T. di Piazza, Vicenza	?	
	Klagenfurt	(Hasse?)	Company Mingotti

Year	Theatre	Composer	Notes
1740	T. Pergola, Florence	?	Pasticcio. G. Turcotti (C)
	Accademia, Verona	J. A. Hasse	With *balli*. M. Camati (C)
	T. Nuovo, Lisbon	A. P. Fabbri	
	T. S. Cecilia, Palermo	M. Gabellone	
1741	Pressburg	J. A. Hasse	Company Mingotti
	T. Pubblico, Modena	P. Pulli	
	Erlangen	(Hasse?)	(Pasticcio)
1742	Regio Ducal T., Milan	?	
	Città di Castello	R. di Capua	
1743	T. S. G. Grisostomo, Venice	J. A. Hasse	With *balli*
	S. Agostino, Genoa	E. R. Duni	
	Court Theatre, St. Petersburg	F. Araja	
	S. Carlo, Naples	D. Sarri	
1744	T. Bonacossi, Ferrara	N. Jommelli	With arias by other composers inserte
	T. Pergola, Florence	?	(Pasticcio). V. Tesi (C). With *balli*
	Hoftheater, Berlin	C. H. Graun	
1745	T. Regio, Turin	C. W. Gluck	

APPENDIX 2

Singers appearing in *Alessandro nell'Indie* on several occasions (select examples)

Giovanni Carestini, castrato soprano:

Rome 1730, Vinci (P)
Milan 1731, Predieri (P)
Naples 1736, Hasse (P)

Gaetano Valletta, castrato soprano:

Livorno 1731, Vinci? (P)
Venice 1732, Pescetti (P)
Lisbon 1736, Schiassi (P)

Faustina Bordoni, soprano:

Turin 1731, Porpora (C)
Dresden 1731, Hasse (C)

Annibale Pio Fabri, tenor:

London 1731, Handel (A)
Bologna 1734, Schiassi (A)
Madrid 1738, Corselli (A)
Lisbon 1740 as composer!

Vittoria Tesi, contralto

Milan 1731, Predieri (C)
Venice 1736, Hasse (C)
Florence 1744, ? (C)

Gioacchino Conti detto Gizziello, castrato soprano:

Naples 1732, Mancini (A)
Covent Garden 1736, Handel (A)

Antonio Montagnana, bass:

Turin 1731, Porpora (T)
Haymarket 1731, Handel (T)

Costanza Pusterla, contralto:

Livorno 1731, Vinci? (C)
Florence 1731, Vinci? (C)

Giustina Turcotti, soprano:

Reggio 1732, Vinci (C)
Venice 1732, Pescetti (C)
Florence 1740, ? (C)

Appendix (*cont.*)

Domenico Annibali, castrato alto:	Dresden 1731, Hasse (A)
	Covent Garden 1736, Handel (P)
Anna Peruzzi, contralto:	Milan 1731, Predieri (E)
	Venice 1732, Pescetti (E)
	Bologna 1734, Schiassi (C)
Anna Girò, soprano:	Turin 1731, Porpora (E)
	Ferrara 1737, Hasse/Vivaldi (C?)
	Brescia 1746, Pellegrini (C)
Angelo Amorevoli, tenor:	Turin 1731, Porpora (A)
	Venice 1736, Hasse (A)
	Naples 1736, Hasse/Di Majo (A)
Filippo Finazzi, castrato soprano:	Venice 1732, Pescetti (A)
	Brescia 1733, Vinci? (A) and Imp
	Bologna 1734, Schiassi (P)
Margherita Giacomazzi, soprano:	Venice 1736, Hasse (E)
	Naples 1736, Hasse/Di Majo (E)
Luigi Antinori, tenor:	Livorno 1731, Vinci? (G)
	Reggio 1732, Vinci (G)
Giuseppe Tolve, tenor:	Rome 1730, Vinci (G)
	Venice 1738, Hasse (A)

Comic traditions in Handel's *Orlando*

T HE LONDON opera season of 1732/3 provided some excitement even to such an inveterate opera and theatre supporter as John Hervey, first Earl of Bristol (1665–1751). Before the first night of the season, he wrote to the Duke of Richmond on 31 October 1732: '...I am going to Lady Pembroke's to hear the new Opera-woman, Celestina. The operas begin on Saturday.'[1] His impression of the première, which he reported, as usual, to his young friend Stephen Fox, was the following (4 November 1732):

I am just come from a long, dull, and consequently tiresome Opera of Handel's, whose genius seems quite exhausted. The bride's recommendation of this being the first night, could not make this supportable. The only thing I liked in it was our Naples acquaintance, Celestina, who is not so pretty as she was, but sings better than she did. She seemed to take mightily, which I was glad of. I have a sort of friendship for her, without knowing why. Tout chose qui me fait resouvenir ce temps m'attendrit; et je suis sûr que ce soir à l'opéra j'ai soupiré cent fois. Mais parlons d'autre chose...[2]

Hervey is referring to his journey to Italy with Stephen Fox in 1729, when they had spent January to March in Naples. They had obviously met 'Celestina' then, and heard her sing.

He may soon have found out that the new Haymarket opera was not by Handel himself, but that it was the pasticcio *Catone* which Handel had arranged from a score of Leonardo Leo and other Italian arias. The London *Daily Advertiser* of 6 November reported on the first night: 'There were present a numerous audience, and Signora Celeste Gismondi, who lately arriv'd here, perform'd a principal part in it with universal applause. We hear that this opera was not compos'd by Mr Handell, but by some very eminent Master in Italy...' (*The London Stage*, Pt 3, p. 243).

If the soprano Celeste Gismondi got the lion's share of what applause there was, this was not only a warm welcome to the only new addition to Handel's cast in this season, but also due to the extraordinary concessions the composer had made to her role in the score. Gismondi sang five brilliant arias, four of which had been replaced during the preparations, probably

249

at her request. Several of her arias had originally been composed by Johann Adolf Hasse for excellent singers such as Antonia Merighi, Giovanni Carestini, Faustina Bordoni and Gaetano Majorano detto il Caffarelli, during the years 1728–32. Her last aria in the score, 'Vede il nocchier la sponda', was a showpiece even by Caffarelli's standards, with extremely difficult coloraturas and a total range from a to c^3 (featuring a leap from c^1 to c^3 as well). As if that were not enough, Gismondi was permitted to end one act (the second) with an aria, a chance not given to Senesino – and she had no fewer than three solo scenes. Two of these were, furthermore, of the renowned 'ombra' type. This actually suited the role: Emilia spends the whole drama in feelings of grief and revenge over her murdered husband, Pompejus.

It is thus with reference to the *music* that the *Daily Advertiser* assigns her a 'principal part' in the opera; dramatically the role is inferior to those of Senesino, La Strada and Montagnana. Gismondi's music differs significantly from that of the other singers by being mainly drawn from the works of Johann Adolf Hasse, whereas the others sung mainly Leo's music, with some admixture of Porpora.

If her singing abilities earned Signora Gismondi the recognition of Handel and of the press, one wonders which talents had earned her the 'friendship' of John Hervey, the close ally of Sir Robert Walpole and friend of Queen Caroline. He met Signora Gismondi *privatim* on the night of the fourth performance (14 November): 'I concluded the day at Miss Skerritt's [Walpole's mistress]. Our Naples friend Celestina sung and supped there with her husband, Mr Hempson, another of our Naples friends, who used to live with the consul and play upon the flute.'[3]

La Celestina's later roles under Handel included Lisaura in his *Alessandro* (25 November 1732), Elisa in his *Tolomeo* (2 January 1733), Dorinda in his *Orlando* (27 January 1733), Jael in his *Deborah* (17 March 1733); she also gave concerts.[4] It is noteworthy that the roles of Lisaura and Elisa had been created for Faustina Bordoni, at the time of her greatest rivalry with Francesca Cuzzoni (1726–8). An analogous competition of personalities as well as singing and acting styles may have obtained between La Strada and La Celestina. The reference to La Strada in the pamphlet *Harmony in an Uproar* (February 1734) (Deutsch 1955, p. 355) under the name of 'Coeleste Vocale' must be a pun on Signora Gismondi's name: the attractions of La Celestina did not lie, as with La Strada, entirely in her vocal powers.

After having sung for the 'Opera of the Nobility' in 1733/4, Celeste Gismondi retired from the stage; she died on 11 March 1735. Her obituary in a London newspaper runs thus:

'Signora Celeste Gismondi, wife to Mr Hempson, an English Gentleman, a famous singer, died on Tuesday after a lingering illness. She performed in Handel's Operas for several winters with great applause, but did not sing this season on any stage, on account of her indisposition' (Deutsch, p. 355).

That the writer exaggerated the length of La Celestina's London career is understandable after the impression she had made on the audiences. She was not a star like Faustina Bordoni or Anna Maria Strada – she was more of a comet.

The identification of La Celestina with the intermezzo soprano Celeste Resse of Naples, which I proposed some years ago (see p. 181), was based on a few simple facts. Around the time when Hervey and Stephen Fox visited Naples and heard La Celestina sing (early in 1729), there was no other opera singer in the town with this first name. The score of a Hasse intermezzo of 1726 identifies Celeste Resse explicitly as 'la buffa Celestina'.[5] Celeste Resse's last role in Naples was that of Eurilla in the intermezzi for F. Mancini's *Alessandro nell'Indie*, Carnival 1732, whereafter she disappears for good from the theatre bills. The many virtuoso arias by Hasse which Signora Gismondi mastered by the time of her arrival in London suggest a previous association with the composer. Celeste Resse was a foremost performer of Hasse's music, if only in intermezzi, from 1726 to 1730. The stylistic gap between the *seria* arias by Hasse, sung by Gismondi, and the intermezzo arias sung by Resse can perhaps be bridged: I propose now that the 'chamber arias' composed by Hasse in the late 1720s on (mostly pastoral) texts by Paolo Rolli were written for private performances with La Celestina (Strohm 1975). It is her 'serious' singing style. The three different last names of the singer are not a genuine obstacle to the identification. She could have been the widow of a Signor Gismondi when she lived in Naples; more attractive is the idea that she simply invented a new artist's name for herself when arriving in London, because 'Resse' sounds dreadful in English.

All this seems, however, to add to the mystery rather than to dispel it. It was not usual at the time for female intermezzo specialists to emancipate themselves to the higher status of a *seconda donna* in the *dramma per musica*.[6] La Celestina is the only female intermezzo specialist ever employed by Handel; only in 1737/8 did he have a *male* intermezzo singer (Antonio Lottini) in his cast, who happened to be available in any case, having come over to sing intermezzi. It is true that Celeste Resse's predecessor in Naples, the famous Santa Marchesini, was a member of the Real Cappella, and did therefore appear not only in intermezzi, but also Court serenatas and some serious roles; but this lack of specialisation was precisely the reason why the Neapolitan court theatre delayed the introduction of self-contained intermezzi until the early 1720s, adhering to the more old-fashioned type of the *scene buffe*. It was Celeste Resse who, from 1725, represented the modern type of the female intermezzo specialist, who depended on success alone without the security of court employment – thus emulating the most famous of them all, Rosa Ungarelli.[7] On the other hand, it is not known that female intermezzo specialists could sing virtuoso arias written for castrati.

La Celestina's artistic emancipation coincided with a social one – her marriage to a British gentleman and friend of the British consul in Naples. The wedding must have been the talk of the town. We do not know its date; it must have been close to the time when J. A. Nelli published his prose comedy *La serva padrona* (1731) and when Gennarantonio Federico and Giambattista Pergolesi created their very different intermezzi of the same title (1733). Both these plays present a topical story: the social ascent of a woman by way of marriage. Was it Celestina's life that was turned into an 'intermezzo'? As the plot had long been a stereotype, one should rather say that she *lived* an intermezzo plot. The marriage prevented La Celestina from creating Serpina in Pergolesi's *La serva padrona*, however. The person who did create that role, Laura Monti, certainly knew Celestina's story, as she sang in Naples in 1729 as well, only on the humbler comic stage of the Teatro de'Fiorentini.[8] There is not the slightest doubt that Federico and Pergolesi were familiar with Celestina's art. Therefore, when we admire Serpina as she knocks the ageing gentleman Uberto out of his wits, we may spare a thought for Mr Hempson. His wife was to sing, in Handel's *Orlando*: 'Amor è qual vento, che gira il cervello!' (Love is a stormwind, which makes your head spin!)

These lines could almost be termed the 'unofficial motto' of Handel's opera *Orlando*. Is not Handel's Orlando just as mad for love as is Pergolesi's Uberto, and all the other 'pazzi per amore' before and after them? Some of these 'pazzi' must have flocked into the auditorium and the *ridotto* of the S. Bartolomeo theatre where Celeste Resse performed; many, surely, populated the steps of Rosa Ungarelli's more international career. As one contemporary has it:[9] 'The actions, the fine manners that she showed to her husband can't be described; I'll say only that her gestures and manner on the stage are something that can't be believed by one who hasn't seen them. For this reason I gave her the name "man-killer"...' And at the end of the season, he notes:

Signora Rosa Ungarelli left this city with Signor Antonio Ristorini... Many gentlemen went to visit them. Certainly she is a shrewd woman; it's enough to say she's a singer, and there are no fools in that profession...she brought to her feet people whose names you would never believe... And the woman was ugly; God help us if she had been beautiful, because she had an inimitable manner, and a way of showing affection that is more than could be described in words. Most favoured by her was Doctor Biagio Desideri, who was one of the impresarios. Even so, he gave her many substantial gifts, escorted her as far as Florence, and entertained her; and this gentleman is a miser, but for this woman he would have gone broke.

Elsewhere, the writer describes her words: 'All the while, she implored him, saying "kill me, but remember our earlier love" in words that would have liquified bronze.' Rosa's partner might then have exclaimed: 'O care parolette, o dolci sguardi, se ben siete bugiardi, tanto vi crederò!'

This is, of course, the text of an aria which La Celestina sang as the shepherdess Dorinda in Handel's *Orlando*. Here she is referring not to her own graces, but to those of the handsome Medoro whom she adores. The jealous madness of Orlando, to which her other aria refers, is not caused by her, but by the beautiful and disingenuous Angelica. Dorinda, the 'pastorella', keeps her head when she realises that Medoro is not for her; she even protects the lovers against Orlando in her hut (or tries to). When the mad Orlando takes her for the goddess Venus and wants to make love to her, she is first flattered and then justly alarmed, especially when Orlando sees in her the ghost of Angelica's slain brother (Act III scene 2). Dorinda is not mad, nor does she need or use magic to save herself, as the lovers do. Whereas Zoroastro wishes to establish 'reason' through magic, Dorinda practices commonsense. Zoroastro, who prophesies and steers the fate of Orlando, Angelica and Medoro, has no power over Dorinda; she has no use for his astrology, his flying geniuses, or stage-craft in producing enchanted palaces, temples, statues, magic rings and grottos. Hers is an 'inferior' role, as far as social status is concerned; but she is in a sense the drama's central character, and the only convincing personality.

Dorinda also differs from all the others in her use of comic language. For her, Amor confuses the 'cervello', whereas the other characters would speak exclusively of 'la mente'. The 'brains' had been banished from the normal vocabulary of the *dramma per musica*. Dorinda also characterises love straightaway as 'un grand' imbroglio' (in Act III scene 5); this vocabulary is drawn from the *buffa*-code, and is often found in the titles of spoken comedies and *opere buffe*. The everyday language corresponds to the way Dorinda feels. In Medoro, she loves his 'buona struttura' (not the 'forme leggiadre') (Act II scene 2). She is not all that secure with grammar, when she advises Zoroastro (Act III scene 9): 'È più sicur a lo lasciar dormire', meaning the potentially dangerous Orlando (perhaps: 'It's safer for to let him sleep').

These are slight but decisive departures from the linguistic code of the *dramma per musica*, including its pastoral variety. Shepherdesses in opera, whether they be the Dorindas of the *Pastor fido* or of the *Tempest* traditions, are not supposed to speak like that. This is not exactly the language of the 'gentil pastorella', but of the 'villana' or comic servant of the intermezzi – it comes from intermezzo roles previously created for and by Celeste Resse.

It is also totally absent from the textual source for Handel's libretto: Carlo Sigismondo Capeci's *dramma per musica* 'L'Orlando, overo La gelosa pazzia' of 1711. The character of Dorinda is present in Capeci's text, with all the attributes of the lovely shepherdess, who reaps only confusion and suffering from her involvement with the great world of chivalry. But Capeci's Dorinda has as little experience of comedy as have all the other pastoral Dorindas of the period – La Celestina has plenty.

Whoever adapted Capeci's libretto for Handel (on this question, see below) went out of his way to introduce a few comic traits into the role of Dorinda, while violating linguistic conventions. Given the fact that Handel had also gone out of his way, musically, in substituting so many arias for her in *Catone*, the suspicion arises that La Celestina had a hand in the planning of *Orlando* altogether. It is clear that only a person of significant artistic standing and theatrical experience could have influenced Handel's text – let alone the music – on the creative level.[10] We must remember that Handel's opera differs from Capeci in more than one respect, including not only the comic traits, but all the magic (enchanted palaces, temples, grottos, statues, flying objects etc.) and the very figure of Zoroastro.

As has been said, Celeste Resse's activity at the theatre of S. Bartolomeo in Naples coincides with the emancipation of the intermezzo genre in this particular operatic centre, belated if compared with the development in northern Italy and also in Florence and Rome – but much more dynamic if one considers that the *scene buffe* of the early 1720s were followed within less than ten years by the amazing little masterpieces of Hasse and Pergolesi. Much of this artistic climax is to be ascribed to the composers, especially Hasse, who contributed eight intermezzo scores between 1726 and 1730;[11] to Gioacchino Corrado, a great bass singer and excellent actor (he was to create not only Pergolesi's Uberto, but also Leo's *commedia* protagonist Fazio Tonti, in 'Amor vuol sofferenza' 1739, see Strohm 1979, pp. 159ff); at least as much, however, to Celeste Resse herself. She was the first important soprano *buffa* in intermezzi (Rosa Ungarelli was a contralto); she turned the dramatic weight of the pieces decisively in favour of the female part, mainly, it seems, by her ability to appear in more than one disguise within the same intermezzo-set, singing and acting male and female, young and old, 'elevated' and servant characters (see the table of her roles in the Appendix to this essay, pp. 268f).

We might distinguish two phases in the development. Apart from the independent intermezzo 'La canterina', which Metastasio wrote for the 1724 production of his *Didone abbandonata* (with music by Domenico Sarri, performed by Santa Marchesini and G. Corrado), the years between 1724 and 1727 saw only a slow increase of independent intermezzo plots within the *dramma per musica*; of the sixteen *drammi per musica* of these years, only eleven had intermezzi at all, five of which were of the *scene buffe* type. By about 1726 intermezzi were more usually given this name, and also carried a separate title, in the libretto; from 1728, they were often printed separately at the end of the libretto of the *dramma* and also attributed individually to their composers. (After 1730, they were no longer usually printed with the *dramma* at all. A similar emancipation concerns the scores of the music.)[12]

It is significant that the five independent intermezzi of 1725–7 were all reworkings of texts by the Florentine pioneer of the genre, Antonio Salvi, produced for the couple Rosa Ungarelli and Antonio Ristorini, mostly with music by G. M. Orlandini; and of these, four were plots derived from Molière. It is likely that 'Il giocatore' (= 'Bacocco e Serpilla') of 1 October 1725, was sung with Orlandini's music, perhaps revised by Leonardo Vinci, and 'L'avaro' (Molière – Salvi) of Carnival 1726 with the music composed in 1720 by F. Gasparini. The remaining three Molière – Salvi texts, however, were newly set by Vinci and Hasse. The latter also composed relatively independent *scene buffe* ('Miride e Damari') for his *Sesostrate* of 1726. In the aria 'Donzellina innocentina' (labelled in the score 'aria della buffa Celestina'),[13] Celeste Resse sang the following lines: 'Con le belle parolette mi rubasti e l'alma e 'l core, e poi questo? Ah, traditore! Le ragazze semplicette in tal modo sai ingannar.' The music is a gigue in 12/8; the mood (and its sudden changes) are just as much La Celestina's style as is Handel's aria with a similar text, quoted above. This text of Handel's appears in Capeci. The *Sesostrate* intermezzi also contain a duet with the text 'Mio caro – mia bella – gentil pastorella – piacesti al mio core – e in premio d'amore – mia sposa ti vo'.' The striking similarity with the trio Handel wrote for Dorinda, Angelica and Medoro is again a generic one – Handel's trio text occurs in Capeci. The text authors of almost all the intermezzi sung by La Celestina are unknown. I believe that they had little freedom, as the action (with the most important *lazzi*, jokes) and apparently much of the text was determined by the interpreters.

This state of things becomes extremely interesting in the second phase of the period (1728–32), when apparently all the intermezzi were newly written and composed for Resse and Corrado. This series includes the splendid Hasse works 'La finta tedesca', 'La contadina', 'La fantesca', 'La serva scaltra' and 'Il tutore'. Of the total of fifteen intermezzo-sets performed by La Celestina in 1728–32, eleven have individual titles and seven of these refer to the female character, mostly indicating her disguise. I believe that she invented many of these plots herself. Let us examine some of them.

In 'L'amante geloso' by Vinci (summer 1729), she is Berina. Her first duet with Forlingo presents jealousy as the main theme. In the second intermezzo, she induces Forlingo to join her in a cave ('grotta') with a statue in it. Forlingo is frightened when she asks him to touch the statue. The statue trembles, smoke comes out, then two other statues appear, one of which grabs Forlingo, the other dances with Berina, then also with Forlingo. In 'La serva scaltra' by Hasse (November 1729), Dorilla encourages Balanzone to court her padrona; then she appears in disguise as her own brother and accuses Balanzone of having lost his ring. She beats him up with the help of several peasant friends. Later, Dorilla reveals that she had also been posing as her own padrona. Balanzone has to marry her, after repenting his misdeeds, which he does in the aria 'Antri ciechi, opachi spechi, nascondete i miei rossori, negli orrori delle vostre cavità'. The motives of the ring, repentance, the grotto ('speco') are all *Orlando* motives. In the intermezzo 'Dorina e Nesso' of Leo's *Semiramide* (Carnival 1730) La Celestina makes the partner fall in love with her in a disguise of a pastoral goddess (Diana). He is a coward and needs her help against an imagined monster, which she kills. Later, she appears as a Turkish woman with her Turkish brother and servants. Obviously, La Celestina was good at directing mute actors, sometimes a whole host of them, and at fighting (the latter occurs also in Hasse's 'Larinda e Vanesio' and 'La fantesca'). In Leo's *dramma per musica*, *Semiramide*, a main character is the Persian king and sorcerer Zoroastro (although he does not have as much power as has Handel's figure).

In Pergolesi's intermezzo 'Nerina e Nibbio', La Celestina is a simple *contadina* (as in Hasse's intermezzo of that title) or *pastorella*. But she has strong friends: Silvio, Dameta, Ormino, Fileno, Aminta... They behave like real peasants, however, not like their namesakes in Guarini and Tasso! Nerina also asks Nibbio to follow her into a cave, supposedly to find hidden treasure in an enchanted vase, which he does not dare touch. Nerina stages a mock necromantic ritual with the aria 'Spirti venite dall'empia Dite', recalling innumerable Seicento intermezzi and serious scenes. The scene ends with the statue and ring motives.

In the intermezzo 'Vespina e Pacuvio' (October 1731), La Celestina is a fake astrologer, using this powerful role against Pacuvio who is actually hunting a hidden treasure (but ends up by marrying the 'astrologer'). She has a train of other fake astrologers with her, who almost beat up Pacuvio; he is also humiliated and driven to repentance. In the second scene, she prophesies wealth to Pacuvio, as she has already traversed for him, in a moment, the 'assi e poli de'cardini celesti zodiaci ed orizzonti'. They also meet in a cave, with a moor posing as a statue, and an image of some god which is later transformed into a tower. The statue moves and embraces Pacuvio; he is freed on condition of marrying Vespina.

The dramatic and scenic motives of Handel's opera, which do not already occur in Capeci, are thus almost completely prefigured in the Neapolitan operas to which La Celestina contributed. Even Zoroastro had appeared there! Apart from that character, however, the motives were all presented in a comical fashion.

Two main questions arise from this. First, that of the *genesis* of the work: is it possible that La Celestina herself influenced the planning of *Orlando* by suggesting all these motifs, going far beyond her own role in the opera? Second, we are confronted with the need of a new *interpretation* of Handel's *Orlando*. Does it show aspects of comedy, beyond Dorinda'a language, perhaps even in the figures of Orlando and Zoroastro? What is Handel's artistic goal in this work?

As regards the genesis of *Orlando*, we can take it for granted that Handel knew the ultimate literary source, Ariosto's *Orlando furioso*, long before 1732. Everyone around him did. Capeci's libretto was very probably known to Handel by 1728 at the latest, when he composed *Tolomeo*, based on a libretto by the same author, with the original music by the same composer.[14] Also, Handel's decision to set an Ariosto subject may predate 1730: by 1729 at the latest, he knew the libretto *L'isola d'Alcina* which he later used for his *Alcina*. Both these operas continue, in their magic and moral traits, the stylistic orientation of *Rinaldo* and *Amadigi*; the pastoral element in *Orlando*, to which Capeci gives strong emphasis, may have recommended this plot to Handel in the particular circumstances of 1732. The sumptuous stage machinery and costumes – elements which were absent from Capeci's drama – were surely among J. J. Heidegger's priorities (but also among those of Aaron Hill, as can be seen from his letter to Handel of 5 December 1732). All these decisions must have been made quite independently from any possible suggestions of Celeste Gismondi. Moreover, the dramatic and scenic motives which she could have suggested, had not actually originated during her activity in Naples. They were much older: when she first met Handel, he knew them already. When creating *Orlando*, Handel and his assistants did not need to invent a single motive that was not present in Ariosto or Capeci. Everything could be found in the various traditions of European theatre in the seventeenth century: in Italian opera, prose comedy, *commedia dell'arte*; French spoken tragedy and *tragédie lyrique* together with their parodies; English, German and Spanish theatre. Handel's personal knowledge of these traditions must have been comprehensive, and this fact – not his acquaintance with Ariosto's *Orlando furioso* – distinguished him from some of his spectators and from most of his modern interpreters. All that La Celestina could do was to *remind* him of his own profound theatrical experience.

There is no space here to plough through the many and varied adaptations of Ariosto in the European Baroque theatre; i.e. this research has largely been done.[15] What remains is to apply its results to Handel. Let us concentrate on those aspects which distinguish his *Orlando* from that of Capeci. They are:

a. the more comical treatment of the character of Dorinda
b. the elimination of the characters Isabella and Zerbino
c. some aspects of Orlando and his madness
d. the figure of Zoroastro and all his magic
e. the moralistic opposition of the allegories 'Amore' and 'Marte'.

Carlo Sigismondo Capeci, as a true member of the Roman *Arcadia*, reacted polemically against the often comical and debased fashion in which Seicento authors had treated Ariosto's shepherds. Ariosto himself had introduced the shepherd and his family, who give shelter to Angelica and

Medoro, as socially inferior, almost realistic figures. Some dramatic elaborations of the Seicento turned these shepherds into genuine peasants or comic servants, who perform *scene buffe*. It seems to have been Capeci's idea to convert these characters into a young shepherdess of the 'rococo' type, who is in love with Medoro, causes confusions and amorous intrigues among the main characters, and thus becomes gentrified at least by reflection. Her language is in the purest 'elevated' style. All this corresponds exactly with the type of serious pastoral opera which the *Arcadia* advocated and produced. Under Handel, Dorinda *regains* comic traits as well as low-class accents. This transformation may well have been caused or at least welcomed by Celeste Gismondi.

The elimination of the chivalrous couple Isabella–Zerbino was perhaps necessitated by Handel having only five singers in 1732/3. Isabella's rescue by Orlando is actually shown on stage (Act I scene 4), although she does not speak. Many of her passages in Capeci's libretto are given over to Dorinda, including the arioso 'Quando spieghi i tuoi tormenti' (Act II scene 1; a Da Capo aria in Capeci) and the encounter with the mad Orlando (Act III scene 3). In the latter passage, Orlando taking his partner for the goddess Venus is new in Handel; the duet 'Unisca amor' as well as Dorinda's concluding aria 'Amor è qual vento' are impossible with the serious character of Isabella. Here is Handel's clearest contribution to La Celestina's theatrical image. As a whole, her Dorinda is more multi-faceted than either Dorinda or Isabella in Capeci. This should remind us that Handel's cast of five singers must have been connected with the presumably high wages for Celeste Gismondi, who combined the *seconda* and *terza donna* characteristics. The elimination of Zerbino is made up numerically, if not dramatically, by Zoroastro. Some lines in Capeci give Zerbino a slightly similar function, however; he calls Angelica to 'reason' ('Non ha mai forza il Fato, quando l'arbitrio è di ragione armato'; p. 50 of Capeci's libretto), and he heals Orlando – without stage machinery – by putting the magic ring on his finger. As he has received the ring from Angelica precisely because his warnings have affected her, causing her to have 'at least pity' on Orlando, his 'ragione' effectively restores peace. All this is different from Capeci's predecessors, and recognisably a rationalist element. It seems symbolical that this place in the drama was to be occupied by Handel's sorcerer Zoroastro!

Although Handel's opera is not actually entitled 'Orlando furioso', Orlando's madness is its main subject. Only his jealousy and madness hold this selection from Ariosto's epic together; without it, there would be no need for the two characters that are not in Ariosto. Orlando's madness takes first place in the many Ariosto dramatisations of the seventeenth century and appears in a variety of dramatic genres. Italian opera and *commedia dell'arte* – according to Nino Pirrotta[16] 'two branches which had grown from the same trunk' – made about equal use of it, although written documentation for the *commedia dell'arte* performances is obviously scanty; in practice, those performances must have exceeded the operatic ones by far. Within the literary theatre, 'Orlando furioso' plays exist with and without music and are of both the 'serious' and 'comic' varieties or combine them. It can, therefore, be concluded that the subject was better known in a comic guise than in a tragic one. This simple aspect of its tradition has, of course, not escaped Handel![17] Madness is an ambivalent phenomenon (and was treated as such by Ariosto); the seventeenth century preferred to expose it to laughter. Rationalists like Capeci and Braccioli (whose 'Orlando furioso' of 1713 toured half of Europe with music by Vivaldi) preferred to view it from a moralistic or even tragic angle. The literary sources within the Italian Seicento tradition[18] exploit three aspects of Orlando's madness for comical effects. The first consists in Orlando's confusing his partners with each other. Already Prospero Bonarelli (1635) makes Orlando take a wild bear for Angelica; M. A. Perillo (1642) and G. A. Cicognini (c. 1640?) introduce comic servants, whom Orlando confuses with his beloved. This idea is clearly the basis for the Orlando–Dorinda scene in Handel (Act III scene 3) and is *absent* from Capeci. It may be significant that Cicognini's prose comedy 'Le amorose furie di Orlando', which seems to have been influenced by Lope de Vega's Orlando comedies and by *scenari* of the *commedia dell'arte*, was still known at the beginning of the eighteenth century; according to Döring, an edition of the work appeared 1707 in Rome and contains, furthermore, a note about a performance which took place that year.[19] Is it an exaggeration to suggest that Handel himself saw this performance? I think not. The second aspect is the involvement, as it were, of the underworld (absent in Ariosto). Orlando in his madness 'meets' the infernal gods, which makes him a comic counterpart of Orpheus, and of Hercules in the 'Alceste' plays. Now this element is common to Bonarelli, Perillo, Cicognini, Capeci and several *scenari* of the *commedia dell'arte*; it can be articulated either towards the horror effect, or to its parodistic opposite. The latter articulation is almost ubiquitous in operatic intermezzi; La Celestina has used it several times. Handel responded positively. His Orlando visits the 'stigie larve', Caronte, Cerbero etc. with music right on the edge between a serious 'ombra' scene (the *accompagnato*) à la Cavalli and the mock-ritual of conjuring the ghosts with the characteristic *sdrucciolo* verses and the triple metre ('Già latra Cerbero'). Handel must have seen the music of Hasse in 'Larinda e Vanesio', where Vanesio conjures 'fagotti e timpani' instead of infernal spirits (Example 1). In the same intermezzo he has to swim without water, the music depicting his movements (Example 2). This is, of course, one of the best-known *lazzi* of all; Kurz-Bernardon seems to have been famous for it. In Handel, Orlando does not actually swim (although he does in Ariosto!), but he enters Charon's boat and 'ploughs'

Example 1

Fa – got – ti e   tim – pa –ni,   vi-o-let -te e   cim – ba - li,   or via   so – na - te,

vi – a,   so – na - te,   so – na – te

Example 2

Ohi-mè,   ohi-mè,   non toc-co ter- ra,   nuo-to in un mar di gua- i,

e sul -la   ri – va non ar-ri- vo mai.

the black waves. It is here that the notorious 5/8 bars occur – they depict
the shaking of the boat. Senesino must act this out; Handel 'helps' him
by twice interrupting his phrase 'già solco l'onde nere' with rhythmic
irregularities (Example 3). The whole passage is so clearly a comedian's joke
that modern interpretations which treat this as serious and 'expressive'
music are in themselves worthy of laughter.

Example 3

The music of this scene has, however, yet another ancestry: in French
opera. The madness scene at the end of Act IV of Lully's *Roland* (1685) is
the obvious model for the whole 'Tempo di Gavotta' in Handel, especially
with its prelude, which was one of the more familiar pieces of Lully for
Handel's audiences.[20] It was, with or without its monologue 'Ah! Je suis

descendu', copied many times, used in parodies of the opera, and its music
was printed in 1730 (2nd edn 1731) for use in vaudevilles and opera-parodies.
The monologue itself is parodied in Dominique's and Romagnesi's 'Arlequin
Roland' of 1727.[21] Here, Arlequin spends the whole scene in the ballroom
of the opera-house and finally smashes all the glasses and furniture when
he realises not only that Angélique is not going to come to the rendezvous,
but also that he has to pay ten francs for a lemonade. The text of the
monologue reads 'Ah! me voilà descendu Sous le theâtre par la trape...'
and is sung to a popular gavotte tune (Example 4). Lully himself had

Example 4 Air 299

maintained a balance between the tragic and the comic here; this was also
what Capeci may have expected from his composer Domenico Scarlatti.
Lully wrote, however, another underworld scene which was openly
parodistic – the encounter of Hercules with Charon in *Alceste*. It cannot be
stressed enough that all these pieces were well known to Handel's audience,
and with them, a certain oscillation between the tragic and the comic was
expected from Handel, to say the least.

The third comical aspect of Orlando is his affinity with the *miles gloriosus*
of Plautian tradition. Senesino's battle arias are perhaps above suspicion,
although the audience must have known that he, like his predecessor
Nicolino Grimaldi, could at times be a real coward. Orlando's aria 'Fammi
combattere' (Act I scene 10) makes him promise to 'muraglie abbattere,
disfare incanti' – the first of these actions occurs, unfortunately, when the
mad Orlando destroys Dorinda's hut with the innocent Medoro in it, the
second takes place in reverse. The most thorough comical exploitation of
false militarism happens in the Spanish-influenced 'Orlando forsennato' by
M. A. Perillo.[22] The figure of the 'Capitano' was ubiquitous in Italian prose
comedy, intermezzi (several instances in Hasse, with Celeste Resse) and later
opera buffa. In Handel's opera, the irony is more subtle. The inglorious
action of Capeci's Orlando of trying to kill Angelica is now immediately
frustrated by Zoroastro who carries her away through the air – visible to
the spectators. Orlando's failure is scenically obvious. In Capeci, one
seriously fears for her life until *later* told that Angelica's fall from the cliff
has been stopped by a shepherd. Again, a relatively small scenic change in

Handel reduces Capeci's earnestness and re-introduces the more mixed taste of the Seicento.

The figure of Zoroastro in Handel's opera would deserve a dissertation by itself. It is completely absent from the 'Orlando' operas up to and including the libretti by Capeci, Braccioli (1713) and Lalli (1715). On the other hand, Handel's character clearly foreshadows Schikaneder's Sarastro, particularly in his cult of 'reason'. Was this figure, after all, an invention of Handel's? Or of his librettist? Or even – of La Celestina, who may have envisaged Zoroastro, her counterpart in the opera, as one of those 'finti astrologhi' of her intermezzi, 'turned genuine'? Let us first examine the Baroque operas where Zoroastro does occur. They are all of the Mesopotamian variety, with Semiramis and her son/lover Ninus as protagonists. Zoroastro is usually a rival king who courts Semiramis or fights Ninus, using his magical powers in his most personal interest. This is the case in the widely known *dramma per musica* '*Semiramide*' by Francesco Silvani (performed, for example, in Naples in 1730); or in the *tragédie lyrique Semiramis* by Destouches (1718) and other French operas, including Rameau's *Zoroastre* of 1749. Only in one branch of this tradition does the sorcerer-king seem to receive a sympathetic treatment, making him almost a 'wise man' (as Handel's libretto preface calls him): these are several 'Ninus und Semiramis' operas performed between c. 1700 and 1730 in Hamburg and Brunswick. In *Nino, overo la monarchia stabilita* by J. H. Wilderer, Zoroastro is killed at his own wishes by a thunderbolt, but reappears at the end from the clouds to restore peace. This work was first performed at the court of Düsseldorf in 1703, and from 1709(?) several times in Brunswick.[23] The closeness to Handel's own background increases when we see that the German version of 1719(?) and 1730, set by G. C. Schürmann, was the work of Johann Ulrich König, a friend of Mattheson and B. H. Brockes in Hamburg. He worked in Hamburg from 1710–16 and after 1730, and as court poet in Dresden from 1720–30. His many libretti were written for Keiser, Telemann, Graun, Schürmann and others. The Zoroastro scenes of his *Ninus und Semiramis* come closer to Handel's text than other versions of this play.[24]

On the other hand, the name of Zoroastro does occur in Ariosto's epic. At the beginning of Canto 31, the poet praises the happiness of love, but laments the disastrous effects of 'quella rabbia detta gelosia'. He continues (st. 5):

'Questa è la cruda e avvelenata piaga
A cui non val liquor, non vale impiastro,
Nè murmure, nè imagine di Saga,
Nè val lungo osservar di benigno astro,
Nè quanta esperienzia d'arte maga
Fece mai l'inventor suo Zoroastro:
Piaga crudel che sopra ogni dolore
Conduce l'uom che disperato muore.'

Not magic liquor, not astrology, not even the magic art of its renowned inventor, Zoroastro, can heal jealousy. And what happens in Handel? It is Zoroastro who does exactly this (and with magic liquor at that), saving Orlando from 'death in desperation'. Whoever introduced Zoroastro into the libretto did this on purpose and after careful reading of the cited stanza. What a reply to Ariosto!

The poet has provided, however, two other prototypes for Handel's Zoroastro. One is the main character in his comedy (in *versi sdruccioli*) *Il Negromante*. This sorcerer, with the help of his apprentice Nibbio, sells his services to young lovers – and to their old opponents at the same time. He certainly is a benign spirit, who exerts great power over loving couples and individuals. This 'necromancer' has become a favourite figure in the *commedia dell'arte* (as has his apprentice), frequently under the name of Zoroastro,[25] and in opera intermezzi. In one *scenario*, 'La forza della magia', Zoroastro helps Pulcinella become powerful and happy, and attract veneration and love. His magic crown causes anyone who wears it to be taken for the beloved object by anyone who sees him; this magic is used with Niso, Dorina and Fileno. La Celestina had already turned this table when *she*, as Dorina, made Nesso admire her as goddess Diana. She did it again as Venus with Orlando.

Ariosto's other prototype is a figure in the *Orlando furioso* itself: the sorcerer Atlante.[26] He is a kind of father-figure for Ruggiero, whom he loves and protects in his inaccessible castle. In order to bar Ruggiero from the dangerous influences of the outside world, he produces an enchanted palace for him, where all the delights of life are at hand. Ruggiero, however, longs to get out of this paradise, because he feels destined for the world of honour and chivalry (an anticipation of Tannhäuser?). Also Bradamante, Ruggiero's spouse, and Orlando are led to the palace and trapped in it, until the palace is destroyed by counter-magic. In Handel's opera, the first scene shows Zoroastro before an image of Atlas who supports the globe. This is a direct hint to the spectators to associate Zoroastro with Ariosto's Atlante. But what happens? Unlike Atlante or the necromancer, who encourage lovers and protect them against the opposing world, Zoroastro dissuades Orlando from following Amor. In magic images, he shows him the 'antiheroic' side of love and orders him to follow Mars. Thus Handel's opera turns Ariosto's Atlante–Ruggiero relationship on its head, while using the poet's own motives. No other dramatist seems to have dared that. Is a bolder reply to Ariosto at all imaginable?

Handel emphasises the opposition Zoroastro–Amor musically by introducing the magician with an ouverture in F sharp minor and the opening *accompagnato* in B minor. Amor is presented with F major. The diametrical opposition of the keys is clearly perceivable in unequal temperament.

Interestingly, Dorinda is introduced with A major, which makes her a different kind of 'antipode' to the ouverture's F sharp minor.

The enchanted palace of Atlante had also found dramatisations in the seventeenth century, for example *Il palazzo incantato* by Rospigliosi and Mazzocchi (1642).[27] In 1734, Leonardo Leo composed an opera *Il castello d'Atlante* for the S. Bartolomeo in Naples.[28]

Zoroastro's command to Orlando, 'Lascia Amor e segui Marte', makes use of a conventional allegory, however. Monteverdi had based his Eighth Book of Madrigals on this opposition. In the theatre, closest to Handel are, in their ways, Perillo's *Orlando forsennato*, where the usual debate in the prologue is conducted by Fama, Marte, Amore and Pazzia, and Quinault's *Roland*. Here, it is actually a sorcerer, Demogorgon, who sets out in the prologue to demonstrate the superiority of 'gloire' over 'amour', referring to the true 'héros', Louis XIV. (Analogously, we can define Handel's opening scene as a kind of prologue.) Again, Handel's references to this figure are predominantly musical. His music for the flying geniuses and for the flight of the eagle from heaven (Act III scene 9) is reminiscent of Lully's fairy music in *Roland*. The sinfonia of the third act, extremely serious in tone, is also remotely Lullyian. In Zoroastro's most programmatic aria, on the other hand, I feel more reminded of Steffani and Keiser.[29] This aria (Act II scene 4) pronounces the 'official motto' of Handel's opera (absent from Capeci): 'In profound darkness errs our mind if guided by the blind god. It is on the brink of ruin (and) imminent danger, if reason does not provide the light.' One can see that the place of the royal hero Louis XIV has been taken by another godlike being: 'Reason'. Zoroastro is its priest and prophet, who steers people away from the errant paths of their passions, as the libretto preface has it. 'Reason' characterises also Zoroastro's cosmology: he despises the 'beautiful obscurities' of the stars, opposing all the fake or genuine astrologers of the Seicento tradition. Most important is his use of the grotto. This place had been the shelter of the happy lovers in Ariosto; Capeci had called it the 'ciechi voragini profonde' ('the dark, profound abyss'), to which Orlando descends. In Handel, the place becomes identical with the 'caligini profonde', the darkness of the love-stricken souls. The caves and grotto's of Celestina's intermezzi are rather unequivocally sexual images. Handel's Zoroastro abhors this place of fury and death, where Orlando seeks his end, and later attempts to kill his beloved. But Zoroastro saves them both from their deaths in the grotto, transforming it at the end into a 'Temple of Mars', where finally the *statue of Mars* appears. It is in front of this statue that the reconciled community celebrates, after Orlando's repentance and Angelica's forgiving, their triumph over the passions: 'Trionfa oggi il mio cor', a Lullyian *rigaudon*. It is a 'trionfo della ragione'.[30] And, Dorinda invites the others to celebrate 'further' in her hut, the home of pastoral innocence (this idea comes from Capeci).'

The climax of the opera with its incredible combination of seemingly diverse ideas and images is too contrived to allow for a purely pragmatic explanation. It is a conscious attempt at a synthesis. Everything is included, from Ariosto to comedy 'à la Celestina', but everything is called to order. This is Handel's *answer* to all the traditions.

One might suspect that the 'order' which now rules, is not entirely unlike that which Demogorgon had glorified. It may be seen in the 'reasonable' and war-loving government of the British Empire – 'La Monarchia stabilita' to use the apotheosis of Wilderer's opera – with Robert Walpole as its 'Atlas' and the Hanoverians as its gods. But Handel did not sell himself out just for that.

The last question: who wrote all this? Even if we assume that an anonymous librettist in Handel's circle was capable of such a synthesis, it is unthinkable that the composer should have waited to be presented with a ready-made text. As regards La Celestina's influence, we must remember that it was Handel's decision to employ her in the first place (no matter how much support she could also muster from Court circles), and he used to plan his casts as long ahead as possible. I do not think that somebody like Rolli would have reacted so sympathetically to Celestina's suggestions. Nor would Rolli have taken on Ariosto so frontally; his style and poetic taste were different in any case. He was, at best, an imitator of Capeci. J. J. Heidegger may have suggested certain things, and he may also have listened with some interest to Celestina'a tales. Aaron Hill admired Handel, whom he tried to recruit for English Opera *because he knew* of his 'Orlando'; but he would still have required an Italian librettist, as in *Rinaldo*. Giacomo Rossi did not even have enough wit to write an aria-text like 'Amor è qual vento'.

For stylistic, dramatic and cultural reasons, Nicola Haym alone qualifies as Handel's assistant. His beautiful elaboration of *Tolomeo*, his succinctness, knowledge of the French theatre and love of Italian poetry, his good standing with the Hanoverians, would have made him an ideal choice for Handel at the planning stage of *Orlando*.

But Haym had died on 11 August 1729. Do we have to close the book over him, then? I have not mentioned before that Handel himself was in Naples early in 1729, where he probably engaged La Strada, met Hasse and – heard La Celestina, as did John Hervey. Handel was then busy collecting material for his operatic productions of the years up to 1735 (the *Alcina* libretto). The last opera which he had produced in London before this travel had been *Tolomeo* with Haym. The riddle is solved if we assume that it was Handel's idea to produce *Orlando* immediately after *Tolomeo* (but the plan was delayed); that he enriched the plan with experiences of his Italian journey, which made him remember Rome of 1707 with Cicognini's play; that he saw intermezzi and read *scenari* of the *commedia dell'arte*, reflected over comic theatre, including the *Beggar's Opera*, decided to bring 'reason' into all this masquerade, and finally – heaped it all on to Nicola Haym on his return (end of June 1729), or even before by letter. The poet was quick to write the additional texts, with Capeci's model already in his hands. The composing of the music had to wait until the London scene was ready for the subject, after significant efforts with Racine and Metastasio, and until La Celestina could be had. Handel was a patient strategist and he had an extraordinary memory. The Lully references in the music, including that to *Arlequin Roland*, could have postdated 1730.

The point of it all is that Handel, not Haym, worked out the new *Orlando* drama to a degree where Haym had only to write the verse.

Handel's *Orlando* is his decisive answer to Baroque comedy – and not to comedy alone, but to theatrical traditions of all kinds. He fuses the comic with the tragic, the rational, the magical, the pastoral – as Ariosto had done. Quite different is Handel's use of comedy in *Serse*. There, he just fills a theatrical framework of the 1690's with new (and not entirely original) music, whereas in *Orlando*, he formulates a comprehensive answer to the past. He himself is the magician who reads the 'hieroglyphs' of earlier ages. He has the wisdom to accept or transform them or dispense with them as 'belle oscurità'. Handel grafted the shoots of reason onto the very trunk of the European Baroque theatre. No one else has achieved that, not even Metastasio. And, besides Handel and Metastasio, no one else has even attempted it.

APPENDIX

La Celestina's comic roles

Bold print indicates that the role was created for La Celestina

Year	Role	Partner's role	Intermezzo title	Opera	Her disguises
1725	Elisa	Tullo		Zenobia: Leo	
	Serpilla	Bacocco	Il giuocatore	Amore e fortuna: Porta + Orlandini	moglie bacchettona
1726	Urania	Clito		Astianatte: Vinci	
	Fiammetta	Pancrazio	L'avaro (Molière)	Lucinda fedele: Porta	pastorella
	Damari	Miride		Sesostrate: Hasse	vedovella
	Erighetta	Don Chilone	L'ammalato immaginario (Molière)	Ermelinda: Vinci	
	Larinda	Vanesio	L'artigiano gentiluomo (Molière)	Astarto: Hasse	maestro di danza, baronessa
1727	**Moschetta**	Grullo		Siroe: Sarri	
	Vespetta	Velasco		Stratonica: Vinci	
	Servilia	Flacco		La caduta de' 10'viri: Vinci	
	Grilletta	Porsugnacco	(M. de Pourceaugnac: Molière)	Gerone: Hasse	
1728	**Perichitta**	Bertone		Oronta: Mancini	
	Carlotta	Pantaleone	La finta tedesca	Attalo: Hasse	finta tedesca
	Scintilla	Tabarrano	La contadina	Clitarco: P. Scarlatti + Hasse	contadina
1729	**Modestina**	Don Pomponio	Il cortegiano affettato	F. Anicio Olibrio: Vinci	
	Merlina	Don Galoppo	La fantesca	Ulderica: Hasse	fantesca, capitan spagnuolo

Year					
	Berina	Forlingo		Farnace: Vinci	villanello
	Dorilla	Balanzone	L'amante geloso	Tigrane: Hasse	
	Arrighetta	Sempronio	La serva scaltra	Tamese: Feo	
1730	Dorina	Nesso	Il vedovo	Semiramide: Leo	cacciatrice ?, turca
	Lucilla	Pandolfo	Il tutore	Ezio: Hasse	pupilla
1731	Madama **Sofia**	Conte Barlacco	La furba e lo sciocco	Artemisia: Sarri	
	Lisetta	Riccardo	La zingaretta	Argene: Leo	zingaretta, egiziana
	Vespina	Pacuvio		Semiramide riconosciuta: Araya	astrologo, finta maga
1732	**Nerina**	Nibbio		Sallustia: Pergolesi	contadina, finta maga
	Eurilla	Don Corbolone	La levantina	Aless. nell'Indie: Mancini	levantina
1733	Dorinda	(Zoroastro? Orlando?)		Orlando: Handel	pastorella

Notes

Abbreviations

HJb	*Händel Jahrbuch*
JAMS	*Journal of the American Musicological Society*
M&L	*Music & Letters*
MQ	*Musical Quarterly*
MGG	*Die Musik in Geschichte und Gegenwart*, ed. F. Blume (Kassel, 1949ff)
New Grove	*The New Grove Dictionary of Music and Musicians*, 20 vols., ed. S. Sadie (London, 1980)
RIdM	*Rivista Italiana di Musicologia*
RMI	*Rivista Musicale Italiana*
VfMw	*Vierteljahrsschrift für Musikwissenschaft*

see also abbreviations in the Bibliography

Libraries are referred to by RISM sigla

271

Alessandro Scarlatti and the eighteenth century

1. See L. Bianconi, 'Funktionen des Operntheaters in Neapel bis 1700 und die Rolle Alessandro Scarlattis', in *Colloquium Alessandro Scarlatti*, pp. 13–111. In the normal diplomatic course the Spanish, or Imperial, Ambassador to the Vatican was subsequently Viceroy of Naples. It is important, however, to remember that in cultural matters the initiative came at regular intervals from Rome.

2. Roberto Pagano in Pagano et al., pp. 126–37. Pagano pays particular attention to the question 'arrangement or original work', but overestimates Scarlatti's activity as an arranger. He had no concern with the following operas – *L'Aiace* 1697 (entirely by F. Gasparini), *Mutio Scevola* 1698 (entirely by G. Bononcini), *Tito Manlio* 1698 (arranged by Luigi Mancia) and *Creonte tiranno di Tebe* 1699 (arranged by Severo de Luca); the source material for this matter is absolutely sufficient, and I am grateful to Prof. Lowell Lindgren for suggestions. On the other hand Pagano himself (pp. 132, 136) establishes *Bassiano* (1694), *Nerone fatto Cesare* (1695) and *Massimo Puppieno* (1696) as entirely new settings on the basis of their libretti; and it may be possible to demonstrate the same in the case of those remaining operas where the ascription to Scarlatti himself in the libretto does not make such clear limitations as is the case with *Odoacre* (1694, see p. 129) and *Penelope* (1696, see p. 136).

3. The reason for the adaptation (by Giuseppe Vignola) of the libretto of *Rosmene ovvero l'infedeltà fedele* is said to be that the original arias had no Da Capo, which is not in fact the case. The libretto of *L'Humanità* 1708, signed by Andrea del Pò and Carlo de Petris, says: 'La musica è del Signor Alessandro Scarlatti, con qualche cosa di più del Signor Giuseppe Vignola'. Thirty-eight of the fifty-five aria-texts differ from Scarlatti's libretto of 1691; but of the arias on the old texts at least eight are by Giuseppe Vignola, to judge from the collection of arias in I-Nc. *Teodora Augusta*, 1709, is probably a similar case. From summer 1702 up to and including autumn 1708, the period when Scarlatti was absent from Naples, some thirty-six *drammi per musica* were performed there; at least fourteen of these were arrangements, mostly of Venetian originals, and the remainder by eleven (!) local composers.

4. For the years from 1701 to 1706 R. and N. Weaver count nineteen *drammi per musica* at the Teatro del Cocomero. Apart from the known Scarlatti revivals *La Caduta de'Decemviri*, *Ariovisto*, *Analinda* and *Agarista* the following titles may be Scarlatti's as well: *Berenice* (i.e. Laodicea e Berenice?), *Odoardo*, *La serva favorita*, *Penelope*. *Berenice* (libretto of 1703 in I-Rsc) is missing in Weaver and Weaver. For further details, see Weaver and Weaver, pp. 188–207. We must ask ourselves whether Scarlatti did not perhaps have personal ties with the Teatro del Cocomero.

5. G. Rostirolla in Pagano et al., pp. 317–57.

6. Olga A. Termini, 'Carlo Francesco Pollarolo: His Life, Time, and Music with Emphasis on the Operas', Ph.D. Univ. of Southern California 1970 (Univ. Microfilms Ann Arbor, 70–23, 190).

7. Reproduced by kind permission of the Music Department, Bayerische Staatsbibliothek (BRD-Mbs, Mus. MS 2985).

8. Reproduced by kind permission of the Music Department, Bayerische Staatsbibliothek (BRD-Mbs, Mus. MS 1036, fol. 1–7; this is a small collection of cantatas originating probably in Rome, c. 1720). Handel's cantata is in HG vol. 51, pp. 59–63, its date of composition is recorded in Kirkendale 1967, p. 255 (doc. 5). Stylistic comparisons have been drawn between Scarlatti's and Handel's solo cantatas (with conflicting results) by E. Harris, 'The Italian in Handel', *JAMS*

33 (1980), pp. 468–500, and J. Mayo, 'Zum Vergleich des Wort-Ton-Verhältnisses in den Kantaten von Georg Friedrich Händel und Alessandro Scarlatti', in *G. F. Händel und seine italienischen Zeitgenossen*, ed. W. Siegmund-Schultze (Halle, 1979), pp. 31–44.

9. Scarlatti's setting is a hitherto unknown composition, not being identical with any of those mentioned in Pagano et al., pp. 528f. For a complete transcription of the new *Salve regina*, see *Colloquium Alessandro Scarlatti*, music app. XIII. The source used is BRD-Mbs Coll. mus. Max. 92, a copy in part-books (C, vl 1, vl 2, vla, oorg. bc) originating fairly certainly in Rome about 1720–40 and probably obtained from the Landsberg Collection for King Maximilian II of Bavaria about 1850 (reproduction by kind permission of the Bayerische Staatsbibliothek). Handel's *Salve regina* is in HG, vol. 38, pp. 136–43.

10. GB-Lbm add. 14168.

Handel and his Italian opera texts

1. Harold S. Powers, 'Il *Serse* transformato', makes a distinction between 'ultimate sources' and 'proximate sources'. Texts not even known to Handel, let alone used by him, could perhaps better be called 'forerunners'. In more than half of Handel's operas the original text-model is either unknown or has been wrongly identified. In the present essay the majority of text-models are given.

2. Opinions are surprisingly controversial. Whereas Flower (p. 96) allows Handel a part even in the origin of the libretto of *Agrippina*, Eisenschmidt (see especially vol. 2, pp. 14ff) believes that Haym, for example, chose the subject-models but Handel decided on their adaptation. See also Lang, p. 147, and Dean 1969, p. 19: 'We may wonder why he ever accepted some librettos, or if he had much choice in the matter: no one knows the answer.'

3. This is only true of Handel's own operas: in the pasticci of other men's work he used exclusively texts by Zeno and Metastasio: see pp. 164–211 in this volume.

4. See particularly Emilia Zanetti, 'Haendel in Italia' in *L'Approdo musicale* 12, Series III, 1960, pp. 39ff; the last chapter, devoted to the later London performances of *Il trionfo del tempo*, is entitled 'Alla "recherche du temps perdu"'.

5. This supports the interpretation given by Winton Dean of Handel's 'borrowings' and the problems of creative psychology which these entail. See W. Dean, *Handel's Dramatic Oratorios and Masques* (London, 1959), pp. 50–61.

6. This is also confirmed by a pamphlet by Barthold Feind(?); see Chrysander, vol. 1, p. 106. Libretto (Brunswick, 1703) in BRD-W, Fedeli's score in BRD-LÜh. The opera was sung in Italian; the libretto includes a German prose translation.

7. Libretto in BRD-W. See Renate Brockpähler, *Handbuch zur Geschichte der Barockoper in Deutschland* (Emsdetten, 1964), p. 377. The author guesses Fedeli to be the composer of the Italian arias, but *Almira* was the only Weissenfels opera in a period of fifty years to contain Italian arias (Brockpähler, *Handbuch*, p. 375). Surely this exception would have been made in favour of Keiser rather than Fedeli. The occasion for the performance was a visit of the Elector Palatine Johann Wilhelm, who was honoured by a *licenza* in this very magnificent production.

8. Since the original publication of this essay, Bernd Baselt has undertaken further research on *Almira*, confirming Keiser's authorship of the Weissenfels *Almira* and characterising him as an influential friend of Handel, not his rival. See B. Baselt, 'Händel auf dem Wege nach Italien', in *G. F. Händel und seine italienischen Zeitgenossen. Bericht über die wissenschaftliche Konferenz...Halle 1978*, ed. W. Siegmund-Schultze (Halle (Saale), 1979), pp. 10ff.

9. On Vittoria Tarquini, see also n. 82 below. Aurelia Marcello, Anna Maria Cecchi and Caterina Azzolina, who were in the employ of Mantua, had fled to Florence on account of the war; see Ursula Kirkendale, *Antonio Caldara. Sein Leben und seine venezianisch-römischen Oratorien* (Graz/Cologne, 1966), p. 38.

10. See a letter of Merlini's dated 24 September 1707 in Deutsch, p. 19.

11. The three arias are preserved, in reduced scoring, in MS XIV 743 of the Minoritenkonvent, Vienna. See F. W. Riedel, *Das Musikarchiv im Minoritenkonvent zu Wien* (Kassel, 1963) (Catalogus Musicus I), p. 97f. In this manuscript of keyboard music once belonging to a German musician who apparently lived in Rome at the time, fols. 34–43 form an insertion copied by a Roman copyist, containing some instrumental pieces (possibly by Handel) and the following arias from *Rodrigo*, the first two being ascribed to 'Hendel': fol. 38r 'Io son vostro', fol. 40r 'Così m'alletti' and fol. 42r 'Allor che sorge'. The first aria is not in Handel's autograph, but its text occurs in the Florentine libretto; it must therefore be assumed that the arias correspond to the latest stage of the preparations.

12. First edition: I-Bc 6260; second edition: I-Bu Aula V. Tab. I. F. III vol. 58,2.

13. See also Hellmuth Christian Wolff, *Agrippina, eine italienische Jugendoper von Georg Friedrich Händel* (Wolfenbüttel/Berlin, 1943).

14. A-Wn, MS 19160.

15. For whose wedding Handel composed the serenata *Aci, Galatea e Polifemo* (see also Flower, pp. 94ff).

16. This is one of the important points in Kirkendale 1967, see p. 239.

17. The most famous translation was by Richard Fanshawe (1647); see Nicoletta Neri, *Il Pastor fido in Inghilterra, con il testo della traduzione secentesca di Sir Richard Fanshawe* (Turin, 1963).

18. It is still there today: BRD-HVl MS IV, 409.

19. There is an operatic setting of *Il Pastor fido* by Carlo Luigi Pietragrua (or C. L. Pietro Grua?), who was then second Kapellmeister in Düsseldorf. It was performed at Venice in 1721, but perhaps even earlier in Düsseldorf.

20. See David R. Kimbell, 'The Libretto of Handel's *Teseo*', *M&L* 44 (1963), pp. 371–9. Eisenschmidt was already aware that the text was based on Quinault's libretto (1941, Plate VI and pp. 132ff). Handel may have been acquainted with Lully's music, which was known from the printed score as well as from copies (in Hanover, among other places: see Georg Fischer, *Musik in Hannover*, 2nd edn (Hanover, 1903), p. 17).

21. J. Merrill Knapp, 'The Libretto of Handel's *Silla*', in *M&L* 50 (1969), pp. 68–75.

22. Duncan Chisholm kindly informed me that Louis d'Aumont himself carried the nickname 'Silla' (as had Cardinal Mazarin before him).

23. All three libretti are in I-Bc.

24. See David R. Kimbell, 'The "Amadis" operas of Destouches and Handel', *M&L* 49 (1968), pp. 329–46.

25. Operas given in London during these years included: *Etearco* 10 January 1711 based on Stampiglia/G. Bononcini, Vienna 1707; *Antioco* 12 December 1711, Heidegger's libretto dedicated to the Countess of Burlington (Fassini 1914, pp. 36ff), based on Silvani/Gasparini, *Il più fedele dei vasalli*, (Venice, 1705); *Ambleto* 27 February 1712, based on Zeno and Pariati/Gasparini, (Venice, 1705); *Dorinda* 10 December 1712 – Haym's chief source was probably A. Scarlatti's *La fede riconosciuta*, Naples 1710; *Ernelinda* 26 February 1713 – Heidegger's chief source was Silvani/Gasparini, *La fede tradita e vendicata*, Venice 1704, with other arias by G. Bononcini and F. Mancini; *Creso re di Lidia* 27 January 1714, a pasticcio arranged by Haym and Heidegger, source unknown; *Arminio* 4 March 1714,

Heidegger's source Salvi, music by Venetian composers (Vivaldi, Ristori, Lotti, Orlandini); *Lucio Vero* 26 February 1715, Haym's text-source unknown, musical source unknown but ?Albinoni; *Clearte* 18 April 1716 arranged by N. Grimaldi, source Pioli/A. Scarlatti, *L'amor volubile e tiranno*, (Naples, 1709).

26. Libretto in B-Bc: L'AMOR/TIRANNICO/Drama per musica/DA RAPPRESENTARSI IN FIRENZE/Nel presente Carnovale/dell' Anno 1712./ SOTTO LA PROTEZIONE/ DEL SERENISSIMO/PRINCIPE DI TOSCANA./ (i.e. Ferdinando de' Medici). The composer is not mentioned. The date '1712' is according to the present-day reckoning, not that of the 'stile fiorentino'. Other librettos of *L'amor tirannico* show greater divergence from Handel's text: Rome 1713 (music probably by Orlandini), Naples 1713 and Innsbruck 1716 (music by Feo), Milan 1714 and Livorno 1716 (music probably by F. Gasparini), Brunswick 1718 (music by Schürmann). Lalli's version is to be distinguished from other pieces with the same subject-matter, e.g. *Il Radamisto* by Antonio Marchi (music by Albinoni, Venice, 1698 and Padua, 1716) and *Il Radamisto* by Nicola Giuvo (music by Fago, Piedimonte/Naples 1707 and Florence 1709).

27. Bressand's *Clelia* was set in Hamburg by Keiser (1695) and Mattheson (1702 as *Der edelmüthige Porsenna*), in Brunswick by Schürmann (1718): Librettos in BRD-HVl and BRD-Hs. The Italian libretto (Wolfenbüttel, 1692) and two other (German) Brunswick versions in BRD-W.

28. On Stampiglia and the Bononcinis, see Lowell Lindgren, 'A Bibliographic Scrutiny of Dramatic Works Set by Giovanni and His Brother Antonio Maria Bononcini', Ph.D. Diss. Harvard University 1972, UM 74–25, 641. Libretto Venice 1712 in I-Bc; Venice 1713 in I-Vcg; Naples 1713 in I-Bu (with musical additions by A. Scarlatti); Rome 1695 and Naples 1698 (Bononcini) in I-Bu; Vienna 1710 in I-Bu and A-Wn, Bononcini's score also in A-Wn 18269/70.

29. See Fassini, pp. 55ff. Bononcini himself dedicated his *Cantate e duetti* (1721) to George I; see Dorris, pp. 80ff.

30. See Konrad Sasse, 'Die Texte der Londoner Opern Händels in ihren gesellschaftlichen Beziehungen', in *Wissenschaftliche Zeitschrift der Martin-Luther-Universität Halle-Wittenberg*, vol. 4 (1955), no. 5, pp. 627–46.

31. Libretti: Venice 1696, Venice 1697 and Ferrara 1697 in I-Bc; Livorno 1706 in I-Bu. A more widely divergent version for Fano, Teatro della Fortuna 1718 (I-Vgc) is dedicated to the Pretender, James Francis Stuart!

32. Salvi's text-model was Thomas Corneille's tragedy 'Le comte d'Essex'. The story of the Earl of Essex is the subject of a play also by John Banks, 'The unhappy favourite', which had been given for many years at the Lincoln's Inn Fields Theatre; see *The London Stage*, Pt 2, *passim*.

33. See Gustav Friedrich Schmidt, *Die frühdeutsche Oper und die musikdramatische Kunst Georg Kaspar Schürmanns* (Regensburg, 1933), vol. 1, pp. 191ff.

34. Documents of 1719 (Deutsch, pp. 93ff) show that the following singers were to be engaged for London: Senesino, Guicciardi, Berscelli, Durastanti as well as Cajetano Orsini and Grunswald (probably the Hamburg bass Grünewald) who were not engaged in Dresden – but not the two prima donnas in *Teofane*, Santa Stella Lotti and Vittoria Tesi.

35. See Alfred Loewenberg, *Annals of Opera*, 2nd edn (Geneva, 1955), vol. 1, col. 94.

36. See Sasse 'Texte', p. 633.

37. Libretto in BRD-HVl. The music for this performance was taken from Handel's *Ottone* and Lotti's *Teofane*. This was repeated at Brunswick in 1725 (libretto in BRD-W). In Hamburg the work was given on 15 May 1726 as *Otto, König in Deutschland* (libretto in BRD-Hs). The German recitative follows Pallavicino

rather than Haym. The arias, however, are no longer Lotti's, being for the most part by Handel and Chelleri, Vinci and Telemann, who also set the recitatives. The 1726 score is in BRD-B Mus. MS 9052. See also Robert D. Lynch, 'Händels *Ottone*: Telemanns Hamburger Bearbeitung', *HJb* 27 (1981), pp. 117–40.

38. I-Bu Aula V.Tab. I. E. III vol. 13.
39. Libretti in I-Bc: Venice 1682, Venice 1687, Florence 1697, Pratolino 1702, Genoa 1702 (all ascribed to Partenio in the catalogue, but this is surely not correct for all of them). Alessandro Scarlatti's authorship is now generally accepted for the Pratolino version.
40. H. C. Wolff, *Die venezianische Oper in der zweiten Hälfte des 17. Jahrhunderts* (Berlin, 1937; repr. Bologna, 1977), p. 53 n. 83.
41. I-MOe Misc. teat. XC. D. 20.5. Prof. Craig Monson kindly informs me that there is an even closer model for Handel's text in a version given at Milan in 1680. This includes the 'Vision of Parnassus' absent in the other versions mentioned here.
42. See Fischer, *Musik in Hannover*, on the manuscript of *Antonino e Pompejano*. An opera 'avec des changements de théâtre sans machines' to which the Duchess Sophie of Hanover was invited in Venice, was more probably *Giulio Cesare in Egitto*. Perhaps the Duchess Sophie (mother of the future George I) kept the libretto and the score of this opera.
43. Facsimile edn of Handel's autograph score: *Italian Opera 1640–1770*, vol. 27. Facsimile edn of *Il Bajazet*: l.cit, vol. 24. Gasparini's opera has also been edited by Martin Ruhnke, Munich 1981 (*Die Oper*, vol. 3). See also the essay 'Francesco Gasparini's later operas' in the present volume. Gasparini's *Tamerlano* of 1711, of which nine arias survive (BRD-B Mus. MS 30330) has also been discussed by H. C. Wolff in *The New Oxford History of Music*, vol. 5 (London, 1975), pp. 93ff.
44. I am indebted to Frau Dr Ortrun Landmann, Dresden, for drawing my attention to this score; Frau Dr Oesterheld of the Staatliche Museen Meiningen facilitated my research by written suggestions and by sending photocopies of the Meiningen score. The score of *Il Bajazet* hitherto familiar (A-Wn MS 17251) is perhaps Borosini's presentation copy for the Viennese Court.
45. See the facsimile edn (n. 43), fol. 127r. The content and the metre of these lines show that they can only have been alternatives, not additions, to 'D'atra notte'.
46. Libretto in I-Bu Aula V. Tab. I. F. III vol. 4,3. See Fabbri 1961, pp. 69–83.
47. Emilie Dahnk-Baroffio, 'Nicola Hayms Anteil an Händels Rodelinde-Libretto', *Die Musikforschung* 7 (1954), pp. 295–300.
48. Salvi's *Astianatte*, closely modelled after Jean Racine's *Andromaque* (1675), was performed at Pratolino in 1701 (libretto in I-Fm).
49. See Giuseppe Riva's letter to Muratori of 7 September 1725, Deutsch, pp. 185f, Fassini, p. 124. The libretto is here entitled *Andromaca*, with reference to Racine. A later letter of Riva's dated 3 October 1726 (Deutsch, p. 197) suggests *ex silentio* that Haym had meanwhile been commissioned to rewrite the text for Bononcini.
50. I-MOe Misc. teat. 83 H 19.
51. Libretti of the Hamburg performances of 1695 and 1726 in BRD-Hs.
52. Libretto of 1690 in BRD-W. See Hugo Riemann, *Agostino Steffani: Ausgewählte Werke*, part 2 (= *Denkmäler der Tonkunst in Bayern* XI, 2, Leipzig, 1911), p. ixf.
53. See Philip Keppler, 'Agostino Steffani's Hannover Operas and a Rediscovered Catalogue', in *Studies in Music History. Essays for Oliver Strunk*, ed. H. Powers (Princeton, 1968), p. 353.
54. G. Ellinger, 'Händels *Admet* und seine Quelle'. *VfMw* 1 (1885), pp. 201–24; Anna Amalie Abert, 'Der Geschmackswandel auf der Opernbühne, am Alkestis-Stoff dargestellt'. *Die Musikforschung* 6 (1955), pp. 214–35.

55. There is a list of performances in A. A. Abert's article 'Aureli' in *MGG*.
56. Libretti: Venice 1660 and Hanover 1679 in BRD-HVl; Hanover 1681 in BRD-W. See also Fischer, *Musik in Hannover*, pp. 14ff, Keppler, 'Steffani's Hannover Operas', p. 351.
57. See n. 53 above and Chrysander, vol. 1, pp. 319ff.
58. See Fischer, *Musik in Hannover*, pp. 15 and 19.
59. See Emilie Dahnk-Baroffio, in *Göttinger Händelfestspiele 1970, Programmheft* (Göttingen, 1970), pp. 87ff; J. Merrill Knapp, 'The Autograph of Handel's *Riccardo Primo*', in *Studies in Renaissance and Baroque Music in Honor of Arthur Mendel*, ed. R. L. Marshall (Kassel/Hackensack, N.J.,1974), pp. 331–58. Rolli's text-model was Francesco Briani's *Isacio tiranno*, performed with music by A. Lotti in Venice, autumn 1710 (libretto in I-Mb, Racc.dramm.3109/3110). The libretto is dedicated to John Churchill, Duke of Marlborough, whose successful campaigns would at this time suggest a parallel with Richard Lionheart. The Duke died in 1722, after Handel's and Rolli's *Floridante* had celebrated him as a political figure.
60. See Squire's description of the sources, pp. 63ff., and Clausen, pp. 205ff.
61. A. H. Mann, 'Manuscripts and Sketches by G. F. Handel', in *Catalogue of the Music in the Fitzwilliam Museum* (London, 1893).
62. Libretto in I-Bc.
63. Both libretti in BRD-Hs.
64. Libretto in I-Bc. For the performance see Ralph Kirkpatrick, *Domenico Scarlatti*, 2nd (German) edn (Munich, 1972), vol. 1, pp. 63ff and vol. 2, pp. 103ff. A score of the overture and Act I has been preserved; facsimile of the overture in Kirkpatrick *Scarlatti*, vol. 1, plate 12.
65. See Kirkendale, *Caldara*, p. 60.
66. Two operas, with intermezzi, were given at Prince Ruspoli's, see Kirkendale, *Caldara*, pp. 57ff. At Cardinal Ottoboni's (Palazzo della Cancelleria) Filippo Amadei's *Teodosio il giovane* was given. Ottoboni was Juvarra's employer.
67. See Rolli's letter to Senesino of 4 February 1729 (Deutsch, p. 237).
68. The only traceable score of this opera, now in GB-Lam, must be the dedicatory copy for James Hamilton, Viscount Limerick, one of the directors of the Royal Academy 1726 and later of the 'Opera of the Nobility' (Deutsch, pp. 199 and 304). The score was formerly in the possession of William Savage. The libretto, dedicated to Hamilton, in I-Vgc. Handel used three arias from *Adelaide* for his pasticcio *Ormisda* in the 1730/1 season. See p. 173 below and Clausen, p. 187.
69. This version was set by Porpora; the arranger of the text is not known.
70. See Fischer, *Musik in Hannover*, p. 14, and Oscar Mischiati, article 'Sartorio' in *MGG*.
71. BRD-Mbs.
72. On the different performances see Robert S. Freeman, 'The Travels of Partenope' in Powers (ed.) *Studies in Music History*, pp. 356–85.
73. Libretto in I-Vcg.
74. Vinci's and Hasse's settings are preserved in numerous scores, but only a few arias of Porpora's setting (in BRD-B Mus. ms. 30123 among other places). Libretti: Vinci and Porpora in I-Vgc, Hasse in BRD-Mbs. All the collected editions of Metastasio follow Vinci's text.
75. He included an aria from this role in a pasticcio of Handel's; see p. 205, this volume.
76. See Squire, pp. 30 and 94. Chrysander, vol. 2, p. 248 considers it possible that other pieces from the project were used in *Ezio*.
77. Deutsch, pp. 272ff (Rocchetti and Salway in *Acis and Galatea* on 26 March 1731)

and pp. 291ff (Mountier in *Acis and Galatea* on 6 May 1732). Handel may perhaps have wanted to engage Mountier for a performance of *Ottone* planned in March (not autumn) 1733: see Clausen, p. 189, n.6.

78. They are the pasticci *Catone, Semiramide, Arbace* and *Didone abbandonata*.
79. The Porpora score in B-Bc 2300; Hasse's score in GB-Lk 22.e.17.
80. Libretto in I-Vgc; score not preserved. All collected editions of Metastasio follow this text.
81. Libretto in I-Bu. On the performance see Mario Fabbri, 'Nuova luce sull' attività fiorentina di G. A. Perti, B. Cristofari e G. F. Händel' in *Chigiana*, XXI, N.S. 1 (1964), p. 156.
82. Vittoria Tarquini is in fact mentioned for the year 1707 as a singer in the service of Ferdinando de' Medici: see Leto Puliti, 'Cenni Storici della vita del Serenissimo Ferdinando de' Medici, Gran-principe di Toscana', in *Atti dell'Accademia del R. Istituto Musicale di Firenze* (Florence, 1874), p. 73.
83. In fact Paolo Rolli says in one of the epigrams in his collection *Marziale in Albion*, which must, from its content, date from 1735/6, on Giacomo Rossi and Angelo Cori: 'Son poeti ed ambo vanno/lor talenti esercitando,/dove il cembalo alemanno/il buon senso ha posto in bando/'; see Carlo Calcaterra, *Paolo Rolli: Liriche* (Turin, 1926), p. 246 (Epigram Nr. xxviii).
84. I-Bc 5133.
85. There is a Zoroaster role in F. Silvani's *Semiramide* (Venice 1713) and also in the Brunswick opera *Ninus und Semiramis* (1730, music by Schürmann?). The libretto (BRD-W) starts: 'The scene represents a magician's cave with all kinds of magical instruments...Zoroaster: 'You terrible gods of the dark abyss!' But at the end of the work Zoroaster appears as peace-maker and reconciler. (See Schikaneder's Sarastro!). For another important aspect of Handel's opera, see pp. 249–69 in the present volume.
86. Compare on the other hand Capeci's text: 'Chi può dir, che l'amor sia follia,/ Quando cangia in diletto il martir./Sol la fiera crudel gelosia/Con Orlando fa amando impazzir./'
87. The 'wise man' is Zoroastro, who is thus represented as not only a magician but also a teacher of Reason.
88. Evidence for the five-year contract in Deutsch, pp. 234 and 237 (= Fassini, p. 85). On *Arianna*, see also pp. 183f in this volume.
89. One of these seems to have been Sir John Buckworth, who certainly lent Handel scores in 1732 (see pp. 177, 180 in this volume); and also perhaps James Hamilton, see n.68 above.
90. The libretti of 1729 and 1721 in I-Bc.
91. For Carestini see Rolli's letter of 16 May 1729 (Deutsch, p. 242), Swiny's letter to Colman of 18 June 1730 (Deutsch, p. 258).
92. Leo 1729: 13 arias in I-Rc 2244 fol. 91–142; three more in I-Rc 2513. Leo's pasticcio 1721: 7 arias in F-PcX. III A. Porpora 1727: autograph of Act II in GB-Lbm add. 14114 fol. 40–98; numerous arias in GB-Cfm 23 F3.
93. Libretto in I-Bc.
94. The overture comes from the early Roman cantata *Cor fedele*; see Rudolf Ewerhart, 'Die Händel-Handschriften der Santini-Bibliothek in Münster', *HJb* 6 (1960), p. 129.
95. Emilie Dahnk-Baroffio, 'Zur Stoffgeschichte des *Ariodante*', in *HJb* 6 (1960), pp. 151–61. Salvi's 1708 libretto (Handel's source) is in I-Bu.
96. The libretti of 1728 and 1729 are in I-Bc.
97. Cf. Hugo Riemann, *Steffani*, p. xi.
98. 1694 libretto in I-Bu. There is also the libretto of an *Atalanta*, music by Clemente

Monari, for Modena 1701. In I-Bc 3029 libretto of a performance of Mazzoleni's setting at Rovigo 1699.

99. See Riemann, *Steffani*, p. xi; libretto in BRD-W, title *Attalanta overo La Costanza in Amor vince l'inganno*. No composer named. G. F. Schmidt dates the performance in October 1711 in *Neue Beiträge zur Geschichte der Musik und des Theaters am Herzoglichen Hofe zu Braunschweig-Wolfenbüttel* (Munich, 1929), Nr.198.

100. Libretto Mantua 1707, composer not named, in I-Bc 6146 (probably Caldara). For Caldara's versions Macerata 1710 and Rome 1711 see Kirkendale, *Caldara*, pp. 56ff.

101. 1715 score in BRD-W Hs. 55. 1719 libretto in BRD-W Nr. 496.

102. Libretto in I-Bc 968. This source is already quoted by William C. Smith in his 'Catalogue of Works', in Abraham 1954.

103. Libretto Innsbruck 1715 in BRD-Mbs; Heidelberg 1722 in BRD-MHrm. Orchestral parts of the original version also in BRD-WD.

104. Libretto in US-Wc.

105. For Pratolino 1703 see Fabbri 1961, pp. 51ff. Libretto in I-Bu. In his preface Salvi mentions as his text-model the tragedy *Arminius* (1684) by Racine's pupil Jean Gualbert de Campistron.

106. Libretto in I-Bc. See Ursula Kirkendale, 'The War of the Spanish Succession reflected in Works of Antonio Caldara' in *Acta Musicologica* 36 (1964), pp. 228ff.

107. See Riemann, *Steffani*, p. xv; Gerhard Croll, 'Zur Chronologie der Düsseldorfer Opern Agostino Steffanis' in *Festschrift Karl Gustav Fellerer* (Regensburg, 1962), pp. 82–7. It is not certain whether the librettist Pallavicino used Salvi's drama.

108. Performance on 4 February 1714; libretto in GB-Lbm. With arias by Vivaldi, Orlandini, Ristori, Lotti and others. The text has much less in common with Salvi's original than Handel's version.

109. See Kirkendale, 'War of the Spanish Succession'.

110. The 1711 libretto in I-Bc, that of 1724 in I-Vgc; the 1724 score (partly Vivaldi's autograph) in I-Tn Foà 34. Powers (p. 91) identifies Handel's text-source. It was Beregan's original, not Pariati's reworking of it, that became so unusually popular; there are six different versions of it in I-Bu alone.

111. Sasse, 'Texte', pp. 643ff.

112. See Fabbri, 'Nuova luce', p. 175. Libretto in I-Bu.

113. There is a list of performances of Pollarolo's opera in Olga Ascher Termini, 'Carlo Francesco Pollarolo: His Life, Time and Music with Emphasis on the Operas', Ph.D.Diss. University of Southern California 1970, University Microfilms, Ann Arbor 70–23, 190, pp. 299ff. Apart from Pollarolo the only notable setters of the text are Nicola Porpora (Naples 1719, libretto in I–Nn) and Francesco Gasparini.

114. Libretto in B-Bc; 24 arias in F-PcD. 4340.

115. That is to say £1000 as outright payment for two new operas and a pasticcio: Chrysander, vol. 2, p. 447.

116. The 1723 libretto in I-Mb. In view of the agreement between this libretto and the anonymous score of *Alessandro Severo* in GB-Lbm (add. 16143) the latter may be attributed to Orlandini.

117. Libretto in I-Bc.

118. See Alberto Cametti, 'G. B. Costanzi, violoncellista e compositore', *Musica d'Oggi* 6(1924), p. 3.

119. See Jacob Maurice Coopersmith, 'The Libretto of Handel's *Jupiter in Argos*', *M&L* 17, (1936), pp. 289–96. For Handel's music see also Chrysander, vol. 2, p. 453; Flower, p. 277; Deutsch, p. 484. There are Lotti scores in BRD-B, DDR-Dlb, BRD-Mbs.

120. On the other hand a third aria ('Deh m'aiutate oh Dei') seems to have found its way from *Jupiter in Argos* to *Imeneo*, where it has been entered at a later date in

the conducting score. See Clausen, p. 158. Both the other arias were originally meant for *Imeneo*, as their texts appear already in Stampiglia (1723).
121. The 1733 libretto in I-Nn: score in DDR-Dlb. The Venice libretto (1726) in I-Vnm. There were later performances of the three-act version at Reggio Emilia 1727, Verona 1727, Treviso 1730 and S. Giovanni in Persiceto (Bologna) 1731. The text was set by G. B. Costanzi (Rome 1727 with the title *Rosmene*) as well as Porpora. In I-MC the score of Porpora's new version of 1742, with the title *Giasone*. I have not yet been able to study the autograph score of yet another setting by Porpora, of 1742, with the title *Rosmene* (in GB-Lbm Add. MS 14113).
122. Paolo Rolli, *Liriche*, ed. Carlo Calcaterra (Turin, 1926).
123. Libretto in US-Wc. I have only been able to consult the libretto of a 1664 repetition in Venice (I-Fm).
124. See Sasse, 'Texte', p. 645.

Francesco Gasparini's later operas

1. *Francesco Gasparini (1661–1727), Atti del primo Convegno Internazionale*, ed. F. Della Seta and F. Piperno (Florence, 1982).
2. See also Strohm 1976, vol. 1, pp. 15ff; Hucke 1961, pp. 253ff.
3. See the essay on Alessandro Scarlatti in this volume, pp. 15–33.
4. *Canto e bel canto*, introduction and appendix by Andrea della Corte (Turin, 1933), pp. 9ff.
5. 'Il *Serse* trasformato'. Powers has also identified other borrowings from this score in Handel's *Giustino* (1737) and, indeed, in *Faramondo* (the aria 'Sappi crudel ch'io t'amo).

Towards an understanding of the *opera seria*

1. Important to any preliminary consideration of these questions is Hucke, 'Die neapolitanische Tradition in der Oper' (1961).
2. See Loewenberg, vol. 1, p. 150.
3. Oskar Hagen, 'Die Bearbeitung der Händelschen *Rodelinde* und ihre Uraufführung am 26. Juni 1920 in Göttingen', *Zeitschrift für Musikwissenschaft* 2 (1920/1), pp. 725–32. Rudolf Steglich, 'Händel's Oper *Rodelinde* und ihre neue Göttinger Bühnenfassung', *Zeitschrift für Musikwissenschaft* 3 (1921/2), pp. 518–34. The piano score of Hagen's edition of *Giulio Cesare* (Peters) appeared in 1922.
4. The 'delayed' execution of recitative-cadences – the instruments playing the dominant and tonic chords after the voice – only became usual about the middle of the eighteenth-century, whereas the cadences in Handel should normally be played as written. See Dean, 1977.
5. Original projects for stage-sets for Handel's London operas or adequately faithful reproductions have not been preserved. The point made by Hagen seems to refer to engravings from the Hamburg performances in 1725, which included *Julius Caesar*. See Eisenschmidt, vol. 2, Plate V.
6. This has in any case been suggested for Handel's opera-theatre in London. The most important recent study of the financial circumstances of the King's Theatre in the Haymarket in Handel's day is *The London Stage* Pt 2, vol. 1, pp. xxviff.
7. See preceding note, and the attempt below to reconstruct the circumstances. The difference in the fees paid to average singers or composers and 'star' singers was greater in London than elsewhere.
8. See the chapter on *Bajazet* in Strohm 1979.

9. Paolo Rolli's letter of 25 January 1729: See Deutsch, p. 235. The original Italian text of the letter is quoted in Fassini, pp. 84ff.
10. Giuseppe Riva's letter of 3 October 1726: See Deutsch, p. 197.
11. A double importance – as both sources for the history of the work and as starting-point for any understanding of the musical setting – may therefore be attached to the original Italian libretti used by Handel and merely arranged for him by his assistants. See this volume, pp. 34–79.
12. See *The London Stage*, Pt 2, vol. 2 covering the season of 1723/4 and 1724/5. Works at other theatres competing at the time with Handel's *Giulio Cesare* included Shakespeare's *Julius Caesar* (Lincoln's Inn Fields and Drury Lane), Dryden's *All for Love* (i.e. *Antony and Cleopatra*; Drury Lane 26 October 1723) and also Colley Cibber's *Caesar in Egypt* (Drury Lane 9 December 1724). It is a remarkable fact that in the 1723/4 season the operas given at the King's Theatre had almost exclusively classical Roman plots. The subject of Grazio Braccioli's *Calfurnia* (music by G. Bononcini), which followed *Giulio Cesare* was not in fact Caesar's wife but a classical Roman virgin of the same name.
13. On this subject see especially Dorris, *Paolo Rolli*.
14. O. E. Deutsch estimated £800 for the Royal Academy, while the figure for 1729–34 is known to have been £1000 – for the whole season, that is. See O. E. Deutsch, 30 (1949) p. 260 and see the appendix at the end of this essay.
15. Since Chrysander did not live to complete the *apparatus criticus* of his edition, source-criticism of Handel's operas may be said to begin with Squire, 1927. Valuable monographs devoted to philological problems are Knapp 1968, 1972 and 1975 and Dean 1975. Handel's performing scores are also of central importance (see Clausen). Winton Dean is at present engaged on a major study of the texts and original histories of all the operas. I should like to express my deep gratitude to him for supplying oral information more particularly on the subject of *Giulio Cesare*.
16. See the description of all three autographs in Squire, pp. 57, 32 and 34.
17. In an otherwise admirable work: Powers, 'Il *Serse* Trasformato'.
18. Mercedes Viale Ferrero, 'Antonio e Pietro Ottoboni e alcuni melodrammi da loro ideati e promossi a Roma', in *Venezia e il melodramma del Settecento*, ed. M. Teresa Muraro, *Studi di Musica Veneta* 6 (Florence, 1978), pp. 271–94 with 8 illustrations.

An opera autograph of Francesco Gasparini?

1. A. Hughes-Hughes, *Catalogue of the Manuscript Music in the British Museum*, vol. II, *Secular Vocal Music* (London, 1908), p. 352.
2. Sources in Strohm 1976, vol. 2, p. 167.
3. The following manuscripts are of Milanese origin (partly with the assistance of copyist B) – G. Bononcini: *L'Arrivo della Gran Madre degli Dei*, score A-Wn 18628 (Milan 1713); A. Bononcini: *Sesostri*, score DDR-Dlb 2209 F4 (M. 1716); A. Bononcini: *Il tiranno eroe*, collection of arias DDR-Dlb 2209 F5 (M. 1715); A. Bononcini: *Griselda*, score A-Wgm Q 1205 (M. 1719); A. Caldara: *La Castità al cimento*, oratorio, score A-Wn 18311 (no performance in M. traceable); A. Caldara: *L'Ingratitudine gastigata*, score BRD-MÜs Hs. 800 (anon. libretto of a Milan performance in I-Bc, ascribed in the catalogue to Albinoni, 1711); Anon.: *La Maddalena ai piedi di Cristo*, oratorio, score A-Wn 17101 with date 1713 added (no Milan performance traceable). Facsimiles of two of the handwritings appearing in the three last named scores, in Ursula Kirkendale: *Antonio Caldara. Sein Leben und seine venezianisch-römischen Oratorien*, Graz/Cologne 1966, Plates 1 and 2. Kirkendale's attribution of the oratorio *Maddalena* to Caldara (p. 108ff) is based

on the similarity of the handwriting to that found in the two established Caldara scores. The copyists were certainly working in Milan between 1710 and 1720. Caldara was active in Milan between August and November 1711, Giovanni Bononcini during the year 1713. Since he too set the *Maddalena* libretto there is the possibility of his being the author, owing to the dating of the score.

4. Between 1708 and 1717 supplementary operatic performances were given in the Teatro delle commedie; the new theatre of the Habsburg period could not be started until after the Treaty of Rastatt (1714) and was not completed until 1717.

5. Gasparini himself also in the year 1713, if he was concerned in the production of his opera *Il comando non inteso ed ubbidito* that year.

6. See Strohm 1976, pp. 274ff and 281f *Astianatte* was also used later in a pasticcio (*Andromaca*), see ibid., p. 267.

7. Important documents concerning Gasparini's work at the Pietà are to be found in R. Giazotto, *Vivaldi* (Turin, 1973), particularly pp. 351ff. Generally about his life and works, see *Francesco Gasparini* 1982.

8. Other settings beside Gasparini's include those by Pietro Torri, Munich 1716, Antonio Bononcini, Venice 1718 and Leonardo Vinci, Naples 1725. The composer of the first performance in Ferdinando de' Medici's private theatre at Pratolino is not known – the name of Antonio Bononcini has been suggested.

9. The long-overdue opportunity of studying an important opera by Gasparini has recently been presented by Martin Ruhnke's edition of *Il Bajazet* (Reggio Emilia 1719), in the series *Die Oper*, vol. 3, 1981 (ed. Heinz Becker).

10. It is well known that Handel sometimes wrote in the chief parts of whole scores and then 'filled in' everything else on a second round of work.

11. The present writer has been guilty of an error of this kind, believing on insufficient grounds that a number of aria manuscripts of 1716 were Gasparini autographs; see Strohm 1976, vol. 2, p.165 – the question 'autograph?' is answered in the negative by the London score.

12. Bologna, 1723. See the facsimile in *Francesco Gasparini* 1982, pl. III a, b and c.

Vivaldi's career as an opera producer

1. See A. Cavicchi, 'Inediti nell'epistolario Vivaldi – Bentivoglio', *Nuova Rivista Musicale Italiana* 1 (1967), pp. 45–79 (letter of 2 January 1739).

2. Ibid., letter of 3 May 1737.

3. For details about the musical sources, see Strohm 1976, vol. 2, pp. 246–59.

4. For details about the individual libretti, see A. L. Bellina, B. Brizi, M. G. Pensa, *I libretti Vivaldiani: Recensione e collezione dei testimoni a stampa* (Florence, 1982).

5. J. W. Hill, 'Vivaldi's *Griselda*', *JAMS* 31 (1978), pp. 53–82.

6. F-Pn X.111 A.

7. M. Talbot, 'Vivaldi and a French Ambassador', *Informazioni e Studi Vivaldiani* 2 (1981), pp. 31–41.

8. Facsimile reproduction in F. Degrada and M. T. Muraro, *Antonio Vivaldi da Venezia all'Europa* (Milan, 1978), pl. 104.

9. See also G. Corti, 'Il teatro La Pergola di Firenze e la stagione d'opera per il carnevale 1726–27: Lettere di Luca degli Albizzi a Vivaldi, Porpora ed altri', *RIdM* 15 (1980), pp. 182–8.

10. J. W. Hill, 'Vivaldi's *Griselda*'.

11. R. Strohm, 'Zu Vivaldis Opernschaffen', in Muraro, p. 246 and n.13.

12. Published in Cavicchi, 'Vivaldi – Bentivoglio'.

13. Omitted in error from the list in Strohm, 1976, vol. 2, p. 255.

14. J. W. Hill, 'Vivaldi's *Griselda*', p. 81.

Handel's pasticci

1. An important attempt to realise and to bridge this gap is to be found in Dean 1969. For theatrical practice, see also Eisenschmidt and *The London Stage*.
2. Our present knowledge of the pasticci comes from Chrysander, Fassini and Deutsch. *HHB* vol. 3 will contain a thematic catalogue of the pasticci, incorporating also the information found in the present essay.
3. J. J. Quantz, *Lebenslauf, von ihm selbst entworfen* (Berlin, 1755): see P. Nettl ed., *Forgotten Musicians* (New York, 1951), p. 305.
4. For this practice in Gluck's case, see K. Hortschansky, 'Parodie und Entlehnung im Schaffen Ch. W. Glucks', *Analecta musicologica* 13 (1973); and the same author's '*Arianna* – ein Pasticcio von Gluck', *Die Musikforschung* 24 (1971), pp. 407–11.
5. The pasticcio *Ernelinda* (text by F. Silvani), performed at the Haymarket on 26 February 1713, has nothing to do with Handel. Heidegger put together the pasticcio after models by F. Gasparini and G. M. Orlandini; individual arias were probably taken from operas by G. Bononcini and F. Mancini. The second act of an opera *Ernelinda* by F. Gasparini is to be found by chance among the Hamburg collection of Handel's conducting scores (BRD-Hs M A/1014), but this corresponds to a version of F. Gasparini's *La fede tradita e vendicata* as given at Turin, 1719. See Strohm 1976, vol. 2, pp. 165 and 274. The Hamburg score may have served as a model for performances in Brunswick and for the pasticcio *Ernelinda*, arranged by Telemann for Hamburg, 1730; see also Strohm 1976, vol. 2, p. 281 (under *Rodoaldo re di Norvegia*). The London libretto of 1713 corresponds to none of these.
6. Cf. Addison's attack in *The Spectator* no. 18, quoted in Fassini, pp. 14ff.
7. See Clausen; the collection is in the Staats- und Universitätsbibliothek Hamburg (BRD-Hs).
8. Performance dates in this essay are taken from *The London Stage* and from A. Nicoll, *A History of Early Eighteenth-Century Drama 1700–1750* (Cambridge, 1925), App. C: Handlist of Plays, II. Italian Operas, Oratorios and Serenatas, pp. 387–400.
9. Not Leonora d'Ambreville as stated in Deutsch, p. 181.
10. GB-Lbm add. 31606.
11. The libretti of Handel's pasticci are all found, unless otherwise indicated, in GB-Lbm.
12. See *BUCEM*, vol. 1, pp. 315f. Both the sinfonia and Senesino's aria 'Un vento lusinghier' can be completed from printed editions.
13. See H. Hell, *Die neapolitanische Opernsinfonie in der ersten Hälfte des 18. Jahrhunderts* (Tutzing, 1971), pp. 452ff. Hell believes on stylistic grounds that the final movement is not by Vinci, but more probably by Handel.
14. All the seven arias newly inserted for the 1725/6 season are printed in 'The Quarterly Collection of Vocal Musick...', see *BUCEM*, vol. 1, p. 316.
15. Chrysander, vol. 2, p. 140; Deutsch, p. 193. Further details in Strohm 1976, vol. 2, p. 273.
16. Chrysander, vol. 2, p. 326; Deutsch, p. 234; see also Rolli's letter of 7 (or 4) February 1729 in Deutsch, pp. 236ff.
17. On the libretti, see pp. 34–79 in the present volume.
18. See Rolli's letter in Deutsch, p. 237. Rolli's observation is confirmed by a note in the manuscript *Catalogo de' Drammi musicali fatti in Venezia dal 1637 al 1778*, I-Mb Racc. Dramm. 6007, under the year 1729.

19. This *Orlando furioso* is not the libretto source for Handel's *Orlando* (see p. 65), but Handel used an aria from Vivaldi's score for his pasticcio *Catone* (see below).

20. As stated in Rolli's letter to Senesino of 16 May 1729; Deutsch, pp. 242f.

21. Frati, p. 479. Rolli wrote on 16 May (Deutsch, p. 242): 'Handel has written that Carestini was emulating Bernacchi.'

22. On her, see below, p. 181, and in the essay on *Orlando*, pp. 249ff.

23. See the statements about her in Deutsch, pp. 247 and 249f.

24. Chrysander (vol. 2, 232ff) suggests a visit of Handel to Hamburg in 1729 only on the basis of the supposed Riemschneider engagement and of a very vague comment by Mattheson which, since it refers also to a trip to Dresden, would fit Handel's travel in 1719 much better.

25. Conducting score in GB-Lbm add. 31551; harpsichord score in BRD-Hs M A/1036.

26. I am indebted to Dr Helmut Hell for the reference to Vinci's oratorio. The incipits of both Vinci's movements in Hell, *Neapolitanische Opernsinfonie*, pp. 540f.

27. It is the copy in B-Bc MS 4670.

28. There too are Italian manuscripts of arias sung in the London *Ormisda*, which perhaps found their way to Brussels from London. The whole group comprises twelve arias (partly with ascriptions) from *Ormisda* (B-Bc 3975, 4101, 4446, 4448, 4670, 4678, 4946, 4950, 5079, 5360, 5369 and 5389), two arias from *Venceslao* (3758, 4679) and one aria each from *Semiramide* (5370), *Arbace* (4677) and *Didone abbandonata* (5015).

29. This statement is in an English eighteenth-century hand. Among the printed *Additional Songs* Strada's 'Agitata dal vento' is entitled 'The last song'.

30. '*Venceslaus* New Opera – did not take', *Opera Register*, p. 219. *Ormisda* appears in the wrong chronological order in the *Opera Register*, and Sasse's n. 64 referring to it contains the misprint 1731 for 1730.

31. Conducting score: BRD-Hs M A/1061; harpsichord-score: BRD-Hs M A/189; Walsh: see *BUCEM*, vol. 2, p. 1036. An aria not printed by Walsh, 'Lascia cadermi in volto', was also performed in the Hamburg pasticcio *Circe* (1734), arranged by Keiser. This pasticcio also contains other arias borrowed from Handel's own works and his pasticci; see Strohm 1976, vol. 2, pp. 270f.

32. A copy of this score is in GB-LBm add. 15993. I have not been able to compare Capelli's recitatives with those of Handel.

33. This happens to be the only aria which had been composed after Handel's trip to Italy in 1729.

34. It later belonged to William Savage and is now in GB-Lam (MS 71). I am indebted to Dr Richard Andrewes, Cambridge, for drawing my attention to the opera collection in GB-Lam.

35. There is a score of Vinci's *Medo*, also prepared by Faelli, in B-Bc 2196, erroneously attributed to Leonardo Leo. I suspect that this score, too, came to Brussels via London.

36. No corresponding performance is mentioned in *The London Stage*. The only possibility would be Monday 22 May 1732, New Haymarket Theatre, where Anderson (from 8 May) and Wignel appeared; see *The London Stage*, Pt 3, vol. 1, p. 217.

37. BRD-Hs M A/1029. This harpsichord-score includes some of the instrumental upper parts.

38. BRD-Hs M A/1012.

39. GB-Lam, MS 75.

40. GB-Lam, MS 81. The collection includes other Venetian scores of the time, for example Porpora's *Ezio* (MS 79) and Leo's *Argeno* (MS 74), both of 1728. The

title 'Argeneo' appears in Kerslake's catalogue of Handel scores, see Clausen, pp. 17f. Perhaps, this was a copy of Leo's *Argeno*, which Handel intended to produce as a pasticcio as well.

41. But another score of Leo's *Catone in Utica* (B-Bc 2194), has a different sinfonia. Hell, *Neapolitanische Opernsinfonie*, p. 462, believes that neither sinfonia is by Leo. See also Strohm 1976, vol. 2, p. 185.

42. J. Hawkins, *A General History of the Science and Practice of Music*, new edn, 2 vols. (London 1875), vol. 2, p. 876. According to Hawkins, Handel heard Farinelli while he was on this journey, 'a young man of astonishing talents, and also Carestini'; he also had J. Chr. Smith senior with him. Since the information about Farinelli is clearly a confusion with the journey of 1729, both the other pieces of information may also refer to that journey. See also Chrysander, vol. 2, p. 332, and Deutsch, p. 331.

43. See n. 21 above.

44. See Swiney's letter to Colman of 18 June 1730 in Deutsch, p. 258.

45. For the sources of Porpora's Ariadne operas, see Strohm, 1976, vol. 2, pp. 206 and 208f.

46. The entry in the *Opera Register*, p. 222, 'Arbaces, a new Opera did not take at all', may well be a confusion with *Caio Fabricio*. The chronology in this last section of the *Opera Register* is muddled in any case. A negative judgement on *Semiramide* can be found in Deutsch, p. 336.

47. W. C. Smith, 'Gustavus Waltz: Was he Handel's Cook?', in: W. C. Smith, *Concerning Handel, His Life and Works* (London, 1948), pp. 178f.

48. References for the three conducting scores of the pasticci: *Semiramide* BRD-Hs M A/1051, *Caio Fabricio* M A/1011, *Arbace* M A/1004. Libretti of the former two in GB-Lbm; that of *Arbace* has not yet been found.

49. An exactly similar account appears in Burney, *General History*, vol. 2, p. 782, regarding Carestini's voice. But this information is taken almost verbatim from Quantz, *Lebenslauf*, and Quantz gives no date for the lowering of the pitch of Carestini's voice. Burney may have mentioned it in connection with the 1733/4 season because he knew that there were passages in Handel's *Arianna* which lay too high for Carestini and were later either cut or transposed – thus confirming Carestini's arrival in London after the completion of the *Arianna* autograph (5 October 1733). The alterations for Scalzi, however, were far more drastic than those for Carestini, who was still at that time a genuine soprano. For Handel's singers, their style of singing and their range, see in particular Rodolfo Celletti, 'Il virtuosismo vocale nel melodramma di Händel', *RIdM* 4 (1969), pp. 77–101.

50. BRD-Hs M A/680 (Acts 2 and 3).

51. The pasticcio certainly goes back to *Belmira in Creta* by G. Giusti, music by A. Galeazzi, performed in autumn 1729 at S. Moisè, Venice. Two of the *Belmira* arias in Smith's collection can be identified: 'Se il duol' is the parody of an aria in Hasse's *Cleofide* (Dresden, 1731) and 'Non disperi peregrino' comes from Orlandini's *Adelaide* (S. Cassiano, Venice, 6 February 1729).

52. On *Terpsicore*, La Sallé, Cecilia Young and John Beard, see Deutsch, pp. 373ff.

53. See Chrysander, vol. 2, pp. 246f; Deutsch, p. 419. Handel's notes described by Chrysander (GB-Cfm 30 H 8) must be understood as instructions to a copyist. The three arias concerned were inserted in *Poro*: 'Per l'africane arene' seems to have been suggested by Handel, as it is by Vinci, occurring both in his *Flavio Anicio Olibrio* (Naples, 1728) and his *Medo* (Parma, 1728); it had been composed for Bernacchi. 'Tiranna tu ridi' was Annibali's final aria in Giovanni Alberto Ristori's opera *Le Fate* (Dresden, 1736), in the role of Ruggiero; 'Mira virtù' was his other most brilliant aria in the same work at the end of the first act. The opera is a close

imitation of Handel's *Alcina*. The source of Ristori's aria 'Quel pastor che unendo al suono' sung by Annibali in *Didone*, has not been identified.

54. The conducting score is in GB-Lbm, add. 31607. Samuel Arnold had in his possession a 'half score', i.e. the harpsichord score. As he noted on the first page of the conducting score, the aria 'Se vuoi ch'io mora' and the voice-part of almost all the recitative were in Handel's autograph in the harpsichord score.

55. It is almost certain that the manuscript of Vinci's opera published in facsimile in *Italian Opera*, vol. 29 (now in Chicago) is the very copy from which Handel worked; there are entries which could be in Handel's own hand and which refer to aria transpositions as became necessary in London in 1737. This manuscript had been written in Rome, c. 1730.

56. BRD-Hs M A/401.

57. The sources for the original operas can be found, for most of the composers concerned, in Strohm 1976, vol. 2.

Leonardo Vinci's *Didone abbandonata*

1. A.-E.-M. Grétry, *Mémoires, ou Essays sur la musique* (Paris, 1789, reprint 1973), conclusion of the first volume (second book).

2. See M. Robinson, *Naples and Neapolitan Opera* (Oxford, Clarendon Press, 1972), *passim*.

3. For a list of his works, see Strohm 1976, vol. 2, pp. 227–46.

4. See Charles De Brosses, *Lettres familières sur l'Italie*, ed. Y. Bézard, 2 vols. (Paris, 1931).

5. Charles Burney, *The Present State of Music in France and Italy* (London, 1771), ed. F. Mercer, *An Eighteenth-Century Musical Tour in France and Italy*, 2 vols. (London, 1935).

6. F. Algarotti, *Saggio sopra l'opera in musica* (Livorno, 1755), in F. Algarotti, *Saggi*, ed. F. da Pozzo (Bari, 1963).

7. See A. De Angelis, *Il teatro Alibert o delle Dame nella Roma papale* (Tivoli, 1951).

8. *Tutte le opere di Pietro Metastasio*, vol. 3, no. 25 (letter of 16 February 1726).

9. De Angelis, *Il teatro Alibert*, p. 145.

10. See ibid., pp. 47ff.

11. *Tutte le opere di Pietro Metastasio*, vol. 1, p. 1386 – where however the effect is erroneously attributed to La Bulgarelli.

12. For a facsimile edition of the work, see *Italian Opera*, vol. 29 (score) and vol. 54 C. (libretto).

13. For a description and edition of this aria, see Strohm 1976, vol. 1, pp. 47–51 and vol. 2, music ex. 107, where the piece is compared with a setting of the same text by Domenico Sarri.

14. See W. Osthoff, 'Mozarts Cavatinen und ihre Tradition', in *Festschrift Helmuth Osthoff zum 70. Geburtstag* (Tutzing, 1969), pp. 139–77.

Handel's *Ezio*

1. See R. Strohm, 'Handel, Metastasio, Racine: The Case of "Ezio"', *Musical Times* 118, no. 1617 (Nov. 1977), pp. 901–3.

Comic traditions in Handel's *Orlando*

1. *Lord Hervey and His Friends 1726–38. Based on Letters from Holland House, Melbury, and Ickworth*, ed. the Earl of Ilchester (London, 1950), p. 145; Deutsch, p. 296.
2. *Lord Hervey and His Friends*, p. 145; Deutsch, p. 296.
3. *Lord Hervey and His Friends*, p. 150f. The same letter also contains a reference to Ariosto.
4. See Winton Dean, article 'Gismondi, Celeste' in *The New Grove*.
5. It is the aria 'Donzellina innocentina' at the end of the first act of Hasse's *dramma per musica Sesostrate* (Naples, May 1726) in the MS *A-Wgm* Q 1477. See also p. 255.
6. On intermezzo singers, see Charles E. Troy, *The Comic Intermezzo: A Study in the History of Eighteenth-Century Italian Opera*, Studies in Musicology no. 9 (UMI Research Press, 1979), pp. 47ff; Franco Piperno, 'Appunti sulla configurazione sociale e professionale delle "parti buffe" al tempo del Vivaldi', in Bianconi and Morelli, vol. 2, pp. 483–97.
7. Troy, *Comic Intermezzo*, pp. 49–54. See also Ortrun Landmann and Gordana Lazarevich, article 'Intermezzo' in *MGG*, supplement.
8. On social differences between intermezzi and the Neapolitan comic opera, see R. Strohm, 'Aspetti sociali dell'opera italiana del primo Settecento', *Musica/Realtà* 5 (August 1981), pp. 117–41.
9. Troy, *Comic Intermezzo*, p. 53f.
10. It might have some significance in this context that Lord Hervey wrote to Henry Fox on 24 January 1730: 'I am of Dorinda's mind, who says "è perduto tutto il tempo che in amar non si spende"' (*Lord Hervey and His Friends*, p. 45). Whose philosophy of life is this? A shepherdess's in a pastoral play, a lady's whose nickname was 'Dorinda', or La Celestina's?
11. See Ortrun Landmann, 'Johann Adolf Hasses Intermezzi', in *Oper heute: Ein Almanach der Musikbühne* vol.5 (Berlin, Henschelverlag, 1982), pp. 46–77. One work by Hasse has been critically edited so far: J. A. Hasse, *L'artigiano gentiluomo* (*Larinda e Vanesio, 1726*), ed. by Gordana Lazarevich, Recent Researches in Music of the Classical Era no. 10 (A-R Editions, 1978); other editions of Hasse by Prof. Lazarevich in the same series are forthcoming. There is a recording (in German) of the intermezzo 'Die listige Magd' ('La serva scaltra'), Staatskapelle Berlin, Otmar Suitner, with sleeve-notes by Ortrun Landmann (Eterna Stereo 827 508), 1982.
12. The following information is mainly based on research carried out on the important libretto collections of the Music Department, New York Public Library, and of the Music Department, The British Library.
13. See n.5 above.
14. Miss Elizabeth Gibson, London, who is working on a Ph.D. dissertation on the Royal Academy, kindly informs me that there is documentary evidence that the libretti of both *Tolomeo* and *Orlando* were sent to London in 1727.
15. The most relevant study is Renate Döring, 'Ariostos "Orlando Furioso" im italienischen Theater des Seicento und Settecento', Ph.D. diss. Hamburg 1973 (Hamburger Romanistische Dissertationen no. 9).
16. Nino Pirrotta, 'Commedia dell'arte and Opera', *MQ* 41 (1955), p. 305. Pirrotta was the first to point out to music historians that the *commedia dell'arte* was not all 'comic' in the modern sense of the word, but embraced many different subjects. Both in opera and *commedia dell'arte*, the performers mattered more than the

subject. The *Orlando* subject would always have required a performer who was able to strike a balance between the tragic and the comic or parodistic.

17. Nor did it escape Edward J. Dent, in his chapter 'The Operas', in Abraham 1954, p. 47: 'Orlando in his madness is rather like Don Quixote, half terrifying and half comic at the same time. Dorinda, the shepherdess, belongs to the pastoral convention, but she is never sentimental, like a shepherdess of Guarini or Tasso; she stands for frivolous common sense.'

18. See Döring, 'Ariostos "Orlando Furioso"', pp. 93–195.

19. Ibid., p. 186 n.5.

20. On the distribution of Lully's music in general, see Herbert Schneider, *Die Rezeption der Opern Lullys* (Tutzing, 1982). The sources of the madness scene are quoted in Herbert Schneider, *Chronologisch-thematisches Verzeichnis sämtlicher Werke von Jean-Baptiste Lully* (Tutzing, 1981), p. 446.

21. *Les Parodies du nouveau Theatre Italien... avec les Airs gravés*, vol. 3 (Paris, 1731), pp. 1–43 (note the correction of the performance date on the preceding errata page).

22. Döring, 'Ariostos "Orlando Furioso"', pp. 158–81.

23. I have seen the undated libretto of Brunswick (1709?) in the Beinecke Library, Yale University.

24. Libretto of 1730 in BRD-W. See also p. 66 and n.85.

25. See Vito Pandolfi, *La commedia dell'arte*, 6 vols. (Florence, 1957–61), vol. 2, p. 287; vol. 4, p. 379; vol. 5, pp. 294 and 308.

26. I am grateful to Prof. Remo Cesarani, Pisa, for drawing my attention to the figure of Atlante.

27. Döring, 'Ariostos "Orlando Furioso"', pp. 141–57.

28. Interestingly, it was in Naples that the first 'Orlando' opera after Handel with comic elements appeared. This was Gaetano Latilla's *Angelica e Orlando* (Teatro Nuovo, 1735). A MS of the work is in GB-Lbm add. 14205. At the end of Act II, the shepherdess Silvia and her partner Armindo have a mock-necromantic scene with Silvia's aria 'Spirti dell'Erebo' and Armindo's reply from inside a cave.

29. This splendid aria is probably another important Handelian response to traditions. It is of a 'Ciacona' type, thematically related to Zoroastro's prologue (falling motives), and also uses the chromatically descending 'Ciacona' bass. One cannot deny that Mozart, in the *Magic Flute*, specifically uses 'Ciacona' bass progressions to characterise the world of Sarastro.

30. It would lead too far to discuss the magic transformation which the B minor music of Zoroastro's prologue undergoes in this finale. One detail must be mentioned: the special relationship of Dorinda's solo with the 'Ciacona' bass. She even has a 'false relation' with the bass at 'festeggia'.

Bibliography

Abraham, G. (ed.). 1954. *Handel. A Symposium* (London)

Bianconi, L. and Morelli, G. (eds.). 1982. *Antonio Vivaldi: Teatro musicale, cultura e società*, 2 vols. (Florence)

BUCEM. The British Union-Catalogue of Early Music. 1957. Ed. E. B. Schnapper, 2 vols. (London)

Burney, Charles. 1935. *A General History of Music* (1776), ed. F. Mercer, 2 vols. (London)

Celletti, Rodolfo. 1983. *Storia del Belcanto* (Fiesole)

Chrysander, Friedrich. 1858/1860/1867. *G. F. Händel*, 3 vols. (Leipzig)

Clausen, Hans Dieter. 1972. *Händels Direktionspartituren ('Handexemplare')*, Hamburger Beiträge zur Musikwissenschaft, no. 7 (Hamburg)

Colloquium Alessandro Scarlatti Würzburg 1975. 1979. Ed. W. Osthoff and J. Ruile-Dronke (Tutzing)

Dean, Winton. 1969. *Handel and the Opera Seria* (Berkeley/Los Angeles)

1975. 'Handel's *Sosarme*, a Puzzle Opera', in *Essays on Opera and English Music in Honour of Sir Jack Westrup*, ed. F. W. Sternfeld et al. (Oxford), pp. 115–47

1977. 'The Performance of Recitative in Late Baroque Opera', *M&L* 58, pp. 389–402

Degrada, Francesco. 1967. 'Giuseppe Riva e il suo "Avviso ai compositori ed ai cantanti"', *Analecta musicologica* 4, pp. 112–32.

Deutsch, Otto Erich. 1955. *Handel. A Documentary Biography* (London)

Dorris, George E. 1967. *Paolo Rolli and the Italian Circle in London 1715–1744* (The Hague/Paris)

Eisenschmidt, Joachim. 1940/1. *Die szenische Darstellung der Opern Händels auf der Londoner Bühne seiner Zeit*, Schriftenreihe des Händelhauses Halle no. 5 and 6, 2 vols. (Wolfenbüttel/Berlin)

Fabbri, Mario. 1961. *Alessandro Scarlatti e il Principe Ferdinando de' Medici* (Florence)

Fassini, Sesto. 1914. *Il melodramma italiano a Londra nella prima metà del Settecento* (Turin)

Flower, Newman. 1959. *George Frideric Handel*, 2nd edn. (London)

Francesco Gasparini (1661–1727). 1982. Atti del Primo Convegno Internazionale, ed. F. Della Seta and F. Piperno (Florence)

Frati, Lodovico. 1922. 'Antonio Bernacchi e la sua scuola di canto', *RMI* 29, pp. 473–91

HG. Georg Friedrich Händel's Werke. 1858–1902. ed. F. Chrysander for the Händel-Gesellschaft (Leipzig/Bergedorf)

HHA. Hallische Händel-Ausgabe. 1955ff. ed. by the Georg-Friedrich-Händel-Gesellschaft (Kassel etc.)

HHB. Händel-Handbuch. 1978ff. ed. by the Georg-Friedrich-Händel-Stiftung. 4 vols. (in progress) (Leipzig)

HJb. Händel-Jahrbuch. 1928–33 and 1955ff. (Leipzig)

Hucke, Helmut. 1961. Die neapolitanische Tradition in der Oper, in *Report of the Eighth Congress of the IMS,* New York and Kassel etc., vol. 1, pp. 253–77

Italian Opera 1640–1770. 1977ff. Ed. Howard M. Brown (Garland Publishing, Inc., New York)

Kirkendale, Ursula. 1966. *Antonio Caldara. Sein Leben und seine venezianisch-römischen Oratorien* (Graz/Cologne)

1967. 'The Ruspoli Documents on Handel', *JAMS* 20, pp. 222–73

Knapp, J. Merrill. 1968. 'Handel's *Giulio Cesare in Egitto*', in *Studies in Music History: Essays for Oliver Strunk,* ed. H. S. Powers (Princeton, N.J.), pp. 389–403

1970. 'Handel's Tamerlano: The Creation of an Opera', *MQ* 56 (1970), pp. 405–30

1972. 'The Autograph Manuscripts of Handel's *Ottone*, in *Festskrift Jens Peter Larsen* (Copenhagen), pp. 167–80

1975. 'The Autograph of Handel's *Riccardo Primo*', in *Studies in Renaissance and Baroque Music in Honor of Arthur Mendel* (Kassel etc.), pp. 331–58

Lang, Paul Henry. 1966. *George Frideric Handel* (New York)

Loewenberg, Alfred. 1955. *Annals of Opera,* 2 vols., 2nd edn (Geneva)

The London Stage (1660–1880). 1960/61. Part 2: *1700–1729,* ed. E. L. Avery, 2 vols.; Part 3: *1739–1747,* ed. A. H. Scouten, 2 vols. (Carbondale/Ill.)

Mainwaring, John. 1760. *Memoirs of the Life of the Late George Frederic Handel* (London)

Muraro, M. T. (ed.). 1978. *Venezia e il melodramma nel Settecento* (Florence)

Opera Register from 1712 to 1734 (Colman Register). 1969. ed. K. Sasse, *HJb* 5, pp. 199–223

Pagano, R., Bianchi, L., Rostirolla, G. (eds.). 1972. *Alessandro Scarlatti* (Turin)

Powers, Harold S. 1961/2. Il 'Serse' transformato, *MQ* 47, pp. 481–92; *MQ* 48, pp. 73–92

Smith, William C. 1970. *Handel. A Descriptive Catalogue of the Early Editions,* 2nd edn (London)

Squire, W. Barclay. 1927. *Catalogue of the King's Music Library. Part 1: The Handel Manuscripts* (London)

Streatfeild, F. A. 1917. 'Handel, Rolli and Italian Opera in London in the Eighteenth Century', *MQ* 3, pp. 428–45

Strohm, Reinhard. 1974. 'Händel in Italia: Nuovi contributi', *RIdM* 9, pp. 152–74

1975. 'Hasse, Scarlatti, Rolli', *Analecta Musicologica* 15, pp. 220–57

1976. *Italienische Opernarien des frühen Settecento (1720–1730),* 2 vols., *Analecta musicologica* 16 (Cologne)

1979. *Die italienische Oper im 18. Jahrhundert,* Taschenbücher zur Musikwissenschaft 25 (Wilhelmshaven)

Talbot, Michael. 1978. *Vivaldi* (London)

Tutte le opere di Pietro Metastasio. 1947–54. ed. B. Brunelli, 5 vols. 2nd edn of vols. 1 and 2: 1953, 1965 (Milan)

Weaver, Robert L. and Weaver, Norma W. 1978. *A Chronology of Music in the Florentine Theater 1590–1750,* Detroit Studies in Music Bibliography no. 38 (Detroit)

Index

'Above' and 'below' in cross-references indicate that the reference is to another subheading under the same heading, not to another heading. Titles of works have been abbreviated by omission of words not necessary for their identification.

291